Restructuring Justice

RESTRUCTURING JUSTICE

The Innovations of the Ninth Circuit and the Future of the Federal Courts

ARTHUR D. HELLMAN

Editor

Cornell University Press

ITHACA AND LONDON

First published 1990 by Cornell University Press.

International Standard Book Number 0-8014-2405-4 (cloth)
International Standard Book Number 0-8014-9686-1 (paper)
Library of Congress Catalog Card Number 90-55129

Printed in the United States of America

*Librarians: Library of Congress cataloging information
appears on the last page of the book.*

♾The paper in this book meets the minimum requirements
of the American National Standard for Information Sciences—Permanence of Paper
for Printed Library Materials, ANSI Z39.48-1984.

To
JAMES R. BROWNING
Chief Judge of the Ninth Circuit
1976–1988

In recognition of his tireless service
to the more effective administration of justice.

Contents

List of Illustrations   ix

Foreword *Hon. William H. Rehnquist*   xi

Preface   xiii

PART I. THE IMPETUS FOR CHANGE

1. The Crisis in the Circuits and the Innovations
   of the Browning Years *Arthur D. Hellman*   3

PART II. ADJUDICATION: COHERENCE AND
         CONSISTENCY

Introduction   25

2. Standards of Review *Maurice Rosenberg*   30

3. Maintaining Consistency in the Law of the Large
   Circuit *Arthur D. Hellman*   55

PART III. ADJUDICATION: EFFICIENCY WITHOUT
          DEPERSONALIZATION

Introduction   93

4. Screening, Delegation, and the Values of Appeal:
   An Appraisal of the Ninth Circuit's Screening
   Docket during the Browning Years
   John B. Oakley and Robert S. Thompson   97

Contents

5. Appellate Justice Economized: Screening and Its Effect on Outcomes and Legitimacy
   Jerry Goldman   138

6. The Bankruptcy Appellate Panel and Its Implications for Adoption of Specialist Panels in the Courts of Appeals *Michael A. Berch*   165

PART IV. ADJUDICATION: ALTERNATIVE PERSPECTIVES

7. Struggling against the Tower of Babel
   Daniel J. Meador   195

8. An Unknown Court: Appellate Caseload and the "Reckonability" of the Law of the Circuit
   Paul D. Carrington   206

PART V. GOVERNANCE AND ADMINISTRATION

Introduction   221

9. Administration of an Appellate Leviathan: Court Management in the Ninth Circuit Court of Appeals *Thomas W. Church, Jr.*   226

10. Governing the Ungovernable: The Theory and Practice of Governance in the Ninth Circuit
    Doris Marie Provine   247

11. The Bar's Role in Circuit Governance
    Stephen L. Wasby   281

PART VI. BEYOND GOVERNANCE: REFLECTIONS ON THE NINTH CIRCUIT EXPERIENCE

12. Independent and Interdependent: The Ninth Circuit and the Federal Judiciary
    Judith Resnik   321

13. Lessons for Smaller Circuits, Caution for Larger Ones *A. Leo Levin*   331

PART VII. THE DYNAMICS OF INSTITUTIONAL CHANGE

14. Judge Browning and the Remaking of the Ninth Circuit's Institutions *John R. Schmidhauser*   345

The Authors   375

Index   379

List of Illustrations

FIGURES

1.1 Caseload relative to 1961, courts of appeals and
district courts   6

4.1 Circuit-by-circuit comparison of rates of disposition
of cases on the merits without oral argument   113

4.2 Proportion of Argued Cases, Informally Screened
Cases, and Screened Cases among 12,677 Study
Group cases   117

4.3 Distribution of 381 Rejected Cases within Study
Group of 12,677 Argued, Informally Screened, and
Formally Screened Cases, with Rejected Cases
enlarged to 10 times normal scale   118

4.4 Comparative docket distributions of major case
types   120

4.5 Rejection rates by case type compared with overall
rejection rate   122

4.6 Distribution of 2,756 cases initially assigned to
screening panels, by case type   123

4.7 Rejection rates of individual screening panel judges   125

4.8 Comparative rates of nonaffirmance and publication,
by group   129

4.9 Comparative rates of nonaffirmance and publication
in cases rejected from screening by parallel versus
serial screening panels   130

4.10 Relative rejection rates of parallel versus serial
screening panels   131

ix

Illustrations

Tables

2.1 Express references to "standards of review" in
published opinions, Ninth Circuit Court of Appeals,
1987–88   33
2.2 Affirmance rates in Ninth Circuit diversity cases,
1981–83 and 1986–88   53
4.1 Comparison of screening models of the federal courts
of appeals   107
4.2 Relative distribution of case types by docket type   119
5.1 Differences between the screening and the regular
docket   146
5.2 Relief rates for screening docket and regular docket
cases, by case weight   153
5.3 Opinion publication rates for screening docket and
regular docket cases, by case weight   153
5.4 Opinion publication rates for regular docket cases, by
case weight   156
5.5 Average number of citations to screening docket and
regular docket cases, by case weight (published
signed opinions)   157
5.6 Relief and publication rates for serial and parallel
screening panels, by case weight   157

Foreword

HONORABLE WILLIAM H. REHNQUIST
Chief Justice of the United States

In the federal court system, the Ninth Circuit has occupied for many years a singular position in terms of size and breadth. It encompasses nine states, more than any other circuit. Its jurisdiction spans the vast distances between Alaska, Hawaii, Guam, the Northern Mariana Islands, and the arid lands of the Great Basin. The circuit extends along several thousand miles of the Pacific coastline and the American borders with both Canada and Mexico. With twenty-eight authorized circuit judgeships and eleven senior circuit judges, the United States Court of Appeals for the Ninth Circuit is larger than any of the courts of appeals sitting in the other twelve circuits. The Ninth Circuit's eighty-six authorized district judgeships and its thirty-nine senior district judges likewise provide a larger complement of judicial strength at the trial level than any other circuit enjoys.

The administration of judicial operations within the Ninth Circuit has been a formidable task, demanding vision and leadership and a dedicated willingness on the part of many individuals to make the system work. Chief Judge James R. Browning has demonstrated that vision and leadership and has provided the innovation needed to make the Ninth Circuit function as effectively as it has. He served as chief judge for twelve years—from 1976 to 1988—at a time when the court of appeals underwent its most dramatic growth in both number of judges and judicial business. During his tenure the Ninth Circuit created a Bankruptcy Appellate Panel, adopted limited en banc review, and explored methods for "screening" cases to determine which disputes might be diverted to a separate decisional track. More attention was paid to defining more clearly the standards governing the scope and depth of review within a large circuit and to improving the circuit council˙and the circuit conference.

As the workload of the federal courts continues to expand, it is more important than ever for the third branch regularly to reassess its organization and procedures with a view to their improvement. In that spirit the essays in this volume make a valuable contribution to the ongoing task of judicial reform.

Preface

For most Americans, the work of the judiciary is defined by the cases the courts hear and the results they reach. Scholars and judges take an interest in the doctrines that underlie the decisions. But few people, even in the legal profession, pay much attention to the structures and internal procedures that provide the framework within which the courts operate.

This indifference, although understandable, is shortsighted. Judicial decision making cannot be divorced from judicial administration. The structures and procedures of our court systems help to determine how, when, and by whom disputes will be resolved. The effect is ultimately felt in the content of the rulings. Structure takes on even greater importance in the courts' performance of their lawmaking functions. Precedent in the American legal system exists not in the abstract but rather through the particular institutional arrangements that give it authority and meaning.

Over the last few decades, tremendous increases in caseload, especially at the appellate level, have challenged courts to find new ways of carrying on their work. Nowhere did that challenge elicit a more vigorous response than in the ninth judicial circuit of the United States. Extending from the Pacific Rim to the Missouri River, the Ninth Circuit has long been the nation's largest in area and population; since 1981 it has also had more cases and more judges than any other. Within a period of two years in the early 1980s, those judges adopted innovations that reshaped one after another of the circuit's structures and processes. Particularly noteworthy were the experiments undertaken by the court of appeals, which was then composed of twenty-three active judges; its reforms proceeded in the face of conventional wisdom that viewed an appellate court of more than fifteen as a monstrosity and a far-flung circuit as an anachronism.

The circuit has now been operating for nearly a decade within the framework established by the revamped institutions and processes, and the time is ripe to assess the results. What has been accomplished through the restructuring of justice in the Ninth Circuit? Have the reforms achieved their goals? Have there been any unexpected adverse consequences? Above all, what lessons can be learned that will help courts elsewhere as their caseloads increase in size and complexity? Those are some of the questions addressed in this volume.

The central figure in the reshaping of the Ninth Circuit's institutions was James R. Browning, who served as chief judge of the circuit from 1976 to 1988. Although Judge Browning would be the first to say that the accomplishments of his tenure could hardly have been achieved by one individual alone, there can be no doubt that his own zeal for experimentation and, later, his commitment to avoiding a division of the circuit gave decisive momentum to the currents of change.

To pay tribute to Judge Browning and to the spirit of reform that animated his regime, the Executive Committee of the Circuit Conference decided to sponsor a volume of scholarly studies, each dealing with an important aspect of the Ninth Circuit's work during the Browning years. An advisory committee was established; an editor was selected; and the editor in turn recruited a group of experienced law professors and political scientists to write the chapters and commentaries. Judge Browning (and later his successor, Chief Judge Alfred T. Goodwin) pledged full cooperation—but also full independence. Two years of research, analysis, and discussion yielded the present volume.

As work on the book was moving into its final phase, the Federal Courts Study Committee appointed by Chief Justice Rehnquist under the Federal Courts Improvement Act of 1988 was starting its own examination of the problems of the federal judicial system. Among the ideas considered by the committee were proposals that would have downgraded or eliminated the role of the regional circuit as a locus of adjudication and governance in the federal judicial system. Reflection on this aspect of the committee's agenda led to the realization that the Ninth Circuit's experiments could be seen not only as a test of the workability of the large circuit but as an attempt to preserve the vitality of the circuit system and the idea of regional decentralization it embodies. Several of the chapters thus consider the Ninth Circuit's innovations from that perspective.

Although the authors have had the benefit of mutual consultation and some exchange of drafts, no effort has been made to reach a consensus on any of the issues addressed. Each of the chapters expresses only the view of its author; the introductions speak only for the editor. None of the opinions or conclusions are necessarily shared by the circuit or its judges.

A study such as this one builds, of course, on its predecessors. What makes this volume unique is the extent to which the institutions of the Ninth Circuit opened themselves up to scrutiny by outside scholars. Several of the authors were given direct access to the court of appeals' operational databases, enabling them to investigate the court's processes both in detail and over time. Internal documents were made available (with some restrictions) on a scale seldom permitted by courts while the participants remain active. Judges submitted to interviews, often more than once; they reviewed drafts for accuracy. The book thus includes not only analyses of the various reforms, but also authoritative "micro-histories" explaining how they were accomplished.

The chapters in Parts IV and VI take a different approach. The authors of those chapters were invited not to undertake original research but to provide additional perspectives on the issues raised by the findings of the study.

The Ninth Circuit's institutions and processes continued to evolve even as they were being studied. In this volume the present tense usually denotes conditions and practices as of midsummer 1988, when Judge Browning stepped down as chief judge.

Except where otherwise indicated, quotations without attribution are drawn from internal court documents, correspondence, and interviews. Copies of the source materials are on file with the authors and, in most instances, with the editor.

In undertaking this project, we received help and support from many people. We owe our largest debt of gratitude to Chief Judge Browning and Chief Judge Goodwin. They submitted to numerous interviews, supplied us with documents, reviewed drafts, and directed the circuit's staff to assist us—without compromising the independence of our work. Other judges, too, gave freely of their time and counsel. As editor, I particularly acknowledge the support of our advisory "committee," Judges J. Clifford Wallace and Dorothy W.

Nelson. They helped in many ways, but above all they were there when I needed them.

Throughout the project we received full cooperation from the staffs of the courts and other institutions within the circuit. Two individuals deserve special mention, for it is literally true that without them much of the research for the book could not have been undertaken. Cathy A. Catterson, Clerk of the Ninth Circuit Court of Appeals, made available the full facilities of her office as well as her own unmatched knowledge of the court's operations. Mary C. Schleier, secretary to Judge Browning, repeatedly demonstrated dedication and resourcefulness in aid of our research; if our requests sometimes verged on the impossible, it was because we knew that, if anyone could help us, it was she. We are also grateful to Circuit Executive Gregory B. Walters and his predecessor, Francis Bremson, for support both personal and institutional. And at the risk of omitting others who helped fourteen authors over a period of two years, we must say thanks to Tom Arthurs, Evelyn Brandt, Francis Gates, Adell Johnson, Alan Koschik, Dinah Shelton, Glenn Tremper, Sue Welsh, and Serge Wilson.

Midway through work on the book the authors took part in the Conference on Empirical Research in Judicial Administration, sponsored by the Arizona State University College of Law. This gathering enabled us to share our preliminary perceptions with one another and also to gain immediate feedback from some of the individuals we were studying—the judges and other participants in the work of the circuit. An edited transcript of the conference proceedings has been published in 21 *Ariz. St. L.J.* 33 (1989). We are grateful to the law school and to Dean Paul Bender; to the law firm of Lewis and Roca in Phoenix, Arizona, which offered generous financial support to make the conference possible; and to John P. Frank, a partner in the firm.

In the summer of 1988 the authors made preliminary presentations of their work at sessions of the Ninth Circuit Judicial Conference. Many people contributed to the success of that effort, but two deserve particular thanks: Judge Jerome Farris, the program chairman, and Mark Mendenhall, Assistant Circuit Executive.

For help in avoiding the pitfalls that lie between writing and publication, we express our thanks to the staff at Cornell University Press, and in particular to our editors, Holly Bailey and Carol Betsch. The volume also benefited greatly from the thoughtful and sharp-eyed scrutiny of copyeditor Kimberley Vivier.

Much of the administrative work required by a project of this magnitude was carried on at the University of Pittsburgh School of Law.

Preface

LuAnn Driscoll and the staff of the word-processing center assisted in the preparation of drafts, surveys, charts, and other documents too numerous to mention. A number of students helped with research and with preparation of the manuscript; particular mention goes to Michael Hnath and John Williams. Finally, I am grateful to Dean Mark A. Nordenberg for his encouragement and support during the lengthy gestation period of the book.

Arthur D. Hellman

Pittsburgh, Pennsylvania

PART I

The Impetus for Change

1

The Crisis in the Circuits
and the Innovations of the Browning Years

ARTHUR D. HELLMAN

In the founding years of the American republic, Congress established a two-tier structure for the federal judiciary, a structure that remained in place for more than a century.[1] Change finally came in 1891 with passage of the Evarts Act, which added a third tier by creating courts of appeals intermediate between the trial courts and the Supreme Court.[2] Today, after the passage of another century, prominent voices suggest that a "crisis of volume" may require another major restructuring of the federal judicial system. The studies in this book, like the innovations they examine, have been prompted by that sense of crisis.

Although caseloads have increased at all levels, the most acute concerns have centered on the appellate courts. This is partly because the rate of growth has been higher, but also because there is a general consensus that increased demand is more difficult to accommodate at the appellate level than in first-tier tribunals.[3] In essence, the problem

---

[1]The Judiciary Act of 1789 actually created three sets of courts—district courts, circuit courts, and the Supreme Court—but the circuit courts were authorized to review district court decisions only in limited classes of cases. Felix Frankfurter and James M. Landis, *The Business of the Supreme Court* 12 (Macmillan Co., 1928). Moreover, the appellate function of the circuit courts soon atrophied, in large part because Congress did not provide them with separate judges. Id. at 32, 69, 87. Thus "[t]he district and circuit courts were in practice two *nisi prius* courts dealing with different items of litigation." Id. at 13.

[2]See p. 12.

[3]See, e.g., Henry J. Friendly, *Federal Jurisdiction: A General View* 31 (Columbia University Press, 1973); Richard A. Posner, *The Federal Courts: Crisis and Reform* 14 (Harvard University Press, 1985).

is one of hierarchy and control. Hierarchy is needed to maintain control, but expansion in the hierarchy, whether horizontal or vertical, is likely to reduce effectiveness of command[4] or simplicity of operation—perhaps both.

"Crisis" is a much overused word. Burgeoning caseloads are nothing new, nor is the sense that the system is on the verge of breakdown.[5] What is new is the perception that the traditional remedies— enlarging the number of judgeships and auxiliary staff, creating new courts, or subdividing existing courts into smaller units—are no longer adequate. Complicating the search for solutions is the recognition that court organization today implicates functions of governance and administration as well as adjudication.

As a result of these developments, scholars, lawyers, legislators, and judges have been looking for new approaches; they have also been reconsidering ideas that might have been rejected in the past. One possibility that has aroused both interest and skepticism is the development of appellate courts substantially larger than has hitherto been thought desirable. A principal purpose of this book is to provide an empirical foundation that will help in assessing the feasibility of that approach. The book also aims to shed light on a related question: the virtues and drawbacks of regional decentralization in the structuring of the federal courts.

To those ends, the studies in this volume describe and analyze the innovations adopted over the course of a decade by the judges of the ninth judicial circuit of the United States. The Ninth Circuit encompasses nine western states, including California, and two territories.[6] In area, population, and caseload, it far exceeds any of the other circuits. With twenty-eight authorized judgeships, the Ninth Circuit Court of Appeals is the largest appellate court in the federal system.

This chapter sets the stage for the detailed analyses that follow. In it, I sketch the outlines of the caseload crisis and the Ninth Circuit's response. I also explain the reasons for thinking that the development of large courts may hold at least part of the solution. That analysis leads in turn to a consideration of the role of the circuit in the federal

---

[4]This is Paul D. Carrington's phrase. For further discussion, see Part II, Introduction.

[5]For example, in the decade preceding the Evarts Act, the Supreme Court's docket "got beyond all control," and the lower courts "were staggering under a load which made speedy and effective judicial administration impossible." Frankfurter and Landis, supra note 1, at 86.

[6]The other states are Alaska, Arizona, Hawaii, Idaho, Montana, Nevada, Oregon, and Washington. The territories are Guam and the Northern Mariana Islands.

judicial system. The chapter concludes with a few words about the general approach taken in the remainder of the book and some reflections suggested by the findings of the individual studies.

Crisis and Response

The numbers tell the story. In 1961, when James R. Browning began his service as a federal judge, the number of cases filed in all the courts of appeals was 4,204, with 443 in the Ninth Circuit.[7] Fifteen years later, when Browning took over as chief judge, filings nationwide had increased to 18,408, of which 2,907 came to the Ninth. In 1988, Browning's last year at the court's helm, 37,524 new appeals were filed in all federal courts, with 6,334 in the Ninth. The volume of appeals thus expanded more than eightfold during Browning's service on the court. During the same period, filings in the federal trial courts grew only 228 percent—a substantial gain, to be sure, but, as shown in Figure 1.1, less than half the rate of increase for appeals.

The number of federal appellate judges has also expanded, but at a pace that lags far behind the growth in filings. If filings per judgeship had remained at the same level as they were when Browning went on the bench, the Ninth Circuit Court of Appeals would now have about 125 judges, four times as many as it actually has. Nor does the picture brighten if we look only at appeals adjudicated on the merits. In recent years each judge has heard about 250 cases a year, an average of more than one each working day.[8] It is not uncommon for judges to author thirty or more signed opinions in a year, and an even larger number of unpublished memoranda. When the complexity and difficulty of some of the cases are taken into account, it is hardly surprising that lawyers feel that cases of seemingly lesser importance may be getting short shrift. By the same token, asking the judges to increase their individual workloads would only bring us closer to assembly-line justice.

By the early 1970s, concern about federal appellate caseloads had grown to the point that Congress established a Commission on Revision of the Federal Court Appellate System to study the problem and make recommendations for change. The study group, known as the Hruska Commission after its chairman, Senator Roman L. Hruska of

[7]The data in this paragraph are taken from the Annual Reports of the Director of the Administrative Office of United States Courts.

[8]Data on workloads of individual judges have been supplied by Clerk of Court Cathy A. Catterson.

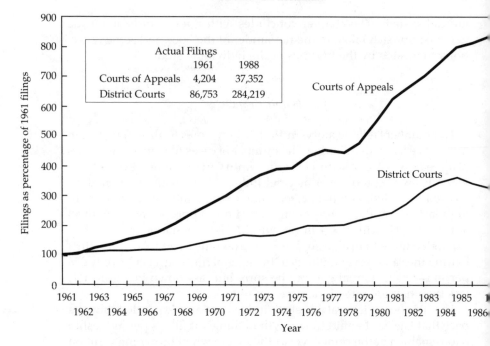

Figure 1.1. Caseload relative to 1961, courts of appeals and district courts
Source: Annual Reports, Director of the Administrative Office of the United States Courts.

Nebraska, urged, among other remedies, that Congress divide the two largest circuits, the Fifth and the Ninth, into four smaller circuits. After some initial controversy the recommendation garnered a generally favorable response from judges and lawyers in the Fifth Circuit, and in 1980 a new Eleventh Circuit was created from the three eastern states of the former Fifth.[9] In the Ninth Circuit, however, reform took a different turn. The state of California accounted for more than 60 percent of the appellate caseload, and the California bar strongly resisted any realignment that would place any of the state's four federal judicial districts in different circuits. The circuit judges, forcefully led by Chief Judge Browning, initially urged Congress to proceed with the addition of much-needed judgeships without awaiting reso-

[9]A brief account of the Hruska Commission and developments relating to the Fifth Circuit is found in Chapter 9. For a detailed history, see Deborah J. Barrow and Thomas G. Walker, *A Court Divided: The Fifth Circuit Court of Appeals and the Politics of Judicial Reform* (Yale University Press, 1988).

lution of the controversy over circuit division; later the judges argued that division was unnecessary because a large circuit could be managed effectively.

The device that enabled Congress to avoid the difficult questions was section 6 of the Omnibus Judgeship Act of 1978. Conceived primarily as a compromise that postponed decision over dividing the Fifth Circuit, the legislation authorized any court of appeals with more than fifteen active judges to "constitute itself into administrative units" and to "perform its en banc function by" a number of judges smaller than the full court. The 1978 statute also created ten new appellate judgeships for the Ninth Circuit, giving it a total of twenty-three. Six years later the authorized complement was expanded to twenty-eight.

The 1978 legislation inaugurated a decade of innovation and experimentation that is probably without parallel in the history of the federal judicial system. Less than a year after the appointment of the sixteenth judge, the court of appeals adopted a rule vesting the decision of en banc cases in ad hoc eleven-judge panels constituted by random selection. The court also created three geographically organized administrative units, each with its administrative chief judge. But the court's innovations were not limited to those specified in the act. A large, highly structured office of staff attorneys was established; among other tasks, it administers an elaborate case-inventory system designed to assist the judges in maintaining consistency in panel decisions. Screening panels experimented with two kinds of procedures for handling cases perceived to be less substantial. In published decisions and in internal discussions the court made intensive efforts to articulate standards of appellate review. Outside the realm of adjudication, a seven-judge executive committee took over many of the responsibilities of governance formerly handled by all members of the court.

The spirit of innovation extended beyond the court of appeals to the other institutions within the circuit. The circuit conference was reorganized in an effort to make it more representative as well as more effective. The circuit council was reduced in size, and its composition was changed by giving district judges representation almost equal to that of circuit judges. The reorganized council established a large network of committees under its overall supervision and put into effect an annual action plan that cut across jurisdictional lines. A conference of chief district judges was organized and met regularly to share ideas about common problems. Alone among the circuits, the

Ninth Circuit established and maintained a Bankruptcy Appellate Panel, a novel system that provides appellate review at the trial court level.

Some of these innovations were inspired, at least in part, by the court's desire to show that a large circuit can be managed effectively; some developed independently of that goal. Some grew out of circumstances unique to the Ninth Circuit; others were prompted by legislation applicable nationwide. What is important is not their origins but their implications for the future. Separately, they represent a variety of approaches that may serve as models for court systems of any size. Together, they may offer a way of meeting the challenge of increased caseloads without resort to more drastic reforms. The studies in this book seek to determine the extent to which these possibilities have been realized.

The Large Appellate Court and the Needs of the Future

The particular focus of this volume comes about in part because of the book's origins, described in the Preface, and because of what the Ninth Circuit is: the largest appellate court in the federal judicial system. Moreover, had Judge Browning been asked to select the theme for the book, it is one he might well have chosen, for Browning has seen the development of large, geographically organized circuits as the direction in which the system should move in the future. But quite apart from the realities of the Ninth Circuit today or Browning's vision of the twenty-first century, the challenge of the large appellate court warrants the attention of all who care about the administration of justice in the United States.

Three premises lead to this conclusion. First, in the years to come, caseloads in both federal and state courts will continue to grow—perhaps not at the same rate as in the last two decades, but at least at the pace of population and the economy. And if the past is any guide to the future, appellate caseloads will expand even faster than filings in the trial courts.

Second, Congress will take no major steps to reduce the jurisdiction of the federal courts.[10] On the contrary, Congress is likely to continue

---

[10]In 1988 Congress raised the minimum jurisdictional amount for diversity of citizenship cases from $10,000 to $50,000. A recent study indicates that this reform will reduce

to create new federal causes of action, though perhaps not with the same frequency as in past decades.[11] State as well as federal courts will feel the impact. In the federal system, appellate review of criminal sentences, authorized under limited circumstances by legislation effective in 1987, will add to the burdens of the courts of appeals.

Third, more cases will require more judges, and the options for designing structures that will accommodate those judges will be severely limited. Proliferation of new regional circuits would further balkanize the law and would probably lead to the establishment of a new court of national jurisdiction intermediate between the courts of appeals and the Supreme Court—a "solution" that would create problems of its own.[12] Creating an array of specialized tribunals could divert a substantial proportion of the business of existing courts, but that approach would have to overcome strong resistance in the legal community. Nor is that resistance merely a reflexive opposition to change; on the contrary, it is solidly grounded in concerns about tunnel vision, interest-group-dominated appointments, and centralization of power.[13] The proposals that have some modest chance of becoming law (e.g., creation of a Court of Tax Appeals or of an Intercircuit Panel) would have at best a minimal impact on the workload of the courts of appeals. Indeed, the Intercircuit Panel—strongly advocated by the former chief justice, the present chief justice, and powerful members of Congress—would actually reduce the capacity of the system at the intermediate appellate level by "borrowing" judges from the courts of appeals. None of the current proposals would give any relief to state courts.

---

the number of diversity cases in the district courts by somewhere between 10 and 40 percent. See Anthony Partridge, *The Budgetary Impact of Possible Changes in Diversity Jurisdiction* 14–15 (Federal Judicial Center, 1988). In 1987 diversity suits accounted for about 13.5 percent of the cases filed in the courts of appeals.

[11]For example, the Americans with Disabilities Act, which was moving toward enactment as this book was in preparation, can be expected to generate a large volume of litigation. The legislation defines disability broadly, applies to almost every aspect of human life, and provides a wide array of remedies enforceable in courts.

[12]For detailed discussion of these problems, see Arthur D. Hellman, "The Proposed Intercircuit Tribunal: Do We Need It? Will It Work?" 11 *Hastings Const. L.Q.* 375, 424–44 (1984).

[13]These concerns are spelled out at greater length in Posner, supra note 3, at 148–60; Arthur D. Hellman, "Courting Disaster," 39 *Stan. L. Rev.* 297, 308–9 (1986); Symposium, The Federal Courts: The Next 100 Years, 38 *S.C. L. Rev.* 363, 442–43 (1987) (remarks of Judge J. Harvie Wilkinson) (hereafter cited as South Carolina Symposium). For contrary views, see id. at 452–54 (remarks of Paul M. Bator); id. at 458–60 (remarks of Daniel J. Meador).

9

This gloomy prognosis finds confirmation, both direct and indirect, in the remarks of Chief Justice Rehnquist to the American Bar Association at its midyear meeting in February 1989. The chief justice likened the federal court system to "a city in the arid part of this country which is using every bit of its water system to supply current needs. We must think not of building new subdivisions, but of conserving water. More accurately, we must think of conserving water and cutting down on some present uses."[14] But when he came to suggesting "candidates for possible curtailment," the chief justice offered only modest possibilities. Of the five ideas on his list, two involved categories of lawsuits that contribute only minimally to federal appellate workloads.[15] Two proposals would have reduced district court caseloads at the expense of the court of appeals,[16] and only one might have provided significant relief at the appellate level.[17]

The upshot is that the federal courts, and in particular the courts of appeals, will have to confront ever-mounting caseloads with no help from the outside except for the occasional addition of more judges. Indeed, apart from everything else, the opposition that develops to any form of structural change virtually ensures that from time to time Congress will respond to the need for increased capacity by creating new judgeships within existing structures. That in turn leads to the conclusion that, even if other reforms are implemented, the future of the federal courts lies in the development of large circuits—appellate courts with substantially more judges than the American legal system has been used to. State court systems may have a greater variety of options, but for many of them too there will be no practical alternative to the creation of large courts.

Even today, all but one of the federal courts of appeals have more judges than the nine that the Hruska Commission Report of 1975 saw

[14]William H. Rehnquist, "Remarks of the Chief Justice" (Feb. 6, 1989, Denver, Colorado), at 8.

[15]The two categories were personal injury suits by railroad and maritime workers and civil RICO actions. The first accounted for only 325 of the 30,000-plus filings in the courts of appeals in statistical year 1987—about 1 percent. Civil RICO actions are so small in number that they are not tabulated separately.

[16]Both proposals involved administrative agency rulings now reviewed initially by the district court, with further scrutiny by the court of appeals. The chief justice suggested that review be confined to the latter.

[17]The chief justice suggested that Congress eliminate the right of in-state plaintiffs to invoke the diversity jurisdiction. The Federal Judicial Center study indicates that this reform would reduce the volume of diversity cases in the district courts by about 44 percent. See Partridge, supra note 10, at 34. As already noted, diversity cases account for about 13.5 percent of appellate filings.

as the maximum for effective and collegial operation. As the federal judicial system moves into the twenty-first century, courts of twenty or more judges will become the norm rather than the exception. Similar expansion can be expected in state appellate systems.

Distinguished members of the legal community have viewed this prospect with alarm. For example, Judge Richard Posner has stated flatly that "[a]llowing the circuits to grow willy-nilly and instituting quasi-en-banc procedures is not the answer to the caseload problem of the courts of appeals."[18] Less emphatically, Chief Justice Rehnquist has expressed the view that "a price is paid in the development of a coherent body of circuit law when we get beyond a certain point" in the size of an appellate court.[19] But if the premises set forth above are correct, it is bootless to lament the drawbacks of the large circuit; rather, lawyers and judges must learn how to make the large circuit work. One purpose of this volume is to assist in that endeavor.

The Role of the Circuit
in the Federal Judicial System

If no more were at stake than finding the least destructive of a generally invidious set of alternatives, study of the large appellate court would be a worthy, even important, enterprise, but not, perhaps, a very inspiring one. What takes it beyond the merely worthy is the vision of Judge Browning—a vision that finds positive virtue not so much in the large appellate court, but in the large circuit of which it is a component. Browning has even gone so far as to suggest that the solution to the caseload crisis may lie in the consolidation of existing circuits. Movement in that direction is highly unlikely, but the underlying perception holds out hope for something better than settling for the least of evils. To understand why, it is necessary to examine the role of the circuit in the federal judicial system.

The idea of the circuit as an organizing device for the federal courts has its origins in the Judiciary Act of 1789. Then as now, the circuit was a division of the country encompassing at least two states and thus less parochial than the districts,[20] but organized geographically and thus

[18]Posner, supra note 3, at 102.
[19]Rehnquist, supra note 14, at 7.
[20]From 1789 to the present, with negligible exceptions, district boundaries have never crossed state lines. See Frankfurter and Landis, supra note 1, at 11 and n.25; Charles Alan Wright, *The Law of Federal Courts* 8 and n.3 (West Publishing, 4th ed. 1983). The state of New York was divided into two districts in 1814; today twenty-four states

respectful of the regional spirit.[21] For the first hundred years, however, the structural role of the circuits was little more than symbolic.[22] The circuit courts had only a limited appellate jurisdiction over the district courts;[23] until 1869 they did not even have judges of their own. Governance and administration scarcely existed in the federal judicial system, but to the extent they did, they took place either within individual courts or (to a very limited degree) at the seat of government.

With the creation of the courts of appeals in 1891, the groundwork was laid for the development of a "law of the circuit." For the first time, appellate tribunals other than the Supreme Court were vested with substantial jurisdiction to review cases from the district courts. Some earlier proposals had called for a single intermediate court with nationwide authority,[24] but Congress rejected that approach, choosing instead to establish separate courts for each of the nine existing circuits. Over a period of time the hierarchical principle, superimposed on a structure defined by geographic boundaries, yielded the rule that the decisions of a court of appeals were binding on all districts within its circuit, but not elsewhere.[25] Nevertheless, recognition of the lawmaking role of the intermediate appellate courts was slow in coming. For three decades it was generally assumed that only the Supreme Court

---

encompass two or more districts. Each of the existing circuits comprises at least three states.

[21]The regional spirit was manifested more in the eastern and southern circuits than in the middle circuit, for the latter included two states north of the Mason-Dixon line (New Jersey and Pennsylvania) and three to the south (Delaware, Maryland, and Virginia). The eastern circuit was composed of four New England states and New York; the southern circuit encompassed South Carolina and Georgia.

[22]From 1816 until 1837, states newly admitted to the Union were excluded altogether from the circuit system because of political deadlock. See Frankfurter and Landis, supra note 1, at 37–48.

[23]See note 1.

[24]Frankfurter and Landis, supra note 1, at 81–83.

[25]Less than two decades after the creation of the courts of appeals, the hierarchical principle and its application were stated by a district judge in New York: "The lower federal courts . . . are . . . bound by the decisions of the Supreme Court of the United States and those of the Circuit Court of Appeals in their own circuit, but are not bound by those of a federal court of co-ordinate jurisdiction, or even the decisions of a federal Circuit Court of Appeals in another circuit. Courts are not mere machines to register and follow the opinions and decisions of some other court, unless that other court be one having appellate power in the same jurisdiction. . . ." Continental Securities Co. v. Interborough Rapid Transit Co., 165 F. 945, 959–60 (C.C.S.D.N.Y. 1908).

would "expound the law [so] as to furnish precedents for the inferior courts in future litigation."[26]

An important step was taken in 1925, when Congress enacted the so-called Judges' Bill, making Supreme Court review of court of appeals decisions largely discretionary. Under that legislation, the Supreme Court was expected to "confine its adjudications to issues of constitutionality and other matters of essentially national importance."[27] This conception of the Supreme Court's function left considerable room for precedential decision making by the courts of appeals, and over the next several decades those courts continued to grow in prestige and authority.[28] One manifestation of their new role was the development of procedures for en banc hearings, pioneered by the Third Circuit "to enable the court to maintain its integrity as an institution."[29] By 1972, Judge Henry J. Friendly could observe that "each circuit [makes] its own federal law in limited areas at least for a short time and occasionally . . . for a long one."[30] Today it is generally recognized that on many issues the governing law *is* the law of the circuit, although there is wide disagreement about the desirability of that state of affairs.[31]

---

[26]Frankfurter and Landis, supra note 1, at 259 n. 13 (quoting 1910 speech by President Taft). See generally Paul D. Carrington, "The Function of the Civil Appeal: A Late-Century View," 38 *S.C. L. Rev.* 411, 416–17 (1987).

[27]Frankfurter and Landis, supra note 1, at 280.

[28]In 1988 Congress further strengthened the authority of the courts of appeals by eliminating the last vestiges of the Supreme Court's obligatory jurisdiction over their decisions. See Bennett Boskey and Eugene Gressman, "The Supreme Court Bids Farewell to Mandatory Appeals," 121 F.R.D. 81 (1988).

[29]Albert B. Maris, "Hearing and Rehearing Cases in Banc," 14 F.R.D. 91, 96 (1954). En banc review is appropriate, the Third Circuit said, for "the occasional case where an important new principle of law or the construction of a new statute or the determination of a new point of procedure of widespread interest is involved." See id. at 97. The distinct resemblance between this description and the language used by Chief Justice Taft in describing the Supreme Court's role under the Act of 1925 serves to emphasize how much the courts of appeals had begun to share in that role. See William Howard Taft, "The Jurisdiction of the Supreme Court under the Act of February 13, 1925," 35 *Yale L.J.* 1, 2–3 (1925). Curiously, the strongest resistance to en banc rehearings came from the Ninth Circuit. See Lang's Estate v. Commissioner, 97 F.2d 867, 869 (9th Cir. 1938); Western Pac. R.R. Corp. v. Western Pac. R.R. Co., 197 F.2d 994, 1013–16 (9th Cir. 1952), vacated, 345 U.S. 247 (1953).

[30]Henry J. Friendly, "The 'Law of the Circuit' and All That," 46 *St. Johns L. Rev.* 406, 412 (1972). For further discussion of regionalism in the national law, see J. Woodford Howard, Jr., *Courts of Appeals in the Federal Judicial System* 33, 52–56, 79–84, 143–47 (Princeton University Press, 1981).

[31]At one extreme is the view expressed by the Hruska Commission in 1975: "Our

Parallel developments in the realm of administration and governance culminated in passage of the Administrative Office Act of 1939. Notwithstanding its innocuous title, the statute wrought, in the words of one of its proponents, "a fundamental change in the judicial system of the country."[32] In particular, the act established a judicial council in each circuit and gave it primary responsibility for supervising the work of the district courts. These councils represented the fulfillment of Chief Justice Hughes's vision of what might be called regional decentralization in the administration of the federal courts. No longer would district judges enjoy almost total independence in the administration of their own courts, but neither would power be concentrated at the seat of the national government. Hughes explicitly invoked the analogy of the states and their role in the national polity: "[Just] as we have the States as foci of administration with regard to local problems pertaining to the States, we have in the various Circuits of the country foci of federal action from the judicial standpoint." The chief justice thus sought, in the words of Peter Fish, "to distribute responsibility to the circuits as a defense against political forays centered on the establishment in Washington."[33]

Dispersion of authority on a regional scale was powerfully reinforced in the Judicial Councils Reform and Judicial Conduct and Disability Act of 1980. That act created a new, stronger mechanism for judicial discipline and placed the principal responsibility for enforcement in the hands of the circuit council. Other legislation vested power in the council to approve or disapprove a variety of actions taken by the district courts within the circuit. Congress also opted for

---

nation is not yet so homogeneous that the diversity of our peoples cannot be reflected to some advantage in the decisions of the regional courts." Commission on Revision of the Federal Court Appellate System, "Structure and Internal Procedures: Recommendations for Change," 67 F.R.D. 195, 235 (1975). In a more tentative vein, Justice Stevens has suggested that "the existence of differing rules of law in different sections of our great country is not always an intolerable evil." John Paul Stevens, "Some Thoughts on Judicial Restraint," 66 *Judicature* 177, 183 (1982). The contrary position has been expressed by Daniel J. Meador: "If the people want a matter to be governed in a diverse and perhaps regionally different way, [we] simply leave the matter to the states. . . . On the other hand, . . . when Congress enacts a statute it is [normally] because we want and need the law administered the same way throughout the nation." South Carolina Symposium, supra note 13, at 457 (remarks of Daniel J. Meador). For further discussion, see Part II, Introduction.

[32]Peter Graham Fish, *The Politics of Federal Judicial Administration* 165 (Princeton University Press, 1973) (quoting Judge John J. Parker).

[33]Id. at 145.

the circuit as the level at which bankruptcy judges would be chosen, although the selection is made by the court of appeals rather than the council.

As a result of these various developments, the circuit serves, even more than in Hughes's day, as a focus for both governance and adjudication in the federal courts. If all were going well, there would be no reason to rethink that role. But all is not going well. And in some respects the circuit system is a natural target for transformation or even abandonment. Although the circuits have been an accepted part of the federal judicial system for two hundred years, nothing in logic or in the constitutional plan requires the continued existence of any geographical divisions larger than the district.[34] Thus, if the circuits were no more than a convenient organizing device, we might be inclined to say that they had outlived their usefulness and to look for alternate structures more suited to the needs of the future.[35] The courts of appeals might be combined into a single national court, with a central en banc panel to resolve inconsistencies. District courts might be given their independence in matters of governance and administration, with limited supervision by the Judicial Conference of the United States.

But there is another way of looking at the circuit—not as an arbitrary division along geographical lines, but as an intermediate structure that makes it possible to carry out the tasks of adjudication and governance from a perspective that transcends the borders of a single district or state, yet without concentrating power in a centralized set of institutions. As Judge Browning suggested in testimony to a Senate subcommittee in 1984, by providing a uniform body of federal law for a territory whose people share important social, political, and commercial interests, the circuit can contribute to social and political unity within its area.[36] More important, "[a] large and vigorous circuit

[34]See Peter L. Strauss, "One Hundred Fifty Cases Per Year: Some Implications of the Supreme Court's Limited Resources for Judicial Review of Agency Action," 87 *Colum. L. Rev.* 1093, 1113–14 (1987). As Strauss points out, geographical organization at the trial level is required in criminal cases by the Sixth Amendment to the Constitution.

[35]Subsequent developments have undercut at least one of the premises of the scheme conceived by Chief Justice Hughes. One of Hughes's reasons for concentrating responsibility for supervision of the district courts at the circuit level was that the court of appeals judges would "know the work of the district judges by their records that they are constantly examining." See Fish, supra note 32, at 153. To the extent that district judges serve on the circuit councils, as they do today, this knowledge will be lacking. See Chapter 10.

[36]For extended excerpts from Browning's testimony, see Chapter 14 at note 39.

15

strengthens the decentralization of the federal court system"—a decentralization twice ordained by Congress against a background of federalism that resists concentration of power at the center.[37]

If these premises are accepted, the caseload pressures that threaten the viability of the circuit may also provide the opportunity for reforms that will invigorate the circuit system and thus reinforce the dispersion of power that the Framers saw as the greatest safeguard against tyranny or overreaching. That prospect, too, provides a reason for studying the innovations of the Ninth Circuit.

The Approach of This Book

The discussion thus far suggests that the structural and procedural innovations of the Ninth Circuit can be measured against three possible levels of ambition. At a minimum, large appellate courts are going to be with us in the foreseeable future, and we would do well to learn what we can about managing them effectively. Beyond that, the large court may provide the structure that will best accommodate the number of judges necessary to satisfy litigant demands in a way that entails minimal sacrifice of other values. Finally, the development of "large and vigorous" circuits may foster a healthy dispersion of power in the federal judicial system.

This last point is to some degree independent of the first two. By the same token, emphasis on the values of a strong circuit system does not necessarily carry with it any position on the still-simmering issue of dividing the Ninth Circuit.[38] To be sure, Judge Browning linked the two concepts by arguing that vigorous circuits would avoid the need for establishing a national court of appeals or national courts of specialized jurisdiction. And it is reasonable to assume that division of any existing circuit would reinforce pressures for creation of new

---

[37]See Andrzej Rapaczynski, "From Sovereignty to Process: The Jurisprudence of Federalism after Garcia," 1985 *Sup. Ct. Rev.* 341, 380–414. Rapaczynski's discussion of the values of federalism is of particular relevance here because of its emphasis on representation and participation rather than sovereignty.

[38]In May 1989 seven senators from the northwestern states introduced legislation to divide the Ninth Circuit by creating a new Twelfth Circuit that would include all of the present Ninth except Arizona, California, and Nevada. S. 948, 101st Cong., 1st Sess. (1989); see 135 Cong. Rec. S5026 (daily ed. May 9, 1989) (remarks of Sen. Gorton). The judges of the circuit mounted a vigorous offensive against the bill, and at the 1989 Circuit Conference overwhelming majorities of both judges and lawyers urged rejection of the proposal. For discussion of earlier attempts to divide the circuit, see Chapter 14.

national tribunals that would further concentrate power at the center. To that extent, a strong circuit system does presuppose no proliferation of additional circuits. Still, the circuit does serve other purposes; moreover, it is hard to believe that having twelve regional circuits rather than eleven would mean the difference between balkanization and tolerable diversity.

Whether the focus is on large circuits or on strengthening the circuit system, the starting point is the same. We take as a given the two principal functions of intermediate appellate courts—lawmaking and review for error—and seek to determine the extent to which the Ninth Circuit's innovations have aided in the effective performance of those functions. Part II examines initiatives that directly address the substance of adjudication—in particular, the judges' efforts to clarify standards of appellate review and to maintain consistency in panel decisions. Part III considers procedural and structural responses to the challenge of volume: screening panels, staff assistance, and specialized review in the trial court.

In pursuing the implications of this research, we have tried to assume no more than is necessary about the future shape of the federal appellate system, but rather to allow our findings to suggest the directions that reforms might take. For example, if the "limited en banc" is successful in making it possible for a large circuit to maintain uniformity of decision, this might support the desirability of having fewer circuits, without the need for a new tier of review below the Supreme Court. At the other extreme, if the Bankruptcy Appellate Panel has provided satisfactory appellate review, especially of nonprecedential cases, this might point to creation of new tiers immediately above the trial courts. Other possibilities are suggested by the essays in Part IV.

The open-endedness of this approach has another purpose as well: as suggested earlier, the lessons learned from the Ninth Circuit's experience should benefit not only the other federal circuits, but also the state appellate courts. Different constraints will be at work, but the essential challenge is the same.

As indicated earlier, we recognize that courts today have administrative as well as adjudicative responsibilities. No analysis of the large appellate court would be complete without consideration of the court's success in managing its own administrative structure. And because the circuit is the locus of responsibility for many aspects of administration and governance in the trial courts, it is necessary to examine the institutions that seek to promote the effective operation of tribunals at all levels in the hierarchy. Parts V and VI of the book thus concentrate on Ninth Circuit innovations that involve administration and governance rather than the decision of cases.

Almost as significant as the substance of the circuit's initiatives is the manner in which they were adopted and implemented. Courts are not generally regarded as organizations hospitable to change; yet over a fifteen-year period virtually all of the Ninth Circuit's institutions were transformed in ways that went to the heart of their operation.[39] Several of the chapters devote some attention to the origins of particular reforms, but in Part VII the focus shifts entirely to the climate and the process of change. That part cuts across subject-matter lines and takes a broader, essentially historical view of the reshaping of the Ninth Circuit's institutions during Browning's tenure as chief judge.

The project that generated this book differs in several ways from other studies of appellate courts. First, although the book deals with a wide range of issues, we have not attempted to provide a definitive treatise on the work of appellate courts or the operation of the federal judicial system. For example, many of the topics addressed by the Hruska Commission have not been treated at all. Some of them do not fit within the overall theme; others have not been particularly significant for the Ninth Circuit.

Second, the contributors have not been asked to consider, a priori, the entire universe of possible innovations; rather, they have taken as their starting point what the Ninth Circuit has already done. Because the Ninth Circuit has undertaken so much innovation over the last few years, there has been ample opportunity for imagination and creativity; at the same time, the focus on what has been done in one circuit has provided a solid factual foundation for the authors' analyses.

Third, the contributors have attempted, to the extent possible, to build on and learn from previous research. It is a common complaint of scholars generally and empirical researchers in particular that it is difficult to know how to conduct a study until after the work has been completed, or at any event is too far advanced to permit a radical restructuring. Thanks to the efforts of the Federal Judicial Center and of other scholars, the contributors to this volume often found that the groundwork had already been laid for their research efforts.[40] At the

---

[39]As noted in Chapter 11, the restructuring of the circuit conference began in the mid-1970s, under the leadership of Chief Judge Richard H. Chambers.

[40]In late 1988 the Federal Judicial Center published a useful compilation of its research reports on the federal courts of appeals. See Michael Tonry and Robert A. Katzmann, *Managing Appeals in Federal Courts* (Federal Judicial Center, 1988).

same time, the ability to check previous findings in a new setting has provided a valuable way of testing hypotheses.

Finally and most important, the project has had the full cooperation of the judges and staff of the Ninth Circuit. For example, the authors could draw on the massive database already in existence as part of the Ninth Circuit's case-processing programs. And several chapters include detailed micro-histories, based on internal documents, that provide unusual insights into the workings of today's judicial structures.

Looking toward the Future

In undertaking a course of experimentation ranging over wide areas affecting both adjudication and governance, the Ninth Circuit self-consciously sought "to test whether a large circuit, and particularly a large court of appeals, can function effectively."[41] The contributors to this volume have drawn their own conclusions about the success of the particular innovations studied, and I shall make no attempt to second-guess them here. Rather, I offer some reflections based on a review of the project as a whole.

One thought that emerges from Parts II and III taken in tandem is that, a century after the Evarts Act, the legal community is still struggling to delineate the appropriate relationship between precedential decision making and review for error in a three-tier structure within a common law system. Anyone who reads Felix Frankfurter's classic 1928 account today will be struck by his insistence that the work of the Supreme Court involves a unique kind of judicial business, denominated "public law." The clear implication is that the courts of appeals and the district courts are relegated to the more mundane task of resolving "the ordinary legal questions" arising in "private law."[42] There is no recognition that all three tiers might be part of a common enterprise, addressing many of the same issues but at different levels of particularity and with different degrees of freedom to innovate.[43]

Paul Carrington has characterized Frankfurter's distinction as "un-

---

[41]See Chapter 14 at note 39 (quoting testimony of Judge Browning).

[42]Frankfurter and Landis, supra note 1, at 307–8, 310.

[43]I think that that much would be common ground in the debate over the adequacy of the present structure. See South Carolina Symposium, supra note 13, at 468–69 (remarks of District Judge Robert E. Keeton). As indicated in the next paragraph of text, the disagreement centers on the amount of lawmaking that is appropriate at the intermediate level.

realistic, even unsophisticated," from a contemporary perspective.[44] Most observers would probably agree, but when it comes to finding a replacement for the Frankfurter model, the consensus breaks down. A widely shared belief is that the Supreme Court does perform a unique function, not because it alone deals with matters of "public law," but because lawmaking decisions by courts of regional jurisdiction are at best provisional and at worst disruptive.[45] That view is reflected in the assumption that seems to underlie many of today's reform proposals—that the law can be made more certain and knowable through the pronouncement of more rules at higher levels in the hierarchy.[46] Others will see this approach as a more sophisticated version of the now-discredited Langdellian orthodoxy and its vision of a self-contained system in which every case can be decided through "analytical reasoning from abstract norms that [are] themselves immanent in the existing case law."[47] I do not want to press the parallel too far, but the similarities are sufficiently striking to suggest caution in seeking to remake the system in order to secure more precedents binding on more people.[48]

[44]Carrington, supra note 26, at 419–20.

[45]The most comprehensive presentation of this view is found in id. at 425–48.

[46]This assumption has been articulated quite explicitly in the writings of Erwin N. Griswold. See, e.g., Erwin N. Griswold, "The Federal Courts Today and Tomorrow: A Survey and Summary," 38 *S.C. L. Rev.* 393, 405–6 (1987). Griswold acknowledged that "[t]he law is never precise and mechanical, and often it must be unclear." Id. at 406. Nevertheless, he adhered to the view that predictability suffers because there are not enough binding precedents. Id. See also Paul M. Bator, "What Is Wrong with the Supreme Court?" 51 *U. Pitt. L. Rev.* No. 3 (Spring 1990).

[47]Thomas C. Grey, "Langdell's Orthodoxy," 45 *U. Pitt. L. Rev.* 1, 40–41 (1983). Grey's article is a comprehensive critique of the Langdellian view of law as a science. The connection between that view and the argument about inadequate appellate capacity has also been noted by Herbert Wechsler. Wechsler expressed concern that Griswold had renounced "the great achievements that have happened in my lifetime in the nature of the judicial function"—the repudiation of "the closed case system in which my father's generation believed." He acknowledged that "the present view of precedent" might mean "that it is harder to advise clients or that there is bound to be a certain element of inequality in the application of law," but accepted that as the lesser evil. South Carolina Symposium, supra note 13, at 446–47 (remarks of Herbert Wechsler). Griswold disclaimed the implication that Wechsler had drawn, id. at 463, but not, to my mind, convincingly.

[48]Many of the difficulties Grey identifies in the Langdellian view are relevant to the structural issues addressed here. For example, when Grey explains why formality did not always produce predictability (Grey, supra note 47, at 45), or praises Cardozo for his "masterfully attentive use of the facts of particular cases" (id. at 47), he could almost be responding to Griswold's denunciation of the "discretionary approach to justice" resulting from "too little appellate capacity." See Griswold, supra note 46, at 402, 406.

In a more optimistic vein, Parts V and VII can be seen as vindicating Chief Justice Hughes's vision of regional decentralization in the governance of the federal courts. The restructuring of the council and of the circuit conference have democratized those institutions and made them more representative in a way that would have been difficult to achieve on a national scale. The reorganized conference has already served as a model for other circuits; the new form of the council may yet do so. Within the court of appeals, the process by which the limited en banc rule was adopted may provide a model for careful, collegial progress toward significant reforms elsewhere in the judiciary. Thus, whatever one may think of the circuits as testing-grounds for the evolution of legal rules, the Ninth Circuit experience strongly supports the utility of regional divisions as laboratories for experimentation in matters of governance and administration.

PART II

Adjudication: Coherence and Consistency

Introduction

During the first several decades under the three-tier structure established by the Evarts Act of 1891, the courts of appeals were confined largely to the task of review for error. The institutional functions of appellate review—declaring and harmonizing general principles—remained in the domain of the Supreme Court.

If that model were still valid, the problem of appellate overload could be dealt with fairly easily through the creation of new geographically organized appellate courts. But geometric increases in caseload and the vast expansion in the scope of federal law have made that model obsolete. On many issues, especially outside the realm of constitutional adjudication, the governing law is the law of the circuit. As a result, geographic fragmentation would only add to uncertainty and disarray. Creation of new courts of national jurisdiction might solve the problem of "appellate capacity," but at great cost.[1]

Against this background, the possibility of simply allowing existing circuits to grow (or even consolidating contiguous circuits) holds considerable promise. And the Ninth Circuit, with twenty-eight active judges and one-sixth of the federal appellate caseload, would be seen as the model for the future rather than as the "monstrosity" perceived by critics. But the desirability of that approach depends on the soundness of two premises, one empirical, the other normative. The empirical premise is that adjudicative unity over a wide geographic area can bring coherence and consistency to the law without the need for

---

[1]See Chapter 1 at note 12.

25

additional institutions of review at the national level. The normative proposition is that on at least some matters governed by national law the content of the rules can appropriately be defined by precedents of regional applicability. The two studies in this part of the book focus primarily on the empirical question, but they also contribute to the debate over the normative postulate.

A full-scale examination of coherence in the law of the circuit would require analysis of the court's work in each of the many areas of federal governance. Such an inquiry is beyond the scope of this book, but there is one issue that cuts across and affects all others: the standards governing the scope and depth of appellate review. These standards take on particular importance in the large circuit. If the appellate court is too zealous in second-guessing the trial courts, the result is to encourage appeals and, perhaps, to contribute to a sense that the law is unknowa because the volume of decisions delineating the application of particular rules is too large to be comprehended and organized.[2] But if the appellate judges are too deferential, the rules may become empty vessels, with the ultimate consequence of subverting "the law of the circuit" as a tool for hierarchical control and a source of everyday guidance.

In the latter part of the Browning era the Ninth Circuit Court of Appeals acted aggressively to articulate, rationalize, and publicize the standards of review applied to different kinds of issues and different kinds of cases. The court's efforts were manifested in several ways, including the convening of en banc panels to consider standard-of-review issues, the preparation of outlines for internal use, and the reiteration of explicit statements in opinions identifying the standard of review applied. The court even attempted to develop what might be called meta-standards for standards of review, that is, standards for determining what the standard should be for a particular issue.

In Chapter 2, Maurice Rosenberg examines and evaluates the Ninth Circuit's approach. He devotes particular attention to the clarity of the standards articulated and to the purposes served by the degree of deference accorded district court determinations on various kinds of issues. Among the areas of the law addressed are the use of summary judgment in civil litigation, the application of Rule 11's new provisions for sanctions, and the review of discretionary rulings by the trial court.

Rosenberg also assesses the Ninth Circuit's program to improve the

---

[2]The premise is that this zeal would be manifested in a higher incidence of reversals, which in turn would lead to a larger number of published opinions and longer explanations attempting to reconcile the various holdings.

quality of appellate review. He examines the court's achievements, the implications of the different standards articulated by the court, and remaining areas where problems persist. The chapter also attempts to look to the future and identify challenges that lie ahead. Of special interest is Rosenberg's recommendation that appellate courts be more specific in expressing reasons for not deferring to trial court decisions in particular cases. This in turn suggests that counsel on appeal should be encouraged or even required to focus more closely on considerations militating for or against deference. The broader implication is that allocating decision-making power in a way that is both appropriate and intelligible is not solely a concern of appellate judges; rather, it requires efforts by bench and bar, each working in its own sphere.

In Chapter 3, I evaluate the Ninth Circuit's efforts to maintain consistency in the law established by its panels. I begin by examining the various institutional devices for avoiding or eliminating intracircuit conflict, with particular attention to the Ninth Circuit's major innovation, the limited en banc panel. The chapter traces the lengthy process that led to adoption of the rule and reports on a detailed study of the cases in which en banc review was requested by a member of the court.

Analysis of the court's en banc work leaves open the question whether the court has succeeded in its efforts to minimize intracircuit conflicts. It is therefore necessary to undertake a broader study not limited to en banc cases. Starting with basic concepts of precedent in a common-law system, I propose an analytical framework for defining intracircuit conflict and identifying the kinds of decisions that are most likely to give rise to actual disarray in the law of the circuit. I then summarize the results of an empirical study designed to estimate the extent of conflict within the circuit. The study finds that actual conflict is rare but that some uncertainty can be seen in cases involving much-litigated legal issues that are governed by fact-specific rules.

Chapters 2 and 3 converge to shed light on the normative question raised by the Ninth Circuit experiment: the role of "the law of the circuit" in the federal judicial system. As noted in Chapter 1, the concept is a controversial one, in large part because the prospect that the law may be applied differently in different parts of the country seems to flout the determination that a matter should be controlled by national law in the first place. This concern is understandable, but its force is blunted by consideration of the way in which federal law actually operates. The matter has both a practical and a political dimension.

The practical dimension involves the need for predictability and

clarity in the law. From that standpoint, however, intercircuit variations pose only a modest threat. For the vast majority of the disputes
and transactions subject to federal jurisdiction, venue will be a given.
For example, in criminal prosecutions, habeas corpus actions, civil-
rights suits, and many others, there will seldom be any doubt as to
where litigation will take place. This means that the law that counts is
the law of the circuit; the fact that another circuit interprets the law
differently is largely irrelevant.[3] In some business-related disputes the
venue options may be wider, but there is little evidence that inconsistent rules of federal law have posed a problem for entities whose
conduct may be challenged in more than one circuit.[4]

In any event, the most thoughtful formulation of the argument rests
not on practical but on political grounds. The premise is that the very
existence of a federal statute tells us that the American people have
made a decision, through their representatives in Congress, that a
matter should be dealt with in the same way throughout the nation.
Regional disuniformity in the application of federal law is seen as
thwarting this determination.

This concern has great force when the meaning of federal law depends on a choice between articulated legal rules. A classic illustration
of this pattern, often invoked by Erwin N. Griswold, is *United States v.
Cartwright*,[5] involving the question whether mutual fund shares in a
decedent's estate should be valued, for tax purposes, at the bid or the
asked price. But in a common-law system, issues of that kind are the
exception rather than the rule.[6] Moreover, the available evidence indi-

---

[3]This proposition must be qualified in one respect. When the Supreme Court over-
rules a circuit precedent, the new law generally will be applied retroactively, thus
frustrating the expectations of those who have relied on the law of the circuit. For a
recent illustration, see In re Cimarron Investors, 848 F.2d 974, 976 (9th Cir. 1988). This
approach is followed even in criminal cases, as United States v. Rodgers, 466 U.S. 475,
484 (1984), indicates. See the discussion in Chapter 3, note 2. However, the *Rodgers*
caveat applies largely to issues that are not only doubtful but discrete, and as indicated
in the text, such issues are relatively uncommon.

[4]Within the Supreme Court, the most zealous monitor of unresolved intercircuit
conflicts has been Justice Byron R. White. Early in the 1988 Term, White flagged fifteen
cases in which he asserted that the Court was denying review despite the presence of a
conflict. See Metheny v. Hamby, 109 S. Ct. 270 (1988) (White, J., dissenting) (collecting
cases). Even assuming that all the conflicts were genuine, few if any created a real risk
that the same conduct of the same actor might be tested by different standards in
different circuits. Eight of the cases arose out of criminal prosecutions; most of the others
involved disputes that could have been litigated only in a single state or circuit.

[5]411 U.S. 546 (1973).

[6]For elaboration of this point, see Arthur D. Hellman, "The Proposed Intercircuit
Tribunal: Do We Need It? Will It Work?" 11 *Hastings Const. L.Q.* 375, 407–13 (1984).

cates that when two or more circuits have chosen different rules, thus creating an actual conflict, the Supreme Court usually steps in to provide a definitive resolution.[7]

Chapter 2 underscores the limited applicability of the *Cartwright* model. On many issues, as Rosenberg's research shows, the articulated rules leave wide leeway for the exercise of discretion at the trial level. In other words, the rules themselves reflect an acknowledgment that there need not be total uniformity in the way the law is administered throughout the country. By the same token, differences in application from circuit to circuit do not thwart the choice made by the people's representatives.

To be sure, even as to these issues there is widespread, though not universal, agreement that appellate review of some kind is required "to protect[] the public from the idiosyncracies and indiscretions of individual district judges."[8] The question then is whether the law of the circuit is an efficient device for maintaining "effectiveness of command"—hierarchical control within the framework established by rules accepted nationwide. Chapter 3 suggests that it is. Admittedly, the study also indicates that it is precisely in the realm of fact-specific legal rules that the law of the circuit is most likely to appear incoherent because of the proliferation of relevant precedents. But the issues that follow this pattern tend to be issues that do not directly govern primary conduct.

This analysis does not necessarily lead to the conclusion that the development of large, geographically defined circuits is preferable to the creation of national tribunals organized by subject matter as a means of coping with increased appellate caseloads. That is a far-reaching question, well beyond the scope of these introductory comments. The analysis does suggest that on at least some matters governed by the Federal Constitution or Acts of Congress the content of the rules can appropriately be defined by "the law of the circuit."

---

[7]See id. at 395–98; see also Arthur D. Hellman, "Preserving the Essential Role of the Supreme Court: A Comment on Justice Rehnquist's Proposal," 14 *Fla. St. U. L. Rev.* 15, 19–20 (1986).

[8]Paul D. Carrington, "The Function of the Civil Appeal: A Late-Century View," 38 *S.C. L. Rev.* 411, 434 (1987).

2

Standards of Review

MAURICE ROSENBERG

The tendency to appeal in the federal courts needs no artificial stimulus. To the contrary, caseload data show how essential it is for the administration of justice that futile appeals be discouraged. Nationwide, in the period 1960 through 1983, federal civil appeals climbed from 8.8 percent of terminations on the merits to 17.6 percent, precisely doubling.[1] Criminal appeals were filed at the rate of 25.1 percent in 1960, rose to 98.1 percent in 1982, and leveled off at slightly below that figure.[2]

Appeals in the Ninth Circuit have not lagged behind. In 1960, 9,824 civil cases terminated in the district courts throughout the circuit. In that year only 236 civil appeals were filed. In 1970, with barely any increase in the number of civil suits terminated, appellate filings in these cases rose to 762, nearly tripling the appeal rate. By 1976 the number of civil appeals had climbed to 1,482, almost twice the 1970 volume; by 1988 the figure had risen to 4,825 civil appeals, a nearly

---

[1]Richard A. Posner, *The Federal Courts: Crisis and Reform* 91 (Harvard University Press, 1985). According to Posner, the rate of civil appeals nationwide rose in nine subject areas and fell in six during the twenty-three-year period. In the increased appeal group were federal contract, federal tort claims, Jones Act, and federal forfeiture and penalty suits. This was not a function of an increased tendency on the part of the courts of appeals to reverse. The reversal rate in United States civil cases fell from 24.9 percent to 20.0 percent in the period studied; in private civil cases it fell from 26.5 percent to 17.8 percent. Id. at 69.

[2]Id. at 90. The year 1960 marked the start of the sharp rise in appellate filings that continues to the present. Compare id. at 59.

twentyfold increase over 1960. In just the twelve years of James R. Browning's chief judgeship the caseload grew to 338 percent of its 1976 size. No one could seriously contend that the court of appeals needs to advertise for business.

Many of the appeals in the Ninth Circuit were hopeless because the decision below was assuredly correct. Many others were hopeless for a different reason—one relating to limitations on the appellate court's function. That is to say, even though the decision below would have been impeachable if appellate review were unrestricted, in point of fact there was no real chance for a reversal because the court of appeals was obliged by established standards to affirm unless, for example, crucial fact findings were not merely in error but clearly so. Discretionary rulings had to be not merely incorrect, but abusive.

Several questions are suggested by those propositions. First, if the limitations on review imposed by the standards were made known to would-be appellants in clear, consistent terms and were reliably applied, would hopeless appeals have been discouraged? Next, are the standards of review too fuzzy? Are they applied irresolutely and inconsistently? Is the consequence that losers are led to harbor vain hopes and to bring foredoomed appeals? Have the court's decisions contributed to the flood of appeals or have they instead laid down such clear standards of review that only foolhardy advocates would risk money, reputation, and possible sanctions by taking appeals from virtually unreviewable decisions? And finally, is there room for further clarification of the standards? These questions received serious attention and determined responses in the Ninth Circuit Court of Appeals under the leadership of Chief Judge Browning. Probably no other circuit has reacted to the problem so resolutely. Have the results repaid the effort? That is the inquiry pursued in this chapter.

Originally, my intention was twofold. Not only would the chapter evaluate the clarity and soundness of the review standards fashioned by the circuit; it would assess their actual effectiveness in deterring hopeless appeals. Direct evidence of effect would presumably appear in the form of a shrinkage in the number of appeals on hopeless issues—a decline that lawyers' reports would attribute to the futility of appealing in the teeth of the review-limiting standards. However, a sufficient quantity of that sort of evidence is not available at this stage. The assessment must rest on indirect evidence, on inferences rather than interviews or hard statistical data. These inferences have been derived from the text of the standards, the cases applying them, and conversations with a sampling of judges and lawyers.

31

Maurice Rosenberg

Devising Standards of Appellate Review

Respected authorities are convinced that standards of review are important in the appellate process. In 1988, apparently acting on that conviction, the Supreme Court took a court of appeals to task for failing to announce the standard it applied when it reversed the trial court's findings. Justice Marshall complained, "The Court of Appeals never identified the standard of review that it applied to the District Court's factual findings."[3]

That complaint could seldom be directed at the Court of Appeals for the Ninth Circuit. That court has adopted a program dedicated to clarifying and adhering to appropriate standards of review. The premise of the program was succinctly expressed by Judge Otto R. Skopil, Jr., in the introduction to his outline on this subject compiling hundreds of exemplary quotations from the cases: "I . . . believe that the standard of review is extremely significant to our decisionmaking process."[4]

A key feature of the standards program is Rule 28–2.5, requiring the appellant to state in its brief the applicable standard of review for every issue.[5] For its part, the court of appeals itself has been quite faithful in identifying the standard of review it follows with regard to major issues. As shown in Table 2.1, 74 percent of the opinions in a recent sample set forth the standard of review in express terms.

Implicit in the effort to formulate rational and workable standards of review is acceptance of the principle that the court of appeals should subordinate its own view and defer to the district court's decision in some situations and to some degree. The standards address two issues: whether the appellate court should defer to the district court and, if so, to what extent. They produce a four-way classification of the nature of issues on appeal: questions of fact; questions of law; mixed questions; and questions of discretion. With regard to each category, the degree of deference accorded to the trial judge is designed to promote the better functioning of the judicial process. The theory is that if deference makes this happen, it justifies departing from the normal presumption that three appellate judges are better able than one trial judge to arrive at the correct decision.

---

[3]Amadeo v. Zant, 486 U.S. 214, 223 (1988).

[4]Otto R. Skopil, "Standard of Review Outline" (July 7, 1986), at 1.

[5]The rule reads as follows: "As to each issue, appellant shall state where in the record on appeal the issue was raised and ruled on and identify the applicable standard of review."

Table 2.1. Express references to "standards of review" in published opinions, Ninth Circuit Court of Appeals, 1987–88

Volume F.2d	Total Cases	Number of References		Relative frequency of references (%)		
		Caption	Text	Caption	Text	Total
846	20	3	8	15	40	55
845	29	5	16	17	55	72
844	21	6	9	29	43	72
843	31	6	17	19	55	74
842	25	2	16	8	64	72
841	49	12	23	24	47	71
840	28	8	13	29	46	75
839	30	8	13	27	43	70
838	24	5	15	21	63	83
837	24	6	12	25	50	75
836	21	4	12	19	57	76
835	16	6	8	38	50	88
834	27	7	15	26	56	81
833	50	12	28	24	56	80
832	28	6	14	21	50	71
831	39	10	22	26	56	82
830	28	5	14	18	50	68
829	44	12	18	27	41	68
828	35	4	20	11	57	69
827	63	11	37	17	59	76
826	17	1	8	6	47	53
817	19	6	11	32	58	89
TOTAL 22	668	145	349	21.7%	52.2%	73.9%

Source: Vols. 817 and 826–846 F.2d; opinions dated from May 18, 1987–May 18, 1988.
Note: Percentages may not add up because of rounding-off.

A strong endorsement of that view was given by Justice O'Connor for the Supreme Court in 1985 in *Miller v. Fenton*.[6] The issue was whether the Third Circuit was correct in treating voluntariness of a confession as a question of fact. Holding that it was not, she pointed out that the decisive inquiry was whether, "as a matter of the sound administration of justice, one judicial actor is better positioned than another to decide the issue in question."[7] If the district court is "better positioned," given the needs and values of the sound administration of justice, some degree of deference is due its decision. If the district court is not better positioned, the court of appeals' review should be nondeferential. For example, in deciding an issue of historical fact, the

[6]474 U.S. 104 (1985).
[7]Id. at 114.

trier of the fact—whether jury or judge—"is usually in a superior position to appraise and weigh the evidence."[8] On the other hand, in identifying or declaring the applicable rule of law, the appellate court has the advantage of superior numbers of judges as well as an opportunity to confer, exchange views, and reason collegially.

The most troublesome step for standard-of-review purposes comes after the facts are determined and the relevant legal rule is selected: deciding "whether the rule of law as applied to the established facts is or is not violated."[9] This is the problem of the mixed question of law and fact. Acknowledging in 1984 that its "jurisprudence concerning appellate review of mixed questions lacks clarity and coherence,"[10] the Ninth Circuit sought to formulate clear guidelines to end the admitted disarray in its precedents by taking en banc an appeal raising for review a mixed question of law and fact. The issue in the suppression-of-evidence case, *United States v. McConney*,[11] was whether police officers, who entered the defendant's house after announcing their identity and purpose, were excused by "exigent circumstances" from having to await admittance or refusal in order to comply with the federal statute. In its effort to clarify the standards of appellate review, the court outlined the guiding principles and underlying policies. A six-member majority declared that, as to district court determinations of pure questions of fact or law,

> [t]he appropriate standard of review for the first two of the district court's determinations—its establishment of historical facts and its selection of the relevant legal principle—has long been settled. Questions of fact are reviewed under the deferential, clearly erroneous standard. . . . Questions of law are reviewed under the non-deferential, de novo standard. . . . These established rules reflect the policy concerns that properly underlie standard of review jurisprudence generally.[12]

With regard to review of mixed fact-law questions, the court adopted a "functional analysis," one that made the pivotal question the impact on administration of justice concerns of applying a deferential rather than a nondeferential standard:

---

[8]See Zenith Radio Corp. v. Hazeltine Research, Inc., 395 U.S. 100, 123 (1969).
[9]See Pullman-Standard v. Swint, 456 U.S. 273, 289 n. 19 (1982).
[10]See United States v. McConney, 728 F.2d 1195, 1200 (9th Cir. 1984).
[11]Id.
[12]Id. at 1200–1201 (footnote and citations omitted).

If the concerns of judicial administration—efficiency, accuracy, and precedential weight—make it more appropriate for a district judge to determine whether the established facts fall within the relevant legal definition, we should subject his determination to deferential, clearly
erroneous review. If, on the other hand, the concerns of judicial administration favor the appellate court, we should subject the district judge's
finding to de novo review.[13]

The court went on to observe that generally the concerns of judicial
administration favor the appellate court, thus justifying plenary (so-
called *de novo*) review. That is because applying the law to facts requires considering the pertinent legal concepts and exercising judgment about the values that animate the relevant legal principles.[14] On
the other hand, if applying the law to the facts calls for an essentially
factual inquiry—one "founded on the fact-finding tribunal's experience with the mainsprings of human conduct"—the concerns of judicial administration favor the district court and call for the clearly
erroneous standard of review.[15]

The court conceded that its functional analysis neither offers a lit-
mus test for all mixed questions nor distinguishes unerringly between
findings of fact and conclusions of law.[16] Still, said the majority, "we
think that if we focus on the nature of the inquiry required in determining whether the established facts fall within the relevant legal
definition, we employ a neutral test that accurately reflects the concerns that properly underlie standard of review jurisprudence."[17] The
critical factors supporting plenary review of the finding of exigent
circumstances were that the determination required the court to balance and make judgments on competing societal values and that the
decision would clearly be of precedential importance.[18] The opinion
was not oblivious to the fact that applying the nondeferential standard
of plenary review requires a greater investment of appellate time and
energy than the less searching clearly erroneous standard.[19]

In the few years since it was rendered, the *McConney* decision has
been heavily cited—more than 560 LEXIS references in the Ninth
Circuit alone and scores of citations in other circuits. The *McConney*

[13]Id. at 1202.
[14]Ibid.
[15]Ibid. (quoting Commissioner v. Duberstein, 363 U.S. 278, 289 (1960)).
[16]Id. at 1204.
[17]Ibid.
[18]Id. at 1205.
[19]Id. at 1201 n.7.

analysis has apparently had an influence on the way the Ninth Circuit looks at the broad issue of fashioning appellate review standards. Its underlying approach also emerges in some of the specific contexts with which the remainder of this chapter is concerned.

Review of Summary Judgments

Few procedural issues generate as sharp divisions as whether a summary judgment should be granted on the ground that there is in reality no factual question requiring trial despite what the pleadings say. Although there is relatively little disagreement with the cost-and-burden-avoidance aims of the summary judgment procedure, there are fierce battles over its application. Rule 56 allows any party to ask for a summary judgment early in the proceeding "if the pleadings, depositions, answers to interrogatories, and admissions on file, together with the affidavits, if any, show that there is no genuine issue as to any material fact and that the moving party is entitled to a judgment as a matter of law."[20] The courts have focused heavily on the phrase "genuine issue as to any material fact," reading it as requiring a close examination to determine whether the evidence warrants dispensing with a trial.[21]

Interest in the standards of review applied in summary judgment decisions has been at an especially high level since the famous trio of cases decided by the Supreme Court in 1986, *Matsushita, Anderson,* and *Celotex.*[22] There are abundant appeals from summary judgments.[23] A computer search turned up 566 Ninth Circuit summary judgment cases decided on appeal between March 26, 1986, when the *Matsushita* decision was handed down, and February 25, 1989, the cutoff date for the search. The decisions awarding a summary judgment under the Rule 56 prerequisite of "no genuine issue as to any material fact and . . . the moving party [being] entitled to a judgment as a matter of law" are divisible into three categories, depending on whether the court found (1) an absence of the minimum evidence necessary to support a material element of the claim or defense; or (2) a defect of

[20]Fed. R. Civ. P. 56(c).

[21]See, e.g., Anderson v. Liberty Lobby, Inc., 477 U.S. 242, 248–52 (1986).

[22]Matsushita Elec. Indus. Co. v. Zenith Radio Corp., 475 U.S. 574 (1986); Anderson v. Liberty Lobby, Inc., 477 U.S. 242 (1986); Celotex Corp. v. Catrett, 477 U.S. 317 (1986).

[23]Because of the final judgment rule, almost all these appeals are from grants of summary judgment.

law in the claim or defense; or (3) a lack of evidentiary or legal support with regard to a mixed question of law and fact.

The Supreme Court's 1986 threesome actually dealt with only the first-listed basis for summary judgment—an insufficiency of evidence to avoid defeat. Cases of this type probably account for fewer than half of all summary judgments. Cases in the second category appear to be at least as numerous as the deficient-evidence type. The mixed law-and-fact category is relatively sparse. The reasons for noting the relative frequency of cases in the various categories are, first, that the 1986 trio provides little guidance for any but the first category, and second, that the standards of appellate review differ with the type of deficiency.

In many of the decisions discussed below, the court of appeals included in its opinion a special section headed "Standard of Review." The court then routinely began its discussion of that subject with the statement, "This court reviews a district court's grant of summary judgment *de novo*." The ordinary meaning of reviewing *de novo* is that the court is not limited to the record made before the first tribunal and will take new evidence.[24] Judge Skopil's *Standard of Review Outline* concurs by giving this definition of the term: "De novo review means trying the matter anew, the same as if . . . no decision had been previously rendered."[25] That plainly is not the meaning the court of appeals intends in reviewing summary judgments. There is no suggestion in the summary judgment decisions that the court has any idea of taking new evidence. The term is apparently designed to make clear that in discharging its review function the court of appeals will be substantially unaffected by the determination of the court below. In a different context that conception of *de novo* review was expressed more helpfully and accurately without invoking the Latin: "We review [the] questions without deference to the district court's legal interpretations."[26] In the summary judgment context, another helpful statement of what is intended by "*de novo* review" appears in *T. W. Electric Service,*

[24]*Black's Law Dictionary* (5th ed. 1979) defines *de novo* as "Anew, afresh; a second time." *Hearing de novo* is "[g]enerally, a new hearing or hearing for the second time, contemplating an entire trial in same manner in which matter was originally heard and a review of previous hearings." The term is used in this sense in other contexts, notably in connection with appeals following court-annexed arbitration awards or administrative agency determinations. See, e.g., 28 U.S.C. § 655 (trial *de novo* in experimental arbitration program).

[25]The definition was quoted from Exner v. FBI, 612 F.2d 1202, 1209 (9th Cir. 1980).

[26]Los Angeles Nut House v. Holiday Hardware Corp., 825 F.2d 1351, 1353 (9th Cir. 1987).

Inc. v. Pacific Electric Contractors: "[W]hen reviewing a grant of summary judgment, this court sits in the same position as the district court and applies the same summary judgment test that governs the district court's decision."[27]

Logically, the depth of the appellate court's review of a summary judgment grant should depend on the nature of the issue presented; often it does. As already indicated, summary judgment may be granted (1) for a defect of fact in the sense that the party has no evidentiary support for an essential element of the case, or so little support it is insufficient to avoid an adverse judgment; (2) for a fatal defect of law in a party's position; or (3) for a flaw affecting a mixed question of law and fact. Reference to the cases illustrates the responses these diverse issues have generated.

Defect of Evidence on Issue of Material Fact

The court of appeals has been prone to reverse a grant of summary judgment when it finds that the district court discounted evidence the jury might have credited. In *Allen v. Scribner*,[28] a public employee suing for on-the-job harassment, retaliation, and other injurious conduct resisted the defendants' motion for summary judgment by offering the supporting affidavits of two co-workers. These contained hearsay in violation of Rule 56(e). After the affidavits went unchallenged in the district court, the court of appeals ruled first that their deficiencies had been waived and then that the affidavits raised issues of credibility requiring trial.

In *Baxter v. MCA, Inc.*,[29] the case turned on whether the musical theme in the movie *E.T.* was "substantially similar" to the plaintiff's earlier composition. The court of appeals held that this fact question was one that depended on circumstantial inference (from the combination of notes and other musical values). The question was therefore for the trier of the facts to decide, not the district judge on summary judgment.

The *Allen* and *Baxter* cases show that the court of appeals will perform a searching review of the record when a summary judgment is

---

[27]809 F.2d 626, 630 (9th Cir. 1987). Seemingly, this means that when the basis of the motion is alleged insufficiency of the evidence to pass the directed verdict test, the court of appeals will pose that test itself for independent determination. When the basis of the motion is an alleged defect in law, the court likewise will accord no deference to the district court's view.

[28]812 F.2d 426 (9th Cir. 1987).

[29]812 F.2d 421 (9th Cir. 1987).

granted for insufficiency of evidence on an issue that turns on credibility or circumstantial inference. But the presence of such issues will not protect an opponent of the motion who fails to adduce supporting evidence when properly challenged to do so. In *Coverdell v. Dept. of Social & Health Services*,[30] the issue was whether the defendants had been motivated by racial bias or class animus in removing the mother's newborn daughter from her custody. Summary judgment for defendants was affirmed on appeal because the plaintiff had not made any showing that there was a genuine issue as to the defendants' motivation. The court of appeals cautioned that, "even in a civil rights action, plaintiff may not survive a motion for summary judgment without offering some evidence in support of her claim."[31]

Many of the cases in which a summary judgment motion is granted for insufficiency of evidence to create a genuine issue of material fact are destined for trial without a jury.[32] In those cases the directed verdict test cannot serve as the standard for deciding the motion (as it does, the Supreme Court has assured us, in cases entitled to trial by a jury).[33] By the same token, the appellate court's review of an "insufficiency of evidence" summary judgment cannot appropriately mirror its review of a directed verdict motion if the case was due for nonjury trial. In the latter event, if the district judge who would try the case has granted summary judgment because the evidentiary materials submitted on the motion do not permit the finding of fact contended for by the opponent of summary judgment, the appellate court should review on the clearly erroneous standard. In short, the standard of review of sufficiency of evidence to resist summary judgment should depend on whether there was a right to trial by a jury.

Errors Regarding Issues of Law

As earlier noted, summary judgments are frequently awarded because of a fatal legal defect in the loser's position. Common examples

---

[30]834 F.2d 758 (9th Cir. 1987).

[31]Id. at 769.

[32]E.g., No GWEN Alliance of Lane County, Inc. v. Aldridge, 855 F.2d 1380 (9th Cir. 1988); Ferguson v. International Ass'n of Bridge Workers, 854 F.2d 1169 (9th Cir. 1988); In re Entz-White Lumber & Supply, Inc., 850 F.2d 1338 (9th Cir. 1988); United States v. King Features Entertainment, Inc., 843 F.2d 394 (9th Cir. 1988); Hutchinson v. United States, 838 F.2d 390 (9th Cir. 1988); Jurado v. Eleven-Fifty Corp., 813 F.2d 1406 (9th Cir. 1987).

[33]See *Celotex Corp.*, 477 U.S. at 323.

of this type are statutes of limitations issues[34] and cases involving the effects of a former adjudication as res judicata (claim preclusion) or collateral estoppel (issue preclusion).[35] In many other cases the decision turns on the interpretation and application of a word or phrase in a statute, regulation, common law rule, or written instrument.[36]

A case in which the district court has determined that one side's legal position is so weak it cannot withstand summary judgment presents a quite ordinary problem of appellate review. The court of appeals is to examine the judgment independently and without deference to the district judge's views. The real question, as noted earlier, is whether the term *"de novo"* is the most helpful expression to convey that function. Although there is probably no harm in the present usage, it seems more meaningful to speak of "independent," "plenary," or "nondeferential" review. In effect, the court would be saying, "We apply our own judgment and decide the issue as a matter of law."

Mixed Questions of Law and Fact

Summary judgments deciding mixed questions present the most difficult problems of review. Their redeeming feature is that they are far less numerous than the Rule 56 cases raising unmixed fact or law questions.

---

[34]E.g., Duncan v. Southwest Airlines, 838 F.2d 1504 (9th Cir. 1988); Sheet Metal Workers Int'l Ass'n v. Air Systems Eng'g, 831 F.2d 1509 (9th Cir. 1987).

[35]E.g., Robi v. Five Platters, Inc., 838 F.2d 318 (9th Cir. 1988); Garrett v. City and County of San Francisco, 818 F.2d 1515 (9th Cir. 1987).

[36]E.g., Matter of Bishop, Baldwin, Rewald, et al., 856 F.2d 78 (9th Cir. 1988) (summary judgment for the defendant bank appropriate after the Supreme Court of Hawaii answered a certified question exonerating the bank from liability for paying certain checks); EEOC v. Boeing Co., 843 F.2d 1213 (9th Cir. 1988) (FAA age-sixty rule for commercial airplane pilots did not establish a bona fide occupational qualification as a matter of law for an airplane manufacturer that removed pilots from active flight duty at age sixty); Eldredge v. Carpenters 46 N. Cal. Counties JATC, 833 F.2d 1334 (9th Cir. 1987) (summary judgment for plaintiff class in Title VII action against union by female applicants for apprenticeships appropriate when defendant failed to show business necessity for employment system that produced disparate negative impact on females); Cohen v. Paramount Pictures Corp., 845 F.2d 851 (9th Cir. 1988) (term in license contract conferring the right to exhibit a film "by means of television" does not include the right to distribute video cassettes of the film); Air Transport Ass'n v. P.U.C. of State of Cal., 833 F.2d 200 (9th Cir. 1987) (state officials violated state law prohibiting telephone customers from eavesdropping); Turner v. McMahon, 830 F.2d 1003 (9th Cir. 1987) (plain language of Social Security Act permits state to recoup overpayments to AFDC recipients made under compulsion of erroneous court order).

Typical problems in this category are like those that arose in the *McConney* case, discussed earlier: Were there "exigent circumstances" within the meaning of the federal law excusing "knock-notice" entry into the suspect's abode despite lack of permission or refusal? In reviewing a summary judgment on an issue of that kind, ought the appellate court's approach be to treat the issue as a question of fact calling for the clearly erroneous test or as a question of law opening the matter to plenary, nondeferential review? *McConney's* functional analysis is the one most frequently applied by the court of appeals. Because it requires subtle and complex judgments, the *McConney* approach is probably not much of a barrier to appealing. The temptation remains strong for the loser to present the mixed question as one of law only so that the panel, reviewing it independently, is freer to reverse than if the fact standard—did the district court clearly err?—applies. A brief list of typical cases will illustrate:

- Was the misstatement in the security offering "material" within the meaning of the statute?[37]
- Were the motion picture clearances given to the competitor of the antitrust plaintiff "reasonable" restraints of trade?[38]
- Was the suspect's consent to a warrantless police search "voluntary"?[39]

In situations like those there clearly is an underlying matrix of facts. In each case these are imbedded in a context such that the court, while making findings of fact, could simultaneously resolve the ultimate, dispositive issues if it is so minded. Or it can instead treat the dispositive issue as a legal question, subject to the purposes and policies of the applicable rule of law. In each case the choice requires hard thought and close analysis; it is not susceptible to global solution.

Suggestions Regarding Review of Summary Judgment

The subject is usually approached as if the dominant question is the one treated in the Supreme Court's 1986 triad. In reality, as has been shown, a large part of the problem is review of summary judgments based on questions of law or mixed law-fact questions. Taking that into account, the court of appeals would do better to avoid reflexive intona-

---

[37]Anderson v. Aurotek, 774 F.2d 927, 931 (9th Cir. 1985).
[38]Theee [sic] Movies of Tarzana v. Pacific Theatres, Inc., 828 F.2d 1395 (9th Cir. 1987).
[39]United States v. $25,000 U.S. Currency, 845 F.2d 857 (9th Cir. 1988).

tion of "We review appeals from summary judgments *de novo*." Instead, the standard of review should be the one appropriate to the category of defect in the opponent's case. If it is insufficiency of evidence, the standard of review should depend on whether the opponent is entitled to a jury trial or not. If the former, the appellate function should mirror the process involved in reviewing a directed verdict or judgment notwithstanding the verdict. If a bench trial was in the offing, the question would be whether the district judge clearly erred in granting judgment. As for the latter cases, the court of appeals might consider adopting a standard that expressly accords due deference to the district court's appraisal of the record.[40] District courts can enhance the chances of appellate deference if the judges follow the practice of expressly identifying (1) the facts they deem material and undisputed and (2) the facts they recognize as disputed but deem nonmaterial.

Review of Rule 11 Decisions

Rule 11 of the Federal Rules of Civil Procedure was radically amended in 1983 in hopes of making it an effective means of curbing the practice of some litigants and lawyers to produce pleadings and motion papers that are unwarranted in fact or law or inspired by improper purposes. By 1983 the earlier version of Rule 11, adopted thirty-five years before, was virtually a dead letter. The 1983 amendments certainly brought the rule to life. The revisions tightened the standards for filing pleadings and other papers and commanded the courts to impose sanctions when the standards were violated. Within a few years the district courts found themselves bench-deep in Rule 11 motions. Numerous issues surfaced. Many have been decided in inconsistent ways by the district courts, and the judges and the bar look to the courts of appeals for guidance. The growing volume of appeals from Rule 11 orders raises anew the challenging question of how to ensure that unclear appellate practice does not stimulate worthless appeals.

One of the Ninth Circuit's best-known efforts to enunciate unam-

---

[40]Even though the "clearly erroneous" limitation of Rule 52 does not apply to review of summary judgments, the Supreme Court has indicated a like standard would be appropriate. See City of Rome v. United States, 446 U.S. 156, 183 (1980) (applying clearly erroneous test to findings of fact on direct review of summary judgment by three-judge district court).

biguous appellate review standards is an often-repeated paragraph in its 1986 decision, *Zaldivar v. City of Los Angeles*.[41] The case involved a dispute over whether the federal Voting Rights Act's requirement that election materials be published in the language of a minority group applied to a notice of intention to circulate a recall petition. By the time the case reached the court of appeals, the election was over, the merits were mooted, and all that remained was the validity of the district court's order assessing counsel fee sanctions against the plaintiffs for assertedly violating Rule 11 of the Federal Rules of Civil Procedure by harassing their adversaries. In reversing the imposition of sanctions for error of law, Judge Charles E. Wiggins for the panel outlined the standard-of-review problem as follows:

> Appellate review of orders imposing sanctions under Rule 11 may require a number of separate inquiries. If the facts relied upon by the district court to establish a violation of the Rule are disputed on appeal, we review the factual determinations of the district court under a clearly erroneous standard. If the legal conclusion of the district court that the facts constitute a violation of the Rule is disputed, we review that legal conclusion *de novo*. Finally, if the appropriateness of the sanction imposed is challenged, we review the sanction under an abuse of discretion standard.[42]

In a footnote the *Zaldivar* opinion explained that this was the court's first effort since Rule 11 was amended in 1983 to declare the appropriate standard of review. It went on to say that the standard adopted was consistent with the Rule 11 standards followed in other circuits, with those the Ninth Circuit itself had applied to Rule 11 prior to 1983, and with the standards applied in similar situations under other provisions of law.[43] *Zaldivar*'s three-ply review test has been invoked regularly at home[44] and has won some acceptance in other circuits.[45]

---

[41]780 F.2d 823 (9th Cir. 1986).

[42]Id. at 828.

[43]These included sanctions for violating 28 U.S.C. § 1927 by vexatiously multiplying litigation; discovery sanctions; fees to prevailing defendants under 42 U.S.C. § 1988; and fees for meritless litigation under the Securities Act of 1933. Id. at n.4.

[44]In 1988 alone, the test was cited in at least six published Ninth Circuit decisions.

[45]See Kurkowski v. Volcker, 819 F.2d 201, 203 n.8 (8th Cir. 1987); compare Donaldson v. Clark, 819 F.2d 1551, 1556 (11th Cir. 1987) (en banc) (adopting similar standard but not citing *Zaldivar*). Several circuits have explicitly rejected the *Zaldivar* approach. See Mars Steel Corp. v. Continental Bank N.A., 880 F.2d 928, 933 (7th Cir. 1989) (en banc) (citing cases). In Cooter & Gell v. Hartmarx Corp., decided June 11, 1990, the Supreme Court considered and rejected the *Zaldivar* approach, opting for the one-ply abuse of discretion standard.

The chief competing approach is the one explicated in 1988 by the Fifth Circuit en banc in *Thomas v. Capital Security Services, Inc.*[46] That was a Title VII case in which the defendant-employer, Capital, prevailed at trial. After plaintiffs appealed, Capital asked for attorney's fees as sanctions against plaintiffs and their lawyers for alleged violations of Rule 11 and several other sources of sanctioning power.

Capital's main accusation (for Rule 11 purposes) was that plaintiffs' claims of discriminatory practices in their lawsuit were far broader than in the complaints they had filed with the administrative agency.[47] The district court, while noting that the plaintiffs' shotgun allegations were evidence of inadequate investigation, thought the law too unsettled on the impermissibility of the broadened complaint to warrant imposing sanctions.[48] On appeal, the Fifth Circuit panel applied a *de novo* standard of review to the Rule 11 decision and remanded for clarification of the district court's order and for findings and conclusions. The full bench, besides attempting to provide guidelines in administering Rule 11, addressed squarely the problem of appellate review standards and rejected the then-recent Fifth Circuit *Robinson* decision expressly adopting the three-ply *Zaldivar* approach.[49] The rationale of the decision was a declaration of the need for deference to the district court:

> We likewise believe that the imposition or denial of sanctions of necessity involves a fact-intensive inquiry into the circumstances surrounding the activity alleged to be a violation of Rule 11. The perspective of a district court is singular. The trial judge is in the best position to review the factual circumstances and render an informed judgment as he is intimately involved with the case, the litigants, and the attorneys on a daily basis. We can perceive of no advantage that would result if this Court were to conduct a second-hand review of the facts from the trial court level, as "the district court will have a better grasp of what is acceptable trial-level practice among litigating members of the bar than will appellate judges."[50]

Fearful of transforming appellate courts into trial courts by reviewing the attorneys' and litigants' conduct too closely, the court declared that

[46]836 F.2d 866 (5th Cir. 1988).

[47]The employment discrimination law requires that claims be filed with the agency before a lawsuit can be brought.

[48]See 836 F.2d at 869.

[49]Robinson v. National Cash Register Co., 808 F.2d 1119 (5th Cir. 1987).

[50]836 F.2d at 873 (quoting Eastway Constr. Corp. v. City of New York, 637 F.Supp. 558, 566 (E.D.N.Y. 1986)).

the "overall umbrella remains abuse of discretion." It added: "Appellate courts are not replacements for district courts and we decline to adopt a standard of review in Rule 11 cases which would effectively usurp the discretion of district courts."

Although one can sympathize with those views, the conclusion reached is hard to square with the clear language and intention of the governing rule. The text of Rule 11 lays down firm requirements and unequivocally commands that if it is shown that Rule 11 has been violated the district court "shall" impose—not "may" impose or "has discretion to" impose—a sanction. Deciding whether there has been a violation of Rule 11 sometimes involves an issue of fact such as whether the accused party (or counsel) examined available witnesses and documents and investigated in other ways to ensure that the paper in question was well grounded in fact. At other times the question of violation turns on an issue of law—whether the accused party had a plausible legal basis for the position asserted, based on the law as it was or on a reasonable argument for its modification or extension. It is hard to see how an appellate court can fail to apply the clearly erroneous standard to a finding that counsel did take certain steps, or how it can shrug off an error of law when an appeal is taken in a Rule 11 situation raising issues of that kind.

In the *Thomas* case itself, the court, after having listed the many "affirmative duties" Rule 11 enjoins, concluded that "a district court *must* impose sanctions once a violation of Rule 11 is found."[51] If the legal duties prescribed by Rule 11 were undefined and amorphous there would be good reason for the *Thomas* court to leave the decision to the district judge. But since the court conceded that Rule 11 clearly sets forth the duties to be complied with, the justifications for deference are absent, and the court of appeals should review for legal error. The *Zaldivar* opinion correctly appreciates the standard of review that should apply to the three main types of issues that may arise when Rule 11 is invoked. I believe that time will show the *Zaldivar* approach to be not only analytically correct in clarifying the standard of review but also quite effective in discouraging improvident appeals.

In 1988 there were twenty-six published court of appeals decisions in the Ninth Circuit on Rule 11. In outcome these decisions amplified a tendency that had become apparent in earlier years, namely, to overturn grants and uphold denials of Rule 11 sanctions. The 1988 decisions produced a 65 percent reversal rate of twenty orders granting and a 100 percent affirmance rate of six orders denying sanctions. The

---

[51]Id. at 878 (emphasis added).

comparable figures for the thirty-four published appeals court decisions in 1985–87 were 46 percent reversal of grants and 83 percent
affirmance of denials.

The *Zaldivar* case was cited in seventeen of the twenty-six published
decisions in 1988, often with seemingly dispositive effect.[52] These
showed a parallel pattern of reversing grants (62 percent) and affirming denials of sanctions (100 percent). Nevertheless, the data are too
incomplete to warrant the conclusion that *Zaldivar* has discouraged
futile appeals of Rule 11 orders. One reason is the lack of information
about the frequency of unreported Rule 11 decisions and the results
they reach. Another is the presence of overriding substantive issues in
nearly all the appeals challenging the grant or denial of a sanction. In
most of those the Rule 11 order was probably not the ruling that led the
appellant to seek a reversal.

Of course, the standard of review is not the only, or even the most
important, determinant of whether to appeal a Rule 11 order. Counsel's decision on appealing may well be more heavily influenced by the
denial-affirmed/grant-reversed trend of the published opinions than
by the standards of review. If so, counsel may be misreading the
situation: the decisions rendered without published opinions probably tend to affirm grants of Rule 11 sanctions nearly always. To the
extent that the net overall effect of appellate review is to reduce the
frequency with which sanctions are ultimately imposed, the explanation may be psychological rather than legalistic. Perhaps because they
are more remote from the court where the offending papers were
lodged and are not as personally involved in the affair, the appellate
judges take a more tolerant view of litigant or lawyer conduct that
departs from Rule 11's norms. At all events, in a few years it should be
possible, by comparing the overall Rule 11 appeal picture in the Fifth
Circuit with that in the Ninth Circuit, to reach a firmer conclusion
about the relative effectiveness of *Zaldivar*-type standards in discouraging hopeless appeals.

Review of Discretionary Orders of the Trial Court

With great frequency litigants who lose in the district court complain
on appeal of rulings the appellate courts hold to be in the district

---

[52]The most recent decision at the time of this writing was King v. Idaho Funeral Serv.
Ass'n, 862 F.2d 744 (9th Cir. 1988). A complete list is on file with the author.

judge's discretion. The way the court of appeals responds to these challenges may have a significant effect on its work. Are potential appellants encouraged to be hopeful that the court of appeals will apply a penetrating standard of review and dig deeply into a discretionary decision, or are they discouraged because they know that the court of appeals operates under review-limiting constraints when dealing with discretionary orders?

The operative concept here has been referred to as *secondary discretion*.[53] That is a type of discretion that recognizes the lower court's limited right to be wrong in the appellate court's view without incurring reversal or modification. It speaks to the relationship between trial and appellate courts, embodying a review-limiting principle. It stands in contrast to *primary discretion*, which gives the decision-making court (at all levels of the judicial system) a wide spectrum of permissible determinations owing to the loose-textured quality of the decisional norm.[54] Primary discretion is in this sense decision-liberating, whereas secondary discretion is review-restricting. It is the latter that concerns us here.

Appellate review of discretionary rulings is a high-volume phenomenon in the Ninth Circuit. A computer search of the published opinions of the court of appeals indicates that in 1988 at least 20 percent contained one or more issues reviewed on an "abuse of discretion" standard. Data on unpublished dispositions are harder to obtain. We have, however, no reason to expect the proportion of discretion-based rulings in those dispositions to be lower.

Among the evidentiary rulings deemed discretionary are those that weigh relevancy and probative value against prejudicial effect,[55] or that refuse to allow impeachment evidence on a collateral matter.[56] Decisions regarding the extent of cross-examination are also subject to the discretionary review principle.[57] Discovery sanctions are reviewed as discretionary rulings.[58]

The central meaning of the concept of discretion is choice. In the present context the sense it conveys is that the option selected by the district judge will not be disturbed on appeal unless the deference

---

[53]Maurice Rosenberg, "Judicial Discretion of the Trial Court, Viewed from Above," 22 *Syracuse L. Rev.* 635, 637 (1971).

[54]Id.

[55]Coursen v. A. H. Robins Co., 764 F.2d 1329, 1333–35 (9th Cir. 1985).

[56]Mitchell v. Keith, 752 F.2d 385, 392 (9th Cir. 1985).

[57]Guillory v. County of Orange, 731 F.2d 1379, 1383 (9th Cir. 1984).

[58]Fjelstad v. American Honda Motor Co., 762 F.2d 1334 (9th Cir. 1985).

ordinarily due the ruling must be set aside for some specific reason beyond the appellate judges' belief that they would have made a different ruling. The generally accepted view is that a trial court with discretion has a right to be wrong in the judgment of the appellate court without incurring reversal—a limited and variable right, to be sure. The Court of Appeals for the Second Circuit made the point in these words:

> Had any one of us been in a position to exercise the discretion committed to a trial judge when such a request is made, we have no hesitancy in stating that the decision would have been otherwise; but as appellate judges we cannot find that the action of the district judge was so unreasonable or so arbitrary as to amount to a prejudicial abuse of the discretion necessary to repose in trial judges during the conduct of a trial.[59]

There are wide variations in how "erroneous" by appellate lights the district judge's exercise of discretion may be and still escape reversal. Gradations of discretion can be calibrated, depending on how impervious to appellate revision the rulings will be. One area of lower-court discretion that is virtually invulnerable is the district judge's decision to hold or forego a pretrial conference. Another is the option of the trial judge to order special verdicts under Rule 49. In *Skidmore v. Baltimore and Ohio Railway Co.,*[60] the trial judge refused the defendant's request for special verdicts and took a general verdict. Judge Jerome Frank wrote an opinion denouncing the general verdict for "shedding darkness" and other serious faults, and urged the superiority of the special verdict. In the end, however, he said, "the federal district judge . . . has full, uncontrolled discretion in the matter" and "we cannot hold that a district judge errs when, as here, for any reason or no reason whatever, he refuses to demand a special verdict. . . ."[61] Allowing the jury to take notes during the trial for use in their deliberations is another example of "Grade A" discretion.[62]

A slightly lower level of protection surrounds the district court's rulings on motions for a new trial or similar relief. In these situations the discretion is Grade B. The appellate court will show deference but

[59]Napolitano v. Compania Sud Americana de Vapores, 421 F.2d 382, 384 (2d Cir. 1970).
[60]167 F.2d 54 (2d Cir. 1948).
[61]Id. at 66–67.
[62]"Whether it is advisable to permit a jury to take notes is a subject of some debate, and reasonable arguments are advanced for and against the practice. The decision . . . is left entirely to the discretion of the trial court." United States v. Vaccaro, 816 F.2d 443, 451 (9th Cir. 1987).

will not be as tolerant as the "for any reason or no reason whatsoever" approach would require.[63] The same is true of many rulings on admissibility of evidence. In *United States v. Solomon,* for instance, the court of appeals said, "The district court's evidentiary rulings will be upheld on appeal unless the court abused its discretion . . . or committed 'manifest error.' "[64] A similar approach can be seen in the oft-repeated statement that the court of appeals reviews "strictly" a district court's exercise of discretion denying leave to amend a complaint.[65]

At the lowest end of the scale is Grade D discretion, where little or no deference is accorded the trial court's ruling. Rulings on applications for declaratory judgments fall into this category. Many appellate courts treat discretion in declaratory actions as so dilute that a mere disagreement with the lower court's choice is enough to call for reversal.[66] Rulings on motions to dismiss on *forum non conveniens* grounds are also examples of low-grade discretion. In *Villar v. Crowley Maritime Corp.,*[67] the district court dismissed a tort action by the widow and children of a Philippine sailor who drowned in waters off Saudi Arabia. In affirming, the court of appeals said its standard of review of the *forum non conveniens* dismissal was for abuse of discretion. But after a careful review of the requirements delineated by the Supreme Court, the opinion concluded that the "district court properly considered the private and public interest factors" and "correctly concluded" for dismissal. This treated the dismissal order as if it were a ruling on a question of law. Unfortunately, that approach has been common in Ninth Circuit decisions reviewing various types of discretionary rulings; indeed, so common that in his *Standard of Review Outline* Judge Skopil offers the following definition of "abuse of discretion": "Under the abuse of discretion standard, a reviewing court cannot reverse unless it has a definite and firm conviction that the court below com-

[63]See Oltz v. St. Peter's Community Hosp., 861 F.2d 1440, 1452 (9th Cir. 1988) (after concluding that excessive damages were awarded by the jury, the district judge may grant a motion for a new trial or condition the grant on a remittitur).

[64]United States v. Solomon, 753 F.2d 1522, 1524 (9th Cir. 1985). The court's treatment of discretion and error as alternative grounds is bound to create confusion and is not commended. As noted in the next paragraph of the text, this kind of confusion is not uncommon.

[65]E.g., Mayes v. Leipziger, 729 F.2d 605, 608 (9th Cir. 1984).

[66]See New York Foreign Trade Zone Operators, Inc. v. State Liquor Authority, 285 N.Y. 272, 275–76, 34 N.E.2d 316, 318 (1941): "[I]f the ground [on which the court refuses to exercise discretion] is untenable, the discretion has been improperly exercised."

[67]782 F.2d 1478, 1483 (9th Cir. 1986).

mitted a clear error of judgment in the conclusion it reached upon a weighing of the relevant factors."[68]

Ninth Circuit decisions generally have not distinguished among the various gradations of discretion. Occasionally the opinions reflect an awareness that different issues call for different levels of deference to the lower court, but they have not been explicit or consistent. Sometimes panels have persuaded themselves that discretionary rulings call for independent, nondeferential (*"de novo"*) review, as in *Greater Los Angeles Council on Deafness v. Zolin*,[69] a declaratory judgment case, in which the court said:

> Whether or not to grant a declaratory judgment is a matter committed to the sound discretion of the district court. . . . But, with declaratory-judgment rulings, unlike many other discretionary acts, we must exercise our own discretion to determine the propriety of the district court's ruling. . . . As a result, we effectively review a district court's decision to grant or deny declaratory relief *de novo.*

Confusion over the treatment of discretionary rulings of various kinds will be dissipated, it seems to me, if attention is paid to the reasons for according protection—deference, that is—to the district court's rulings. This can be done by applying the functional inquiry employed by the Supreme Court in *Miller v. Fenton* and the court of appeals in *McConney*. An especially vivid example occurred in *United States v. Layton*,[70] the Jonestown mass suicide case, in which the court sustained the trial judge's *in limine* ruling against the admissibility of the "last hour tape." The ground for deferring to the district judge was that "he is in the best position to assess the impact and effect of evidence based upon what he perceives from the live proceedings of a trial, while we can review only a cold record."[71] Similarly, in *Pierce v. Underwood*,[72] the Supreme Court marshaled as follows the arguments in favor of deferential, abuse-of-discretion review of a decision that the government's position was not "substantially justified," thus warranting an award of attorneys' fees: "By reason of settlement conferences and other pretrial activities, the district court may have insights not conveyed by the record, into such matters as whether particular evi-

[68]Skopil, supra note 4, at 2 (citing Fjelstad v. American Honda Motor Co., 762 F.2d 1334, 1337 (9th Cir. 1985)).

[69]812 F.2d 1103, 1112 (9th Cir. 1987).

[70]767 F.2d 549 (9th Cir. 1985).

[71]Id. at 554 (quoting United States v. Ford, 632 F.2d 1354, 1377 (9th Cir. 1980)); see also United States v. Shaffer, 789 F.2d 682, 689 (9th Cir. 1986).

[72]108 S. Ct. 2541 (1988).

dence was worthy of being relied upon, or whether critical facts could easily have been verified by the Government."[73]

In lieu of "abuse of discretion" as the touchstone for reversal, an appellate court might better communicate its reasoning to the lower courts by declaring that it will not defer to the lower court for the reason that one of the following statements is true.

- There are applicable rules or standards and they were not correctly applied.
- Some material factors were disregarded.
- The choice the district court made lacks a sound or practical basis because . . .
- The record gives us as full an opportunity to make an informed choice as the district judge enjoyed, and we see the matter differently.

Impact of McLinn-*Style Review on Appealing*

In *Matter of McLinn,*[74] decided en banc in 1984, a closely divided court held that henceforth in reviewing questions of state law it would use the same nondeferential standard as in reviewing questions of federal law. This was a departure from the prevailing practice of panels that had usually accorded "deference" or even "substantial deference" to the district judges' determinations of state law.[75] The majority saw "no sound reason why we have a lesser appellate duty to the parties to make a correct, independent determination when the question is one of state law" than of federal or foreign law.[76] As its rationale the majority urged that the same policy concerns and structural advantages were involved in reviewing questions of state law. The dissent, in addition to arguing that the district courts were close to their own states' law, worried that the majority had transmitted "signals to litigants that reversals will be easier to obtain, thus encouraging more appeals" on state law issues.[77]

Has that occurred? That it might occur is not implausible. The

[73]Id. at 2547.

[74]739 F.2d 1395 (9th Cir. 1984).

[75]See, e.g., Gaines v. Haughton, 645 F.2d 761 (9th Cir. 1981); Vu v. Singer Co., 706 F.2d 1027 (9th Cir. 1983); Philpott v. A. H. Robins Co., 710 F.2d 1422 (9th Cir. 1983); In re Big River Grain, Inc., 718 F.2d 968 (9th Cir. 1983); Houston v. Bryan, 725 F.2d 516 (9th Cir. 1984); Safeco Ins. Co. of America v. Schwab, 739 F.2d 431 (9th Cir. 1984).

[76]739 F.2d at 1398.

[77]Id. at 1406.

standard of review does make a difference. In *McLinn* itself, the en banc majority pointed out that the outcome on appeal might depend entirely on the standard of review: "The panel indicated that if the question of law were reviewed under the deferential standard that we have applied in the past, which permits reversal only for clear error, then they would affirm; but if they were to review the determination under an independent de novo standard, they would reverse."[78]

To test the more-reversals-more-appeals hypothesis, two separate lines of empirical inquiry were followed. One was to look at the affirmance-reversal outcomes in a sample of pre-*McLinn* cases turning on questions of state law and comparing it with a set of post-*McLinn* cases.[79] When that was done with approximately equal numbers of cases in the before and after groups, the results were patternless.[80] The second approach was to compute the affirmed/reversed/modified rate in diversity cases in three pre- and three post-*McLinn* years, on the assumption that state law questions generally play a dominant role in the outcomes of diversity actions.[81] Table 2.2 shows the results, both for published opinions and for all dispositions on the merits.

[78]Id. at 1397.

[79]"Affirmed" is a less ambiguous disposition than either "reversed" or "modified." The last two do not necessarily mean that the outcome was ultimately favorable to the appellant, but an affirmance nearly always conveys the clear meaning that the appellee prevailed. Accordingly, Table 2.2 uses the affirmance rate as the basic parameter.

[80]Of seven pre-*McLinn* decisions, four were affirmed and three were reversed (with two of the latter containing expressions of deference to the district court's interpretation of state law). Affirming were Houston v. Bryan, 725 F.2d 516 (9th Cir. 1984); Vu v. Singer Co., 706 F.2d 1027 (9th Cir. 1983); Philpott v. A. H. Robins Co., Inc., 710 F.2d 1422 (9th Cir. 1983); and Gaines v. Haughton, 645 F.2d 761 (9th Cir. 1981). Reversing were Safeco Ins. Co. of America v. Schwab, 739 F.2d 431 (9th Cir. 1984); In re Big River Grain, Inc., 718 F.2d 968 (9th Cir. 1983); and Allen v. Greyhound Lines, Inc., 656 F.2d 418 (9th Cir. 1981).

Of the eight post-*McLinn* group reviewing nondeferentially, three cases affirmed: Ford v. Manufacturers Hanover Mortgage Corp., 831 F.2d 1520 (9th Cir. 1987); Ortiz v. Bank of America Nat'l Trust and Sav. Ass'n, 824 F.2d 692 (9th Cir. 1987); Matsumoto v. Republic Ins. Co., 792 F.2d 869 (9th Cir. 1986). Three cases reversed: FBW Enterprises v. Victorio Co., 821 F.2d 1393 (9th Cir. 1987); Sutherland v. Kaonoki Ohana, Ltd., 776 F.2d 1425 (9th Cir. 1985); In re Thomas, 765 F.2d 926 (9th Cir. 1985). Two cases affirmed in part and reversed in part: Stinnett v. Damson Oil Corp., 813 F.2d 1394 (9th Cir. 1987); Piatt v. MacDougall, 773 F.2d 1032 (9th Cir. 1985). (Cases in the earlier group were identified through key phrases ["state law," "deference"]; cases in the later group, through citation to *McLinn*.)

[81]The cases were those (a) identified as diversity cases by the staff attorneys at the inventory stage and (b) disposed of after hearing or submission by a panel of judges. (For a description of the inventory process, see Chapter 4.) Cases that were dismissed were excluded from the tallies. Spot checking of published cases confirmed the overall accuracy of the staff attorneys' classifications.

Table 2.2. Affirmance rates in Ninth Circuit diversity cases, 1981–83 and 1986–88

	Published opinions				All cases		
Year	Total	Affirmed	Modified	Affirmance rate (%)	Total	Affirmed	Modified	Affirmance rate (%)
1981	47	24	23	(51)	148	98	50	(66)
1982	50	23	27	(46)	190	131	59	(69)
1983	49	36	13	(73)	139	103	36	(74)
1986	73	41	32	(56)	176	122	54	(69)
1987	78	36	42	(46)	219	142	77	(65)
1988	64	38	26	(59)	193	137	56	(71)

Source: Computed from Ninth Circuit Court of Appeals operational databases (ARMS and SADB).

Note: "Modified" includes all cases in which the appellee did not prevail; i.e., the judgment was reversed, remanded, or affirmed in part and reversed in part. Dismissals were excluded from the totals and in calculating affirmance rates.

As can be seen, the data offer no support for the hypothesis. As one would expect, affirmance rates were consistently lower for published opinions than for all cases, although in one apparently aberrational year (1983) the two figures were very close. But in each group the affirmance rates in the post-*McLinn* period remained within the same range as for the pre-*McLinn* years. Nor do the data show any disproportionate increase in the number of diversity cases adjudicated.[82] The upshot is that neither of the empirical approaches permits us to say with confidence what impact *McLinn* has had. Probably the most that is permissible is the negative inference that so far there has not been a dramatic upsurge of either appeals or reversals in cases raising state law questions.

Concluding Thoughts

Recurring to the questions posed at the start of this chapter, we can venture a few responses that are not quite answers. First, in the main the court of appeals has done a good job of articulating plainly the standards of review it applies. The *Zaldivar* three-ply approach seems analytically correct, informationally clear, and operationally practical. The *McConney* opinions illuminate the complex problem of reviewing

[82]Of course, any conclusions based on the assumption that the affirmance/reversal rates in diversity cases are evidence of the *McLinn* effect are highly problematical. The same is true with respect to before-and-after rates of appealing. Too many variables are at work here to allow confident conclusions regarding the effect of any one of them.

mixed law-fact issues by suggesting how the appellate court may determine whether the law or the fact aspect predominates. Instead of using *"de novo"* to mean independent, plenary, or nondeferential review, the court should use those terms or others that realistically convey the approach it will follow.

As important as clear articulation is the need for consistent application of the standards. Here, too, the court of appeals receives high marks. Although perfect adherence to the announced standards of review is not an attainable goal, the departures noted in the course of reviewing hundreds of published opinions are remarkably few. One of them that could readily be remedied is the tendency of some judges, when reviewing orders they term "discretionary," to test their correctness as if the ruling were a matter of law rather than discretion. Instead of treating the order with deference, these judges subject it to exacting scrutiny to ensure fidelity to legal rules.

The explicit reference to the standards of review in three-fourths of the published opinions is a commendable practice. It should impress on the bar the fact that the court of appeals takes the standards seriously. It also serves as a self-reminder to the reviewing court and in that way probably increases consistency in applying the standards.

Obviously, even clarity, consistency, and determination on the part of the court of appeals will not avoid hopeless appeals if the bar disregards the standards in deciding whether to seek appellate review. One experienced appellate lawyer opined that the standards are relatively unimportant factors in the decision whether to appeal. The three factors that influence the decision to appeal, he said, start with the question whether the outcome in the district court is tolerable to the client. If the judgment appears ruinous to the loser, an appeal is almost inevitable, however remote its chance of success. A second determinant is whether the outcome below seems just or unjust. If it seems unjust, an appeal is indicated. The exact issues to raise are secondary. Finally, if a question of law inviting independent appellate review can be found, the inducement to take the appeal is greater than if only fact questions can be raised. Even if we grant that these factors have an important influence on the decision whether to appeal, there seems little doubt that in close cases the review standards can and do make a difference, and a helpful one.

3

Maintaining Consistency
in the Law of the Large Circuit

ARTHUR D. HELLMAN

Starting in the 1970s, prominent voices in the legal community have expressed concern that one Supreme Court of nine justices can no longer provide adequate authoritative guidance to maintain uniformity in the application of federal law. To increase the "national appellate capacity," they have proposed creating a new appellate court, such as an "Intercircuit Tribunal," that would serve as an auxiliary to the Supreme Court. But the prospect of a fourth tier within the federal judicial system encounters strong resistance from judges and lawyers alike. Other approaches to structural reform, such as creation of specialized appellate courts, have attracted even less support. Thus, even among those who agree with the diagnosis, the search continues for solutions.

Judge Browning has suggested that the need for increased appellate capacity can be met without creating additional courts through effective management of large circuits. The premise is that, with a smaller number of circuits, there will be fewer conflicts for the Supreme Court or any national court to resolve. Not everyone agrees with this premise, but even if it is correct, the success of the idea will depend on whether it is possible to maintain consistency and stability in the law of the circuit when cases are decided by hundreds of shifting three-judge panels on a large court. Otherwise, we would simply be trading intercircuit conflict for intracircuit conflict—a much more pernicious phenomenon.

The Ninth Circuit as it has existed since 1980 provides a unique testing ground for Browning's plan. The circuit extends over nine states and two territories and generates almost one-sixth of all appeals in the twelve regional circuits. The court of appeals adjudicates about twenty-five hundred cases each year; more than nine hundred of them are decided by published opinions that can be cited as precedent. The decisions are made by as many as twenty-eight active judges, ten senior judges, and a long parade of visiting judges, almost invariably sitting in panels of three.

In theory, the large number of judges and the fact that decisions are made by panels of three should have no effect on the consistency of the law of the circuit. The reason is that the Ninth Circuit, like all the courts of appeals, is committed to the rule of intracircuit stare decisis: panel decisions are binding on subsequent panels unless overruled by the court en banc.[1] In addition, the court has put into place an elaborate series of mechanisms designed to maintain intracircuit consistency. Finally, where irreconcilable conflicts do develop, a mechanism is available to restore coherence to the law: review by an en banc panel of the court.

Notwithstanding all of the mechanisms and rules, many lawyers and trial judges believe that inconsistency continues to be a serious problem. For example, in a survey conducted for this volume, members of the Ninth Circuit Judicial Conference were asked if they agreed or disagreed with the statement, "When intracircuit conflicts do arise, the Court of Appeals generally resolves them through modification of opinions or en banc rehearings." Two-thirds of the district judges disagreed; among lawyer members the extent of disagreement was even higher. In contrast, the court of appeals judges tend to think that with occasional lapses the court has generally succeeded in maintaining consistency; only two of the twenty-one circuit judges who responded disagreed with the quoted statement.

Although the court of appeals judges may differ with their constituents on the extent of disuniformity in the court's decisions, they do not dispute the underlying premise: consistency in the law of the circuit is

[1]In some circuits a subsequent panel is permitted to overrule an earlier decision if the proposed opinion is circulated to the full court and the other judges agree (or do not vote for en banc rehearing). This procedure is sometimes referred to as a "mini en banc." See Steven Bennett and Christine Pembroke, "'Mini' In Banc Proceedings: A Survey of Circuit Practices," 34 *Cleveland St. L. Rev.* 531 (1986). Occasional ad hoc attempts by individual Ninth Circuit panels to invoke this procedure have always been rebuffed. There is a narrow exception to the general rule for panel decisions that are found to be inconsistent with intervening Supreme Court rulings. See LeVick v. Skaggs Cos., 701 F.2d 777, 778 (9th Cir. 1983).

not only a virtue but a necessity if the system is to serve its intended functions. I share that view, and at the risk of reiterating the obvious, I note the principal concerns supporting the conclusion. First, the ideal of equality is violated when similarly situated persons receive disparate treatment because two panels of the same court have attached different legal consequences to facts that are identical in all relevant respects. Second, inconsistent appellate decisions create uncertainty about what the law requires or permits. That uncertainty encourages wasteful litigation; and where litigation cannot be avoided, the uncertainty adds to the costs and other burdens of court proceedings. Third, intelligent planning and structuring of transactions is frustrated when the relevant precedents in the governing jurisdiction give conflicting guidance on what the law is.

The values underlying these concerns are implicated far more seriously by conflicts within a circuit than by conflicts between circuits. If a district judge finds apparently conflicting authority from outside his circuit, he can ignore it, but if decisions within the circuit point in different directions, he must do his best to reconcile them. Similarly, a lawyer seeking to advise a client generally need not worry if another circuit has laid down a different rule, but if the apparently inconsistent holdings come from his own circuit, he ignores them at his peril.[2] The principal question addressed in this chapter, therefore, is whether the Ninth Circuit Court of Appeals succeeded in its efforts to maintain consistency in its law during the Browning years.[3]

Mechanisms for Avoiding Intracircuit Conflicts

The measures adopted by the court of appeals to preserve uniformity can be broken down into three stages, with the second and third each involving successively greater commitments of judicial resources. First, a primary mechanism, designed to head off conflicts

[2]The distinction is not absolute, even when criminal penalties are involved. The Supreme Court sees no unfairness in convicting a defendant under an interpretation of a criminal statute rejected by the defendant's own circuit, as long as "the existence of conflicting cases from other Courts of Appeals [made a contrary decision by the Supreme Court] reasonably foreseeable." United States v. Rodgers, 466 U.S. 475, 484 (1984).

[3]For an earlier study, examining the subject from the perspective of the Ninth Circuit's judges, see Stephen L. Wasby, "Inconsistency in the United States Courts of Appeals: Dimensions and Mechanisms for Resolution," 32 *Vand. L. Rev.* 1343 (1979).

before decisions are issued, operates through the court's support staff and its three-judge panels. Next, backup procedures allow nonpanel judges to intervene without necessarily involving the full court. Finally, if all else fails, the safety valve of the en banc process gives all of the active judges a chance to participate in restoring coherence to the law.

The effort to maintain consistency begins in the Office of Staff Attorneys before any judge has seen a new appeal. Upon the filing of the briefs, the staff attorneys "inventory" the case using detailed issue-identification codes. This information is then fed into the computer, so that cases raising the same issue can be calendared before the same panel if scheduling constraints permit.[4] Where that is not possible, the different panels are informed of the pendency of the other cases.[5] Under the court's internal rules, "when identical issues are pending before two or more panels, the panel to whom the issue was first submitted has priority," and other panels are required to defer or vacate submission so that they can follow the law established by the first panel.[6]

The priority-of-submission rule comes into play only when later panels know that the issue has previously been submitted to another panel. Absent that knowledge, the first opinion to be filed controls. On occasion, confusion and ill feeling have been created when one panel published an opinion without realizing that one of the issues it addressed had been submitted to another panel at an earlier date. Successful operation of the rule thus requires accurate classification of issues by the staff attorneys and effective communication with the judges.

The inventory system works well overall, but it does not always prevent the situation of two panels considering the same issue at the

[4]For a more extended description of the inventory system, see Arthur D. Hellman, "Central Staff in Appellate Courts: The Experience of the Ninth Circuit," 68 *Calif. L. Rev.* 937, 957–64 (1980).

[5]The principal obstacle to having similar cases heard by the same panel is the court's practice of regional calendaring. Court sessions are held in San Francisco and Pasadena every month and in other cities at longer intervals. Cases are ordinarily scheduled for argument in the region or state of origin. Thus, if the same issue were to arise in cases from Oregon and Southern California, it would not ordinarily be possible to calendar them before the same panel. Even if the apparently similar cases come from the same district, simultaneous calendaring may be precluded because the appeals reach the court at different times or because one case is ready for argument long before the other.

[6]The rule now in force was not adopted until 1983. A similar rule was approved in August 1981 but rescinded a month later.

same time, each in ignorance of the other. This can happen for several reasons. In areas of the law characterized by elaborate reticulation of rules, the staff attorneys may not accurately predict which line of precedents will be viewed by the panel as most relevant. Novel issues may wind up in different classifications, especially if the cases are inventoried many months apart. Cases involving multiple issues present special problems, since the computer looks only for the first four, and an issue that appeared to be of lesser importance may turn out to be the one that is resolved differently by different panels. Procedural questions and those involving standards of review may cut across subject-matter areas in a way that does not become apparent until the opinions are published. Nor can the staff always anticipate the issues that may arise only if one of the questions emphasized by the parties is resolved in a particular way.

To a large extent, these limitations are unavoidable. Staff attorneys are not judges, nor can they devote the amount of time to a case that the judges do. Nonetheless, one reform might substantially improve the utility of the process: reclassification of cases upon the filing of the opinion. Although new decisions are made available to judges within days in slip opinion form and almost as quickly on computerized databases, these sources lack indexes or other finding tools. Moreover, the very issues that are most likely to fall through the cracks during the initial inventory (particularly issues of procedure, jurisdiction, and the scope of review) are equally likely to escape the eye of the judges as they browse through the slips. Finally, a written update from the staff attorneys' office would be especially useful during the period of greatest vulnerability: while the opinion is being reviewed by the nonwriting judges on the panel.[7]

Unlike the practice in some of the other courts of appeals, dispositions in the Ninth Circuit are not ordinarily circulated to nonpanel judges before filing. The only exception is when the staff attorneys have identified similar issues as currently pending before more than one panel. Then, if all works as it should, the opinion of the panel with

---

[7]This period may actually begin somewhat earlier, depending on the practices of the particular judge. Some judges have their law clerks prepare draft opinions that the judge then reviews and edits. Under this approach, a week or more may elapse between the time the law clerk finishes work and the time the judge puts the opinion in final form for circulation to the other panel members. Other judges do their own first drafts, then ask their law clerks to check the citations and look for errors or omissions. If the law clerk raises questions that the judge wishes to consider further, only limited additional research may be done before the opinion is sent to the other chambers.

priority of submission will be circulated to the other panels. Usually, the others will conform their dispositions to the first panel's holding, even to the point of abandoning a draft opinion that has reached an advanced stage of preparation. The upshot is that conflict is averted without the public's ever knowing that a contrary disposition was in the making.

Conformity does not always occur without some stress, however. Occasionally there are memoranda of protest or remonstrance before the turbulence subsides.[8] Moreover, if the issue is especially important, or if feelings run deep, the second panel may refuse to back down. Where that occurs, one or both panels will request en banc review so that a larger number of judges can establish the law of the circuit. This does not happen often, and the procedure is not necessary to prevent conflict, but it does provide an escape hatch for those situations where it is most obvious that differences in judges' "can't helps" would otherwise control.[9]

The suggestion is sometimes made that for-publication opinions should be circulated as a matter of routine to all active judges before filing. But in a court that issues published opinions at the rate of more than seventy-five per month, the idea is not practical. Either the judges would give the opinions only the most superficial review, or the disposition of cases would be delayed to an extent that would understandably dismay litigants and the public.[10]

---

[8]Tension will not necessarily reflect disagreement over results. Frustration may occur when a panel that has completed its work quickly must wait for a panel that is proceeding at a slower pace to consider some antecedent or related issue. At one point the court considered modifying its rule to provide that the first panel would lose its priority if it did not reach a decision within a limited period of time. The change was not made, largely because of the court's strong commitment to panel autonomy and out of concerns for collegiality.

[9]In the six years 1981 through 1986 there were seven cases in which judges requested en banc review to settle an issue on which panels were prepared to differ. En banc hearing was granted in four of the cases.

[10]In the late 1980s it seemed to some court watchers that an equivalent practice had come in through the back door. A large number of cases, it appeared, were being amended after publication, sometimes more than once. The effect was to give published opinions a provisional status that in some ways created more uncertainty than the delays that would have been occasioned if the opinions had not been issued until nonpanel judges had had a chance to review them.

Amendments to a published opinion do not necessarily reflect disagreement within the court. Rather, a petition for rehearing may call attention to a mistake that must be corrected somehow. At the same time, the panel may continue to believe that the disposition is correct. Sometimes the judges struggle for months (occasionally aided by off-panel judges) in an effort to correct ill-advised or inaccurate statements without altering the result.

The second stage in the court's efforts to maintain uniformity thus begins with the filing of the panel opinion in slip form. Starting in 1985, these "slips" have been printed by a commercial firm in San Francisco and mailed to the circuit judges on the date of filing. Under section 5.3 of the court's General Orders (GO; the court's name for what other circuits refer to as Internal Operating Procedures), off-panel judges have twenty-one days from filing in which to communicate with the panel about concerns generated by the opinion. Judges expressing such concerns are not required to circulate their memoranda to the full court, though sometimes they do so.

The GO 5.3 procedure was not designed as a conflict-avoidance mechanism. Rather, its purpose is to give the panel a chance to correct misstatements or substantive omissions before the case is published in the Federal Reporter and even before a petition for rehearing is filed. If an off-panel judge has a "bottom-line disagreement" with the panel opinion, or believes that the opinion creates an intracircuit conflict or that the result is so wrong that an en banc hearing will be needed, the judge is expected to use the more formal procedures of GO 5.4, triggered by the filing of a petition for rehearing.[11] However, the line between misstatements or omissions, on the one hand, and conflicts or errors, on the other, is far from clear. Thus, judges who think that a panel opinion has muddied the law of the circuit do not always hold off in saying so until the losing litigant seeks to bring the problem to the attention of the full court. In at least five of the thirty-six cases that generated an en banc ballot in 1987, the exchange of memoranda between off-panel judges and members of the panel began before any petition for rehearing had been filed.[12]

The court's central legal staff also plays a role in this second phase of the effort to maintain uniformity. The court has instructed the staff to review all published opinions for potential conflicts with other opinions and to suggest modifications where appropriate to avoid inconsistency. From time to time staff attorneys do send memoranda calling panels' attention to apparent conflicts, and on occasion panels have made changes in their opinions in accordance with those suggestions. The court keeps no records on how often this happens, however, and

---

[11]Under the Federal Rules of Appellate Procedure, a petition for rehearing must be filed within fourteen days of the entry of judgment. Judgment is ordinarily entered on the date the opinion is filed. The time for filing a rehearing petition thus overlaps with the time in which judges may circulate GO 5.3 memos.

[12]For further discussion of communications between panel and off-panel judges, see Stephen L. Wasby, "Communication in the Ninth Circuit: A Concern for Collegiality," 11 *U. Puget Sound L. Rev.* 73, 104–6 (1987).

other staff duties generally take priority over the task of flagging possible inconsistencies. The responsibility for discovering conflicts thus rests primarily with the judges and with the lawyers.

The En Banc Process in the Ninth Circuit

Notwithstanding their reliance on the conflict-avoidance mechanisms described in the preceding section, the court of appeals judges recognize that these devices will not always have the desired effect. When that occurs, the only remedy is to invoke the court's procedures for en banc hearing. Study of the en banc process should therefore shed light on the extent and significance of intracircuit conflict in the Ninth Circuit during the Browning years.

I have used the term *en banc process* rather than *en banc hearing* because there are really three levels of decision making. The first stage involves the determination whether to conduct a ballot on taking a case en banc. Any litigant may make the suggestion, but a vote is taken only if one or more judges request it. Second, there is the vote itself and the exchange of memoranda that precedes it. At that stage all active judges are eligible to participate, and if a majority of the non-recused judges vote in the affirmative the case will be heard en banc. Finally, there is the en banc court itself. That consists of eleven judges, the chief judge and ten other judges selected at random.

The Origins of the En Banc Rule

In the Ninth Circuit, as in the other courts of appeals, cases are ordinarily "heard and determined" by three-judge panels (28 U.S.C. § 46(c)). Under the Federal Rules of Appellate Procedure, en banc hearing "is not favored and ordinarily will not be ordered except (1) when . . . necessary to secure or maintain uniformity of . . . decisions or (2) when the proceeding involves a question of exceptional importance." Within fourteen days of the filing of a panel opinion, litigants are permitted to "suggest" rehearing en banc,[13] and when they do, the petitions are circulated to all active judges. However, lawyers have not proved helpful in identifying true disuniformity or questions of "exceptional importance."[14] Lawyers' petitions may call attention to cases

---

[13]Litigants are also permitted to suggest initial hearing en banc, but it is rare for them to do so and even rarer for the court to accept the suggestion.

[14]See Neil D. McFeeley, "En Banc Proceedings in the United States Courts of Appeals," 24 *Idaho L. Rev.* 255, 267–74 (1987–88).

that warrant a second look, but beyond that first stage the entire en banc process rests with the judges.

Traditionally, the determination whether to hear a case en banc has been made by the same group of judges that would decide the merits if the hearing is granted: all the circuit judges in regular active service.[15] However, when Congress expanded the Ninth Circuit Court of Appeals from thirteen to twenty-three judgeships in the Omnibus Judgeship Act of 1978, it also made special provisions for large circuits. Section 6 of the act authorized any court with more than fifteen active judges to "perform its en banc function by such numbers of members of its en banc court as may be prescribed by rule of the court of appeals." Although two of the twelve circuits are now eligible to exercise this option, only the Ninth Circuit has done so. Under Circuit Rule 35–3 (formerly Rule 25), the en banc court[16] consists of the chief judge and ten additional judges drawn by lot from the active judges of the circuit.[17] The power to select cases for en banc hearing remains, as the statute apparently requires, with the full court.

The present Ninth Circuit rule emerged from lengthy discussion that began even before Congress enacted the authorizing legislation.[18] As early as May 1977, when the omnibus judgeship bill was stalled by an impasse over division of the Fifth Circuit,[19] some members of the Ninth Circuit Court of Appeals were exchanging memoranda on possible methods for composing an en banc court of less than all the active judges.[20] In February 1978 the matter was included on the agenda for the "Symposium," the judges' annual retreat, which took place at Rancho Santa Fe near San Diego.[21] There the judges gave their ap-

---

[15]There is one exception to this equivalence: under current law, senior judges do not vote on the decision to go en banc, but they are "eligible to participate . . . as a member of an in banc court reviewing a decision of a panel of which [the particular] judge was a member." See 28 U.S.C. § 46(c).

[16]Circuit Rule 35–3 refers to the "en banc court." The court's internal rules sometimes refer to the "en banc panel."

[17]The rule provides that any judge who is not drawn for any of three successive en banc courts will automatically be placed on the next en banc court.

[18]The account in this chapter is based on interviews and on internal memoranda that were made available to me with the stipulation that I not quote from confidential material or identify individual judges' positions.

[19]See Deborah J. Barrow and Thomas G. Walker, *A Court Divided: The Fifth Circuit Court of Appeals and the Politics of Judicial Reform* 195 (Yale University Press, 1988).

[20]A few of the judges had discussed the subject at hearings held by the Commission on Revision of the Federal Court Appellate System (Hruska Commission) in 1975. The commission endorsed the basic idea of a limited en banc court in its June 1975 report but opted for seniority as the basis for selecting the members.

[21]For an account of the origins of the Symposium, see Chapter 14.

proval to proposed legislation that would have explicitly authorized the Ninth Circuit to reduce the number of judges on the en banc court.[22] They then turned to the composition of the limited en banc court and debated the issue at some length. When Judge Browning indicated that he would like to have a proposed rule to present to Congress if asked, the judges adopted in principle a rule that provided for a nine-member en banc panel consisting of the chief judge, the members of the original three-judge panel, and additional judges selected by lot for each case.[23]

The impasse in Congress was finally broken by a compromise provision that became section 6 of the Omnibus Judgeship Act.[24] The compromise was announced on September 20, 1978, and within days the matter was placed on the agenda for the November meeting of the court. Some discussion took place at that meeting, but the judges recognized that they needed more time to think about the issues individually before they would be ready to confer as a group, and the topic was put off until December. When the judges convened for their regular December meeting, however, they concluded that the complexity and sensitivity of the issues required still further thought and, perhaps, a more informal atmosphere for discussion. The subject was thus set for consideration at the Symposium scheduled for February 1979, again at Rancho Santa Fe.

In the meantime, ideas and comments flew back and forth in a remarkable exchange of memoranda. From late October through early January, at least eleven of the thirteen active judges and three senior judges took part in a vigorous and earnest debate over the best way of constituting the en banc court.[25] Significantly, there was no debate over two crucial points. First, no judge questioned the threshold decision that the court would exercise the option afforded by the new law to reduce the size of the en banc court.[26] Second, all judges agreed that

[22]This particular proposal appears to have been drafted within the court. Similar proposals had been discussed in correspondence between judges and members of the House Judiciary Committee in connection with the pending judgeship bill.

[23]It is not clear whether the draft rule was ever submitted to Congress. The conference committee considering the omnibus judgeship bill did discuss various ways of composing a limited en banc court. See Congressional Record, Oct. 7, 1978, pp. 34546–47 (remarks of Sen. Kennedy).

[24]Barrow and Walker, supra note 19, at 215.

[25]Strangely enough, the fact that the judges had adopted a rather detailed rule "in principle" at the February 1978 Symposium appears to have carried no weight with anyone. None of the memoranda even allude to the earlier decision.

[26]I cannot find any record of the court's actually having voted on this point before the

the determination whether to take a case en banc would continue to be made by the full court.[27] Of lesser importance, it was also assumed that the chief judge would serve as a member of the en banc court.

Two issues received greatest attention in the exchange of memoranda. The first was the size of the en banc court. The numbers discussed ranged from seven to fifteen, with nine receiving the greatest support. Judges who placed a high value on efficiency pressed for an en banc court of seven or nine to avoid the delays and procedural complications inherent in a larger decisional group. Other judges argued that unless the en banc court included a majority of the full court of twenty-three it would not satisfy the values of representation and participation.

The second and more complex question was how the judges should be selected. Two basic approaches soon emerged. Under the "ad hoc" model, the judges (other than the chief judge) would be chosen on some random basis for each en banc case. Under the "permanent rotation" system, the judges would serve for a designated period of time, with new judges rotating on at staggered intervals.[28]

Superimposed on these questions were others. Should members of the original three-judge panel sit by right on the en banc court? What role, if any, should seniority play in the selection of the judges? For example, should the judges be chosen from two separate pools, one composed of the more senior half of the active judges, the other composed of the junior group?[29] Once a case was selected for en banc consideration, should other members of the court be permitted to participate informally in the en banc decisional process or to issue their own opinions?

Pasadena Symposium in March 1980. At the 1978 Symposium the judges did express support for legislation authorizing a limited en banc court, but they did not commit themselves to adopting such a provision; in any event, the vote could not have been binding under the 1978 act until a sixteenth judge had been appointed. From all available evidence, it appears that there was a consensus from the beginning that the court would implement section 6.

[27]Some judges flirted briefly with the idea of requiring less than a majority of the active judges to select a case for en banc consideration, along the lines of the Supreme Court's "rule of four." This approach appeared to run contrary to the language of the statute, and no mention of it appears in the later memoranda.

[28]"Permanent rotation" was the phrase used by the judges, although as indicated in the text, only the chief judge would sit as a permanent member.

[29]Early in the debate, some judges argued that judges should not become eligible for the en banc court until they had served on the circuit for a year. This idea aroused opposition and soon disappeared.

After four months of exchanging views largely through written memoranda, the debate climaxed in a four-hour discussion at the February Symposium. In what must have been an exhilirating if exhausting session, the judges began by talking about the function and purpose of the en banc procedure, the criteria for selecting en banc cases, the benefits derived from the process by the court, and criticisms of current procedures. The discussion then turned to the composition of the limited en banc court. There was widespread recognition that in designing a system the judges would have to take into account two competing values. On one side, the interest in stability and continuity suggested a rotation system. On the other, the interest in collegiality pointed to the ad hoc model, which would enable all members of the court to participate actively in the process within a short period of time.

In the course of the meeting, however, a third consideration—one that appears not to have been mentioned at all in the initial memoranda—came to the fore: the desirability of avoiding distortion in the voting on taking a case en banc. The premise was that the determination whether to hear a case en banc should not turn on the anticipated result; the concern was that knowledge of who would sit on the en banc court would lead at least some judges to vote on that basis. The judges also began to realize that a random selection of the en banc panel after the vote on rehearing would probably produce fewer en bancs. Because the members of the court would not know who the deciders would be, they would not vote for en banc unless there was a true conflict in the circuit or the case was so clearly important that it had to go en banc no matter who would sit on the panel.[30]

When the discussion ended, it appeared that the idea of a permanent rotation system, with changes or rotations of some members of the en banc court every six months and eventual service by all active judges within a two-year period, had garnered general support. At the same time, the judges were becoming increasingly sensitive to the concerns about maintaining collegiality and avoiding distortion in the initial en banc voting—concerns that could most easily be met through a pure ad hoc system. The judges may also have been influenced by the fact that the court was committed to random assignment of cases to

[30]Although there is no evidence that the judges considered the point, the actual operation of the rule suggests that "voting in the dark" (as one judge termed it) would also permit en banc rehearing when a panel's decision was so obviously aberrant that it would be overturned by a majority no matter who was chosen. See, e.g., Jensen v. City of San Jose, 806 F.2d 899 (9th Cir. 1986), reversing 790 F.2d 721 (9th Cir. 1986).

three-judge panels. If the policy made sense in that context, as just about everyone agreed it did, why should it not be extended to en banc business?[31] But there was no need to reach an immediate decision.[32] The judges had already agreed not to take action until the sixteenth judge had been appointed, and now one member of the court was asked to draw up and present for future consideration three options for limited en banc procedures.

Consistent with the results of the "consensus votes," the task was assigned to a judge who had championed the permanent rotation system. But when the judge reported to his colleagues two weeks later, he had changed his mind. After further reflecting on the argument that many judges would find their votes on en banc hearings colored by knowledge of who would sit on the en banc court, the judge concluded that the ad hoc system was preferable, at least initially. Further thought had changed other minds as well, and the court was now ready to move toward a new consensus in favor of random selection.

There matters stood for nearly a year while President Carter proceeded at an agonizingly slow pace to nominate judges for the positions created by the 1978 legislation. In June 1979 Browning summed up the situation in a speech to a group of lawyers:

> The court has . . . devoted many hours to considering the size, composition, and procedures of an en banc court of less than the full court of 23. We have gone through several changes of mind and come to about this: (1) the most acceptable model *may* be an en banc court of nine, consisting of the chief judge and eight associates drawn by lot; (2) further consideration . . . should await the arrival of our new judges so they too may participate in the discussions . . . ; and (3) the approach must be pragmatic—whatever proposal is adopted should be experimental, limited to no more than a year, for in this area experience is essential, and experience is now totally lacking. [Emphasis in original.]

The debate over the limited en banc rule resumed in early 1980, after nine of the new judges had joined the court. At the February court and

[31]The ad hoc model had the additional virtue of simplicity, and after wrestling at length with the mechanics of the alternative approaches, the judges may have placed a higher value on simplicity than they did when the meeting began.

[32]The 1979 Symposium did resolve one issue: it gave the coup de grace to the idea—which at one time had wide support—that judges who were members of the original panel should sit by right on the en banc court. No one advanced this suggestion when the discussions resumed in 1980.

council meeting the judges considered the issue briefly, then agreed to continue the discussion and reach a decision at the court's Symposium the following month in Pasadena. Again memoranda were circulated in advance of the meeting, although fewer judges participated and the effervescence that characterized the earlier interchange had abated considerably. One new idea came to the fore: several judges thought that the rule should include some provision for rehearing by the full court, either as an option in the initial voting or as a safety valve after the limited en banc panel had issued its decision.

When the judges convened in Pasadena, they began by discussing the composition of the en banc court in general terms, then took a series of votes to shape the en banc rule. The first step was to accept the basic plan for a limited en banc court. This the judges did, but in accordance with the late-emerging idea they tempered the concept by allowing for the possibility of a second rehearing by the full court.[33] Next came the issue of size. A motion that the en banc court consist of nine judges was defeated, as was a motion that set the number at thirteen. A proposal that the en banc court consist of a number constituting a majority of the full court failed on a tie vote. In retrospect, it is hard to believe that the judges would have adhered to a rule that for the foreseeable future would have yielded an even number (twelve out of twenty-three) and a real prospect of affirmances by an equally divided court. In any event, the options were rapidly diminishing, and the judges agreed that the en banc court would consist of eleven judges.

Finally the judges turned to the selection process. After formally agreeing that the chief judge should be a member of every limited en banc panel, the judges considered a motion that the remaining ten judges be chosen by random selection, with a corrective mechanism to ensure that no judge would be excluded too long from the panels. By this time, the outcome was no longer in doubt. The motion passed, and the permanent rotation model, once the preference of a majority, died without ever coming to a vote. The session came to an end with the approval of a motion authorizing Judge Browning to appoint a committee to draft rules of procedure that would embody the decisions just reached.

[33]In allowing for the possibility, the judges did not anticipate that the safety valve would be used very often. Probably not more than one or two judges thought that the full court should ever overrule the limited en banc court except perhaps in extremely unusual and unforeseeable circumstances.

Immediately upon his return to San Francisco, Browning designated three judges to serve on the committee, and two weeks later the committee circulated the draft of a proposed rule, along with revisions of the court's internal procedures relating to en bancs. The drafts were approved in principle at the court's April meeting, with the understanding that the committee would make several changes in wording and style. The committee proceeded in accordance with those instructions but concluded that the emendations it had made were substantial enough to warrant further scrutiny by the full court.[34] The judges considered the matter again at their June meeting and approved in principle the revised version. Meanwhile, the proposed procedures were circulated widely to district judges, members of the bar, and the public. Responses were received from lawyers and bar associations; comments and suggestions were also submitted by the court's staff. Final approval, with further slight revisions, came at the court meeting of August 15. Four days later the Clerk of Court drew names for the first limited en banc court. The historic experiment was under way.

The plan adopted by the court in August 1980 closely resembled the one outlined by Browning in June 1979, which in turn largely tracked the resolution suggested in the memorandum prepared for the judges after the 1979 Symposium. Three changes had been made, however. The number of judges on the en banc court was increased from nine to eleven; the idea of adopting the rule for only a limited period of time was dropped; and the provision for a second rehearing by the full court was added. The abandonment of the "experimental" label is particularly striking. The probable explanation is that after talking about the proposal for so long and in such detail the judges no longer saw it as such a leap in the dark; at the Symposium there was not even a motion to limit the time during which the rule would remain in effect. (The judges may also have felt that such a motion was unnecessary, on the theory that whatever the court did, it could undo.)

The court has now been operating under the plan for almost a

---

[34]Curiously, the rule as initially drafted by the committee provided for en banc hearing by the full court as an alternative to hearing by the limited en banc court. This option was not reflected in the proposed revisions to the General Orders, and when the disparity was called to the judges' attention, they revised the draft rule to make clear that rehearing by the full court could be ordered only after a decision by the limited en banc court. At first blush it is puzzling that the drafting committee could have misunderstood the intent of the judges as expressed at the Symposium, but perhaps the decisions did not emerge from the discussion with total clarity. For example, at least one of the judges who was present did not recall that a consensus had been reached for allowing rehearing by the full court under any circumstances.

decade. No judge has ever requested rehearing by the full court of a decision by the limited en banc court,[35] nor has the rule been revised in any substantial way. When the court expanded from twenty-three to twenty-eight judgeships, there was some talk of increasing the number of judges on the en banc court, but the proposal never reached the stage of a formal motion.[36] Later the possibility was raised of eliminating the provision that the chief judge would sit on every en banc panel. After a discussion that one participant remembers as "quite spirited," the judges chose not to make the change.[37]

The Operation of the En Banc Process

Even before adoption of the limited en banc rule, the Ninth Circuit Court of Appeals had developed an elaborate set of procedures to govern the en banc process. The rules occupied eight pages of the General Orders, and a member of the court, designated the "en banc coordinator," supervised compliance with deadlines and monitored

[35]In July 1980, while the limited en banc rule was in the final stages of consideration, the judges voted to deny rehearing by the full court of a case submitted to the en banc court before any of the new judges had taken their seats. See United States v. Penn, 647 F.2d 876, 889 (9th Cir. 1980) (Fletcher, J., dissenting from denial of rehearing en banc). The 5–4 decision generated an intense emotional response, and almost certainly it would have been reversed if the full court had heard the case. Under these circumstances, the denial of further review signified a genuine commitment on the part of the judges to the principle underlying the new rule: a willingness to accept decisions with which they disagreed made by less than majority of the court.

On one later occasion a judge asked for a vote on withdrawing a case from the limited en banc court before it had issued a decision. The request was soon withdrawn "in the interest of institutional unity," and no balloting ever took place.

[36]A search of the court's records reveals no evidence that the idea was ever considered by the court's executive committee, let alone by the full court.

[37]Having the chief judge sit on every en banc panel was seen as serving at least three important purposes. First, it maintained continuity in procedure, especially in the assignment of opinions. It was thought that the chief judge would be better informed than anyone else about the caseloads of individual judges, the number of en banc opinions previously written by those judges, and the various subjective considerations that go into the distribution of work. Second, the court could benefit from having the person with the longest institutional memory presiding. Finally, at least some judges perceived a symbolic value in having the chief judge preside when the court was speaking as the whole court in the lawmaking role.

Other judges argued in favor of a full random draw presided over by the senior person drawn. Apparently, a majority of the court did not feel that the abstract value of undiluted randomness outweighed the perceived advantages of continuity in the central seat.

the constant flow of memoranda. In the eight years between the expansion of the court and the transfer of leadership to Judge Goodwin, the rules grew into an eighteen-page maze of such complexity that even experienced judges sometimes got lost.[38]

At the risk of oversimplification, I have chosen to treat as the starting point for the en banc process the panel's circulation of a notice pursuant to GO 5.4(b)(3) recommending rejection of a party's suggestion for rehearing en banc. Until that point, nonpanel judges who express concerns about an opinion are not obliged to share their memoranda with the full court. Moreover, although copies of an en banc suggestion are forwarded to all active judges immediately upon filing, nonpanel judges are not supposed to circulate memoranda commenting on the suggestion until the panel has expressed its view.

Once the 5.4(b)(3) notice is sent, a judge who has objections to the panel disposition can signal his concerns in one of two ways: through a "stop-clock" memo or through a request for en banc review. According to the General Orders, the purpose of a stop-clock memo is to suggest "further reflection by one or more judges [that] may be necessary or helpful in aid of early disposition of a possible en banc question." More concretely, the procedure is designed for cases in which the off-panel judge thinks that the panel may be able to meet his concerns by amendment and thus avoid an en banc vote. The judges are discouraged from using the stop-clock procedure to gain additional time in cases where from the beginning the concerns are so substantial that an en banc call is almost inevitable.

Stop-clock memos are circulated to all active judges, sometimes prompting further suggestions to the panel by other members of the court, still without a call for an en banc vote. Through this device, apparent inconsistencies in language or approach can be cleaned up without any public indication that judges other than those sitting on the panel have taken part in the process. Or the judge who initiated

---

[38]To some extent the increased complexity was inevitable: matters that can be handled informally in a court of thirteen require more structured processes in a court of twenty-three. However, some judges had the sense that the shifting ideological makeup of the court—an initial infusion of liberals under President Carter, followed by conservative appointments under President Reagan—also played a role. As one judge put it, "Certain things weren't done [in earlier times]. Judges started playing hardball under the old, more open-ended rules," and new rules had to be adopted "more or less under emergency conditions" to address particular problems. Not suprisingly, a series of ad hoc revisions over a period of eight years did not yield a particularly unified or coherent body of rules. (This type of rule growth is not unique. See Aside, "The Common Law Origins of the Infield Fly Rule," 123 *U. Pa. L. Rev.* 1474 (1975).)

the process may be persuaded that the panel decision is acceptable after all.

The court kept no records on "stop clocks" before 1987. During the twelve-month period beginning April 1, 1987, stop-clock requests were filed in forty-seven cases. Nineteen of these led to requests for en banc rehearing. Amended versions of opinions were published in twelve of the remaining cases. On the basis of available records, it is not possible to determine how many of those amendments were triggered by assertions of intracircuit conflict; however, examination of the amendments suggests that concerns about conflict probably played only a minor role in the intracourt debates.

If the stop-clock correspondence does not resolve the disagreement, or if the gulf is so wide that the procedure would be a waste of time, the next step is to request an en banc vote. Even at this stage, the panel may amend its opinion in a way that satisfies the requesting judge. At this point, too, the parties are brought back into the picture. If the panel has not previously called for a response to the losing litigant's en banc suggestion, it does so. And if the en banc request comes sua sponte, both parties are given the opportunity to comment on the appropriateness of the case for en banc hearing.[39]

The formal request and the receipt of responses from the parties initiate the period during which the judges circulate memoranda supporting or opposing en banc review. Sometimes only one or two memoranda are circulated; other cases generate a blizzard of paper that may tax even the court's electronic mail system. The exchange of views may lead to modification of the opinion, and in some cases the requesting judge withdraws the request for an en banc vote.[40] Here, however, the process may leave its traces in the publication of an amended opinion with a notation that rehearing en banc has been denied.

Only if all of these procedures have failed does the court actually vote on a judge's request for en banc hearing. Those votes are, of course, important, but as the preceding account demonstrates, they represent only part of the en banc process in the Ninth Circuit. And in

---

[39]For most of the 1980s, no provision was made for ascertaining the views of counsel in cases in which the en banc process was initiated within the court. Only in August 1987 was the rule changed to ensure that the lawyers would have their say on whether the case was enbancworthy.

[40]Occasionally, a request is withdrawn to give the panel a chance to do further work on the case, only to be renewed because the new opinion does not satisfy the requesting judge's concerns.

considering the data on en banc grants and denials presented in the next section, it is important to remember that these are not the only cases in which judges other than those on the regular panel have participated in the formulation of the court's precedents.

The Results of the Process: An Empirical Study

To ascertain the role of the en banc process in the court's efforts to maintain a consistent body of law, I examined all of the cases in the six years 1981 through 1986 in which a judge requested an en banc ballot.[41] This means that I excluded cases in which litigants suggested en banc rehearing but failed to persuade even a single judge that the procedure was warranted. Given the routine nature of many of these suggestions and the widespread misunderstanding of the purposes of en banc review, I have no doubt that casting the net wider would have uncovered at best a tiny number of additional unresolved conflicts at the cost of an enormous amount of effort. I am more troubled by the omission of cases that generated stop-clock memoranda or other exchanges of views short of an en banc ballot, but as previously indicated, the court kept no comprehensive records of those cases, and consideration of them must await another day. (I did include cases in which a judge asked for an en banc vote but withdrew the request before polling was completed.)

For purposes of the study, I was given access to the memoranda exchanged by the judges in the course of deciding whether to grant en banc review. I used those memoranda to identify the issues that were thought to require en banc resolution and the reasons one or more judges thought en banc review was necessary. Obviously, I cannot quote from those memoranda in a way that would identify particular cases or attribute positions to individual judges. The reader will have to take on faith the accuracy of my characterizations.

The fate of en banc requests. The first and most important finding is that en banc ballots were rarely requested and even more rarely successful. In the six years of the study there were fewer than 160 cases in which a judge called for a vote on en banc rehearing.[42] Fewer than

---

[41]A few cases generated two separate requests at different stages in their history, e.g., before and after the panel had issued its opinion or before and after the Supreme Court had directed reconsideration. One case was the subject of three separate ballots.

[42]For three reasons, the figures given in this section are not exact. First, the court kept no single comprehensive list of en banc calls during this period. My own list was

one-third of those cases—forty-nine in all—were actually heard en banc. In that same period, the court adjudicated more than twelve thousand cases, five thousand of which received published opinions. This means that en banc decisions accounted for less than 1 percent of the court's precedential rulings.

The raw figures alone thus suggest that en banc hearings played only a minor role in maintaining consistency in the law of the circuit. Scrutiny of the opinions and internal memoranda strongly reinforces that conclusion. More than half of the en banc requests made no assertion at all that the panel decision created an intracircuit conflict. In fifteen cases (about 10 percent of the total) the requesting judge acknowledged a controlling circuit precedent and sought en banc review for the purpose of overruling it.[43] The other nonconflict cases were a varied lot. In some, the memoranda emphasized the precedential significance of the panel's decision;[44] in others, the judges pointed to the number of people who would be affected,[45] the likelihood of

---

compiled from two others, and it is possible that a case here and there slipped through the cracks. Second, there is room for disagreement over which cases to count. Should a case be counted if the request was withdrawn before the completion of the balloting? (As indicated in the text, I did count these cases if I knew about them, but it is possible that not all such requests were recorded in the lists I had, especially in the early years of the study period.) What about cases that were the subject of more than one en banc ballot? (Generally, if the balloting was completed, I counted the calls separately, but if the balloting was interrupted while the panel resumed work on the case, I did not.) Finally, the files of the cases I did study were not necessarily complete, and missing memoranda might well have caused me to modify some of my characterizations.

[43]It has been suggested that en banc hearing in cases of this kind does serve, albeit indirectly, to foster intracircuit consistency. The argument is that if the court fails to use the en banc process to correct an old precedent that a majority of the judges believe is wrong, the old case will die a slow death over the years by being distinguished in one decision after another. The effect will be to create confusion in the law of the circuit. I can see no ready way of testing this hypothesis: in cases of this kind in which en banc review was rejected, it is impossible to determine whether the judges were willing to live with an erroneous precedent or simply did not agree that the old case was wrong.

[44]Illustrations of this pattern can be seen in published dissents from denial of rehearing en banc. See, e.g., Miller v. Rumsfeld, 647 F.2d 80, 90 (9th Cir. 1981) (Norris, J., dissenting); California State Council of Carpenters v. Associated General Contractors, 648 F.2d 527, 545 (9th Cir. 1981) (Sneed, J., dissenting), rev'd, 459 U.S. 519 (1983); International Olympic Comm. v. San Francisco Arts & Athletics, 789 F.2d 1319, 1326 (9th Cir. 1986) (Kozinski, J., dissenting), aff'd, 483 U.S. 522 (1987); Golden Eagle Distrib. Corp. v. Burroughs Corp., 809 F.2d 584 (9th Cir. 1987) (Noonan, J., dissenting).

[45]See, e.g, United States v. Harvey, 711 F.2d 144, 145 (9th Cir. 1983) (Kennedy, J., dissenting from denial of rehearing en banc).

Supreme Court review if the panel decision remained unreversed,[46] or simply the egregiousness of the panel's error.[47] The common thread was the absence of any suggestion that the panel decision posed an immediate threat to uniformity within the circuit.

This leaves barely seventy-five cases in six years in which a judge requested en banc hearing to resolve an intracircuit conflict. But even that figure overstates the role of conflict resolution in the en banc process. In more than one-quarter of the cases that I have classified as involving claims of conflict, concerns about inconsistency were clearly secondary to other reasons for questioning the panel decision. For example, in one case the initial memorandum described the issue as one of "great importance" without pointing to a conflict; a later memorandum by another judge went no further than to say that the panel decision was "not in keeping with the spirit of" a Ninth Circuit precedent that involved very different facts. In at least two of the "conflict" cases that did receive en banc consideration, the en banc opinion made no mention of the allegedly inconsistent decisions.

En banc requests that claimed intracircuit conflicts had about the same success rate as en banc requests generally: one in three. Of the successful calls, however, fewer than twenty generated an en banc decision that actually resolved a conflict.[48] In addition, three requests led panels to change the result of published dispositions, after which the requests were withdrawn. In about a dozen other cases the panel amended the opinion without changing the result; with two exceptions the modifications did not satisfy the requesting judge. Overall, there were no more than thirty cases in six years in which the en banc process led to the reversal or overruling of a decision asserted to be in conflict with another precedent.[49]

[46]In two of the cases that generated published dissents from the denial of en banc rehearing, the dissenting judges pointed out that the Ninth Circuit decision had created a conflict with another circuit. Both cases were reviewed by the United States Supreme Court. Financial Inst. Employees v. NLRB, 750 F.2d 757, 758 (9th Cir. 1985) (Kennedy, J., dissenting), aff'd, 475 U.S. 192 (1986); Pangilinan v. INS, 809 F.2d 1449 (9th Cir. 1987) (Kozinski, J., dissenting), rev'd, 108 S. Ct. 2210 (1988).

[47]See, e.g., Students of California School for the Blind v. Honig, 745 F.2d 582 (9th Cir. 1984) (Sneed, J., dissenting), vacated, 471 U.S. 148 (1985).

[48]An en banc decision was counted as having resolved a conflict if it overruled a precedent that the judges viewed as inconsistent with other Ninth Circuit cases or if it reversed the original panel *and* cited with approval an earlier ruling that was said to be in conflict with the panel decision.

[49]Arguably, the tally should include the seven cases in which en banc voting was

The effect of en banc decisions.   When I began work on this project, I thought that an important part of the study would be to determine whether en banc decisions had succeeded in bringing consistency to areas of the law previously characterized by disarray. In light of the findings discussed thus far, that inquiry becomes largely irrelevant. The point is well illustrated by immigration law, the area most often mentioned by people who think that intracircuit conflict is a problem in the Ninth Circuit. In the six years of the study, judges requested en banc review in seventeen immigration cases, more than in any other area of the law except search and seizure. But rehearing was granted in only three of the cases, and none of them proved to be a major precedent.[50] Contrariwise, several immigration cases in which rehearing was denied played central roles in the later development of the law.

Outside of immigration law, no more than a dozen of the en banc decisions during the period of the study can be said to have become major reference points in the work of the court. The two most often cited opinions involved standards of appellate review.[51] Three cases, argued on the same day in 1984, attempted to clear up the admitted disarray in the court's decisions on the relevance of state remedies to the availability of relief under the Civil Rights Act of 1871.[52] There were six en banc rulings on searches and seizures and three on employment discrimination, but only one in each group proved to be a significant precedent.[53] In many important areas of federal law there was not a single en banc decision during the period of the study. Among these were antitrust, labor preemption, freedom of speech, freedom of religion, and police interrogation.

The conclusion is inescapable: en banc decisions contributed only

---

triggered by the recognition that two panels with similar issues under submission were prepared to reach different results. See text at note 9. However, the judges appear to have assumed that, if en banc review was denied, one panel would back off, and indeed that is what happened in the three cases in which the request failed to gain a majority.

[50]The court also granted en banc review of three cases involving constitutional issues arising out of immigration proceedings. Two of these washed out without a decision on the merits, and the third was reversed by the Supreme Court.

[51]These cases, United States v. McConney, 728 F.2d 1195 (9th Cir. 1984), and Matter of McLinn, 739 F.2d 1395 (9th Cir. 1984), are discussed in detail in Chapter 2.

[52]The principal case was Haygood v. Younger, 769 F.2d 1350 (1985).

[53]The one important search and seizure case was United States v. McConney, better known for its holding on standards of appellate review. The employment discrimination case was Atonio v. Wards Cove Packing Co., 810 F.2d 1477 (9th Cir. 1987), rev'd on other grounds, 109 S. Ct. 2115 (1989).

minimally to the preservation of uniformity in the law of the circuit. But does that mean that the en banc *process* was a failure? Not necessarily. On the contrary, one possible explanation for the low incidence of en banc calls is that the mere availability of en banc review had a restraining effect on the three-judge panels. Judges knew that if they strayed from the law as established by earlier decisions, they would expose themselves to internal attack, an en banc call, and perhaps to the public rebuke of reversal by the en banc court. As a result, notwithstanding the hundreds of shifting three-judge panels and the widely perceived ideological division within the court, there simply were not very many intracircuit conflicts.

That is one way of interpreting the data, but it is not the only way. To begin with, some people will find it implausible if not ludicrous to suggest that the prospect of en banc reversal would ever influence life-tenured Article III judges to reach a decision other than the one indicated by their own reading of the applicable authorities. The phenomenon would seem especially improbable in the Ninth Circuit, where the composition of the en banc court depends on the luck of the draw and the judges have no way of knowing at the stage of panel deliberations (or indeed at the time of voting on en banc rehearing) who would sit on the particular case if it did go en banc.

Fear of reversal, however, is not the only way in which the en banc process may have affected the decisions of three-judge panels. There can be no doubt that the judges of the Ninth Circuit accept the principle of intracircuit stare decisis as an essential rule of the institution. At almost every Symposium, with no outsiders present, the judges "pray with each other" on the subject and renew their commitment to consistency. Against that background, the en banc process described in this chapter may have influenced the court's work in a way that the numbers cannot measure. Time and again, en banc requests generated thoughtful exchanges over the scope of a precedent and the obligations of stare decisis. Often the discussion was couched in a personal vein and manifested a self-conscious mode of analysis seldom seen in published opinions.[54] This flow of memoranda served as a constant reminder that to ignore relevant cases or draw untenable distinctions was to violate the underlying institutional and collegial agreements that bound the court together. The en banc process could thus be

---

[54]My impression is that with rare exceptions the memoranda exchanged in the en banc process were written by the judges themselves, with little assistance from law clerks.

viewed both as an instrument and as a symbol that helped the judges to internalize a commitment to consistency.

Yet such a commitment, even if widely shared, would not necessarily have kept intracircuit conflicts at the low level suggested by the en banc data. It is one thing to adhere to stare decisis as a principle; it is another to follow it in practice. Some judges may have been more concerned about reaching "correct" results in individual cases than about maintaining consistency between cases. Or the judges may have taken an extremely tolerant view of what constitutes a conflict. Or—of particular significance in the present context—the judges may have acted on a shared sense that the court could not increase its en banc activity in any significant measure without impinging dangerously on the time available for panel dispositions.

The data presented in this section tell us that during the period of the study the court was resolving conflicts through the en banc process at the rate of about five a year. The question that remains is whether this figure approximates the rate at which conflicts were created. Was the incidence of conflict really that low, or does the rather modest level of en banc activity reflect an unwillingness or inability on the part of the judges to use the process to maintain consistency? To find out, I undertook an empirical study not limited to en banc cases.[55]

Defining the Intracircuit Conflict

The first step in measuring the extent of inconsistency in the Ninth Circuit's panel decisions is to define the intracircuit conflict. Scholars, lawyers, and judges have struggled for years to answer the question, What is a conflict between circuits? The inquiry is no less difficult when the search is for conflicts within the circuit.

At one end, some people will look at a pair of cases involving the same kind of legal question, and if they see that the cases reach different results, immediately their suspicions are aroused. Their suspicions ripen into certainty if they read the cases and discover that the language or rationale of one decision, if taken to its logical extreme, would compel a different result in the other case.

In my view, however, that alone does not create a conflict. It is part of the genius of the common law that it does not take propositions—

---

[55]A more complete account of the study is found in Arthur D. Hellman, "Jumboism and Jurisprudence: The Theory and Practice of Precedent in the Large Appellate Court," 56 *U. Chi. L. Rev.* 541 (1989). In the account here I have omitted many details and some minor qualifying observations.

holdings, rationales, or even principles—to their logical extremes. Instead, the proposition found to be controlling in one case comes up against a competing proposition, the lessons of experience, or even limitations inherent in the initial exposition. To see conflicts every time that happens is to disavow the flexibility and capacity for growth of our common law system.

But it is also possible (though not very common) to go too far in the other direction. In this view, as long as a careful lawyer *could* find a distinguishing feature, however obscure, that would justify differential treatment of apparently similar cases, there is no conflict. The amount of effort required to identify or understand the distinction would be irrelevant; it might even be irrelevant whether the distinction was actually relied on by the later court. That approach simply is not practical. It is not reasonable to expect busy lawyers and judges to prepare the equivalent of a law review note simply to understand the relationship between a pair of precedents relevant to advising a client or ruling on a motion.

As a rule of thumb, it is tempting to say that, if it takes a reasonably intelligent lawyer more than fifteen minutes to understand why two decisions are not in conflict, then for all practical purposes they are. For this project, however, I needed a somewhat more scientific definition, and I have come up with a hypothesis that I think is useful. The hypothesis consists of three sequential propositions, each of which addresses one of the possible relationships between a particular new decision and existing law in the circuit.

First, if losing counsel cannot point to relevant circuit precedents that reach results different from the panel's result in the case being considered, there is no possibility of conflict or uncertainty of the kind that arouses legitimate concern among judges and lawyers. Second, the cases that offer the greatest potential for conflict are those in which the panel distinguishes a circuit precedent that losing counsel has reasonably relied on as *requiring* (not simply supporting) a different result. Third, to the extent that the distinctions drawn by the later panel are clear and cogent, the potential for disarray will not be realized.

This formulation, I believe, will go far to assist in evaluating claims of intracircuit conflict and in distinguishing conflicts from the evolutionary shifts inherent in a common law system. Each of the elements requires brief elaboration.[56]

---

[56]For detailed explication, with numerous illustrations, see Hellman, supra note 55, at 555–70.

Step one. In determining whether a panel decision contains the seeds of intracircuit disarray, the threshold question is whether there is a relevant circuit precedent that reaches a result different from the panel's result in the case being considered. A precedent is "relevant" in this sense if a reasonable lawyer would invoke it as supporting a legal argument on a disputed proposition in the case. The "result" is "different" if, on the issue being considered, the earlier court ruled against the interest or claim that prevailed in the later case or vice versa.

Of particular significance, the first step of the analysis rests on the view that dictum, especially dictum that points in the opposite direction from the holding, cannot give rise to an intracircuit conflict. Some lawyers and judges will regard this approach as unduly narrow, but I think it follows from basic doctrines of precedent. In a democratic society, treating statements that do not contribute to the result as nonbinding dicta helps to confine the lawmaking powers of judges to the minimum necessary to serve the values underlying the doctrine of precedent. And from a utilitarian standpoint, such statements are properly treated as dicta because of the high likelihood that they will not have received thorough consideration.

Step two. If there is a relevant circuit precedent that reached a contrary result, the next question is whether the precedent is one that losing counsel reasonably relied on as *requiring* the same result. It is not enough that the earlier case is "relevant" in the broad sense contemplated by the first step—that is, that the earlier case would *support* the holding sought by losing counsel. Rather, counsel must be able to assert, with strong support in the relevant legal materials, that any distinctions between the two cases are irrelevant as a matter of law. For purposes of this inquiry I would deem the losing counsel's argument to be reasonable if (a) it was accepted by the district court; (b) it was accepted by a dissenter in the court of appeals; (c) it was accepted by other circuits; or (d) the panel itself recognized that the argument was strong (albeit ultimately unpersuasive). A precedent could also be "arguably compelling" if the earlier panel's rationale, taken as a whole, fit the facts of the later case as well. Conversely, a precedent could *not* be "arguably compelling" if the earlier decision explicitly adverted to facts or considerations not present in the later case.

Step three. The analysis thus far suggests that there is at least the appearance of conflict, and consequently a serious potential for uncertainty, whenever a panel has distinguished a relevant circuit precedent that losing counsel has reasonably relied on as requiring a contrary result. But these circumstances do not necessarily mean that the conflict is genuine or that the coexistence of the two (or more) decisions creates significant uncertainty for lawyers and lower courts. Whether conflict has been avoided and uncertainty minimized depends on the cogency and clarity of the distinctions drawn by the later panel.

Cogency and clarity are distinct criteria. The former asks whether the distinction drawn by the later opinion is grounded, through reasoned explanation that comports with the norms of legal argumentation, in the policy considerations underlying the rules; the latter asks whether the distinction has been articulated in a way that later courts and lawyers can readily apply.

Step three differs from step two in that step two looks at the law as it existed before the later panel issued its decision; step three takes the decision and its rationale into account. But step three does not depend on whether the distinction drawn by the later panel can be found in the earlier opinion. What the later panel is obliged to respect is the result, not the stated rationale, of a precedent. Of course, the later panel cannot simply say that the earlier case was "different" or insist, without elaboration, that the facts are "distinguishable." Nor is it enough to offer a new verbal formulation without showing how the new rule requires (or at least permits) different results in the two cases. But if the later panel, making legitimate use of the "leeways of precedent," reformulates the "rule" of the earlier case in a way that preserves the result while allowing for a contrary result on the new facts, it has not done violence to the doctrine of stare decisis. Nor has it created a conflict. To put it another way, an unnecessarily broad statement of the "rule" of a case can properly be treated as dictum.

When I presented a preliminary version of this chapter to the Ninth Circuit Judicial Conference, commentators argued that this approach is too narrow. In their view, a later panel is obliged to respect not only the "rule" of an earlier case, but also the purpose of the rule, that is, what the earlier panel was attempting to accomplish. Some judges have gone even further, stating that the binding effect of a decision extends to anything that the earlier panel *intended* to be part of its resolution of an issue in the case. "Dicta" would be limited to statements that the earlier panel explicitly labeled as beyond the scope of its decision.

The narrower view, however, is firmly grounded in the theory of precedent as a device that at once recognizes and limits the authority of courts to make law as a corollary of their power to decide cases.

Under that theory the judges of one panel cannot, by casting their rule in unnecessarily broad terms, preempt later panels from reconsidering (or, more accurately, considering) aspects of the same legal problem that were not present in the earlier case. The contrary view would freeze the development of legal rules in a way that is quite inconsistent with the tradition of the common law. It would be especially pernicious in the federal courts, where gradual adjustment and modification of existing law enables a life-tenured judiciary to reflect, over time, changes in the will of the people as manifested in the election of a new president.

The three-step formulation does not fully address two precedential patterns that may create disarray in the law of the circuit. First, a later panel may fail to mention or distinguish an arguably compelling contrary precedent. If so, the panel has by definition created a conflict, because without an articulated distinction lawyers and other courts have no way of knowing which situations fall on one side of the line rather than the other.

Second, the discussion thus far has posited a situation in which no more than one or two circuit precedents are "relevant" to the question raised by a new appeal, and the object has been to determine whether the panel's decision has created, or is likely to create, an intracircuit conflict. But much of the concern about inconsistency in the law of the circuit has focused on a different phenomenon: a multiplicity of decisions already on the books addressing the same legal problem, with some coming out on one side, some on the other. For example, from 1981 through 1986 the court issued more than twenty-five published opinions construing the "extreme hardship" provisions of the immigration laws. In a period of only three years in the mid-1980s the court published fifteen opinions on the weight and credibility of subjective testimony on levels of pain in Social Security disability cases and nearly as many on the weight to be given to the testimony of the treating physician. More recently, a nine-month period generated six opinions by five different judges on the question whether an allegedly infringing work was "substantially similar" to a copyrighted work.

Issues like these have several characteristics in common. The litigated disputes are numerous. The legal rules are fact-specific. The governing law does not point strongly in one direction rather than another; often the law is in a state of evolution. Second-level rules may provide some degree of predictability, but they do not fully constrain the discretion vested in the panels by the primary rules. Finally, many of the issues implicate deeply felt choices between competing societal values.

Almost invariably, the combination of these circumstances will result in the phenomenon I have described: a large number of decisions on point, some supporting the claim in question, others rejecting it. And when that pattern occurs, it would be difficult if not impossible for any new panel to distinguish all of the contrary precedents in a way that is both clear and cogent. Thus, under the three-step analysis, I would generally conclude that a conflict exists. Indeed, intuition too would tell us that under the circumstances posited, a certain degree of disarray is inevitable, at least when the decisions are not invariably made by the same groups of individuals.

One caveat is in order, however. Lawyers often talk about "extreme hardship," "substantial similarity," "disparate treatment," and the like as though the phrases encompass unitary issues. Thus, if an alien seeks suspension of deportation on the ground of extreme hardship, counsel will probably regard all extreme hardship cases as "relevant" in the sense used here. Yet it is quite possible that, if one looked at the decisions carefully, one could identify discrete subcategories of cases in which there were no contrary results, or in any event no arguably compelling contrary precedents. Nevertheless, at this stage I shall make no attempt to pursue that line of inquiry; instead, I shall assume that multiple relevant precedents reaching different results do constitute intracircuit conflicts, and I will seek to determine whether instances of that pattern have created substantial disarray in the law of the circuit.

Measuring the Incidence of Intracircuit Conflict

Armed with the theory just described, I proceeded as follows in my effort to estimate the extent of intracircuit conflict in the Ninth Circuit. I began by selecting two large samples of published opinions handed down by the Ninth Circuit, one group from 1983, the other from 1986. The sample for each period consisted of all Ninth Circuit panel decisions in every fifth volume of the Federal Reporter from that year. Each decision was analyzed in accordance with the three-step formulation. For cases not eliminated at the first stage (i.e., because there were one or more relevant circuit precedents that reach a contrary result), I also identified the precedent that most strongly supported the losing party.

For each case that was not excluded at the first step, I attempted to trace the subsequent history of the common issue to determine if the coexistence of arguably inconsistent decisions had created confusion or uncertainty. In other words, I did not assume the correctness of my distinction between "supporting" and "compelling" precedents; rather, I sought to determine if that distinction would hold up in practice. In addition, I Shepardized all cases in the sample with a view to discovering actual or potential conflicts created by the panel's failure to mention an apparently inconsistent ruling.

Indicia of confusion were apparent inconsistencies in the later decisions, disagreement within panels, disagreement between appellate panels and district courts, and frequent litigation. If one or more of these indicia were present, I examined the cases further to determine the extent to which the confusion was produced by the coexistence of the apparently conflicting decisions rather than by other factors. I also hoped to talk to lawyers and district judges to discover any evidence of confusion or disarray not manifested in published materials; however, that phase of the work remains incomplete.

I was particularly interested in uncovering conflicts created by a panel's outright failure to mention relevant precedents that reached contrary results. My assumption was that, if silent conflicts existed, they would become manifest in later decisions when judges and law clerks, using a full array of research tools, discovered the arguable discrepancy.

The 1983 sample yielded a total of 175 cases.[57] In 40 percent of them the court cited no contrary precedents on any issue. Research into later caselaw revealed fewer than a dozen instances of what I would call omitted precedents—contrary decisions that should have been cited but were not. And in all but one of these cases the omitted precedents were at best supporting for the losing party. The panels did not create conflicts by failing to cite the contrary rulings; at worst the new decisions introduced some unnecessary uncertainty into the law.

What about the cases in which there *were* relevant contrary precedents? In the overwhelming majority, the earlier decisions were no more than supportive of the losing party. In fact, although I was not doing it consciously, I realized afterward that basically I was applying the fifteen-minute test alluded to earlier. And in most of the cases it took me no more than fifteen minutes to conclude that there were obvious distinctions between the contrary precedents and the sample case, and that no reasonable lawyer would have argued otherwise.

---

[57]The research proved much more time-consuming than I had (perhaps unreasonably) anticipated, and study of the 1986 sample was still in progress as this chapter went to press. For a detailed analysis of the 1983 sample, see Hellman, supra note 55, at 576–94.

That leaves perhaps twenty-five cases in which an existing precedent could be deemed "arguably compelling" for the losing side. However, a few of these were cases in which there were already multiple precedents pointing in different directions. I decided to treat these with the other multiple-precedent cases in order to permit a more accurate estimate of the number of intracircuit conflicts created in the course of a year.

In all but six of the step-three cases the 1983 panel articulated a distinction that I thought was clear and cogent—one that could be understood and followed even if it was not apparent in the earlier decisions. If we extrapolate from the sample, the results would suggest that about thirty such decisions were issued by the Ninth Circuit Court of Appeals during the year. However, the analysis cannot stop there. To question the clarity and cogency of a distinction is not to say that the panel has created a conflict; it is only to say that the panel's decision has a strong potential for doing so. Unfortunately for the urge to quantify, the subsequent history of the issues in these cases provides a dubious base from which to estimate the total number of intracircuit conflicts created by panel decisions in the course of the year. The subset of cases is so small, and the outcomes turn out to be so varied,[58] that any attempt to extrapolate would be attended by a high margin of error. But this does not mean that no conclusions can be drawn from the data. On the contrary, perhaps the most significant finding is that in all but two of the cases the uncertainty created by the panel decisions had been largely if not entirely dissipated within three years.

Twelve cases in the 1983 sample involved issues that had already generated multiple precedents pointing in both directions. Four decisions considered appeals by aliens seeking to avoid deportation on the ground of extreme hardship. Two involved claims of attempted monopolization under section 2 of the Sherman Act. Four cases arose out of criminal proceedings; all but one turned on fact-specific legal rules that by their nature require case-by-case interpretation.

How significant are the multiple-precedent issues? Several observations are suggested by the cases in the study. First, the issues tend to be concentrated in areas of the law like criminal procedure where legal rules do not directly influence the structuring of transactions or other primary activity. Second, many of the rules are heavily weighted in favor of deference to first-line decision makers. At the appellate level,

[58]See id. at 588–90.

the bulk of cases can be resolved without the need to examine the full range of the court's jurisprudence.[59] Third, in most instances the disarray caused by the existence of multiple relevant precedents eventually yields to a dominant trend or to some outside force.

In any event, the study suggests that the pattern exemplified by high-visibility issues like "extreme hardship" and "attempted monopolization" is not characteristic of Ninth Circuit jurisprudence generally. Nor is intracircuit conflict. To recapitulate: in the 1983 sample, nearly half of the cases did not cite any contrary precedents. When contrary precedents did exist, they were usually no more than supporting for the losing party. And when the losing party could cite arguably compelling precedents, the panel generally succeeded in distinguishing them in a way that avoided conflict for the future.

Inconsistency and the "Luck of the Draw"

Neither the three-step test nor the empirical study addresses the concern expressed by some lawyers in the Ninth Circuit that the result in the court of appeals will often depend on the composition of the panel that hears the case. This is not because the phenomenon does not exist; even the court of appeals judges agree that it does. And it is understandable that lawyers would feel uncomfortable with what appears to be an element of the lottery in appellate outcomes. Nevertheless, I think the concern is misplaced.

First, any study that concentrates on published appellate decisions inevitably overstates the extent to which the law is unstable or uncertain. In the familiar metaphor, cases decided by published opinions stand at the apex of a much larger pyramid. For the vast majority of transactions and disputes, the law provides sufficient guidance that no rational person would think of going to court at all. Of the disputes that do wind up in court, many, perhaps most, involve the application of settled law to particular facts, so that litigation ends at the trial level. Even among the cases that are appealed, more than half are decided by unpublished opinions because they raise no new legal issues.

Second, it is important not to equate uncertainty or unpredictability with inconsistency. Inconsistency leads to uncertainty, but uncertainty may have many other causes. In particular, the legal consequences of

---

[59]The standard of review does not ease the burden of lawyers and adjudicators in the trial courts and agencies, yet even there it is likely that extended exegesis and comparison will be required only in close or difficult cases.

primary conduct may be unpredictable not because the precedents point in different directions, but because there are no precedents very closely on point. For example, the result may depend on the interpretation of a statute not previously construed. The Supreme Court may have recently handed down a decision that sets the law on a new course. The facts may bear little resemblance to those of cases already on the books. Or the facts may fall squarely between those of existing precedents. In situations like these, the outcome may well depend on the predilections of the panel that happens to hear the case. But there is no reason to expect that unpredictability of this kind would be more common in the larger circuit. Indeed, the larger circuit will probably have a larger number of precedents relevant to any given issue, and that in turn might actually reduce the number (or at least the proportion) of cases in which the panel has freedom to decide either way without creating a conflict.

Yet even if that proposition is accepted, it does not fully address concerns about the "luck of the draw," for there remains the argument that aberrant decisions (as distinguished from decisions that create conflicts) will be more readily corrected through en banc rehearing in the small circuit than in the large circuit. Two responses are in order. To begin with, the argument assumes that judges are predictable, even knee-jerk, in their responses to novel issues. That has not been the experience of the federal courts in the last few years, even after eight years of appointments by an administration more concerned with ideology than most. Thus, where the outcome is uncertain because of the absence of closely relevant precedents, en banc rehearing will not necessarily add to predictability. Beyond this, even judges with strong views about the substantive issues will temper them with a recognition of the institutional harm that would result from treating panel decisions as merely provisional pending consideration by the full court. Especially when one considers the shifts in national political power that have characterized the twentieth century, it is clear that the system would break down if judges were not willing to live with decisions that they would not have rendered if they had been on the panel.

Third, a certain degree of unpredictability is an inevitable consequence of panel autonomy—a principle on which the judges of the Ninth Circuit place a very high value. Their commitment can be seen in the court's unwillingness to use the "mini en banc,"[60] in the rejection of time limits that would qualify the priority-of-submission rule,

[60]See note 1.

and especially in the repudiation of the permanent rotation model for the limited en banc court. Judge Browning has argued that panel autonomy promotes stability in the long run, "because periodic shifts in the ideological roots of the majority [would otherwise] produce sharp and unsettling shifts in the law."[61] I think he is right, but it must be acknowledged that in the short run panel autonomy may undercut predictability and consistency. By "protect[ing] the opportunity of all, and not just the majority, to play a part in the development of the law," the present arrangements give latitude to the minority to announce binding rules that would be rejected if the full court were voting. Of course, panels must recognize that they operate as part of a larger institution, but the constraints imposed by that role operate only retrospectively. Panels are obliged to respect what other panels have done in the past; they have no obligation to anticipate what the court as a whole might do in the future. And even the retrospective obligation is limited by the "leeways" of precedent.[62]

It is possible to imagine a different approach, one that would call upon individual judges to give some weight to the position of the larger entity, at least when that position could be predicted with some confidence.[63] But the principle of panel autonomy is probably too deeply engrained to expect any group of federal judges to adopt that stance. More important, by permitting a dialectic between majority and minority perspectives, panel autonomy fosters the wise evolution of legal rules.

Finally, I believe that much of the concern about unpredictability in a multijudge court of appeals rests on an impatience with the case-by-case mode of adjudication that is the essence of our common law system. But over the years, society has concluded that that approach, with all its open-endedness, is preferable to the more structured regime of codification, especially in view of the availability of the legislative deus ex machina whenever disarray or lacunae in decisional law become too much to bear. For that reason as well as the others, I think

[61]Annual Judicial Conference, Second Judicial Circuit of the United States, 106 F.R.D. 103, 161–62 (1984) (remarks of Judge Browning).

[62]See Karl N. Llewellyn, *The Common Law Tradition: Deciding Appeals* 77–91 (Little, Brown, 1960).

[63]A hint of this attitude appeared in a discussion of whether a limited en banc panel could "dis-enbanc" a case after the full court voted to grant en banc rehearing. Some judges thought a limited en banc panel might take that step in order to avoid an en banc ruling that would not reflect the views of the entire court. If this were to occur, the members of the en banc majority would indeed be subordinating their own views to those of the larger entity. However, there is no evidence to suggest that this ever happened.

it is sound to concentrate on inconsistency, which I agree reflects a malfunction in the system, and not to worry overmuch about unpredictability, which is to a large extent unavoidable.

Implications for the Future

At the beginning of this chapter I suggested that the Ninth Circuit's efforts to maintain consistency in the law of the circuit deserve attention in part because the development of large, geographically organized appellate courts may provide an alternative to more radical structural reforms in the federal system. Yet in assessing the results of the study, it is necessary to keep in mind some important limitations.

First, I have made no effort to investigate possible conflicts in unpublished opinions. To be sure, from the standpoint of lawyers and district courts any such conflicts would be irrelevant because unpublished opinions cannot be cited as precedent. But they would be troublesome from the standpoint of the court's obligation to treat like cases alike—the more so since the profession has no way of monitoring this aspect of the court's work.[64] Thus, I hope that some other scholar will take a look at the unpublished opinions in the not-too-distant future.

Second, more work remains to be done in exploring the nature and extent of multiple-precedent issues. I acknowledge that, even where the three-part test would not necessarily lead to the conclusion that a conflict existed, the need to reconcile multiple precedents itself places a burden on judges and lawyers that must be taken into account in evaluating the workability of the large appellate court. At the same time, I do not think it unreasonable to assume at least a modest level of care in defining the "issue" in a case.

Third, even if the study could provide complete data on the incidence of actual conflicts, there would still be room for disagreement over the degree of freedom that panels ought to have in treating existing precedents. Just as with intercircuit conflicts, variations in approach that would be seen by some as nothing more than the common law "work[ing] itself pure from case to case"[65] will be regarded by others as creating an undesirable level of uncertainty and unpredictability.

[64]There is reason to believe that panel majorities sometimes agree to decide a case by unpublished memorandum as the price of avoiding a dissent.
[65]Graham Hughes, "Are Justices Just?" *N.Y. Rev. Books*, Nov. 19, 1981, at 41, 42 (quoting Lord Mansfield).

Fourth, the study cannot quantify the hidden costs of maintaining consistency in the large circuit: the additional burdens on the judges which will not be reflected in their published work. Members of the court acknowledge that they spend a substantial amount of time reviewing opinions and exchanging memoranda in order to iron out apparent inconsistencies without calling an en banc hearing.[66] Thus far, however, there is little evidence to suggest that these efforts have interfered with the judges' productivity.

Finally, evaluation of the findings of this study must be comparative, not absolute. Whatever the inadequacies of the Ninth Circuit's efforts to maintain a consistent law, and whatever the costs of those efforts, both must be weighed against the costs of alternative solutions to the crisis of volume in the federal appellate system.

---

[66]Indeed, at one point some members of the court actually suggested that the judges' overall caseload should be reduced so that they could shoulder the burden of monitoring the law of the circuit without a reduction in the quality of their opinions. Other judges pointed out that Congress was not likely to be sympathetic to this idea, and the suggestion was not pursued further.

PART III

Adjudication:
Efficiency without Depersonalization

Introduction

Although discussion of the large circuit tends to focus on the lawmaking functions of appellate courts, the shaping of precedent in a common-law system takes place only as a by-product of the court's primary function—doing justice in individual cases. The crisis of volume that has led to the development of large courts has also had its effect at this more basic level in courts of all sizes.

The effect has not been uniform across the spectrum of the courts' work. Cases obviously destined for precedential status are not handled very differently today from the way they were fifty years ago. Rather, concern has centered on the cases that appear to involve only review for error. When cases are decided without oral argument, without published opinions, and with heavy reliance on the work of staff attorneys and law clerks, it is all too easy for lawyers and the public to conclude that "no judge ever sees those cases." But for courts engulfed by the flood of appeals, there is no turning back to the more leisurely and more individualized processes of earlier years.

The studies in Part III examine some of the Ninth Circuit's efforts to meet the challenge of volume. Two of the chapters focus on procedures within the court of appeals—in particular, the practice of "screening" cases to identify those that can appropriately be diverted to a separate decisional track involving a significantly smaller degree of personal attention from the judges. The remaining chapter in Part III analyzes an experiment that vests appellate review in specialized tribunals at the trial-court level. The chapters in Part IV explore the implications of these findings as well as those of the Rosenberg and Hellman studies in Part II.

In Chapter 4, John B. Oakley and Robert S. Thompson begin by delineating the threat to the values of appeal posed by screening procedures. The concern most often expressed is that screening requires the use of staff; staff means bureaucratization; and bureaucratization gives primacy to goals that are foreign and indeed antagonistic to the norms of traditional appellate adjudication. A related fear is that high-volume, low-status cases will get short shrift because so many are sure losers. Drawing on a mass of statistical information extracted from the Ninth Circuit's operational databases, the authors attempt to determine whether the court has succeeded in controlling the process so as to minimize the impact of preconception on outcome.

Overall, the study provides reassurance that the cases diverted from the traditional "track" are those that any competent decision maker would decide in the same way. The authors also conclude that the court of appeals is conscious of the "needles" that may be hidden in the "haystack" and has made real efforts to locate them.

In evaluating the Ninth Circuit's procedures, the authors suggest that the court may be denying itself the full benefit of the adversary process as a tool for developing and refining the information necessary to a sound judicial decision. This assessment underlies recommendations for improvements in present screening practices which would make better use of adversary dialectic. However, the authors conclude that in the long term the best hope for preserving the values of appeal for nonprecedential cases may be to create appellate magistrates within the court of appeals.

In Chapter 5, Jerry Goldman analyzes screening from a perspective that emphasizes the importance of procedure as a contributing element to the legitimacy of judicial decisions. After reviewing the theory of screening and the procedures adopted by the Ninth Circuit to increase efficiency, the author presents the fruits of an empirical study relying on the Ninth Circuit's database, citation information, and litigant interviews. Does screening (i.e., no oral argument, absence of face-to-face case conferences, and substantial staff assistance) affect case outcomes and opinion publication? The data support the proposition that assigning cases to the screening docket reduces the likelihood that the judges will issue published opinions. On case outcomes, however, screening appears to have no significant effect. In a related vein, Goldman explains why the screening guidelines may fail to distinguish adequately between criteria for summary disposition and criteria for nonpublication.

Turning from instrumental to symbolic concerns, Goldman argues that legitimacy depends to a large extent on litigant perceptions of procedural fairness. That in turn requires greater visibility in the appellate decision-making process. To that end, he suggests consideration of a plan first proposed by Shirley Hufstedler in 1971 as a way of dealing with caseloads that even then seemed to be straining the traditional structure almost to the breaking point. The essence of the idea is that appellate review for cases having no precedential importance would be vested in the trial court.

The attraction of the Hufstedler plan is that it bypasses the complementary concerns about volume and bureaucratization in the courts of appeals by creating institutions of appellate review in a tier that can absorb larger numbers of judges more easily. Prompted by very different concerns, Congress in 1978 authorized a unique alternate system of appellate review for bankruptcy cases that in many respects resembles the earlier, hypothetical model. Alone among the circuits, the Ninth Circuit implemented this plan and created a Bankruptcy Appellate Panel (BAP).

In Chapter 6, Michael A. Berch examines the operation of the BAP and considers its implications for other kinds of cases. The evidence indicates that the BAP has reduced the number of bankruptcy cases taken to the court of appeals; it has helped to articulate and develop the law in its specialized area; and it has won the respect of the bar and bench in the circuit. The one troublesome finding is a high reversal rate of BAP decisions by the court of appeals, although, as Berch points out, that finding may reflect a single aberrant year.

Berch suggests that the apparent success of the BAP may point the way to two distinct models for structural reform within the circuit. Rather than dispersing the review function vertically through the establishment of an appellate division in the trial court, the alternate plan would facilitate horizontal expansion through the creation of specialist panels of judges of the court of appeals. Berch explains why specialist panels bring most of the advantages of specialized courts, but without the drawbacks.

The idea of specialist panels is further elaborated in Chapter 7 by Daniel J. Meador. Meador begins with the proposition that appellate organization should foster uniformity in the articulation of rules and predictability in their application. The key factor in pursuing those goals, he argues, is "continuity of decision makers," and that is what specialist panels would provide. Moreover, like the Oakley-Thompson proposal for appellate magistrates, this arrangement would have the virtue of strengthening the ability of the regional circuits to cope with increased caseloads.

That virtue also characterizes the novel plan offered by Paul D.

Carrington in Chapter 8. The Carrington plan resembles the Hufstedler model in that it establishes distinct tracks for the error-correcting and lawmaking aspects of appellate review, but it substitutes circuit judges for trial judges and adds elements of the Meador proposal for specialized panels. The common thread in these ideas is that they would enable the circuits to accommodate enough judges to give individualized judicial treatment to all cases, without requiring new structures at higher levels that would further concentrate power at the center.

Carrington's proposal differs in one important respect from Meador's. Meador assumes that a large volume of appeals will generate a large body of precedential decisions, and he seeks to design a structure that will bring the greatest possible degree of coherence to those decisions. Carrington shares the concern for coherence, but his proposal addresses the problem by substantially reducing the number of cases in which precedential opinions would be issued. This approach represents a sharp departure from the tradition of the common law, in which legal rules are given meaning through their application in a series of cases. But Carrington suggests that, in an era with a predilection for vague standards and multiple-factor "tests," the common-law process does not operate to narrow the range of uncertainty; instead, it produces a vast body of decisions that no one can master anyway. If that is so, perhaps we should admit it, publish only opinions that contribute significantly to the professional literature, and rely on oral argument and a vigorous adversary process to keep trial courts within the bounds established by the rules.

4

Screening, Delegation, and the Values of Appeal: An Appraisal of the Ninth Circuit's Screening Docket during the Browning Years

JOHN B. OAKLEY
AND
ROBERT S. THOMPSON

Lacking discretion to deny plenary review of cases reaching them from the district courts, United States courts of appeals first and foremost must decide these cases.[1] When caseload overtaxes the capacity of appellate judges personally to review, collegially to discuss, and collectively to endorse a written statement of the reasons for decision in each case on their docket, the imperative to decide is in tension with other fundamental values of appeal. If mechanisms are not developed to cope with docket overload, the court cannot satisfactorily meet its obligation to individual litigants—the correction of trial court error—much less its institutional obligations to declare precedent and to supervise the district courts. But unless caseload control mechanisms are structured both to permit adequate participation by the parties in the proceedings that determine their fate and to preserve

The authors gratefully acknowledge the information and counsel generously provided by Gordon Bermant, Leon Bloomfield, Dede Campagna, Cathy Catterson, Joe Cecil, Jerry Goldman, Mark Langer, Thomas Marvell, Dinah Shelton, and Donna Stienstra. We also acknowledge with thanks the valuable research assistance of Gary Schwebach.
[1]The narrowly circumscribed discretionary jurisdiction of the federal courts of appeals under the Interlocutory Appeals Act of 1958, 28 U.S.C. § 1292(b), accounts for only a few tenths of 1 percent of the cases filed in the courts of appeals. See Charles Alan Wright, *The Law of Federal Courts* 715–16 (West Publishing Co., 4th ed. 1983).

the courtlike characteristics that legitimate the exercise of judicial power, other significant values of appeal are in jeopardy.[2]

The principal caseload control mechanism developed by the United States courts of appeals and similarly burdened state appellate courts is the practice of "screening" their dockets to identify cases appropriate for procedural shortcuts. In one way or another screening programs seek to divert the least difficult cases to a separate decisional track involving a significantly lesser degree of personal attention by judges. The federal courts uniformly forego oral argument in screened cases, and most courts further reduce the unit cost in judicial time of decisions in their "fast-track" cases by placing primary reliance for the operation of the screening process on a centrally organized, parajudicially supervised group of staff attorneys.[3] The central premise of screening programs is that fast-track procedures and substitution of staff for judicial time in the adjudication of screened cases can achieve procedural economies with no significant impact on substantive results. Generally, this premise is defended on the ground that screening programs remove from conventional appellate processing only simple cases destined to a single, obvious, and foregone result at the hands of any qualified decision maker.

Our task in this chapter is to analyze and evaluate from a normative perspective the screening program of the Ninth Circuit Court of Appeals during its six and a half years of operation under the administration of Chief Judge James R. Browning.[4] We use statistical information drawn from the court's operational databases to gauge whether the Ninth Circuit's approach provides an appropriate model for appellate courts seeking to enjoy the procedural efficiencies of screening without undue compromise of the values of appeal.[5] Throughout the

---

[2]For a fuller exposition of these values, see Robert S. Thompson and John B. Oakley, "From Information to Opinion in Appellate Courts: How Funny Things Happen on the Way through the Forum," 1986 *Ariz. St. L.J.* 1, 9–10.

[3]See, e.g., Paul D. Carrington, Daniel J. Meador, and Maurice Rosenberg, *Justice on Appeal* 46–51 (West Publishing Co., 1975). Formal screening for the purpose of denying oral argument and achieving summary disposition does not necessarily require dependence on staff. It can be accomplished by judges without staff intervention, as is the regular practice in the Third Circuit. See Joe S. Cecil and Donna Stienstra, *Deciding Cases without Argument: An Examination of Four Courts of Appeals* 118–20 (Federal Judicial Center, 1987), hereafter cited as Cecil and Stienstra. "Informal screening" occurs when argument panels decide that they do not wish to hear oral argument in particular cases on their calendars. See pp. 108, 116–17.

[4]For an account of the origins of the program, see Chapter 5.

[5]For another report of the empirical research presented in this chapter, see John B. Oakley, "The Screening Docket of the Ninth Circuit" (law review publication forthcom-

chapter we rely implicitly on assumptions that we have proposed and defended elsewhere.[6] These assumptions are:

1. It is important that appellate judges decide cases by personally developing the reasoning that disciplines their decisions. It is not enough that judges merely accept responsibility for decisions made by others.[7]

2. Nevertheless, assistance rendered by aides to judges is both legitimate and necessary to the judicial function. Where judges are faced with rising caseloads, this assistance properly includes some form of screening to segregate those cases most calling for the personal attention of the judges.

3. Cases suitable for screening to decision with minimum judicial review of the staff product should be those in which the decision is essentially rule-bound. Cases in which the result turns on principle that is indeterminate as applied should be rejected from screening.

4. In cases screened to decision, the staff product should supply the judges with information adequate to support the memorandum's statement of controlling precedent and of the facts in the record that render the doctrine applicable.

5. The greater the degree of appellate judicial discretion inherent in a question, the more important it is that the discretion be exercised with the fullest information feasible. Issues of whether trial court error was harmless, whether an issue raised on appeal is timely, whether trial court factual findings survive the clearly erroneous test, and whether trial court discretion has been abused fall within this category of cases.

6. The adversary system can be, and generally is, a trustworthy and effective device for assembling and processing information to be used by judges in their decisions.

---

ing 1991). The article includes extensive documentation and detail omitted here for reasons of space.

[6]See Thompson and Oakley, supra note 2, at 9–10, 13–14, 52–56; Robert S. Thompson, "Judicial Independence, Judicial Accountability, Judicial Elections and the California Supreme Court: Defining the Terms of the Debate," 59 *S. Cal. L. Rev.* 809, 830–33 (1986).

[7]One defender of judicial delegation of opinion-drafting seemingly takes for granted a distinction between reasoning as a process of decision and the writing out of reasons as a process of articulation. See B. E. Witkin, *Manual on Appellate Court Opinions* 16 (West Publishing Co., 1977): "[C]ourts need not seek excuses for delegating part of the opinion-writing function to talented experts, with superior legal training and experience in writing. It is the task of stating reasons for the decision, not the authority to decide, that is delegated." We find more persuasive the observations of judges who find that the reasoning process is not complete until it has been tested through writing. E.g., Roger Traynor, "Some Open Questions on the Work of State Appellate Courts," 24 *U. Chi. L. Rev.* 211, 218 (1957); Wade McCree, "Bureaucratic Justice: An Early Warning," 129 *U. Pa. L. Rev.* 777, 790–91 (1981).

Where we refer in this chapter to *error* in the screening process, we use the term primarily to denote a conclusion recommended by staff that would not have been reached by the panel of judges adopting the conclusion if these judges, fully informed by oral argument and uninfluenced by a central staff memorandum, had heard the case without screening.[8]

The Conflict of Values and Volume in Modern Appellate Administration

There are important reasons to provide parties with a right to appeal decisions by courts of first resort. At least four values are served by the right to appeal.

First, appeal is a mechanism for *correcting mistakes* by trial courts in resolving disputes about law or fact. Society places a high value on having individual cases rightly and consistently decided. The more leisurely pace of appeal vis-à-vis trial and the sharper focus on discrete issues by both counsel and the appellate court are important guarantors of the correctness of a judicial decision that has been tested by appeal.

Second, there is value in having a mechanism for *reviewing institutional impact*. Institutional impact takes three forms. First, some trial judges may not be operating their courts properly. Appeal serves to keep trial courts on the procedural tracks laid down by the general legal system. Second, in responding to the facts of particular cases, trial courts may propound rules likely to be applied in other cases. This is especially likely where there is a practice, as in the federal courts, of publishing trial court opinions. Lawmaking by the judicial spokes of a legal system needs to be bound by the reviewing authority of an appellate hub and its circumscribing precedent. Third, and conversely, trial courts may reach unpublished resolutions of issues of law that should be considered and memorialized in an opinion published

[8]Of course, the word *error* could have other meanings. For example, it could mean error in the abstract despite the impossibility of proving this sort of error. It might mean that most qualified observers would find the result of the case wrong, or that these observers would find the reasoning of the opinion or staff memorandum to be wrong. The definition used in the text derives from the purpose of this chapter. Our concern is the compatibility of screening mechanisms with decisions by duly commissioned Article III judges.

by an appellate court for the future guidance of other trial courts and the public.

The third value of appeal is to foster a sense of *participation* by the parties in the fate of their lawsuit at the hands of the state. Adjudication of a dispute is distinctly different from settlement by executive fiat. The participation of parties in the formulation of issues and the opportunity for parties to persuade the decision maker according to by-and-large preexisting rules are important elements in the distinction between the rule of law and the rule of a totalitarian state.[9] The sense of party participation in the binding but nonviolent resolution of disputes according to general rules is enhanced by placing the first-instance decision maker under the yoke of party-driven review and possible reversal.

Finally, there is *legitimation* of the judicial decision by a process that draws upon form and ritual to inspire a sense of duty to obey judicial decisions even when the substantive premises or outcomes of such decisions are controversial or unpopular. We all sense, by intuition or experience, that the determinations of courts in cases brought before them by others may ultimately bear on disputes in which we later become personally involved. Through precedent we are governed by law declared without our vote or participation. The integrity of the judicial process, including the important feature of appeal, thus serves to legitimate a system of dispute resolution that governs even the uninvolved, the unrepresented, and the unwitting.

In sum, it is difficult to conceive of a functional and acceptable judicial system, one more dependent for its efficacy on acquiescence than coercion, that would operate without a comprehensive system of appeal. The idea that justice demands the right of appeal may not yet be understood as a principle of due process under our enacted Constitution. But in the old and still true sense of our British legal inheritance, the right to appeal is part of our unwritten constitution. Although diminishing returns argue against an undue number of levels of appeal, at least one appeal from a trial court decision inheres in our present social conception of what just adjudication requires.[10]

[9]See generally John B. Oakley, "The Legality of a Political System: Positivism, Political Morality and the Point of Theories of Law," in Eugene Kamenka, Robert S. Summers, and William L. Twining, *Sociological Jurisprudence and Realist Theories of Law* 83, 89–92 (1986) (Rechtstheorie Beiheft 9).

[10]See generally American Bar Association Standing Comm. on Federal Judicial Improvements, "The United States Court of Appeals: Reexamining Structure and Process after a Century of Growth," 125 F.R.D. 523, 531, 547, 549 (1989) (justice requires effective

The constant struggle of the modern intermediate appellate court is to maintain the values of appeal in the face of overloaded dockets.[11] There are practical limits to the number of judges who can operate consistently and harmoniously within a given appellate court, and to the number of courts that can consistently and harmoniously share appellate jurisdiction at the same intermediate tier of a judicial hierarchy. These practicalities have made an increase in per-judge caseload, rather than an increase in judges per court and courts per jurisdiction, the favored means of dealing with the crisis of volume while preserving the values of appeal. But judges' days still have but twenty-four hours. There are substantive limits to the productivity we can expect of the ordinary mortals whom we recruit, by and large, to wear judicial robes.[12] We have probably exhausted the utility of exhorting judges to work harder; like any set of galley slaves, they must surely be tempted to increase their tempo quantitatively by qualitatively shortening their strokes. It is no less idle to expect further substantial gains in judicial productivity through streamlining the processing of cases by individual judges. The length of briefs may be restricted, the time for argument shortened, the incidence of publication of opinions reduced—but the compound effect of successive rounds of cutbacks in the time judges allot to the discrete tasks of appellate adjudication would soon have judges going through the motions and little else. We are already operating at the margin of the efficiency with which traditional appellate adjudication can be delivered.

The only realistic way to increase the productivity of individual judges past the point that can be achieved through diligence and exhortation, while keeping pace with the increase in caseload, has

---

process for correcting trial court mistakes); Judith Resnik, "Tiers," 57 *S. Cal. L. Rev.* 837, 860–62 (fundamental but unwritten right to appeal has evolved in the United States through two hundred years of procedural innovation).

[11]The problem is not confined to the federal system. See Thomas B. Marvell, "State Appellate Court Responses to Caseload Growth," 72 *Judicature* 282, 282 (1989): "The [state] appellate caseload explosion and the resulting pressures on the courts are hard to exaggerate. Appeals have been doubling about every decade since World War II, placing extreme demands on judges to increase output."

[12]Some judges possess extraordinary capacities, of course, but current conditions conspire to reduce rather than to increase the number of super-lawyers among the judiciary. See Richard A. Posner, *The Federal Courts: Crisis and Reform* (Harvard University Press, 1985) 34–45 (low salaries and overloaded dockets reduce attractiveness of federal bench to outstanding lawyers); id. at 46–47 (state court conditions even worse, especially in states where judicial elections deter lawyers from accepting judicial appointments).

been to adopt efficiency devices that drastically reduce the mean amount of individual judge-time required to decide *some* appeals, thereby increasing the productivity of appellate judges when averaged over *all* appeals. Abridgment of traditional methods of appellate adjudication in selected cases enables the court to maintain an acceptable net rate of disposition while continuing to offer traditional adjudicatory procedures in the remaining cases. But this compromise has not generally been conceived as advantageous to the litigants who receive the nontraditional treatment. The fear is that in appellate decision making, as in most of life, acceleration entails a trade-off between the goal of the quick and the risk of the dirty. This presents an overloaded appellate court with the difficult issue of which cases to decide under summary but arguably more error-prone procedures.[13]

One method of speeding up appellate adjudication would be an evenhanded rationing of judicial time, giving every case an equal but less-than-ideal amount of personal judicial attention. Common sense has prevailed, however, and the firmly established norm is to discriminate among cases according to the complexity or difficulty of the issues they appear to present. The goal is to identify early in the appellate process cases so routine or hopeless (or both) that any judge must reach the same result. Such cases clearly exist in abundance in the caseload of any modern American appellate court with a mandatory jurisdiction. Here, surely, conventional appellate procedure is most wasteful of judicial time better spent on more difficult cases, and the risk of error from acceleration is least—provided that such simple cases can be accurately identified by means more efficient than conventional appellate procedure.

---

[13]We refer to *error* in the sense previously noted: a difference in outcome from that which would have occurred had a case been processed in the traditional fashion. An apparent example of the phenomenon has been furnished by Supreme Court Justice John Paul Stevens. A panel of the Fifth Circuit Court of Appeals, in an unpublished opinion, rejected a criminal defendant's claim that the district court had improperly departed from the Sentencing Guidelines. The identical claim was found to be meritorious by another panel in a published opinion issued two days later. (Both cases were decided without oral argument.) Justice Stevens commented, "It is unfortunate that the summary disposition of petitioner's case by the Fifth Circuit and this Court may require petitioner to serve [a longer prison sentence than the Sentencing Guidelines provide]. That, however, is the kind of burden that the individual litigant must occasionally bear when efficient management is permitted to displace the careful administration of justice in each case." Taylor v. United States, 110 S. Ct. 265, 265–66 (1989) (opinion of Stevens, J., respecting the denial of certiorari).

John B. Oakley and Robert S. Thompson

Screening and the Problem of Bureaucracy

Thus we arrive at screening as a prevalent modern response to the crisis of volume at appellate courts.[14] A screening program seeks to filter from the flow of cases those of such an apparently meritless or routine nature as not to require full-scale judicial involvement. Because it can quickly become counterproductive to expend judge-time in deciding which cases do not merit judge-time, staff attorneys commonly play a major role in the screening process. For reasons partly constitutional and partly traditional, the ultimate act of decision in screened cases is still performed by commissioned judicial personnel. But the decision generally will not have been informed by oral argument,[15] and if announced in an opinion at all, the opinion will usually be unpublished and not intended for the guidance or scrutiny of nonparties.[16]

This screening process risks considerable dilution of the values of appeal. If the screening is too crude and the treatment of a screened case too summary, trial court errors may go uncorrected. Moreover, the abbreviated treatment forecloses full party participation and reduces the social legitimacy of result and process. The legitimation value of appeal is particularly threatened by the bureaucratic apparatus of screening. Snap judgments by judges unaided by staff about which cases are to be disposed of summarily—screening and decision occurring virtually simultaneously—risk a merger of the quick and the dirty that is inappropriate where society by statute or constitution has

---

[14]For discussion of such other responses as increasing the number of judges, courts, and parajudicial personnel, or altering traditional appellate procedures by curtailing oral argument or deciding cases with unpublished opinions or no opinions at all, see Posner, supra note 12, at 94–129; Marvell, supra note 11, at 282. Some of these other responses may be adopted by an overloaded appellate court not as alternatives to screening but rather as constituents of a screening program, which generally entails increased use of parajudicial staff, curtailment of argument, and the abbreviation and nonpublication of opinions announcing appellate judgments. See id. at 282 n.3.

[15]Systematic exclusion of cases from the oral argument track is definitional of "screening" in federal appellate practice. Some state court systems, such as California's, operate under a local constitutional requirement that all appeals be orally argued absent waiver of that right. Such systems nevertheless have procedures for disposing of routine cases that are functionally equivalent to the screening of cases in the federal courts of appeals. See Thompson and Oakley, supra note 2, at 23.

[16]As reported in Figure 4.7, published opinions are issued in only 6 percent of the cases decided on the merits by the Ninth Circuit's screening panels.

afforded the litigants appeal as of right rather than at the grace of the judges. Careful administration of a screening program that achieves a significant increase in productivity per judge thus requires the use of staff, and the use of staff introduces an element of bureaucracy into the performance of the adjudicatory function.

We do not refer to the concept of bureaucracy in a pejorative sense. It is what modern appellate justice requires. But we must look carefully at the characteristics of the bureaucratized decision making which screening programs generally employ.

The goals and procedures of a bureaucratized process differ from the norms we associate with traditional appellate adjudication. Virtually by definition, bureaucracies give primacy to quantitative goals, and even in the qualitative realm they emphasize goals of conformity, consistency, and cohesion rather than innovation or reinterpretation. In order to achieve efficiency and consistency across the great mass of decisions that bureaucracies are charged with, internal norms may develop by which presumptions replace analysis in the determination of which cases are routine and appropriate for low-cost bureaucratic processing.[17]

The great challenge for an appellate court seeking relief from the crisis of volume through a screening program is to shape a bureaucratic system that processes only those cases that are appropriate for bureaucratic disposition. Screening loses its value if too much of already scarce judicial time is devoted to the classification process. This sets up the problem of the bureaucracy making its own choice of which cases to feed itself.

Our previous work has identified what we consider to be significant obstacles to the accuracy of bureaucratic assessment of whether cases in fact fall into the routine categories fit for bureaucratic treatment.[18] The net result is that certain kinds of cases may be treated by staff in a routine fashion with inadequate attention to actual merit. This may occur with the best of intentions because the perception of their role by bureaucratic participants leads them to view and describe cases in a way that minimizes their novelty and maximizes their apparent suitability for staff-generated bureaucratic disposition.

[17]See Thompson and Oakley, supra note 2, at 35–36.
[18]See, e.g., John B. Oakley and Robert S. Thompson, *Law Clerks and the Judicial Process* 66, 85–86, 136–38 (University of California Press, 1980); Thompson and Oakley, supra note 2, at 61–62.

John B. Oakley and Robert S. Thompson

Screening Programs in the Federal Courts

Screening in the federal courts of appeals is authorized by Rule 34(a) of the Federal Rules of Appellate Procedure. Although the first sentence of the rule contains what appears to be a ringing commitment to oral argument,[19] the rule as a whole allows wide discretion to the courts to adopt summary procedures. The "minimum standard" set by the rule is that oral argument will be allowed "unless (1) the appeal is frivolous; or (2) the dispositive issue or set of issues has been recently authoritatively decided; or (3) the facts and legal arguments are adequately presented in the briefs and record and the decisional process would not be significantly aided by oral argument."

In the early years of screening, the usual justification for considering oral argument in screened cases to be futile was the limitation of the screening docket to simple cases in which any qualified decision maker could reach only a single result.[20] But the third of the disjunctive criteria in Rule 34(a) apparently permits assignment of a case to the screening docket even when it presents difficult issues of first impression, provided only that the judges unanimously agree on the subjective and necessarily speculative judgment that oral argument would not be helpful. The text of the rule thus allows a screening program to grow beyond a sorting device for hopeless cases to become a means for more generalized expression of judicial antipathy to the very idea of oral argument as a valuable feature of the appellate process. Although that approach is surely contrary to the spirit of the rule, some lawyers think it is already a reality.[21] Our research attempts to shed light on the matter.

Table 4.1 summarizes the seven approaches to screening practiced by the federal courts of appeals. The first two entries in the table are reminders that screening can occur circumstantially or informally as well as by formal procedure. The Second Circuit's "null" model of

[19]"Oral argument shall be allowed in all cases unless pursuant to local rule a panel of three judges, after examination of the briefs and record, shall be unanimously of the opinion that oral argument is not needed."

[20]See, e.g., Daniel J. Meador, *Appellate Courts: Staff and Process in the Crisis of Volume 37* (West Publishing, 1974); Witkin, supra note 7, at 57.

[21]Illustrative is the response of attorney John P. Frank to a preliminary presentation of research for this volume: "When you do your work on argued cases, I hope that you will give very serious attention to the bar attitudes. So far as we are concerned, and I think I speak for a large number, we regard screening as a device to push the lawyer out of the law entirely. We just don't count anymore." Conference on Empirical Research in Judicial Administration, 21 *Ariz. St. L.J.* 33, 126 (1989).

Table 4.1. Comparison of screening models of the federal courts of appeals

Model of screening	Attributes of screening
Second Circuit	The "null" model of screening. The court has a strong norm favoring oral argument. Every case is orally argued except in the cases of pro se incarcerated litigants or where argument has been waived by both counsel with the approval of the presiding judge.
Informal Screening	Argument panels acting ad hoc order cases to be submitted on the briefs without oral argument. Such cases are otherwise disposed of in traditional fashion, after face-to-face conference of the panel judges, with the assistance of in-chambers staff, and generally by written opinion.
Fifth Circuit	Staff attorneys screen cases for assignment to special screening panels.
Sixth Circuit	Staff attorneys screen cases for decision without argument by regular argument panels.
D. C. Circuit	Staff attorneys screen cases for decision by special screening panels; additional cases formally screened and decided without argument by regular argument panels.
Third Circuit	Regular argument panels perform the formal screening function without staff assistance. There is a strong norm against oral argument. Most cases are screened, which results not only in decision without oral argument but also (in most such cases) decision without written opinion.
Ninth Circuit	Staff attorneys screen cases for decision by special screening panels operating in distinct parallel or serial fashion. There is a general preference for oral argument.

screening limits dispositions without oral argument to the bare minimum required by circumstances independent of court control. Informal screening by argument panels is also an important factor in the curtailment of frequency of orally argued appeals. Next in order are the Fifth Circuit's formal screening model; the variations found in the Sixth, District of Columbia, and Third circuits; and finally the Ninth Circuit's blend of the Fifth Circuit model with the Second Circuit's strong norm in favor of oral argument.[22]

The Second Circuit has eschewn a screening program because of a particularly strong belief in the value of oral argument among the judges of that court. We nonetheless include this "null" model in our collection of screening program models because even in the Second

---

[22]Our description of the models of screening practiced by the Fifth, Sixth, and Third circuits is based on the Federal Judicial Center's recent study of variations in screening programs among the federal courts of appeals. Cecil and Stienstra, supra note 3.

Circuit circumstances and procedures combine to result in significant numbers of cases being heard without oral argument. Some of these are cases that cannot be argued because they involve uncounseled incarcerated litigants; in others, both parties have waived oral arguments and the presiding judge of the argument panel has permitted the waiver to take effect.[23]

Our next model involves a practice we call *informal screening*. It occurs when cases are assigned to regular argument panels but nonetheless are decided by these panels without oral argument. In some cases this is because of the waiver or impossibility of argument, as in the Second Circuit, but in other cases it is because the argument panels have decided for themselves that oral argument is not likely to be of substantial benefit. It is important to recognize not only that there are substantial numbers of these informal screening cases, as we shall see below with respect to the Ninth Circuit, but also that this model leads to a process of decision that is distinctly different from decision in those cases that remain on the formal screening track. In an informally screened case the decision is generally reached by judges acting through some form of conference, rather than individually and in isolation; there is input from in-chambers staff; and finally, the panel will generally issue an opinion.[24]

The Fifth Circuit model is the oldest and the most common of the formal screening models. Its key features are the use of staff attorneys to process cases recommended for screening and the use of special panels to decide screening cases without oral argument. The six circuits not otherwise mentioned in this summary (the First, Fourth, Seventh, Eighth, Tenth, and Eleventh) have adopted screening programs that follow the basic contours of the Fifth Circuit model.

The Sixth Circuit, whose model is also used by the Federal Circuit, follows the Fifth Circuit model in the use of staff attorneys to process screening cases but diverges from the Fifth Circuit by routing screening recommendations to regular argument panels. These panels then

---

[23]See id. at 7 n.2; id. at 15 n.22; see also Joe Cecil and Donna Stienstra, *Deciding Cases without Argument: A Description of Procedures in the Courts of Appeals* 7 n.14 (Federal Judicial Center, 1985).

[24]The model of informal screening proceeds much like the Third Circuit model to which it is compared in Figure 4.1. The key difference is the preparation of opinions in screened cases. Under the informal screening model, the submission of the case on the briefs does not fundamentally change the process of justifying the court's decision. The Third Circuit's practice has been to decide many screened cases summarily and without opinion, a practice we see as fraught with great danger to the values of appeal.

decide screening cases as part of their normal daily calendars, generally on the ratio of five argued to two nonargued cases per day per panel.

The District of Columbia Circuit assigns formal screening responsibilities to both staff attorneys and regular argument panels. All cases are inventoried by staff attorneys, who classify nearly one-half of the cases as suitable for disposition without oral argument. Except for a few complex cases, the rest are scheduled for submission to regular argument panels. A second formal screening process operates at the argument panel level. For each case calendared before a particular argument panel, there is a designated screening judge who, with the concurrence of the balance of the panel, can order the case submitted to the panel without oral argument.[25]

The Third Circuit routes the entire flow of cases to the argument panels without any staff input on cases suitable for screening. The argument panels themselves decide which cases to set down for oral argument and which cases to decide on the briefs.

The Ninth Circuit's "Submission Without Argument Program" instituted in 1982 a formal screening program modeled basically on that of the Fifth Circuit, but with distinctions important enough to merit separate classification.[26]

The Ninth Circuit Model

Like the Fifth Circuit, the Ninth Circuit (a) uses staff attorneys to process cases once they are placed on the screening track and (b) routes these cases to special panels for decision on the merits. The Ninth Circuit's use of staff attorneys for analysis and evaluation of screening cases is more extensive than at the Fifth Circuit, where only about half the cases routed to screening panels are accompanied by staff memos. In the Ninth Circuit, every case set for decision by a screening panel is accompanied by a staff memorandum.[27]

All the screening panels of the Fifth Circuit review screened cases in "serial" fashion, one judge at a time until one of the three judges has rejected the case from screening or all three judges have concurred in

---

[25]The District of Columbia Circuit's screening program went into effect in August 1986. For a fuller account of its features, see Oakley, supra note 5.

[26]Cecil and Stienstra, supra note 3, at 16, 67–68.

[27]See p. 146.

the proposed disposition prepared by the first judge. In adopting a screening program modeled on the Fifth Circuit's, however, the judges of the Ninth Circuit insisted on allowing panels to operate in parallel rather than serial fashion if they wished to.[28] The judges of a parallel panel deliberate simultaneously on whether a particular case is appropriate for the screening docket, generally conferring by telephone or electronic mail.[29] During the period of our study, parallel panels processed 43 percent of the cases assigned to the Ninth Circuit's screening docket.

The mechanics of formal screening at the Ninth Circuit are founded on the inventory process. All cases are inventoried by central staff attorneys as soon as they are fully briefed. The inventory process checks for jurisdictional defects, codes issues for future tracking and docketing of cases presenting similar issues, and assigns each case a weight of S, 3, 5, 7, or 10, according to the difficulty of the issues and the complexity of the record.[30]

Case weights are the linchpins of the court's calendaring system. They are used to balance the workload of the argument panels, with each day's calendar of argued cases being bundled into a set of case weights equaling 18.[31] Of more immediate concern here, weights are also used to determine whether a fully briefed case is assigned to an argument panel at all or to a screening panel instead. Case weights are thus the attribute that symbolically is caught when the court's caseflow is screened. The S weights stick to the screen, while the other weights pass through to qualify for calendaring before the argument panels.

The case weight of S was introduced at the Ninth Circuit in the spring of 1988, during the waning days of the Browning era. For most of our study period—from January 1, 1982, when the screening program began, through June 15, 1988, the last day of Browning's tenure as chief judge—the least difficult cases were classified as either 1 or 3L,

[28]See Chapter 5; see also Cecil and Stienstra, supra note 3, at 76–78.

[29]There has been some convergence in practice between the procedures employed by the two types of panels, continuing the trend reported by Cecil and Stienstra. See Cecil and Stienstra, supra note 3, at 78–80. Our discussions with judges of the Ninth Circuit have disclosed that parallel panels now confer principally by electronic mail rather than telephonic "real-time" conferences. Judges of serial panels considering rejection of a case now sometimes poll the other panel judges first to see if there is consensus in principle or if the other judges wish first to review the case for themselves.

[30]See Arthur D. Hellman, "Central Staff in Appellate Courts: The Experience of the Ninth Circuit," 68 *Calif. L. Rev.* 937, 963 (1980).

[31]See Joe Cecil, *Administration of Justice in a Large Appellate Court: The Ninth Circuit Innovations Project* 28–29 (Federal Judicial Center, 1985).

and these weights were automatically assigned to screening panels rather than argument panels. The advent of the S, or *screener*, designation simply replaced the 1 and 3L classifications without substantive change.[32] A screening-level case weight automatically results in a case's being assigned by the clerk to the calendar of a screening panel rather than an argument panel. During the study period 22 percent of all cases disposed of on the merits after calendaring had initially been routed to screening rather than argument panels.

There are three stages of review of the initial staff attorney's inventorying decision to assign a screening-level case weight to a particular case. It is helpful at this point to put aside the metaphorical elaboration of "screening" as literally a process of filtration of sludge out of the case flow, and instead to treat screening simply as a generic process of classification. This allows us the license to put a new metaphor in play, whereby we conceive of the reviewing stages of the Ninth Circuit's screening process as a search for any "needles"—our term for misclassified cases—within the haystack of the screening docket.

The Ninth Circuit looks for needles on three occasions. Each occasion is like the passing of a magnet through the screening docket. The first pass occurs when the case weights assigned by staff attorneys to individual cases are discussed during the weekly division-chief reviews of staff attorney cases and work product. There are three divisions, and between fifteen and thirty cases are reviewed each week within each division. The division chief relies on the attorney's thumbnail sketch of a case (a summary only a paragraph or two in length)[33] in making a snap judgment whether the case weight accorded to it by the reporting staff attorney "sounds right." Absent a false note in the summary, this is not an occasion at which the assessment of the facts and legal contentions of a case by the reporting staff attorney will be reviewed by independent examination of the case record.[34]

---

[32]The use of this two-tiered set of screening-level weights during most of the study period was procedurally advantageous to us in our research. It allowed us to distinguish between cases inventoried as truly "bottom-of-the-barrel" cases—the 1 weights—and cases assigned to the screening track with explicit recognition that they were at the margin of the degree of difficulty or complexity meriting oral argument—the 3L weights.

[33]For instructive examples of these summaries, reprinted from the March 1987 screening calendar of the Ninth Circuit, see Cecil and Stienstra, supra note 3, Appendix D, at 201–20.

[34]In the spring of 1989 the court approved the recommendation of an internal committee that the entire inventory function be shifted from the Office of Staff Attorneys to the Clerk's Office. Under the new system, the staff attorneys in the research division would

The second pass of the magnet is the opportunity for reconsideration of the screening classification when a staff attorney prepares the bench memorandum that accompanies the case to a screening panel for decision.[35] There is a disincentive against a staff attorney's recommending reclassification from the screening to the argument docket after expending substantial effort at drafting a bench memorandum, however. Staff attorneys have monthly quotas of bench memoranda, and they receive no credit for the research and writing they would moot by "kicking" a case from the screening docket after commencing work on its bench memorandum.

We thus focus our attention on the third and last pass of the magnet: the review of a screened case by the screening panel of three judges before whom it has been calendared for disposition. As previously explained, every screened case in the Ninth Circuit comes before a screening panel accompanied by a bench memorandum. The screening panels organize themselves to take action either serially or in parallel, with the serial method predominating.[36]

The screening panels are governed by Rule 34(a) of the Federal Rules of Appellate Procedure, quoted earlier, and by related Ninth Circuit Rule 34–4. These rules require advance notification to the parties that a case has been assigned to the screening docket, giving them an opportunity to object to the screening classification. By requiring unanimity of the three-judge screening panel, the rules also permit a single judge to "reject" a case by finding it unsuitable for decision without oral argument according to the criteria of Rule 34(a).

---

no longer divide up the cases for inventory purposes, assess weights, or assign issue codes. Instead, these tasks would be performed by two full-time attorneys working with the case management staff in the Clerk's Office. In all likelihood, these attorneys would occupy career positions. In this chapter we describe the inventory process as it operated throughout our study period. We hope that future researchers will be able to study the effects on the screening program of concentrating the inventory function in a way that promises greater consistency and efficiency but, perhaps, presents greater risks of bureaucratization.

[35]This attorney is usually (but not necessarily) the attorney initially responsible for the inventorying of the case and its assignment to the screening docket. There is no court policy of assigning the writing of bench memoranda in screened cases to an attorney other than the inventorying attorney in order to ensure a fresh look at the merits of the case. Since the initial inventory process is expected to take only thirty to sixty minutes of attorney time, we question whether reassignment of the case to the same attorney for the writing of the bench memorandum saves sufficient attorney time to justify the loss of "fresh look" reevaluation of the screening classification by the prospective author of the bench memorandum.

[36]During our study period 57 percent of screened cases were processed by serial as opposed to parallel panels.

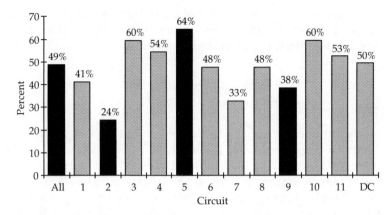

Figure 4.1. Circuit-by-circuit comparison of rates of disposition of cases on the merits without oral argument

Source: 1987 Annual Report of the Director of the Administrative Office of the United States Courts, Table 6. Includes merits dispositions by motions panels.

To put the work of the Ninth Circuit's screening panels in perspective, we direct attention to Figure 4.1. Figure 4.1 compares the overall rate of oral argument in the Ninth Circuit with that of the other regional circuits. The vertical bars display the percentages of appeals terminated on the merits but without oral argument. The data are from statistical year 1987, which was the twelve-month period ending June 30, 1987. Of particular interest are the four highlighted columns.

Starting from the left, the overall rate for all circuits of cases decided on the merits but without oral argument is 49 percent. Lowest among the circuits, at half the overall rate, is the Second Circuit. But even with that court's strong norm in favor of oral argument, nearly a quarter of cases decided on the merits nonetheless are heard on the briefs alone. At the other end of the spectrum is the Fifth Circuit, with nearly two-thirds of its cases decided on the briefs. The Ninth Circuit stands third among the circuits in its overall affinity for oral argument, with only the Second and Seventh circuits hearing argument in a higher proportion of their cases.[37] Thus the Ninth Circuit's approach to screening

[37]The criteria used by the Administrative Office of the United States Courts (A.O.) to identify dispositions "on the merits" inflate the proportion of unargued to argued cases by including some forms of motion panel dispositions. The Ninth Circuit's rate of 38 percent by the A.O. criteria is 31 percent by our criteria as applied to our Study Group cases. Published A.O. data for 1988 and preliminary figures for 1989 indicate that the circuits ranked about the same in their affinity for oral argument as they did in 1987 and that the Ninth Circuit's percentage remained steady at somewhat over 60 percent.

113

must be understood in the context of a court that remains unusually committed to oral argument as the rule rather than the exception when the court is adjudicating the merits of an appeal.

Statistical Analysis of the
Ninth Circuit's Screening Docket

We now propose to take a statistical look at the screening program of the Ninth Circuit, developing profiles of its screened cases and their outcomes and comparing these with profiles of cases disposed of by the conventional argument panels. The latter will include cases originally assigned to screening panels and reassigned to argument panels after rejection from screening by one or more of the screening panel judges. Finally, we shall use these comparisons to judge how well the system is working.

The statistics we present have been generated with an eye to our overall project of examining the administration of the circuit during the Browning years. Thus the study period is defined as beginning January 1, 1982, when the screening program officially started, and ending at close of business on June 15, 1988, the final day of Browning's tenure as chief judge.

The principal source of our figures is the Appellate Records Management System (ARMS), the Ninth Circuit's computerized docketing database throughout the study period.[38] There are three data sets within ARMS: the Appellate Docket, the Screening Docket, and the Staff Attorneys Data Base. We deal here with statistics drawn from the Appellate and Screening dockets.

Dimensions of Screening at the Ninth Circuit

We begin our analysis with some gross comparisons of the court's workload overall, its calendared cases, and its screening docket.[39] We

---

[38]See generally Joseph F. Weis, Jr., and Gordon Bermant, "Automation in the Federal Courts: Progress, Prospects and Problems," *Judges' Journal*, Fall 1987, at 14, 15–16. ARMS is resident on a mainframe computer of the Administrative Office of the United States Courts. Chief Judge Browning and his successor, Chief Judge Goodwin, graciously arranged for us to have password privileges for timesharing access to ARMS via modem and personal computer. In addition, the Ninth Circuit supplied us with computer tapes of ARMS data. We combined the ARMS data with data we had independently compiled to produce our own database on a computer at the University of California at Davis.

[39]We use the terms *appellate docket* and *screening docket* without capitalization to refer

start with the total number of cases disposed of during the study period in any fashion whatsoever: this beginning figure is 32,034 cases. However, to get an informed sense of the role of screening in the court's work, we have to refine this raw figure to focus on the part of the court's business that screening affects, and to count cases in ways that accurately reflect the court's handling of them. This winnowing process entails successively eliminating six categories of cases.[40]

1. Thousands of cases terminate because of settlement, lack of prosecution, lack of jurisdiction, or other procedural grounds not requiring adjudication of the merits. Other cases (many fewer) are disposed of on the merits under expedited procedures afforded by the court in exigent circumstances. Screening has no impact on these cases. We therefore restrict our analysis to only those dispositions that occurred after briefing had been completed, any preliminary motions had been survived, and the cases had been placed on the calendar of a panel of three judges as ripe for disposition on the merits.[41]

2. Since the screening program could have no effect on cases calendared before the screening panels were created, we also exclude cases placed on calendar before January 1, 1982, even if they were disposed of during the study period.[42]

3. A few cases settled or otherwise washed out after calendaring but before submission to a panel. These cases, too, have been eliminated from the study group.

4. We further limit the study group to lead or single cases, excluding

---

generically to the entire set of cases filed with the Ninth Circuit (appellate docket) and to the subset of those cases assigned to the calendars of screening panels (screening docket). When we refer to the *Appellate Docket* and the *Screening Docket* with capitalization, we refer to the ARMS data sets bearing these names. Thus *screening docket* refers to a collection of cases, and *Screening Docket* refers to a collection of records about those cases.

[40]As part of the winnowing process we excluded from the study groups any cases that did not have valid codes for the ARMS fields in question—i.e., those with missing or unrecognized values for the fields used to determine each of the six categories of excluded cases. For a more detailed account of the winnowing process, see Oakley, *supra* note 5.

[41]We refer to assignment of a case to the docket of an argument panel or screening panel as *calendaring* that case or as putting the case *on calendar*. The cluster of cases assigned to be heard on a particular day by an argument panel has traditionally been called that day's *calendar* of cases. The terminology has been carried over to the cluster of cases scheduled to be submitted on any given day for decision by a screening panel.

[42]The screening program officially began on January 1, 1982, and we use this date to define our study period. But New Year's Day 1982 fell on a Friday, and the first business day of 1982 was therefore January 4. On that day twenty-four cases were placed on calendar, with two of them being assigned to the new screening panels.

consolidated or otherwise associated cases that were not really discrete cases requiring a full measure of decisional time and attention.

5. We include only cases decided by the court's regular panels of judges (either argument or screening panels) rather than by motions panels or other ad hoc decisional panels.

6. We include only cases disposed of on the merits in the strict sense that the nature of the disposition recorded by ARMS was not a procedural dismissal, transfer, or vacation of the appeal, but reached and resolved the merits by letting the action below stand, reversing or modifying that action in whole or in part, or remanding for further action below.

This six-step winnowing process reduces the initial gross figure of 32,034 cases disposed of during the study period to a net of 12,677 cases meeting all of our study criteria. We call these 12,677 cases our *Study Group,* and they constitute the master set for purposes of all further analysis in this chapter. The major subgroups within the Study Group are illustrated in Figures 4.2 and 4.3. A more detailed picture of the composition of the Study Group, including the relative distribution of case types within each subgroup, can be found in Table 4.2.

Figure 4.2 shows how the Study Group breaks down into two components, one of which also reduces into two further subgroups. The 12,677 Study Group cases consist of 8,717 cases that were submitted after oral argument (69 percent) and 3,960 cases that were submitted on the briefs (31 percent). We call the 8,717 cases the *Argued Cases.* The 3,960 cases that were not argued consist first of 1,583 cases decided without oral argument but by argument panels rather than screening panels. In accordance with our previous discussion, we call these the *Informally Screened Cases.* The remainder of the nonargued cases are the 2,377 cases that were assigned to the screening docket, were not rejected from screening, and were finally decided on the merits by the screening panels. We call these the *Formally Screened Cases.*

Figure 4.3 presents more information on the important subset of 381 cases within the Study Group that were originally assigned to the screening docket but were rejected by screening panels. We call this group the *Rejected Cases* and note that they constitute a slice of cases figuratively drawn from the marginal area of the Argued Cases and the Informally Screened Cases in Figure 4.2. Most of the Rejected Cases were duly argued. Thus 280 of the Argued Cases are drawn from the 381 Rejected Cases. We call these 280 cases the *Argued Rejects.*

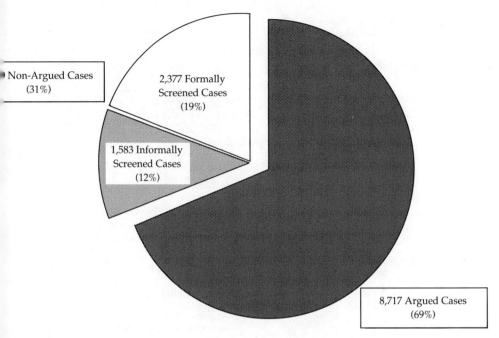

Non-Argued Cases
(31%)

2,377 Formally
Screened Cases
(19%)

1,583 Informally
Screened Cases
(12%)

8,717 Argued Cases
(69%)

Figure 4.2. Proportion of Argued Cases, Informally Screened Cases, and Screened Cases among 12,677 Study Group cases

But 101 of the Rejected Cases were decided by argument panels without having heard oral argument. These 101 Rejected Cases thus belong to Figure 4.2's group of Informally Screened Cases. In Figure 4.3 we call these 101 cases the *Nonargued Rejects.*

Two conclusions stand out from these data. First, only 22 percent of the court's cases were even placed on the screening docket,[43] and only 19 percent were actually disposed of by screening panels. This is a conservative use of screening by a busy court. Second, informal screening by argument panels accounted overall for 12 percent of the court's dispositions on the merits. In terms of effect on the court's rate of dispositions after submission but without oral argument, informal screening by argument panels is almost as significant in the Ninth Circuit as is the formal screening program.

[43]If the 381 Rejected Cases are added to the 2,377 Formally Screened Cases, the total of 2,758 cases initially assigned to the screening docket constitutes 22 percent of the 12,677 Study Group cases.

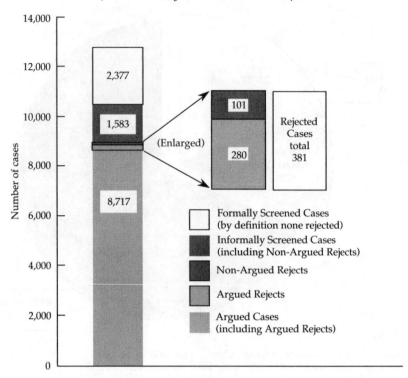

Figure 4.3. Distribution of 381 Rejected Cases within Study Group of 12,677 Argued, Informally Screened, and Formally Screened Cases, with Rejected Cases enlarged to 10 times normal scale

Needles in the Haystack

We next seek to evaluate the success of the Ninth Circuit in screening cases without leaving needles in the haystack. It would obviously be an immensely burdensome and probably unpersuasive procedure for us to sit down and read all or some substantial selection of the cases under study in order to offer our subjective judgments about how many might usefully have been orally argued. Instead, we have generated statistical profiles of the Study Group cases and the various subgroups that allow us to compare screened and unscreened cases according to distribution of case types, nonaffirmance rates, and publication rates.

The data on case-type distributions are presented in Table 4.2 and Figure 4.4. Table 4.2 presents the data on relative distributions of case

118

Table 4.2. Relative distribution of case types by docket type

Case type as coded in ARMS[a]	Study Group Cases submitted[b]	Study Group % submitted	Argued Cases argued[b]	Argued % argued	Formally Screened Cases screened[b]	Formally Screened % screened	Rejected Cases rejected	Rejected % rejected
Administrative agency (AGCY)	417	3.29	315	3.62	56	2.36	6	1.57
Bankruptcy (BKCY)	204	1.61	169	1.94	14	0.59	2	0.52
Civil rights (CIVR)	653	5.16	311	3.57	245	10.32	41	10.76
Criminal (CR)	2,845	22.48	2,034	23.37	435	18.32	70	18.37
Habeas/prisoner's rights (total)	251	1.98	110	1.26	97	4.08	22	5.76
State habeas corpus (SH)	*158*	*1.25*	*80*	*0.92*	*54*	*2.27*	*18*	*4.72*
Federal habeas corpus (FH)	*51*	*0.40*	*26*	*0.30*	*20*	*0.84*	*1*	*0.26*
Other habeas corpus (OH)	*4*	*0.03*	*1*	*0.01*	*1*	*0.04*	*1*	*0.26*
Prisoner's rights; not habeas (PR)	*38*	*0.30*	*3*	*0.03*	*22*	*0.93*	*2*	*0.52*
Immigration (AINS)	658	5.20	315	3.62	267	11.24	69	18.11
NLRB (ANLR)	261	2.06	222	2.55	20	0.84	7	1.84
Private civil (CIV)	6,485	51.23	4,671	53.66	999	42.06	142	37.27
Tax court (TAXC)	336	2.65	170	1.95	131	5.52	5	1.31
U.S. defendant (CIVD)	419	3.31	269	3.09	109	4.59	14	3.67
U.S. plaintiff (CIVG)	79	0.62	74	0.85	2	0.08	1	0.26
Bail (BAIL)	1	0.01	1	0.01	0	0.00	0	0.00
Civil grand jury (CVGJ)	3	0.02	3	0.03	0	0.00	0	0.00
Revenue (REVN)	10	0.08	8	0.09	0	0.00	1	0.26
Writ (WRIT)	30	0.24	28	0.32	0	0.00	0	0.00
Other (OTHER)	6	0.05	5	0.06	0	0.00	1	0.26
TOTAL	12,658	100.00%	8,705	100.00%	2,375	100.00%	381	100.00%

[a]The categories are listed in the order of their presentation in Figures 4.4 through 4.6.
[b]The case-type totals for Study Group, Argued Cases, and Formally Screened Cases are slightly less than the totals for each group stated in Figure 4.2 and in the text. We lack valid case-type data for 19 of the 12,677 cases in the Study Group, including 12 of the 8,717 Argued Cases and 2 of the 2,377 Formally Screened Cases.

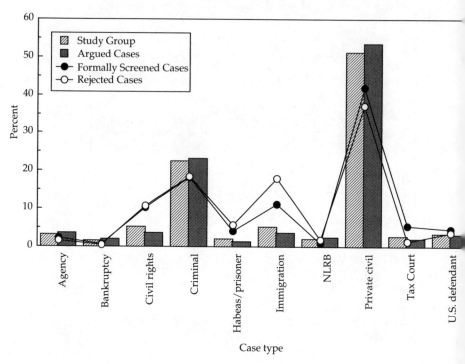

Figure 4.4. Comparative docket distributions of major case types

types for all cases in the Study Group as a whole, and then for three previously identified subgroups: Argued Cases, Formally Screened Cases (cases screened to decision), and Rejected Cases. The case types are those identified in the ARMS database. Figure 4.4 recasts the data, lumping the habeas corpus/prisoner's rights categories together and omitting case-type categories with fewer than one hundred cases in the Study Group.

Our primary interest in the Formally Screened Cases now lies in comparing them with the Argued Cases rather than with the Informally Screened Cases. We shall refer to the Formally Screened Cases as the screening track and the Argued Cases as the argument track.

Figure 4.4 graphically demonstrates that there are few major discrepancies in the case-type distributions across the groups under study. The distribution of case types within the entire Study Group is very close to the distribution of case types within the Argued Cases as to every case type. There is a slightly higher incidence of private civil cases on the argument track and a slightly lower incidence of immigration and civil rights cases, for example, but the differences are hardly dramatic.

There are more pronounced differences in the case-type percentages for the screening track vis-a-vis the argument track and the entire Study Group. Immigration and civil rights cases each account for more than 10 percent of the screening track, compared with less than 4 percent of the argument track and fractionally more than 5 percent of the docket as a whole. Habeas corpus/prisoner's rights cases constitute three times the percentage of the screening track that they do of the argument track; the figure is twice their percentage in the Study Group. Appeals from the Tax Court are also overrepresented on the screening track (especially in comparison with the argument track); so, to a lesser degree, are civil cases in which the United States Government is the defendant (U.S. defendant cases). Private civil cases and, interestingly, general criminal cases (where the lack of any disincentive to indigent appeals is commonly thought to produce a higher than normal proportion of meritless appeals) are underrepresented on the screening track.

The data also reveal, however, that the screening panels are acting with considerable independence in their rejection of cases from screening, providing dynamic feedback to the screening staff to expand or check the screening of cases in under- and overrepresented categories. Figure 4.5 shows how rejection rates in particular categories of cases compare not only with each other but also with the overall rejection rate of 13.81 percent. Figure 4.6 presents a side-by-side comparison of the absolute number of cases of each category that were initially assigned to screening panels during the study period.[44]

In the category of case with the greatest overrepresentation on the

[44]The overall rejection rate of 13.81 percent in Figure 4.5 is derived from the data presented in Figures 4.2 and 4.3 for the entire Study Group. This figure is the result of dividing the number of Rejected Cases (381) by the sum of all cases initially assigned to screening panels (2,377 Formally Screened Cases + 381 Rejected Cases = 2,758 cases initially assigned to screening panels). As noted in Table 4.2, the data used to analyze case-type distributions and to generate Figures 4.4, 4.5, and 4.6 yield a total of 2,375 cases in the Formally Screened category, rather than the total of 2,377 Formally Screened cases featured in Figures 4.2 and 4.3, because we lack valid case-type data for 2 of the Study Group's 2,377 Formally Screened cases. When these 2 cases are excluded, the rejection rate becomes 13.82 percent (381 divided by 2,756).

The numbers in Figure 4.6 are derived from Table 4.2 by adding the number of Rejected Cases for each category to the number of Formally Screened Cases (the cases actually decided by screening panels).

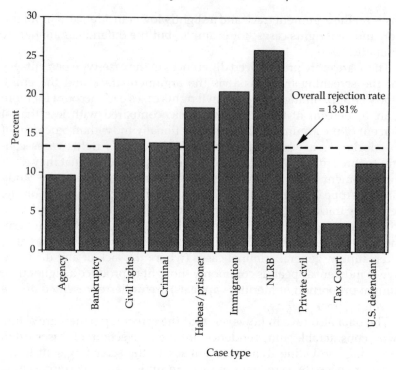

Figure 4.5. Rejection rates by case type compared with overall rejection rate

screening track, immigration cases, the rejection rate is substantially above the norm—almost half again as high as the overall rate.[45] This suggests that screening panels are conscious of the imbalance and are cautious about agreeing with a staff screening decision in this over-represented area. The same pattern can be seen in the habeas corpus/prisoner's rights category: substantially overrepresented on the screening track, it generates the third highest rejection rate among the ten case types. (The category with the highest rejection rate consists of appeals from the National Labor Relations Board (NLRB), but as can

[45]Immigration cases have been extremely controversial within the court of appeals. In 1985 then-Circuit Judge Anthony M. Kennedy pointed to deportation appeals under the 1980 Refugee Act as exemplifying an area in which the court was "quite frankly in disarray." *Los Angeles Daily Journal*, Oct. 18, 1985, at 18. More recently, the judges engaged in an internal debate over the appropriateness of deciding immigration cases via the screening docket. See also Cecil and Stienstra, supra note 3, at 82 n.109.

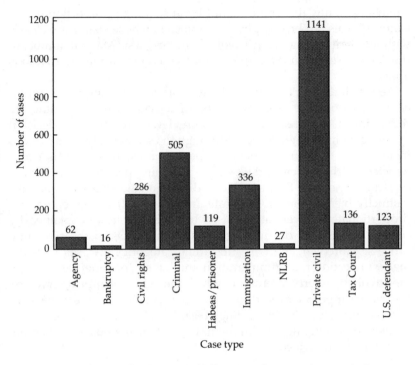

Figure 4.6. Distribution of 2,756 cases initially assigned to screening panels, by case type

be seen in Figure 4.6, the number of NLRB cases initially routed to screening panels was quite small, thus reducing the significance of the rejection rate.)[46] Conversely, the staff assigns disproportionately few private civil cases to the screening docket, but the screening panels reject a somewhat lower than average proportion of the cases in this category that do come before them. Far from encouraging staff to be conservative in the screening of private civil cases, this behavior provides a modest incentive to the staff to be more liberal in designating such cases for the screening route.

The one type of case which is overrepresented on the screening track without triggering a disproportionate number of screening panel rejections consists of appeals from the Tax Court of the United States.

[46]The relative numbers of cases within each category assigned to the screening docket—the size of the pool from which rejected cases were withdrawn—can be gauged from the figures given in Table 4.2 and charted in Figure 4.4.

Almost certainly, this comes about because a high proportion of Tax Court appeals are brought by tax protesters whose claims are clearly without merit if not actually frivolous. Indeed, a substantial number of the cases resulted in the imposition of sanctions for filing a frivolous appeal.[47]

We conclude that case-type distribution does not suggest a significant likelihood that cases deserving of rejection from screening are remaining on the screening track after review of the screening decision by the screening panel judges. Although the screening track is skewed in favor of screening particular types of cases, this skew is counteracted by the rejection rates of the screening panels. There is only one category of case that is both adjudicated on the screening track at a distinctly higher than normal rate and rejected from screening at a proportionately lower rate, and its treatment is easily explained by considerations that do not suggest systemic flaws in the screening process. Moreover, the two substantial categories of cases with the highest rejection rates (immigration and habeas/prisoner) are categories involving liberty interests in which the values of appeal served by traditional appellate procedure have a particular call on the conscience of the court. Overall, the findings bespeak a system conscious of the dangers of leaving needles in the haystack and anxious to catch them by means of the rejection process.

Idiosyncrasy and Efficiency in the Rejection Process

We next turn our attention to Figure 4.7, which shows great variation in the rejection rates of individual screening panel judges. Data are given only for judges who participated in at least fifty decisions as members of screening panels. The rates vary from 12.54 to 0.99 percent, although most are within two points of the average rejection rate of 4.46 percent.[48]

The data presented in Figure 4.7 suggest that the process of rejecting (or not rejecting) cases from the screening docket is dependent on

---

[47]See, for example, Wilcox v. Commissioner, 848 F.2d 1007 (9th Cir. 1988) (screening panel case), one of the few cases of this kind that was decided by published opinion.

[48]Since there are three judges on each screening panel and any one of them can reject a case, the overall rejection rate is three times the average per-judge rejection rate. For this particular data set, which excludes judges with fewer than fifty screening panel participations, the rejection rate per panel is 13.38 percent rather than the overall rejection rate of 13.81 percent reported earlier.

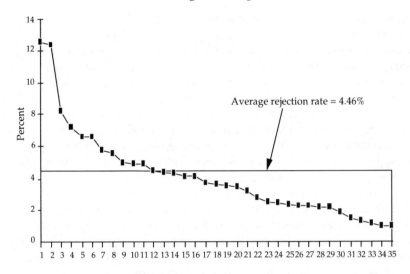

Figure 4.7. Rejection rates of individual screening panel judges
  Note: Minimum 50 participations per judge.

idiosyncratic judicial attitudes favoring or disfavoring oral argument. This in turn leaves open the possibility that the court's search for needles in the haystack is unfocused and inefficient, and therefore is at risk of finding phantom needles and missing real ones.

We have a means of testing whether the significant variation in individual judge rejection rates is indeed a sign of fundamental flaws in the rejection process. Except when chance dictates otherwise, the three judges of the oral argument panel that hears a case after it has been rejected from screening are not the same three judges who rejected the case from the screening docket. Rejected cases thus are independently reevaluated when decided by argument panels. The nature and form of the dispositions reached by argument panels in rejected cases ought to tell us whether significant numbers of cases rejected from screening are so routine as to have merited remaining on the screening docket all along. The same mode of analysis can also shed light on the converse and more important question: whether the rejection process is failing to identify some cases that are *not* routine.

Our reasoning takes the following steps. A routine case will typically be affirmed on appeal by an unpublished opinion or order. A controversial case is more likely to involve some modification of the judgment entered by the court below and to warrant publication of the reasoning on appeal. We would expect to find distinct differences in the degree of controversiality of outcome in the disposition profiles of cases screened to decision (decided by screening panels) vis-à-vis cases disposed of conventionally (decided by argument panels without ever having been assigned to screening panels). Cases assigned to the screening docket and not rejected from it are supposed to be routine cases. The disposition profiles of these cases should show a distinctly lower degree of controversiality than cases disposed of conventionally. In other words, screening docket dispositions ought to have lower rates both of nonaffirmance of the decision under review[49] and of publication of the opinion announcing the disposition.

In contrast to the low degree of controversiality of cases screened to decision, the degree of controversiality of cases assigned initially to the argument docket ought to be in the middle range. We would not expect every case decided by an argument panel to result in reversal by published opinion, but we would expect such results more frequently from argument panels than from screening panels.

Our starting point, then, is that the disposition profiles of particular groups of cases may be ranked by degree of controversiality, measured by nonaffirmance and publication rates. With that idea in mind, we can ask how we would expect the disposition profiles of rejected cases to compare with (a) the expected low degree of controversiality of dispositions in cases screened to decision and (b) the expected medium degree of controversiality of dispositions in cases assigned from the start to the conventional argument docket.

If we were to find that rejected cases reach outcomes with a low degree of controversiality despite their submission for decision by conventional argument panels, it would indicate that the rejection process is not catching and correcting improper screening classifications. The cases diverted from the screening docket are reaching just the outcomes we would expect had rejection not occurred. In other words, cases rejected from screening are turning out, when subjected to the independent reevaluation and more searching scrutiny of regular argument panels, to be just the sort of routine cases that *should* be assigned to the screening docket, and should remain there.

We would conclude from this scenario that the screening panels'

[49]The common significance of nonaffirmance dispositions is that in every such case the appellant benefited in some way from the appeal—the effect of the decision below was in some way blunted after consideration of the merits by the appellate panel.

rejection process is a costly waste of time. The low degree of controversiality in the outcomes of the rejected cases would indicate that the rejection process is failing to find a significant number of needles in the haystack of the screening docket. Moreover, the rejection process would ironically be causing some of the least meritorious cases to receive consideration by as many as six judges (depending on the type of screening panel and the point at which rejection occurred) rather than the statutorily required three. And finally, this unnecessarily elaborate process of decision would be creating delays in the disposition of some of the court's easiest cases.

If we were to find, however, that the disposition profiles of rejected cases show a significantly higher degree of controversiality than the disposition profiles of cases screened to decision, we would have evidence that at least some needles are indeed being detected and diverted to the regular docket by the screening panels' review and rejection process. The degree to which the rejection process is underinclusive or overinclusive would be revealed by the degree of controversiality of rejected cases relative to the regular docket.

In this scenario, if the rejected cases showed a high degree of controversiality—distinctly higher than the middle range of controversiality we would expect of the dispositions in cases assigned to argument panels from the start—we would probably have an underinclusive rejection process. That is, if nearly every rejected case were proving to be controversial (nearly every one a needle), this would suggest that only the most obviously controversial cases were being rejected, leaving other less obvious needles undetected among the unrejected cases destined for the summary procedures and routine results of adjudication by screening panels. But if the rejection process were to properly catch only cases that should never have been screened in the first place, those cases should come to exactly the same distribution of outcomes—in the middle range of controversiality—as the regular docket.

To the extent that the disposition profiles of the rejected cases were to show a higher degree of controversiality than the unrejected cases that are screened to decision, we could conclude that some needles were being caught, but to the extent that this degree of controversiality of the rejected cases was less than that of the regular docket as a whole, we would also have to conclude that the rejection process was overinclusive. In this scenario some cases are being rejected (out of an excess of caution) that are proving ultimately to be routine cases destined for routine outcomes, and this is lowering the degree of controversiality of the rejected cases relative to the regular docket cases. Thus, ideally, rejected cases should have disposition profiles showing the same middle range of controversiality as the court's conventional docket.

As shown in Figure 4.8, the Ninth Circuit's rejection process approximated this ideal result during the study period. The rates of nonaffirmance and publication of opinions in the 381 Rejected Cases are much more similar to those of the 12,677 Study Group cases and of the 8,717 Argued Cases than to the rates of nonaffirmance and publication of the 2,377 Formally Screened Cases. The argument panels that decided the rejected cases clearly did not treat them as routine cases that should have remained on the screening track. The incidence of nonaffirmance is nearly 250 percent higher; the incidence of issues deemed worthy of publication is nearly 500 percent higher.

The rejected cases have not proven to be *more* controversial than the mainstream cases, however. On the contrary, the disposition profiles of the 381 Rejected Cases are slightly more routine than the disposition profiles of the 8,717 Argued Cases. Thus we can conclude that the Ninth Circuit errs, but only slightly, in favor of underscreening by rejecting too many cases from the screening docket. To put it another way, a few more cases are being rejected than appears warranted by the rate at which needles are actually turning up when the argument panels reexamine the rejected cases. The fact that the court's screening panels tend to underscreen by overrejecting—erring in favor of reassigning the doubtfully routine case to the argument panels—confirms our earlier conclusion that the Ninth Circuit makes cautious use of screening for such a busy court.

One other aspect of the screening program deserves examination. Figures 4.9 and 4.10 offer statistical comparisons of the two screening panel methods. Figure 4.9 indicates that the disposition profiles of cases rejected by parallel as opposed to serial panels are similar. However, if the rates of nonaffirmance and publication subsequent to rejection are accepted as indicators of efficacy at rejecting cases constituting true needles in the screening haystack, parallel panels are marginally more effective at the rejection process. Figure 4.10 suggests that parallel panels operate not only more effectively but also more efficiently, since their more accurate identification of needles is achieved despite a 25 percent lower rate of rejection. In short, parallel panels reject fewer cases than serial panels, but the cases they do reject are more likely to

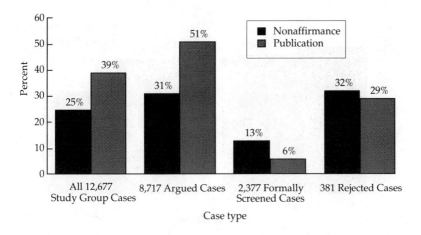

Figure 4.8. Comparative rates of nonaffirmance and publication, by group

be found interesting or meritorious by the argument panels than are the cases rejected by serial panels.

Improving the Process for the Immediate Future

Our analysis of the disposition profiles of screened cases that have been rejected by screening panels suggests that during the period of our study the Ninth Circuit's rejection process was working well at finding the needles in the screening haystack. The rates of nonaffirmance and publication in rejected cases were close to, but slightly below, the rates for all cases decided by argument panels. On the basis of these data, we have concluded that there was a modest degree of underscreening after the screening docket had been pared down by the rejection process. Rejected cases reach noncontroversial outcomes slightly more frequently than mainstream cases, indicating that screening panels are erring in favor of rejection, and hence in favor of underscreening, when they find that an arguably troublesome case has been assigned to the screening docket.

Goldman's research in Chapter 5 indicates that cases screened to decision would be perceived as more significant (i.e., more worthy of publication), but would not be decided differently, if screening were disestablished and these cases were returned to the mainstream of the

129

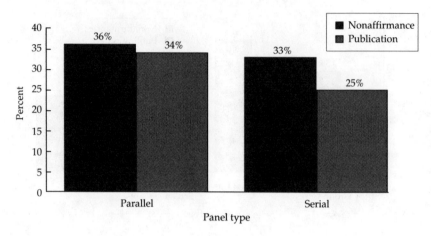

Figure 4.9. Comparative rates of nonaffirmance and publication in cases rejected from screening by parallel versus serial screening panels

court's docket for decision after calendaring before regular argument panels.[50] Nonetheless, he finds that screening threatens substantial impairment of litigants' perceptions of appellate justice.[51]

Taking both studies into account, we conclude that the "product" of screening at the Ninth Circuit is satisfactory and that recommendations for improvement should focus on reducing the "cost" of screening in terms of judicial resources and perceptions of illegitimacy. Are there innovations or alternative procedures that promise to refine the screening process so that fewer cases need to be rejected (and hence reviewed twice by panels of judges), while maintaining the Ninth Circuit's good record at confining screening to truly noncontroversial cases and also improving the perceptions of legitimacy of losing litigants whose cases are screened to a decision of affirmance? We offer four.

Modification of the staff memorandum. In one of the most intensive studies of screening, Thomas Y. Davies examined the operation of one division of California's intermediate appellate court. He concluded that unconsciously internalized bureaucratic norms had resulted in

[50]See pp. 152–54.
[51]See pp. 161–62.

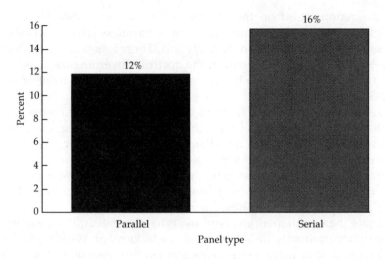

Figure 4.10. Relative rejection rates of parallel versus serial screening panels

error-prone screening decisions in particular categories of cases.[52] His study identified four categories of problem cases: (1) where appeal was based on claimed lack of sufficient evidence to support the judgment; (2) where appeal was based on claimed abuse of trial court discretion; (3) where appeal was based on a claim of trial court error that was arguably harmless; and (4) where the error appealed from was arguably waived by failure properly to object to the trial court.[53]

In hindsight, and in light of the cases in which the error-prone screening occurred, Davies's discovery seems unsurprising. The mistakes he identified were not caused by any failure of capacity or effort on the part of the judges involved. Rather, the problems were caused by the nature of the issues on appeal, the nature of the doctrines governing these issues, and a lack of recognition of the significance of this congruence for the screening decision.

The appellate decision whether application of the "clearly erroneous" rule or the "abuse of discretion" standard requires reversal in the unique circumstances of a given case involves exercise of substan-

---

[52]Thomas Y. Davies, "Affirmed: A Study of Criminal Appeals and Decisionmaking in a California Court of Appeal," 1982 *Am. B. Found. Res. J.* 543.
[53]Id. at 551, 584–86, 591–605.

tial discretion based on the "flavor" of the record.[54] So also does appellate determination of the question of harmless error or whether an issue was timely raised in the trial court. These issues are not tightly rule-bound. In practice, however, the doctrine governing their resolution results in affirmance in by far the bulk of cases in which one of the issues arises.

Contentions that factual findings do not survive the clear error test or that trial judges have abused their discretion are frequently the straw to which the sinking appellant clings. Other similar straws are claims that error relating to some minor point was so prejudicial as to warrant reversal, and the assertion on appeal of issues that were not preserved in the trial court. Staff attorneys and judges, conditioned by case after case in which these claims have been rejected, come to associate them with meritless appeals. What the staff attorney expects to see when such an issue is raised is that it lacks merit. What the judge reviewing a staff memorandum recommending rejection of such a contention expects to see is that the memorandum properly rejected it. The teaching of cognitive science is that expectation has a powerful influence on perception.[55]

Buried within such stacks of straw, however, are needles in the form of cases in which the contention has merit. Expectation can influence misperception of lack of merit, and, as the Davies study demonstrates, has done so in some of these cases. This leads us to suggest a simple modification in the staff memorandum used by the Ninth Circuit. Where one of these issues, or some other issue involving broad judicial discretion, is determinative of the decision to screen, the issue should be clearly flagged at the beginning of the memorandum. Aware of the always-possible needle in this straw, judges will be better equipped to guard against any staff misperception caused by staff expectation. Such cases may well keep the present rejection rate at or near its present level of approximately 15 percent.[56] But our suggested revision would make the detection of such categorically rejection-eligible cases both more dependable and less resource-expensive for the judges of the screening panels.

---

[54]See Chapter 2.

[55]See, e.g., Alexander L. George, *Presidential Decisionmaking in Foreign Policy: The Effective Use of Information and Advice* 20 (Westview Press, 1980); Allen Newell and Herbert A. Simon, *Human Problem Solving* 55, 78–80 (Prentice-Hall Publishing Co., 1972).

[56]This is roughly the average rejection rate nationwide. See Cecil and Stienstra, supra note 3, at 3–4, 164.

Using the Adversary System as an Aid to Screening. Discussion of the pros and cons of the adversary process of trial and appeal has tended to obscure the value of the process in developing and refining information to assist the judicial decision. Long before the terminology was coined by cognitive scientists and used in schools of business and public administration, the common law had developed a sophisticated "information-processing system." The opposing self-interests of contending counsel expressed dialectically constitute a powerful tool in developing and refining information for eventual decision by a disinterested judge.[57]

One aspect of screening as now practiced departs significantly from the function of the adversary process as an information-processing system. Vital to the operation of the system is the ability of the contending counsel to respond to communication that may influence the decision.[58] Yet in the present process the staff memorandum remains untested by advocate response. Counsel communicate to the court by briefs, and the appellant responds to new matter in the appellee's brief. However, counsel have no opportunity to respond directly to the staff memorandum, whose information is influential to the eventual decision. When oral argument is not allowed, the court's last opportunity to query counsel on the thrust of the staff memorandum is forgone. It is ironic that, based on their interviews with judges, Cecil and Stienstra recommend that Rule 34 objections to screening made by counsel "state with specificity the manner in which oral argument will benefit the deliberations of the court"[59] while counsel remain uninformed of the staff rationale for a conclusion that oral argument will not be helpful.

We suggest that Rule 34 be modified to provide that a copy or extract of the staff memorandum accompany the Rule 34 notice to counsel. The memorandum would serve to focus counsel's objection tightly on specific findings or authorities that appear to control the disposition. (If the focus is not narrow, this would raise doubts as to whether the case is appropriate for screening at all.) Subject to a strict limitation on the length of the response, counsel would then be able intelligently to do as Cecil and Steinstra recommend. By subjecting the staff memorandum to adversarial testing, the response should go far in revealing

[57]For more extensive development of this proposition, see Thompson and Oakley, supra note 2, at 36–38.
[58]For example, permitting *ex parte* communications to judges on pending cases would, we believe, be unthinkable to most judges.
[59]See Cecil and Stienstra, supra note 3, at 163.

to the court error in the staff product in the few situations where it occurs. If counsel have been afforded an opportunity to respond, the screening panel judges need spend little time reviewing screening memoranda to which no responses have been received. When there has been an adversarial response, judicial review of a screening recommendation can concentrate immediately on its weakest link. This will save judges time in the long run, as overall the sharper focus imparted by the opportunity for adversarial response will offset the burden of an occasional extra document for the judges to read.[60]

Clarifying Standards for the Appointment of Counsel in Pro Se Cases. There seems no feasible alternative to a bureaucratized decision-making process in pro se cases. Current procedure calls for assignment of a pro se case to the argument track (even if it cannot be argued because the appellant or petitioner is incarcerated) if the case will benefit from closer judicial scrutiny or a conference of judges on the panel. But this same procedure instructs staff attorneys to consider the appointment of counsel only "[i]f the appeal presents important issues."[61]

We suggest that these instructions to staff should be clarified. The word *important* is ambiguous in the sense that virtually all cases are important to the litigants, and hence it can be interpreted as limiting appointment of counsel to cases of wide-ranging importance. The instructions should not preclude consideration of appointment of counsel in cases where a reading of the record indicates that assistance of counsel will give the proceeding a substantial chance of success, even if the case lacks importance from an institutional or precedential perspective.

Addressing Litigants' Perceptions of the Legitimacy of Screening. Goldman's findings about the effect of screening on litigant perceptions are not surprising. Secrecy fuels suspicion. There seems to us to be a growing distrust of the operations of governmental agencies, courts included. We recommend public disclosure of the mechanics of screening, albeit with care taken to enhance confidence that the process of decisions retains the essentially courtlike characteristics of decision by impartial judges collectively responding to adversary argument. In addition, firsthand publicity is needed of the fact that the

---

[60]For discussions of similar proposals we advanced in 1986 and 1975, respectively, see Thompson and Oakley, supra note 2; Robert S. Thompson, "One Judge and No Judge Appellate Decisions," 50 *Cal. St. B.J.* 476 (1975).

[61]See Cecil, supra note 31, at 53 (quoting Ninth Circuit staff attorney handbook).

formal process is followed in practice. It is simply too easy for the suspicious to assume that screening allows and results in judicial abdication.

Planning for the Future

The caseload of the Ninth Circuit Court of Appeals is expected to increase substantially in the future. Intelligent long-range planning requires that the court's primary mechanism for coping with overload, its screening process, be tested for its efficacy as overload increases. In our view the current process, even if modified as we suggest, is likely at some quantum of increased volume of cases to fail the test.

There is a limit to devices designed to increase individual judge productivity in the disposition of cases. At some point emphasis on speed detracts too much from quality in the sense of correctness of outcomes. This possibility, along with the indications of the incidence of mistakes in the screening process today, cautions against undue increase in the proportion of cases that are screened. A large increase in the current rate of screening must be accompanied by either a commensurate increase in the size of the court's staff or a decrease in the time spent by individual staff attorneys on their cases. The first alternative promotes the bureaucratic and less courtlike character of the court of appeals. The second seriously risks an enhanced degree of staff error in screening and hence diminution of the worth of the staff product to judges. Both involve a greater number of staff-processed cases that must be reviewed by judges, and this review will consume more judicial time. Time spent on this review reduces the time spent by judges on cases that are not screened, and the court's judges are already taxed to the limit in this endeavor.

Substantial increase in the court's volume of cases will exacerbate a present problem of too few judges for too many cases. We leave to others the question of whether this problem can be resolved feasibly by increasing the number of judges of the Ninth Circuit either in its present form or as the circuit might be divided. We suggest an alternative to this solution.

Increase in the number of judicial officers available to meet increased caseloads is not limited to horizontal expansion—for example, adding to the number of judgeships authorized for the Ninth Circuit Court of Appeals. Expansion can also be accomplished vertically by the creation of additional tiers in the judicial hierarchy, as occurred when intermediate courts of appeal were created, when magistrates appeared in the district courts, and (to a limited degree) when the Bankruptcy Appellate Panel was established.

In a sense such an additional tier already exists in the Ninth Circuit and other courts of appeals employing central staff screening. The central staff supervisors and staff members are performing a judicial function subject to control and supervision by judges in much the same fashion as a district court magistrate. Despite the functional similarity, a central staff is distinguished from a corps of magistrates by the staff's lack of formal status, its anonymity, the lack of visibility of its work product, and the lack of any interaction with interested parties and their advocates. These distinguishing factors argue against the relative acceptability and effectiveness of adding more staff rather than making use of magistrates once the staff has grown large in proportion to the number of judges it serves.

We suggest that the elevation of key staff members, the present supervisors and their equivalents if more are needed, to the position of appellate magistrate (or commissioner) merits consideration for the future if predictions of increased case overload come to pass. Sufficient for the purposes of this chapter, we sketch the function of these magistrates only in broad terms.

1. A magistrate assigned the task (or the present staff supervisor) will control the present process of screening cases. Cases of the type currently screened, together with cases not screened simply because of their length and somewhat more problematic cases, will be diverted to original decision by a magistrate.
2. Oral argument to the magistrate will be permitted.
3. After submission of the case, the magistrate will prepare a report in the form of an opinion resolving the appeal or petition.
4. To avoid the unseemly—and possibly unconstitutional—prospect of reversal of the judgment of a district court judge by a non-Article III judicial officer, all magistrates' reports recommending reversal will automatically transfer the case to the oral argument track before a panel of the court.
5. In all other cases in which the magistrate issues a report disposing of the case, the aggrieved party will be entitled to petition the court for review of the magistrate's opinion by a panel of the court. Review by judges of the court will be discretionary and not as of right.
6. Where review is granted, the case will be transferred to the oral argument calendar of the court. Where review is denied, the magistrate's report will be adopted as an unpublished opinion of the court.

In the end the decision in all cases will be that of duly commissioned Article III judges of the circuit, a fact that should alleviate concerns about the constitutionality of the plan. Concerns aroused by bureaucratic process are less easily allayed, but several aspects of the scheme should go far toward doing so: the status of the magistrates as judicial officers, their visibility, their interaction with counsel, and the visibility of judicial review of the magistrates' product. No one would argue that this is an ideal solution, but surely it is preferable to the development of massive staffs acting in secret if the caseload of the court reaches mammoth proportions.[62]

[62]Justice Richard L. Jones of the Supreme Court of Alabama, writing as chairman of the Appellate Judges' Conference of the American Bar Association's Section on Judicial Administration, has reported that the conference is giving active consideration to "[t]he creation of appellate magistrates or commissioner positions to ease the burdens of appellate judges." Richard L. Jones, "Appellate Judges' Conference: Committee Work," *Judges' Journal*, Winter 1989, at 27.

5

Appellate Justice Economized:
Screening and Its Effect
on Outcomes and Legitimacy

JERRY GOLDMAN

How government decides affects what government decides. Procedure matters to individuals and interests affected by government. Judith Resnik captured the importance of procedure when she declared that "[p]rocedure . . . embodies deeply held, albeit often unarticulated, views of human relationships, of the importance and difficulty of passing judgments on individuals' conduct, and of the place of government in citizens' lives."[1] Procedure is both a mechanism for expressing political and social relationships and a device for producing outcomes.[2] Changes in judicial process raise the prospect of changes in judicial outcomes.

These propositions apply in full force to the practice of screening— selecting cases for disposition by nonrotating three-judge panels without argument by counsel and generally without a face-to-face judicial examination of the merits. Screening aims to economize scarce judicial resources. One investigator identified the Ninth Circuit's screening program as "the most controversial of the major innovations."[3] Studies in the Ninth Circuit and elsewhere have generally supported the use of screening on the ground of efficiency. The purpose of this chapter is not to replicate those investigations but to test critically

I am grateful to John Oakley for his counsel and Jeffrey Potts for his assistance.

[1]Judith Resnik, "Tiers," 57 *S. Cal. L. Rev.* 837, 840 (1984).
[2]Id.
[3]Joe Cecil, *Administration of Justice in a Large Appellate Court: The Ninth Circuit Innovations Project* 47 (Federal Judicial Center, 1985).

some of the assumptions that provide the administrative foundation for screening in the Ninth Circuit and in appellate courts generally.[4]

Appellate Courts and the Theory of Screening

Appellate courts are inaccessible institutions to most Americans. The average citizen is unfamiliar with the functions appellate courts perform and the procedures they employ. In the late 1980s the Public Broadcasting System sought to penetrate the inaccessibility of the nation's highest court—the Supreme Court of the United States—in a two-part television series titled "This Honorable Court." In one segment, Justice Antonin Scalia reflected on the value of oral argument. Prior to his appointment as associate justice, Scalia (then a federal appeals court judge) thought that oral argument added little to a court's deliberations. His view changed dramatically following his appointment. Experience had taught him the value and necessity of oral argument.

Today, although the length of the standard argument is half the one-hour-per-side norm of 1960, the Supreme Court still hears oral argument in most of the cases it decides on the merits. In the courts of appeals, however, the proportion has dropped from almost 100 percent to about 50 percent. If a case is argued at all (and, as seen in Chapter 4, the size of that "if" depends on the circuit in question), the parties will generally be allotted less than twenty minutes per side.[5] Yet for all but a handful of federal cases, the courts of appeals are the courts of last resort.

If oral argument is necessary in the nation's highest court, what is the justification for curtailing it and foregoing other elements of the judicial process in the courts of appeals? One possible response is that, in the Supreme Court, considerations of policy dominate the issues presented for resolution. In the courts of appeals, disputes tend to focus more on particular facts and their significance for relatively narrow choices among legal rules. But this difference in function might suggest that oral argument would be even more important to the

---

[4]This research has benefited from the detailed study of the Ninth Circuit's screening practices published by the Federal Judicial Center. See Joe S. Cecil and Donna Stienstra, *Deciding Cases without Argument: An Examination of Four Courts of Appeals* (Federal Judicial Center, 1987).

[5]Richard A. Posner, *The Federal Courts: Crisis and Reform* 119–20 (Harvard University Press, 1985).

courts of appeals than to the Supreme Court, rather than the other way around.

The explanation lies not in functional differences but in the combination of jurisdictional imperatives and caseload pressures. Unlike the justices of the Supreme Court, circuit judges must decide all cases that properly arrive in their courts. In essence, the curtailment of oral argument in the federal courts of appeals has been more severe because the judges lack a docket-control mechanism.

The truncation of appellate procedures through active intervention of the judges began in the early 1960s in the Court of Appeals for the Fifth Circuit.[6] Today nearly every circuit employs truncated procedures for a portion of its docket.[7] Side by side with abbreviated processes has come an increase in the number of law clerks (or judicial supernumeraries, as they are sometimes called disparagingly). Each appellate court judge has three law clerks who work in the judge's own chambers ("elbow" clerks); each court has legal assistants (staff attorneys) to assist in the management and resolution of appeals.

The general justification for these programs is efficiency: the saving of judicial time and resources. As appellate dockets grow to the point where it is infeasible simply to add judges in order to continue processing cases under existing procedures, it becomes necessary to modify the procedures in order to maximize the most important values. This may result in infringement of other, less dearly held or more dimly viewed, values. The modification of oral argument is one such example. The value of providing all litigants with prompt judicial processing is thought to outweigh the benefit of having oral argument in certain types of cases.

Efficiency does not come without cost. Citizen trust in the fairness of government institutions is vital to legitimacy, which is the basis of judicial power. And legitimacy may be affected by procedural shortcuts such as the elimination of oral argument. The curtailment of oral argument may also sweep away other deliberative elements of the appellate process such as the face-to-face conference in which judges resolve submitted appeals. Taken separately, these curtailments may appear benign, but together they suggest fundamental changes in the appellate process which impose system-wide costs in exchange for particular benefits.

Researchers initially examined efforts to dispense with oral argu-

[6]Charles R. Haworth, "Screening and Summary Procedures in the United States Courts of Appeals," 1973 *Wash. U.L.Q.* 257.

[7]Cecil and Stienstra, supra note 4, at 7; see also Table 4.1.

ment when the movement toward alterations in appellate process was in full bloom.[8] Most studies concluded that curtailment of oral argument poses few risks for appellate justice. One typical study argued that screening enabled the judges of the Fifth Circuit to decide more cases and overcome a growing backlog of cases awaiting argument.[9] Following the Fifth Circuit's lead, other appellate courts quickly adopted their own versions of the disposition-without-argument program.[10]

In addition to the value trade-off in the face of a burgeoning docket, the reduction in oral argument can perhaps be viewed as an initial step by the courts of appeals to create a discretionary docket similar to that of the Supreme Court. By statute, the jurisdiction of the courts of appeals is mandatory. The courts cannot take away the right to appeal. What they can do is to modify the substance of that right. The segregation of cases into different programs, each involving a different set of procedures and a different amount of judicial attention, suggests that the circuits are employing incremental procedural changes to effectively control their dockets. The basic premise behind procedural curtailment is that some cases do not truly need a full set of appellate procedures to determine the outcome. By giving those cases more abbreviated treatment, the courts are able to devote more of their time and energy to the cases that do require the full set of procedures.

The minimum standard governing oral argument is spelled out in the Federal Rules of Appellate Procedure, which govern all courts of appeals. As noted in Chapter 4, Rule 34(a), the vehicle for accomplishing the case-differentiation goal, declares: "Oral argument will be allowed unless (1) the appeal is frivolous; or (2) the dispositive issue or set of issues has been recently authoritatively decided; or (3) the facts and legal arguments are adequately presented in the briefs and record and the decisional process would not be significantly aided by oral argument." The standards articulated in the rule are a curious amalgam. Two of the three criteria ("frivolous"; "recently . . . decided") are relatively specific but are not likely to cover many cases. The third criterion is so general as to be almost infinitely expandable. The effect is to allow individual circuits to experiment and create programs that will be suitable for their particular needs.

---

[8]See, e.g., Steven Flanders and Jerry Goldman, "Screening Practices and the Use of Para-Judicial Personnel in a U.S. Court of Appeals: A Study in the Fourth Circuit," 1/2 *Justice System Journal* 1 (March 1975).

[9]Haworth, supra note 6, at 281–89.

[10]Cecil and Stienstra, supra note 4.

As screening programs have matured, the justification for the practice has seemed subtly to shift. Whereas supporters once emphasized the overall amount of time saved and the ability to process an ever-larger number of cases, screening programs are now primarily lauded for their ability to increase the convenience to judges of expeditiously handling the screened cases. As one study puts it, "[t]he benefit of screening programs is not that they may save the court the thirty minutes or so that would be spent on oral argument, but that they permit judges greater flexibility in deciding those cases that are not argued."[11] Not only does oral argument require the judges to put aside other work and be in a particular place at a particular time; for most appellate judges it also requires traveling to another city. The flexibility that comes with screening is especially important in a far-flung circuit like the Ninth, but even in smaller circuits judges understandably feel that every day away from their home chambers reduces their capacity to work effectively on opinions and other dispositions.

The original justification of a generalized time-saving implied benefits to all the participants in the judicial process: judges, court personnel, attorneys, and litigants. The shift in the justification now restricts the benefits to the judges alone. If this line of reasoning is accepted, the cost-benefit analysis of the program may have been unnecessarily limited.

Of course, it can be argued that increased efficiency for the judges also benefits litigants and the public by reducing delay and avoiding the cost of additional judgeships. Research results reported later in this chapter explore the consequences of screening for the outcomes of appeals and for litigant perceptions of Ninth Circuit procedures. Before presenting those results, it will be useful to describe the factors that led to screening in the Ninth Circuit and the operation of those procedures, which were officially denominated the "Submission-without-Argument Program."[12]

The Ninth Circuit's Screening Experience

The Ninth Circuit established an initial screening program in 1970[13] but abandoned it for criminal cases in 1972 and for civil cases in 1974.[14]

[11]Id. at 3.

[12]"Submission-without-Argument Program" is a misnomer since the elimination of oral argument is only one element of the Ninth Circuit's program. Henceforth, I shall refer to the Ninth Circuit's program by the generic label *screening*.

[13]In re Amendment of Rule 3, 440 F.2d 847 (9th Cir. 1970).

[14]Some published reports erroneously date the abandonment of screening as 1975.

For most of the 1970s, criminal cases were scheduled for specified calendar days: as many as seven criminal cases would be calendared before a single three-judge panel, with the panel having the right to screen any case for decision on the briefs without oral argument. Civil cases were handled through a "sprinkle" system: cases reviewed by staff attorneys and found to be appropriate for summary disposition were added to the calendars of regular panels. The panels would then decide whether or not to allow oral argument.

The Ninth Circuit's resistance to a Fifth Circuit-style screening program underscored the continued value the judges placed on oral argument as long as it did not impede their ability to clear their dockets. Mounting caseloads made this stance difficult to maintain, however. In the spring of 1980, after extensive discussion, the court adopted a plan that called for adding as many as fifteen lightweight cases to the agenda of each motions panel. (Motions panels ordinarily hear such matters as applications for provisional relief in cases not yet calendared, motions to dismiss appeals because of jurisdictional defects, and nonroutine requests for waiver of procedural rules.) This experiment lasted for about six months; high administrative costs and inefficient use of judicial time combined to bring about its downfall.[15]

In July 1980, Judge Browning wrote to the Federal Judicial Center (FJC) offering the Ninth Circuit as a "laboratory" to test various procedures and approaches that might increase the productivity of individual circuit judges without sacrificing an acceptable level of quality. The FJC agreed, and over the next year it engaged in a wide-ranging study that included interviews with most of the judges and extensive consultation with the court's staff. An initial report early in 1981 contained modest recommendations, some of which were adopted later in the year.

The first phase of the FJC study coincided with the period when the motions panel experiment was in progress. At the February 1981 Symposium, when the experiment was terminated, the court considered two proposals for increasing its capacity to handle insubstantial appeals. One proposal was to reinstitute a "sprinkle" system; the other was to assign lightweight cases to special panels—in essence, a screening program. A majority voted to adopt the sprinkle system as an immediate interim measure. The court also heard a suggestion from Browning that it ask the Judicial Center for "drastic" proposals aimed at reducing the backlog.

---

[15]Another experiment, in which appeals were decided on oral argument alone, without briefs, proved equally disappointing.

In August 1981, the director of the FJC project submitted to the court's executive committee a final draft of a second and more ambitious report. Although the consultant recommended increasing the proportion of cases decided without oral argument, he explicitly declined to endorse a summary disposition procedure modeled on that of the Fifth Circuit.

One point emphasized by the FJC study was the need to establish "production targets." This idea struck a responsive chord with Browning, and while the final draft was being considered by the executive committee, he directed the court's own staff to develop "productivity goals" for the court. More concretely, the target was to bring the Ninth Circuit at least to the national median in postsubmission terminations per judgeship. As the staff proceeded with its analysis, however, it became clear that this goal could not be achieved in the immediate future without more drastic measures than the ones proposed in the FJC final draft. The upshot was a final report, circulated to the court early in September, that recommended adoption of a screening plan. The recommendation was endorsed by Browning.

Three possible approaches were presented in the FJC report: a plan modeled closely on the Fifth Circuit's approach, a Fifth Circuit approach modified to permit simultaneous review of case materials by the judges, and a variation on the "sprinkle" system. In September 1981, the court adopted a screening program based on the Fifth Circuit's procedures, with panels having the option of receiving case materials either simultaneously or in serial fashion. Screened cases would supplement, not replace, cases on the argument track; in fact, the court also voted to increase the number of sitting days for each active judge.[16]

What accounts for the court's ready acceptance of a plan that entailed not only a substantial departure from existing practices, but also a significant increase in the workload of each judge? Several factors appear to have played a part. The heavy backlog and the court's poor showing in comparison with other circuits were something of an embarrassment.[17] The data presented by Browning made it clear that

[16]The court agreed that active judges would sit five days a month for nine months a year rather than four days a month for ten months. It was also contemplated that the court would reduce its use of visiting judges. For further discussion, see Cecil, *supra* note 3, at 27–29.

[17]Some of the judges initially expressed skepticism about data purporting to show that other circuits were more productive, but members of the court had called friends in those circuits to ascertain what the workload actually was—how many cases the judges

the court could not substantially improve its position simply by tinkering with existing procedures—for example, by adding a case or two to each day's calendar. The court had already experimented with less drastic measures for coping with the backlog, and none appeared very promising. Finally, in September 1981 a majority of the judges had been on the court for less than two years. They had no great commitment to existing ways; at the same time, they might well have felt they were ready to take on heavier workloads than they did in their first months on the bench.

In short, the Ninth Circuit adopted screening because the judges became convinced that there was no other way of eliminating the backlog. Referring to screening generally, Cecil and Stienstra suggest that "the recent increase in the overall percentage of appeals disposed of without argument is due to increases in appellate terminations of the types of cases that are especially likely to be decided without argument."[18] The growing number of Ninth Circuit cases that were amenable to screening—in particular, prisoner and Social Security cases—may well have made the screening plan more palatable, but it was not the immediate reason why the Ninth Circuit's judges abandoned their opposition to the procedure.

Screening and the Role of Staff Attorneys

Notwithstanding its official title, submission without argument is not the distinguishing feature of the Ninth Circuit's screening program. The court decides all screened cases without oral argument, but oral argument is also denied in many cases on the regular docket. Rather, screened cases call for a greater degree of staff attorney involvement and dispositions by fixed, three-judge panels, usually without a face-to-face exchange of views. In contrast, all cases assigned to the regular docket are resolved by a face-to-face conference of the judges with the assistance of elbow clerks, each working under the supervision of a single judge. Table 5.1 summarizes the differences.

As described more fully in Chapter 4, the screening process begins in the staff attorneys' office. The staff attorneys "inventory" fully

---

heard, how many opinions they wrote. These reports convinced the skeptics that the Ninth Circuit was indeed a laggard.

[18]Cecil and Stienstra, supra note 4, at 25–26.

Table 5.1. Differences between the screening and the regular docket

	Screening docket	Regular docket
Oral argument	none	frequent
Three-judge panel		
composition	nonrotating	rotating
face-to-face meeting	no	yes
Assistance		
staff attorneys	substantial	minimal
"elbow" law clerks	moderate	substantial

briefed cases and assign a numerical "weight," an estimate of the degree of difficulty, to each case. Low-weight cases (1 and 3L) are sent to screening panels; other cases are assigned to three-judge rotating panels on the regular docket.

For each screening case, a staff attorney prepares a bench memorandum. Typically under twenty-five hundred words, the memorandum contains an overview of the appeal and its procedural posture; a discussion of the facts; a statement and analysis of issues on appeal, including citations to authority; and a recommended disposition of the appeal on the merits.[19] The case then goes to one of the three-judge screening panels. Judges report that they always read the staff attorney memos, the appellant's brief, and the appellee's brief. Other documents are examined far less frequently.

The most striking feature of the relationships among the staff attorneys, judges, and elbow clerks is the minimal degree of interaction. The judges rarely confer directly with the staff attorneys regarding cases on the screening docket.[20] The staff attorneys rely primarily on the weekly staff meetings for feedback, a situation that makes it difficult to convey meaningful evaluation by judges of individual staff attorney work. Judges' rejections of screened cases also constitute a form of feedback, but it is not clear how systematically these determinations or the reasons for them are communicated to the staff attorneys.[21] Nor do the judges necessarily seek assistance from their elbow clerks; according to Cecil and Stienstra, nine of twenty-two

[19]Id. at 72.

[20]Id. at 82.

[21]The staff attorney handbook properly notes that such rejections ought not to generate resentment. Rather, they should provide reassurance that the judges, not the staff attorneys alone, are making the judgments in appeals identified for screening. Handbook for Court Law Clerks at 6–9 (Office of Staff Attorneys, June 1987).

judges reported that they alone review the case materials, five reported using their elbow clerks for specific problems, and only eight reported using their law clerks to review and prepare the draft disposition.[22] It appears to be quite possible that judges, especially those using the serial procedure, might decide a screening case without ever discussing it with anyone—either other judges or a law clerk.

When originally adopted, the screening panels were supposed to evaluate sixty cases a month and to dispose of roughly 25 percent of the total cases submitted. The court, however, has generally been unable to meet the target because of a shortage of cases amenable to the screening program and of staff attorneys to prepare the cases for screening panels.[23]

Serial and Parallel Panels

As already noted, the court established two types of screening panels, the serial type and the parallel type. The serial panel, as originally conceived, consisted of a three-judge panel in which the initiating (or lead) judge would receive the case files following the preparation of a bench memorandum by a staff attorney. The judge would decide which of the cases should be disposed of through screening procedures and which should be returned to the pool for placement on the regular docket. After rejecting any case of the latter kind, the initiating judge would pass on the remaining cases to the next judge, along with a proposed disposition that would frequently rely on the staff memorandum. The second judge would proceed in similar fashion, then send the materials to the third judge, who would either reject the case or complete the process and assent to the proposed disposition.

The major advantage of the serial panel, in addition to the saving of judicial time, was that it permitted individual judges to review the cases at their convenience. The major drawback, apart from the inherent desirability of oral argument, was that this type of "panel" really consists of three individual decisions, perhaps a weaker sort of decision making. Many commentators and judges maintain that the elimination of oral argument may sweep away from a three-judge panel the focused and active consideration of cases; omitting the conference of

[22]Cecil and Stienstra, supra note 4, at 81.
[23]Id. at 74–75.

the judges only compounds the harm by removing the one remaining opportunity for focused collegial attention.

The parallel panel procedure provides an alternative for those judges concerned about the lack of direct communication among the panel members under the serial system. The parallel panel is composed of three judges who each receive a copy of the case materials, review them, and then confer in order to discuss which of the cases should be transferred to the regular docket and which should be disposed of by the screening panel. As with serial panel decisions, the authoring judge frequently relies on the staff memorandum. It should be noted that a conference for a parallel panel does not imply a physical meeting. The geographic dimensions of the Ninth Circuit and the dispersal of the judges have usually mandated the use of the telephone (and later, electronic mail) for conferences on screening cases.

With the adoption of both the serial and parallel panels, the Ninth Circuit became the only circuit to offer its judges the luxury of choosing between two procedures for screening cases. The judges' preferences were initially split about evenly between the two types of programs. But it did not take long before both models underwent modification. By 1985, Joe S. Cecil could report that the serial panels had come to involve more interaction among judges, while the parallel panels involved less interaction, at least in the form of conferences.[24] Two years later, Cecil and Donna Stienstra pointed to the difficulty the judges had in arranging a mutually convenient conference time as one of the reasons for the modification of the parallel procedure.[25]

In the years since 1987, the judges have increasingly come to rely on the use of electronic mail; telephone conversations are used less and less. In its 1986 biennial report to Congress, the Ninth Circuit Judicial Council made the blanket statement that "[t]his new technology [electronic mail] has virtually eliminated any barriers to communication and collegiality created by great distances between judges' chambers."[26] But communication and collegiality require interaction, and it is not clear that the judges have taken full advantage of computer mail to ensure the interchange of ideas as a substitute for the face-to-face conference.

The question is illuminated by a body of research not often directly

[24]Cecil, supra note 3, at 57–58.

[25]Cecil and Stienstra, supra note 4, at 79.

[26]Judicial Council and Court of Appeals for the Ninth Circuit, *Third Biennial Report to Congress on the Implementation of Section 6 of the Omnibus Judgeship Act of 1978 and Other Measures to Improve the Administration of Justice in the Ninth Circuit* at 10 (July 1986).

connected with judicial decision making. In effect, the serial panel is a series of three individual decisions, and the parallel panel is to some extent a group decision-making process. Research on the effectiveness of individual versus group decision making suggests that different decision-making "tracks" affect decision results.[27] For example, one study involving performance testing first examined individual scores and later the scores of groups with different combinations of high- and low-ability members. The investigators concluded that, in general, groups outperform individuals. Group achievement increases when the ability level of the members of the group is characterized by a larger number of high-ability individuals in comparison to an equivalent set of individual decision makers.[28] While recognizing that other variables, such as the willingness of the individuals to work in a group format, can affect performance level, this study lends support to the parallel panel procedure. Of course, evidence from nonjudicial settings can never establish the existence of effects in appellate courts. But group decision-making theory does lead one to anticipate that there will be discernible differences between the two forms of screening in the Ninth Circuit.

Testing Screening Effects: A "Natural" Experiment

Does screening affect the outcome of decisions? This question lies at the core of procedural change, for if the answer is in the affirmative, then track assignment *vel non* will alter the outcome. Only one test of this group-decision hypothesis has involved appellate court judges as subjects.

In a study conducted in a state appellate court, the effects of face-to-face deliberations coupled with oral argument appeared dramatic.[29]

[27]See, e.g., Roy Payne and Cary L. Cooper, *Groups at Work* (John Wiley, 1981); Gayle W. Hill, "Group versus Individual Performance: Are $N + 1$ Heads Better Than One?" 91 *Psychological Bulletin* 517–35 (1982) (group process generally superior to individual process).

[28]Patrick R. Laughlin and Lawrence G. Branch, "Individual versus Tetradic Performance on a Complementary Task as a Function of Ability Level," 8 *Organizational Behavior and Human Performance* 201 (1972). In a related finding, the investigators observed that the addition of more persons to the group (even those with high ability) added little to the group score.

[29]Jerry Goldman, "Oral Decisions in the California First District Court of Appeal, Division Four: An Experiment in Appellate Advocacy" (August 1980) (unpublished paper).

Appeals normally screened by the staff were randomly assigned to two groups. In one group, cases were routed back to the judges without the benefit of a staff-prepared disposition. Furthermore, attorneys were encouraged to argue their appeals. The judges also agreed to reach a preliminary judgment following oral argument and to announce their decision from the bench. In the second group, the cases were screened according to the routine procedures adopted by the court (review by a staff attorney accompanied by a proposed disposition, no oral argument, and serial review by the panel).

The results strongly suggested that the outcome of panel decision making varied with the procedures employed. The proportion of non-affirmances in the oral-argument group was significantly higher in comparison to the no-oral-argument group. Of course, this difference in outcome may have resulted from the judgment-from-the-bench procedure, from the oral argument, from the active interaction of the panel, or combinations of these three variables. Unfortunately, the experiment was short-lived, and the data from it can only suggest, but not establish, the effects of group deliberation and oral argument on appellate court decision making.

The ideal test of the effect of screening on case outcomes would require the random assignment of comparable "screenable" cases to the screening docket or the regular docket tracks. If the outcomes differed greatly across the tracks, it would be legitimate to attribute that difference to the difference in procedures. Although this experiment was never mounted, actual practice in the Ninth Circuit Court of Appeals permits a very close (perhaps even an identical) match to this ideal.

From 1982 to 1988, about one thousand low-weight cases (1 and 3L) were transferred to the regular docket.[30] These transfers filled up vacancies in regular docket assignments and reduced the backlog of cases awaiting staff attorney workup. In effect, low-weight cases were routed to screening panels and to the regular docket simultaneously, a circumstance that almost replicates the random assignment of the state court experiment. This study concentrates only on the transferred cases because they may serve as an undisturbed comparison to

[30]Although Oakley and Thompson (Chapter 4) and I used the same database and similar search criteria to identify cases for our respective analyses, our purposes were not identical and our evidence differs, sometimes substantially. Bear in mind, however, that the goal of this chapter is to assay the importance of the regular docket versus the screening docket. Oakley and Thompson draw comparisons between orally argued cases and screened cases.

cases on the screening docket.[31] And because screened cases include both 1 and 3L weights, all comparisons were made between cases of identical weight.

Two outcome measures were used to test the effects of the court's differential procedures. The first was the relief rate, which is defined as the ratio of successful relief for the appellant to all dispositions.[32] The second outcome measure was publication rate. Appellate courts publish only cases of potential precedential value.[33] Although likely precedential value is only one of the criteria used in weighing cases,[34] comparable groups of cases having the same weight should have comparable potential precedential yields as measured by publication rate. Operationally, the publication rate is the ratio of published opinions (signed or per curiam) to all decisions.

If screening operates solely to make the court more efficient, there should be no difference on these outcome measures between the transferred cases on the regular docket and those on the screening docket. If differences emerge in relief rates or publication rates, however, these differences may be attributable to the difference in procedures between the screening docket and the regular docket. Such evidence would question the desirability of screening in a fundamental way.

It is possible, of course, that the transfer of screening cases to the regular docket might reflect some hidden bias that would intrude on any analysis. As a check against one such flaw, the distribution of case types (criminal appeals, civil rights, prisoner petitions, tax, etc.) was evaluated within case weights and across tracks. Regardless of tracks—screening docket or regular docket—the case-type distributions in each case weight were nearly identical. This provides an additional measure of assurance that, but for the track, cases of the same weight started out alike.

The data reported in the following tables come from the Ninth

[31]Cases rejected by screening panels as inappropriate for screening are not included in the comparisons between the regular and the screening dockets. See note 35.

[32]Relief rate includes any reversal or remand. Dismissals (e.g., for want of jurisdiction) are not defined as relief but are counted as dispositions in the denominator of the rate. This definition departs slightly from that of Oakley and Thompson, since they exclude dismissals entirely from their measure, which they label *nonaffirmance rate*.

[33]See 9th Cir. Rule 36-2; William L. Reynolds and William M. Richman, "An Evaluation of Limited Publication in the United States Courts of Appeals: The Price of Reform," 48 *U. Chi. L. Rev.* 573 (1981).

[34]Arthur D. Hellman, "Central Staff in Appellate Courts: The Experience of the Ninth Circuit," 68 *Calif. L. Rev.* 937, 963 (1980).

Circuit's records. This evidence represents only decisions of regular judge panels for cases docketed after January 1, 1982 (the putative beginning of the screening docket), and terminated on or before June 15, 1988 (the end of Browning's tenure as chief judge). Appeals rejected by screening panels and decisions by motions and en banc panels have been excluded. Thus, the only comparisons are between groups of identical cases assigned at random to the screening docket or the regular docket.

Recall that in the state appellate court study the judge/group process accounted for a significantly higher proportion of nonaffirmances than the staff/individual process. Would the same results occur here? Screening critics might argue that litigants are more likely to get some relief when claims are reviewed by judges as a group. Since group interaction is a function of regularly docketed cases, not screened cases, these critics would predict a significantly higher relief rate for cases on the regular docket in comparison with cases on the screening docket.

As can be seen from Table 5.2, the relief rates of the screening docket and regular docket cases are nearly identical regardless of case weight.[35] There is a slightly higher likelihood of relief to the appellant under the regular docket, but the differences are within the range likely to occur simply by chance. The higher-weight cases reflect a greater degree of difficulty, which may translate into a stronger case for the appellant. These data affirm the screening docket's overall outcome neutrality for litigants.[36]

Screening docket critics might also maintain that different procedures for supervising the preparation of dispositions could result in

---

[35]Screening panels reject some appeals and place them on the regular docket. Screening cases that were transferred to the regular docket were never examined by screening panels. Thus, these transferred cases contain some "rejectable" cases. Removing rejected cases from the screening docket is simple. Removing the "rejectables" from the transferred cases requires estimation according to the following formula:

$$J_c = (J_t - J_r R)/(1 - R)$$

where J_c is the corrected relief rate for a given case weight; J_t is the transferred case relief rate for a given case weight; J_r is the rejected case relief rate for a given case weight; and R is the rejection rate from the screening to the regular docket.

The effects of "rejectable" cases are hardly noticeable. The corrected values actually bring the relief rates closer together. The corrected value for the relief variable (weight = 1) on the regular docket is 0.12; the corrected value for the relief variable (weight = 3L) on the regular docket is 0.14.

[36]The dismissal rate did not vary under either docket. It remained at 5 percent regardless of case weight.

Table 5.2. Relief rates for screening docket and regular docket cases, by case weight

| | Relief rate | |
Case weight	Screening docket	Regular docket
1	11%	13%
(N)	(1,403)	(351)
	t = 1.05	p = n.s.
3L	14%	15%
(N)	(971)	(632)
	t = 0.58	p = n.s.

Note: Here and in Tables 5.3 and 5.6, the *p* value measures the probability of observing a difference of the magnitude actually found between the screening and regular dockets, given the assumption that the relief rate (or other measure) is identical across dockets. An observed difference between the two dockets is treated as significant only if there are fewer than 5 chances in 100 that the difference could have occurred by chance. If the *p* value is greater than 0.05, the results are not considered statistically significant ("n.s."). If the *p* value is less than 0.05, the results are deemed statistically significant and the assumption of identicalness is rejected. The *t* value identifies the particular statistical test and its assumptions.

opinion differences. In screening docket cases, judges rely to a substantial degree on the work of staff attorneys, whereas in regular docket cases, judges rely heavily on the assistance of their own law clerks. Does the difference in tracks yield a difference in publication rates?

Table 5.3 reveals that regular docket panels generated substantially more published opinions than comparable screening docket panels. The differences are most pronounced for signed opinions. Were it not for the screening docket, the proportion of signed, published opinions would increase between 8 and 14 percent for cases with weights of 1

Table 5.3. Opinion publication rates for screening docket and regular docket cases, by case weight

| | Signed opinions | | Per curiam opinions | |
Case weight	Screening docket	Regular docket	Screening docket	Regular docket
1	3%	14%	2%	5%
(N)	(1,403)	(351)	(1,403)	(351)
	t = 8.46,	p < .001	t = 3.75,	p < .01
3L	5%	19%	2%	3%
(N)	(971)	(632)	(971)	(632)
	t = 8.75,	p < .001	t = 1.4,	p = n.s.

and increase between 11 and 17 percent for cases with weights of 3L. In other words, if a screened appeal is assigned to the regular docket rather than the screening docket, the likelihood that the court will issue a signed, published opinion increases by a factor of two to three.

What accounts for this substantial increase in publishability? There are several possible reasons, and each one has a measure of plausibility. First, the assignment to the regular docket generally means that the panel will meet face-to-face to discuss the merits. Perhaps the opportunity to engage the attention of the panel yields more interest in the issues and a more careful rendering of their resolution.

Second, the organization of a judge's office may account for the increased likelihood of publication. Cases on the regular docket become the responsibility of individual elbow law clerks working in close proximity to the writing judge on a panel. Once an elbow clerk has put in the hard work of drafting a proposed disposition, publication may follow as an appropriate reward.

Third, the assignment of a case to the regular docket may carry a presumption that it merits serious review. Only cases with weights of 3 or higher are normally assigned to the regular docket. This presumption of importance may raise expectations about publication, and the expectations in turn become self-fulfilling prophecies, especially if the judges are "blind" to the weight assigned each case.

This last point deserves more extended attention. The architects of screening claim that the decision to eliminate oral argument is independent of the decision concerning publishability. Though oral argument and publishability may be correlated, even strongly correlated, the criteria employed for one decision are not the same as those used for the other, or at least they should not be. Yet there is some disturbing evidence that the criteria have come to be regarded as interchangeable. This development can be seen most easily in the screening instructions given to the staff attorneys. According to these instructions, screening cases must satisfy one or more of four standards: (1) the result is clear; (2) the legal standard is established and undisputed; (3) the appellant or petitioner is proceeding pro se (and may be incarcerated); or (4) the briefs are well focused.[37] The application of the second standard introduces the confusion as follows:

---

[37]Inventory Codebook 33–35 (Office of Staff Attorneys, July 1987). The fourth standard has been phrased in different ways at different times. See Cecil, supra note 3, at 54 ("bus trip test").

Even where the result is not clear, the case may be suitable for submission to a screening panel if the legal standard to be applied is clear and undisputed and the result is not likely to be precedential. For example, an appeal may raise the issue whether police officers had probable cause to search a closet. *Even if the outcome is close*, the probable cause issue is straightforward, unlikely to be precedential, and might suitably be decided without oral argument.[38]

The assumption of a close outcome means that the case will turn on a careful examination of the facts in possession of the police at the time of the search. This is precisely the type of case that would profit from a dialogue between the judges and attorneys concerning the particular facts and how they compare to prior cases in which probable cause was or was not found. Oral argument is desirable here regardless of the precedential value of the conclusion.

A counterexample reaches the right result but reinforces the notion that suitability for oral argument coincides with apparent precedential significance:

[A]n appeal raising the novel question whether police have probable cause to search a particular computerized database might be unsuitable for the screening program, not because the legal standard is complex, but because the disposition might well be precedential.[39]

Precedential value is the putative reason for not screening this case. That makes sense: in a novel situation the judges would probably be aided by a more searching examination of the factual setting and the comparison of the issue in its setting to the prior cases. And this will be so even if the facts are clear and the briefs thorough. Thus, in this kind of case the higher weight and assignment to the regular docket properly suggest a presumption toward publication. The problem lies in the implication that without the likely precedential importance the case would be suitable for screening.

Table 5.4, which reports publication rates by case weight, lends plausibility to some of this speculation. Publication rates increase as case weights increase. A comparison of Tables 5.3 and 5.4 suggests that, if a regular docket panel is blind to case weight, the "given" rate

[38]Inventory Codebook, supra note 37, at 33 (emphasis added), quoted in Cecil and Stienstra, supra note 4, at 73–74.

[39]Inventory Codebook, supra note 37, at 33–34, quoted in Cecil and Stienstra, supra note 4, at 74.

Table 5.4. Opinion publication rates for regular docket cases, by case weight

Case weight	Percentage decided with published opinion	N
3	38	4,506
5	59	3,467
7	75	524
10	81	87

of publication is much higher. This may account for the increased likelihood of publication as a consequence of assignment to the regular docket.

Three plausible explanations were offered to account for the substantial increase in published opinions apparently occasioned by assignment of cases eligible for screening to the regular docket. Regrettably, there is no convincing evidence to prefer one of these explanations to another. The finding thus suggests a kind of traffic problem: is the court producing too few opinions through the screening docket or too many published opinions through the regular docket? If the latter, at least some of the published low-weight cases should prove to be of minimal precedential value. One way to test this hypothesis is to examine the frequency of citations in subsequent opinions.[40]

The citation activity of all 1-weight and 3L-weight cases published before 1986 was examined.[41] This amounted to 113 published opinions, of which 102 were signed and 11 were per curiams. The data, summarized in Table 5.5, reveal a slight tendency to cite regular docket opinions more frequently than screening docket opinions in the Ninth Circuit and overall, but the differences appear inconsequential. These findings suggest that, if more cases were assigned to the regular docket, they too would be found to be of value as precedent in later disputes.

Finally, the data can shed some light on the effects of serial versus parallel screening. Cases are randomly assigned to screening panels,

[40]Posner, supra note 5, at 120–21.

[41]*Citation activity* means where and how often published opinions were cited (e.g., in federal or state courts; inside or outside the Ninth Circuit). It is reasonable to assume that a Ninth Circuit opinion cited frequently throughout the federal system represents a more valuable contribution to the law than a Ninth Circuit opinion that is never cited or that is cited only in the Ninth Circuit.

Table 5.5. Average number of citations to screening docket and regular docket cases, by case weight (published signed opinions)

	Average number of citations				
	In Ninth Circuit		In all circuits		
Case weight	Regular docket	Screening docket	Regular docket	Screening docket	N
1	3.6	3.3	8.2	7.2	61
3L	4.4	3.4	8.9	8.7	41

Table 5.6. Relief and publication rates for serial and parallel screening panels, by case weight

	Rate of relief		Rate of publication	
Case weight	Serial	Parallel	Serial	Parallel
1	10%	11%	5%	6%
(N)	(786)	(577)	(786)	(577)
3L	14%	12%	5%	10%[a]
(N)	(544)	(368)	(544)	(367)
All	12%	11%	5%	8%[a]
(N)	(1,330)	(945)	(1,330)	(944)

[a]$p < 0.05$.
Note: Missing cases = 99.

and screening panel composition changes yearly. Some panels use the parallel format; others the serial format. The screened cases are comparable except for the panel format. Differences in outcomes beyond the level of chance variation can be attributed to the panel format.

With regard to relief rates, as shown in Table 5.6, the outcomes of cases are nearly identical regardless of screening format. This pattern stands when controlled for case weight. However, publication rates differed significantly between formats; most of the overall difference is attributable to the differences for 3L cases. Parallel panel assignments are estimated to increase the likelihood of a published opinion by 3 to 5 percent above the serial publication rate.

This evidence offers support (but only weak support) for the group decision-making theorists. Parallel panels seem to provide more opportunities for contact and interaction than serial panels. This contact may generate more lively exchanges or provoke more thought and involvement.

157

Jerry Goldman

Screening, Perception, and Legitimacy

In a democratic society, courts derive their power from the public perception that they are institutions worthy of exercising power. As Alexander Hamilton observed two hundred years ago, courts have "neither FORCE nor WILL, but only judgment." The willingness of citizens to accept the actions of the courts is the cornerstone of judicial power. There is reason to think that screening programs may jeopardize that cornerstone.

Society functions effectively when citizens comply voluntarily with decisions of duly constituted authority. Citizens are more likely to obey the law when they view legal authorities as legitimate, that is, as possessing a right to dictate behavior in a certain area. Legitimacy thus acts as a "reservoir" of loyalty from which leaders draw, giving them the discretionary authority they require to govern effectively.

Until recently, legitimacy was a commonly held explanation for obedience to law, but it lacked solid empirical demonstration. Then, in a path-breaking study of compliance and legitimacy, Tom R. Tyler demonstrated that legitimacy does play an important role in promoting compliance with law.[42] Moreover, a central element in the complex equation of legitimacy is procedural fairness.[43] Tyler found that citizen assessments of procedural fairness affected citizens' views about legal authorities, and that these effects were independent of citizen assessments of the fairness of outcomes. Even when citizens judged outcomes to be of high quality, those outcomes did not necessarily lead to feelings of fair treatment. Rather, "[p]eople have a tremendous desire to present their side of the story and value the opportunity in and of itself."[44]

Tyler found that a key to procedural fairness is the opportunity for citizens to participate in the decision-making process. This concern for participation implicates three elements: an opportunity for citizens to present their arguments; the willingness of decision makers to consider the arguments; and evidence that the decision makers have considered the arguments.

Tyler's research suggests that litigants who are denied the opportunity to participate in the appellate process will regard that process as

[42]Tom R. Tyler, *Why People Obey the Law* (Yale University Press, 1990).

[43]Tom R. Tyler, "What Is Procedural Justice? Criteria Used by Citizens to Assess the Fairness of Legal Procedures," 22 *Law and Society Rev.* 103 (1988).

[44]Tyler, supra note 42, at 147.

unfair regardless of the outcome. If Tyler is correct, appellate processes that reduce or eliminate participation will erode judicial legitimacy. Does Tyler's theory apply to appellate courts? There are good reasons on both sides. On the affirmative side, procedural justice effects have been found by other investigators in other settings. Citizens count procedural fairness in their evaluations of many institutions; there is no reason a priori to expect appellate courts to be immune from procedural justice effects. On the negative side, Tyler's research was based on a large-scale public opinion survey drawing on citizen contacts with police and trial courts. Tyler made no direct assessment of citizen contact or reaction to appellate courts. The public is far less aware of the functions of appellate courts, and only a minute proportion of the population has any involvement in appellate litigation.

Analysis is complicated by the fact that litigants may approach appellate court proceedings with expectations colored by their attitudes toward the U.S. Supreme Court. Generally, the public appears unaware of the Supreme Court's decisions.[45] Nevertheless, the public expresses much more confidence in that Court than in Congress or the executive branch. It is probably no coincidence that the Court's processes (including oral argument in most cases) and decisions are still mainstays of newspaper copy and television news. Seldom can that be said of other appellate courts. If the public sees the procedures of the Supreme Court as representing the norm for appellate courts generally, litigants in screened cases may judge the procedures as unfair.

In screened cases, citizens—through counsel—have the opportunity to present arguments in written form, but the elimination of oral argument sweeps away the evidence of receptivity. With no opportunity to confront the judges directly, litigants must take on faith the assertion that their written arguments have been read and evaluated by the judges themselves. Finally, many screened cases lack adequate evidence of consideration because they are resolved by brief, unpublished opinions (called *memoranda* in the Ninth Circuit). The terse memorandum format may not meet Tyler's consideration condition.[46]

The directions to staff law clerks for the preparation of memoranda call for the inclusion of (1) a statement of the court's reasons for

---

[45]Thomas R. Marshall, *Public Opinion and the Supreme Court* (Unwin Hyman, 1989).
[46]Some unpublished memoranda are quite long and detailed, satisfying the consideration condition.

accepting or rejecting the appellant's contentions, with appropriate citations, and (2) a statement of the result. The memorandum "may but *need not contain*" (3) a statement of the nature and posture of the case and (4) a statement of the appellant's contentions on appeal.[47] The absence of the fourth element in a screened case memorandum will fuel doubt that the judges actually considered the appellant's arguments.

Most litigants are represented by counsel. If clients entrust their lawyers to the details of an appeal, procedural fairness should prove less important than outcome fairness. But to the extent that clients remain actively involved in their appeals (either from their own initiative or from their lawyers'), procedural fairness should take on greater importance. Finally, a small but nontrivial number of cases involve pro se litigants, individuals who have chosen to represent themselves. Some are foolish, others eccentric. The fact that they have chosen to represent themselves does not, ipso facto, rule out the relevance of their perceptions concerning procedural and outcome fairness in the courts.[48] A comparison of their impressions with the impressions of litigants represented by counsel should embellish an understanding of screening effects.

It should be emphasized that this discussion is not a full-scale replication of Tyler's work in the context of appellate courts and screening. A survey of the public would reveal few if any respondents with experience in appellate courts. A general survey of litigants in the Ninth Circuit would have been ideal. With the exception of pro se litigants, however, there is no direct and representative way to identify and poll litigant-respondents through the public record.

To test Tyler's theory, detailed telephone interviews were conducted with thirty appellants whose cases fell into one of three groups: orally argued civil cases on the regular docket in which the appellant was

[47]Handbook for Court Law Clerks, supra note 21, App. E.

[48]Judge Richard Posner argues that the inability of a pro per litigant in a civil case to obtain a lawyer is a satisfactory demonstration that the claim is insubstantial. See Merritt v. Faulkner, 697 F.2d 761 (7th Cir. 1983) (dissenting opinion). Posner's view fails to acknowledge the litigant who attaches a high value to his loss relative to his total worth. A person may find great consequences in his case, even when an attorney finds such a case beneath the threshold for representation. Posner would dismiss the appellant as irrational; others might say he was unfortunate.

Many judges and court watchers may disagree, but the evidence suggests that the pro per respondents in my survey were as articulate and rational as respondents represented by counsel. Of course, the research hardly qualifies as a judgment of all litigants, since many were unavailable at the time I conducted my interviews.

represented by counsel (Group A); civil cases on the screening docket in which the litigant was represented by counsel (Group B); and civil cases on the screening docket in which appellants represented themselves and paid their own fees (Group C).[49] If Tyler's theory is sound, litigants in the last two sets of cases will harbor more negative assessments of procedural fairness than those in cases on the regular docket.

Though this evidence is impressionistic, it is consistent with Tyler's theory. For the most part, respondents were familiar with the main events of the appellate process. The most striking characteristic in Group A was that litigants tended to attach greater importance to procedural fairness than to outcome fairness. Some respondents were often satisfied with procedural fairness even when they were not satisfied with the outcome and vice versa.

Respondents in Group B were satisfied with the fairness of the court as a general proposition, but they expressed concern about the inability to participate in the process in their cases. Some appellants felt that they were left in the dark by their attorneys; others deferred to their attorneys and trusted their judgments.

The Group C respondents were more equally divided on overall assessments of the Ninth Circuit. In the particulars of their appeals this group also revealed a strong correlation between outcome and procedure assessments. Nonetheless, almost all the respondents in this group rated outcome and procedure in their cases as very unfair. When asked the reasons for outcome unfairness, these respondents spoke in great detail of procedural concerns. The most frequently cited reason for outcome unfairness was lack of oral argument ("Without being able to speak, I didn't have my day in court." "No oral argument makes a difference." "Judges aren't making decisions."). The procedural concerns of these respondents seemed driven by the feeling that they had little or no opportunity to present their cases to the court and that the court gave little or no consideration to their claims. Virtually all felt that they had little influence on the court's decision.

The evidence from this survey tells us that litigants can differentiate and evaluate outcomes and procedures. The more they know about their cases, the greater their ability to make such evaluations. Procedural curtailment in the form of screening may provide an opportunity for dissatisfied litigants to focus on the perceived unfairness of

---

[49]None of the respondents were incarcerated at the time of the interviews. The interviews lasted between 25 and 120 minutes and were conducted in late 1988 and early 1989.

the court's procedures rather than on the weakness of their cases. If litigants expect the traditional model of appellate procedure that includes oral argument, the denial of oral argument and the issuance of terse unpublished opinions will remove the sense of participation that appears vital to the long-term legitimacy of powerful institutions.

Legitimacy does not disappear overnight. It declines through a process of erosion as expectations are worn down by experience. Removing litigant participation from decision making may yield short-term benefits of expenditure and delay reduction. In the long term, however, this erosive force may leave the judiciary weaker in the public's eyes than it is today. It is plausible that oral argument will cease to be a part of the expected process. With a new set of expectations, legitimacy will come to rest on other procedures.[50]

Conclusion

This study of the Ninth Circuit has attempted to measure the effects of screening during a period of considerable administrative ferment. The court has held true to the traditional process of deciding appeals with oral argument, face-to-face judicial deliberation, and published opinions for a substantial portion of its docket. In the remaining cases screening has no apparent effect on the outcome of appeals, but it has had substantial consequences for the publication of dispositions. The publication effect is modest to trivial between screening formats.

The absence of face-to-face deliberations in screened cases may account for the smaller proportion of published opinions. It is not possible, however, to determine whether the court is publishing too many opinions (when cases appropriate for screening panels are assigned to the regular docket) or whether it is publishing too few opinions (when cases appropriate for the regular docket are screened). The author inclines to the latter view, though admittedly the evidence does not squarely support this proposition.

The skeptic who reviews research on screening will observe a strong, even universal, tendency to test program effectiveness by reference solely to the court and its cases. Although such evidence is

---

[50]I do not explore the role that attorneys play. In screened cases they may use the elimination of oral argument as a target for the disappointment of clients who have lost, or they may deflect criticism of the court by assuming responsibility and discouraging client intervention. The relationship between appellant and counsel is beyond the scope of this study.

necessary to any evaluation, it is not sufficient to the larger purpose of courts in a democratic society. The perception of litigants is a vital but largely unexplored domain in the arena of appellate justice. Even when trial courts render judgments in conflict with litigant self-interest, perceptions of the fairness of legal procedure help to put into perspective the laments of disappointed litigants (as well as the satisfaction of those who are successful).

A study of litigant attitudes, although impressionistic, suggests that screening takes its toll on perceptions of procedural fairness. Judicial legitimacy may suffer unless the court restores one or more of the participation elements in screened cases. At minimum, the court should employ a more generous format for all unpublished memoranda which would summarize the appellant's argument in a few paragraphs and then address his arguments or dismiss them in a reasoned manner. This small step would provide additional evidence that decision makers have considered the arguments of litigants, a key element in maintaining legitimacy.

Grand reforms are to the judiciary as the Chicago Cubs are to the National League Pennant: hope outdistances reality at the start of the season. Despite the long odds, it is appropriate to resurrect a plan that rethinks the appellate process while bearing in mind the concerns about legitimacy raised by cases that today receive short shrift. This plan would tackle the requirement of appellate review from a new angle: the trial court.

The idea, first proposed by Judge Shirley Hufstedler, would vest initial review of a trial court judgment in a three-judge panel in the trial court. District judges (excluding the trial judge) would staff this appellate division with occasional help from circuit judges. The panel would hear oral argument and reach its judgment after a face-to-face conference. The panel would then make any disposition that the trial judge or an appellate panel can now make. The panel would offer reasons, either written or oral, but the statements would not carry precedential value. Dissatisfied litigants could appeal to the court of appeals, but this step would become discretionary. Freed from the burden of error correction, the court of appeals would concentrate on policy making.[51]

[51]Shirley M. Hufstedler, "New Blocks for Old Pyramids: Reshaping the Judicial System," 44 *S. Cal. L. Rev.* 901 (1971). Paul D. Carrington recently revived the Hufstedler plan and has made a strong case that this recast appellate court would require fewer judges, fewer circuits, and larger panels. See Paul D. Carrington, "The Function of the Civil Appeal: A Late-Century View," 38 *S.C. L. Rev.* 411, 433–34 (1987).

The advantage of the Hufstedler plan is that it would provide visibility as well as speed for cases without apparent precedential value. This in turn would give an added assurance of legitimacy in all appeals as of right. The cost would be another layer of review, a fourth tier in the judicial pyramid.[52] But only a small number of cases would reach the fourth tier. Under the current structure, the differentiation of appeals is approaching the discretionary model for a large proportion of the cases, but without the visibility and accountability that the Hufstedler plan would afford.

In fairness, the Ninth Circuit's screening program has not generated the intense opposition that earlier screening ventures prompted from commentators, lawyers, and judges in other circuits. But the absence of criticism does not ensure broad-based public approval of screening. Left undisturbed, procedural curtailment harbors erosive force that will not be visible until the damage is grave. Public support of the judiciary is vital, wrote George Washington, because "the true administration of justice is the firmest pillar of good government." In the spirit of Washington's admonition, the federal courts should embrace a fourth tier and establish procedures that will enhance, rather than diminish, its power.

---

[52]Judith Resnik maintains that the courts' legitimacy declines as the forces of finality, resource conservation, and deference to trial courts chip away at levels of decision making, or tiers. Though she adduces no empirical evidence in her analysis, her argument is consistent with the data presented here. See generally Resnik, supra note 1.

6

The Bankruptcy Appellate Panel
and Its Implications for Adoption of
Specialist Panels in the Courts of Appeals

MICHAEL A. BERCH

> *Often do the spirits of great events*
> *stride on before the events, for in today*
> *already walks tomorrow.*
> *—Samuel Taylor Coleridge*

Shortly after passage of an implementing statute in 1978, the Ninth Circuit established the Bankruptcy Appellate Panel (BAP), a unique alternative system for review of bankruptcy cases by a specialist panel of bankruptcy judges. Ever since, the circuit has consistently and enthusiastically supported this innovation. This chapter examines the BAP and its impact on the adjudication of bankruptcy cases. After determining that the BAP has been a success and investigating the reasons why, the chapter advocates that to relieve the mounting burdens in the circuits, the courts of appeals should follow the BAP model and create specialist panels. It also suggests that the Court of Appeals for the Ninth Circuit establish a specialist panel to ensure uniformity and predictability in bankruptcy law.

The call for a specialists to perform judicial tasks in highly technical fields has been justified largely by the need for expertise to promote consistency, uniformity, and efficiency. Recall Learned Hand's comment:

I cannot stop without calling attention to the extraordinary condition of the law which makes it possible for a man without any knowledge of even the rudiments of chemistry to pass upon such questions as these [in a patent case]. . . . How long we shall continue to blunder along without the aid of unpartisan and authoritative scientific assistance in the administration of justice, no one knows; but all fair persons not conventionalized by provincial legal habits of mind ought, I should think, unite to effect some such advance.[1]

In assessing any reform, it is imperative to weigh the benefits achieved against any costs incurred. In evaluating a specialized court system, several factors should be examined: speed of disposition, correctness of result, predictability of outcomes, and frequency of appeals to and from the specialized system. We must also consider financial and other costs to the system and to the litigants. In this assessment we should be particularly alert to concerns about tunnel vision, interest-group-dominated appointments, and centralization of power.[2] But if the proponents of reform can satisfactorily demonstrate its benefits by empirical and other methodologically sound research, the burden should shift to its opponents to demonstrate that the costs outweigh the benefits.

After discussing the BAP with practitioners and judges and reviewing official reports and documents of government agencies, I conclude that the BAP is a success.[3] Analysis of the reasons for its success suggests other innovative techniques using several elements of the BAP model which the courts of appeals might adopt to cope with their

---

[1]Parke-Davis & Co. v. H. K. Mulford Co., 189 F. 95, 115 (S.D.N.Y. 1911). Hand's prescient comment of four-score years ago is even more relevant today. As recently stated in the report of the American Bar Association Standing Committee on Federal Judicial Improvements, "The United States Courts of Appeals: Reexamining Structure and Process after a Century of Growth," 125 F.R.D. 523, 533 (1989) (hereafter cited as ABA Standing Committee), "[a] federal circuit judge today decides a vastly wider range of cases than Judge Learned Hand, when he was appointed to the Second Circuit in 1924 and even when he retired in 1951. All of the New Deal legislation followed his appointment as a circuit judge and most of the modern civil rights, consumer, and environmental legislation and the expansive interpretation of constitutional rights occurred after he had retired."

[2]See Chapter 1, note 11.

[3]This is also the view of the present chief judge of the Ninth Circuit. In June 1989 Chief Judge Goodwin circulated a position paper prepared by the Circuit Executive's Office in response to a pending bill to create a new twelfth circuit by separating several states from the Ninth Circuit. The position paper commented on the BAP as a "highly successful court of experienced bankruptcy judges [that] has developed a body of uniform, high-quality bankruptcy precedents, and relieved both the district courts and the court of appeals in the Ninth Circuit of a substantial burden."

overwhelming burdens. But we must do something—and soon. A few years ago Judge Richard A. Posner stated, "[T]he wolf really does seem to be at the door."[4] By now the wolf has entered.

Negative reaction to specialist panels, though pervasive, is unwarranted. Many judges, including members of the Executive Committee of the Ninth Circuit Court of Appeals, have reacted adversely to the idea of creating specialist panels.[5] Critics, however, do not always distinguish between specialized courts and specialist panels.[6] Not so with Judge Posner, who expressly recognized the difference when, in his attack on specialized courts, he confessed to not addressing the kind of specialization that consists of rotating judges among specialized divisions of their court.[7]

This chapter takes up where Posner left off. It also analyzes the unarticulated assumption that specialist panels are subject to the same inherent problems as specialized courts and concludes that, although the evils commonly associated with specialized courts do not inhere in specialist panels, the benefits do. I therefore advocate an experiment with the use of specialist panels in the courts of appeals—on a modest scale at first.[8]

---

[4]Richard A. Posner, *The Federal Courts: Crisis and Reform* 317 (Harvard University Press, 1985).

[5]When Judge Browning submitted a proposal for specialist panels to the executive committee, the vote was 8 to 1 against it. Conference on Empirical Research in Judicial Administration, 21 *Ariz. St. L.J.* 33, 44 (1989) (remarks of Judge Browning).

[6]Supreme Court Justice Antonin Scalia commented on the use of specialized courts: "I understand the aversion that all we common-law lawyers have for the 'specialist' judge; even in a matter as specialized as tax, the disadvantage of inexperience is often more than made up by the advantage of a fresh outlook and broad viewpoint. . . . It would be wonderful to give all federal litigants, and all cases, the benefit of an old-fashioned, generalist federal judge. . . . [But if] through such specialized courts a substantial amount of business could be diverted from the regular federal courts, the latter would have a chance of remaining in the future what they have been in the past." Remarks by Justice Antonin Scalia before the Fellows of the American Bar Foundation and the National Conference of Bar Presidents 9–10 (February 15, 1987). The specialist panel of the generalist court, advocated in this chapter, would not produce the problems associated with the specialist court described by Scalia. Scalia proposes a specialized Article III Social Security Court, the decisions of which would be subject to discretionary review in the regional courts of appeals.

[7]Posner, supra note 4, at 148.

[8]The courts of appeals may implement specialist panels by circuit rule. Section 46(a) of the Judicial Code, 28 U.S.C. § 46(a), provides that "[c]ircuit judges shall sit on the court and its panels in such order and at such times as the court directs." Thus, unlike other reforms that must await legislation, the innovations suggested in this chapter can be accomplished through internal restructuring.

Before examining the BAP and its implications for specialist panels in the Ninth Circuit, I wish to emphasize that refusing to implement reforms in light of the ever-increasing demands on the courts of appeals may lead to one or more unfortunate consequences: (1) If the number of appellate judges in a circuit is increased, the number of three-judge decisional units will also increase, potentially causing greater confusion and uncertainty in the law. (2) If the number of appellate judges is not increased, the present cadre may have to delegate more of the decision-making process to its professional staff. (3) Further fragmentation of the circuits may weaken regional perspectives and may add to the Supreme Court's burdens in resolving inter-circuit conflicts.[9] Therefore, any concerns about the prescriptions offered in this chapter and elsewhere in this book should be weighed carefully against these consequences. But considering the crisis facing the courts of appeals, Daniel J. Meador's statement appears fitting: The ideas cry out for testing.[10]

The Bankruptcy Appellate Panel

Bankruptcy law is, in essence, a branch of debt-collection law. It has two principal goals: (1) to provide, under stated conditions, a fresh start for bankrupts and (2) to give creditors a forum to determine their share of the debtor's assets. Bankruptcy law is federal. The Constitution grants Congress the power to establish uniform laws on bankruptcy throughout the United States. The principal source of bankruptcy law today is the Bankruptcy Reform Act of 1978, commonly referred to as the Bankruptcy Code. The portions of that act embodied in the Judicial Code vest jurisdiction over bankruptcy cases and proceedings in the United States district courts. Bankruptcy courts are "units" of the district court; their judges are appointed for a term of years. They do not possess their offices during good behavior or without diminution of salary.

Bankruptcy litigation accounts for an enormous volume of cases,

[9]See Chapter 1; see also Chapter 14 at note 39. For discussion of the consequences of increasing the number of decisional units within a circuit, see Chapters 3, 7, and 8. For an examination of the consequences of delegation, see Chapter 4.

[10]Daniel J. Meador, "An Appellate Court Dilemma and a Solution through Subject Matter Organization," 16 *U. Mich. J. L. Ref.* 471, 485 (1983). In March 1989, an ABA committee issued a report that reached many of the same conclusions contained in this chapter. See ABA Standing Committee, supra note 1.

ranging from the simple and mundane to the complex and novel. Between 1981 and 1985 the mean annual number of bankruptcy petitions filed approximated 362,000, equal to one thousand petitions per day, day in and day out, throughout the year. In 1986 total filings nationwide increased dramatically, by more than 31 percent, to 477,856; in 1987 the number had increased to 561,278; and in 1988 the filings grew to 594,567.[11] There is no reason to believe that the overall number of bankruptcy cases in the court system will decrease appreciably in the foreseeable future.

Of course, mere numbers do not tell the whole story. One large Chapter 11 reorganization consumes greater judicial effort and more resources than the run-of-the-mill Chapter 7 liquidation. Indeed, contested matters and adversary proceedings that require large amounts of judicial resources have remained relatively stable over the past few years. This perhaps accounts for the fact that bankruptcy appellate litigation is not increasing in proportion to the dramatic growth of bankruptcy filings or in relation to other types of cases.

The Ninth Circuit has the largest number of bankruptcy filings, approximately one-fourth of the nation's output. In 1987, a total of 143,956 bankruptcy cases were filed in the Ninth Circuit; in 1988 the number increased to 150,427. Although terminations during these periods increased by approximately 30 percent, more than 200,000 cases were pending in the bankruptcy courts of the circuit at the end of statistical year 1988. These cases represent the core from which appeals may be taken.

Before 1978, the virtually exclusive avenue of initial appellate review of bankruptcy cases was via the district court.[12] Most district court judges, viewing bankruptcy cases as only slightly preferable to the plague, longed for relief.[13] Rescue appeared on the horizon with the passage of the Bankruptcy Reform Act of 1978, which, among other things, created a unique alternative system of appellate review for

---

[11]The statistics are taken from the Annual Reports of the Director of the Administrative Office of the United States Courts. The reporting is done on a July 1–June 30 statistical year.

[12]By consent of the parties, certain cases could be directly appealed to the court of appeals.

[13]Two recent cases evidence district court judges' desire to rid themselves of this burden. In In re Elcona Homes Corp., 810 F.2d 136 (7th Cir. 1987) and In re Minrerex Erdoel, Inc. v. Sina, Inc., 838 F.2d 781 (5th Cir. 1988), federal district judges referred appeals to the United States Magistrate. In both instances the court of appeals held that the district court had acted improperly.

bankruptcy cases—the Bankruptcy Appellate Panel, composed of bankruptcy judges—to hear appeals from bankruptcy judge rulings that would otherwise be heard by district judges. The decision whether to implement the system rested with the judicial council of each of the regional circuits.[14] The Ninth Circuit's council seized the opportunity to relieve the district courts of these cases "while assuring litigants a specialized appellate mechanism for the uniform development of bankruptcy law."[15] In its report to Congress on measures to improve the administration of justice, the Ninth Circuit stated its reasons for adopting the BAP: "(1) to provide a convenient and economical forum for the bankruptcy appellate process; (2) to provide a uniform body of quality decisional law for the Ninth Circuit; (3) to expedite appeals; and (4) to permit argument in an appellate setting."[16] This chapter attempts to determine whether the BAP has achieved these goals.

Analysis of the BAP is complicated because the system spans a number of different, and at times overlapping, periods. The first period commenced on February 1, 1980, with the filing of the first appeal to the BAP. At that time the BAP had been implemented only in the District of Arizona and the Central District of California. On November 30, 1982, the BAP was extended to all districts within the Ninth Circuit. During this period the Judicial Conference Committee on Court Administration as well as the Ninth Circuit Committee on Bankruptcy Appeals Panels recognized the heavy workload of the BAP as its most pressing problem.

The Supreme Court decision in *Northern Pipeline Construction Co. v. Marathon Pipeline Co.*[17] ushered in the second period by declaring unconstitutional certain portions of the 1978 act creating the bankruptcy trial court. This decision, together with its several stays before entry of final judgment, caused considerable confusion regarding the

---

[14]The First Circuit adopted the BAP in 1980, but in Massachusetts v. Dartmouth House Nursing Home, Inc., 30 Bankr. 56 (1st Cir. 1983), a First Circuit BAP decision held the BAP unconstitutional. Although the court of appeals did not concur in the reasoning of that decision, it discontinued the BAP (see Dartmouth House, 726 F.2d 26 (1st Cir. 1984)), and its interest in the process has not revived. The Sixth and the Eighth circuits have recently expressed interest in establishing the BAP. Interview with Jed Weintraub, Clerk of BAP, Pasadena, California.

[15]Judicial Council and Court of Appeals of the Ninth Circuit, *Report to Congress on the Ninth Circuit's Implementation of Section 6 of the Omnibus Judgeship Act of 1978 and Other Measures to Improve the Administration of Justice within the Ninth Circuit* at 34 (June 1982).

[16]Id.

[17]458 U.S. 50 (1982).

BAP's constitutionality and nearly sounded the death knell for the idea of three bankruptcy judges sitting as an appellate court. During most of this period the BAP heard only cases that had been entered by bankruptcy judges before the filing of the *Marathon* judgment. On July 3, 1984, the Ninth Circuit resuscitated the BAP by holding that *Marathon* struck down only the trial court jurisdiction of the bankruptcy judges.[18] A week later, on July 10, Congress passed the Bankruptcy Amendments and Federal Judgeship Act (BAFJA). The new legislation retained the BAP, subject to circuit council and district court implementation, as an alternative method of appellate review of bankruptcy cases.[19] It attempted to avoid constitutional infirmity by making consent of the litigants a prerequisite to BAP review.

The third stage in the history of the BAP began on August 14, 1984, when the Ninth Circuit reinstated BAP review upon litigant consent. Because of the affirmative consent feature, few cases were transferred to the BAP. The fourth stage, which commenced on May 20, 1985, and continues to the date of this writing, operates under an opt-out rule whereby appeals from the bankruptcy court are heard by the BAP unless one of the litigants opts out within the designated period. The bulk of the raw data for the BAP analysis contained in this chapter derives principally from this most recent period.

As noted, BAP review is designed to provide uniform and expedited appellate consideration by specialists independent of the district courts. The judicial council selects the BAP judges from the pool of bankruptcy judges within the circuit. During the period of this study the BAP consisted of six judges who heard appeals in panels of three.[20] The BAP judges do not review decisions from within their own districts. Parties may appeal as of right to the court of appeals a decision of either the BAP or the district court.

The appellate work assigned to the BAP judges supplements their ordinary bankruptcy jurisdiction. In their appellate capacity the BAP judges ride the circuit. In 1986 panels were convened in Los Angeles, San Francisco, Pasadena, Sacramento, San Diego, Phoenix, Seattle, and Spokane. Honolulu was added to the list in 1987, perhaps in an attempt to reduce the opt-out rate from the District of Hawaii. The combined trial and appellate workload, together with the burden of

[18]In re Burley, 738 F.2d 981, 983 (9th Cir. 1984).
[19]This provision of the act was codified at 28 U.S.C. § 158(b). Congress's decision to retain the BAP option can be attributed in part to vigorous lobbying by Judge Browning while the legislation was under consideration. See p. 270.
[20]In March 1988 a seventh judge was appointed to the BAP.

riding the circuit, has caused considerable strain on the BAP judges. Although this heavy workload was recognized even at the early stages of the BAP, little was done until 1988 to mitigate it.[21]

In the BAP's few years of existence, minimally sufficient information has been generated to enable researchers to study its effectiveness. The clerk of the BAP periodically submits special reports to the BAP judges and to the chief judge of the circuit. In the summer of 1982, after *Marathon* had been decided but before the effective date of the Supreme Court's judgment, the Ninth Circuit Judicial Council conducted a survey of the opinions held by judges and lawyers who had appeared before the BAP during May and June 1982. More recently, the Federal Judicial Center (FJC) undertook a rather exhaustive study of the BAP; in connection with that study, the FJC sent questionnaires to bankruptcy lawyers seeking information on the functioning of the panel.[22] Although the FJC did not issue its final report until this study was in its final stages, preliminary reports were made available to me in the course of my work, and I have relied on some of their facts and conclusions.[23]

BAP as an Alternative to District Court Review

Perhaps the most striking feature of the BAP is the opt-out provision, under which either party can insist on district court review. Initially, the BAP was the exclusive avenue of appellate review for most bankruptcy cases. After *Marathon*, Congress required that both parties consent to BAP jurisdiction. As noted earlier, the consent feature was designed to overcome possible constitutional problems. Affirmative consent by both parties proved cumbersome and inefficient, resulted in very few cases being transferred from the district court to the BAP (as few as four cases per month), and lasted only a matter of months.

Under current practice, a party is deemed to consent to BAP juris-

---

[21]In 1988 the Ninth Circuit Judicial Council authorized a reduction of up to 25 percent in the regular bankruptcy caseload of judges participating in the panel.

[22]The FJC mailed approximately fifteen hundred questionnaires to lawyers participating in the first-level bankruptcy appeals filed in the Ninth Circuit during calendar year 1987 and obtained a usable return rate of approximately 60 percent.

[23]The FJC's final report, including the results of the survey, was published in the spring of 1989. See Gordon Bermant and Judy B. Sloan, "Bankruptcy Appellate Panels: The Ninth Circuit's Experience," 21 *Ariz. St. L.J.* 181 (1989).

diction unless it files a written objection with the clerk of the bankruptcy panel within twenty-one days from the date of the filing of the notice of appeal. Since May 1985, the opt-out rate throughout the circuit has remained relatively stable at approximately 30 to 38 percent. Interestingly, the Central District of California, which accounts for the largest number of appeals, had an opt-out rate in 1987 of 23 percent. The opt-out rate of the smaller districts has varied substantially, from zero percent in the District of Oregon in 1987 to 77 percent in the District of Hawaii in 1986.[24]

The reasons for these disparities have not been satisfactorily established, and many bankruptcy judges and lawyers have speculated about the considerations that influence the opt-out rate. One contributing factor may be the cost of traveling to the BAP. That assumption prompted the circuit to add Honolulu as a site. The observation may have been accurate; the opt-out rate in that area dropped substantially.

Attorneys may opt out for vastly differing reasons. Interviews with several bankruptcy practitioners suggest that some lawyers who desire a "rubber stamp" of the bankruptcy judge's decision may prefer to opt out.[25] These lawyers reason that district court judges are likely to defer to the expertise of the bankruptcy judges. Moreover, they may assume that the district court, having perhaps been involved in the appointments process, may not truly be independent of the bankruptcy judge.[26] A comparison of the reversal rate of bankruptcy decisions appealed to the district court and that of cases appealed to the BAP provides some interesting information on this subject. With respect to the outcomes of 330 appeals terminated by the BAP on the merits (the complete inventory for appeals decided between May 20,

---

[24]Anecdotal evidence indicates that magistrates—who, like bankruptcy judges, are Article I judicial officers—have been given extensive responsibility in the District of Oregon. A WESTLAW search provides some support for this proposition: in 1988 the Ninth Circuit Court of Appeals issued six published opinions reviewing judgments entered by magistrates in Oregon, and none from Arizona, a much larger district. One might hypothesize that the Oregon bar is receptive to the idea of treating Article I and Article III judges interchangeably.

[25]Appellants who opt out apparently do not subscribe to the rubber-stamp rationale. Unfortunately, the FJC survey did not identify the status of the litigants who opted out.

[26]Today bankruptcy judges are appointed by the court of appeals. See 28 U.S.C. § 151. Until 1978, however, bankruptcy judges (then known as referees in bankruptcy) were appointed by district judges, and many of the individuals holding office in 1978 continued to serve during the 1980s. See Matter of Koerner, 800 F.2d 1358, 1361–66 (5th Cir. 1986), for the convoluted history. Even today, district judges may have (or be thought to have) a voice in the selection by the court of appeals.

1985, and June 1, 1988), the BAP affirmed the bankruptcy courts in approximately two-thirds of the cases. Unfortunately, record-keeping disparities have created severe obstacles to a systematic comparison of the terminations in the BAP and in the district court. As the FJC study noted, the "outcomes of bankruptcy appeals in the district courts are not uniformly collected." The FJC did, however, undertake a comparison for four districts—Central, Northern, and Southern California, and Oregon—and concluded that the numbers do not suggest a systemic difference between the BAP and district courts in affirmance rates. A preliminary version of the study added the following admonition:

> [W]e emphasize that these comparisons cannot be used to assess definitely whether district judges are more or less likely than the [BAP] to affirm the decision of the bankruptcy court. The reason is that the parties and their lawyers have controlled the forum to which the appeal has been sent, and they have done so for various reasons which may have made the two sets of cases dissimilar in significant ways. Absent a detailed analysis of the substance of the cases in the two sets, or better, results from a randomized experimental assignment of cases to the two fora, we may draw only a tentative and limited conclusion.

In the meantime, lawyer perceptions whether district judges are more or less likely to affirm bankruptcy court decisions remain just that, with no verification. Further research along these lines should be undertaken to reveal the differences in results, if any, between generalist review and specialist review of this highly specialized area.

Another factor that may affect the opt-out rate is the speed with which BAP cases are heard and decided.[27] The FJC questionnaire probed lawyers' perceptions regarding the speed with which appeals move through the two systems. According to the FJC, many lawyers perceive the BAP as slower than the district courts in processing appeals. But only 5 percent of the responses to an open-ended question mentioned this factor as the best reason for opting out. We do not know what proportion of those responding to these questions represented appellants or appellees.

---

[27]It seems paradoxical that some lawyers who assume that the district court will "rubber stamp" a bankruptcy court ruling also believe that the district court takes longer to reach a final disposition than does the BAP. Beyond that, it is not entirely clear who benefits from delay, although perhaps it can be inferred that the party believing he or she has the weaker case would assume the benefits.

In 1987, BAP cases were set for oral argument within eight weeks after completion of briefing. The 1987 Annual Report to BAP judges provides the following additional information:

> The goal [of speedy resolution of appeals] is clearly being met with dispositions being filed in 60 percent of the cases in less than 90 days after submission. Decisions were rendered in 23 percent of the cases between 91 and 180 days, which is down from 36 percent in 1986. In 1986 4 percent of the cases required more than 180 days to reach a disposition and in 1987, 16 percent of the cases fell into this category.
>
> The average time from submission to decision for memorandums and orders was 92 days in 1987 and 83 days in 1986. Published opinions, which usually take longer to complete, averaged 117 days in 1987 as compared to 115 days in 1986. The shortest time for the completion of an opinion was 5 days, the longest, 321 days.

The Annual Report's optimism must be measured against a concern that the BAP faces a major problem of mounting backlog. As long as BAP judges continue to have significant trial court jurisdiction and circuit-riding duties, the backlog will probably increase, assuming no appreciable decrease in the rate of appeals to the BAP.

As it did with statistics regarding district court outcomes, the FJC noted problems in assessing the time required for appeals to move through the district courts. Until such data become available and widely disseminated to the practicing bar, comparison between BAP and the district courts in speed of disposition will remain impressionistic, based on the responding practitioner's experience.

Although we may question whether the BAP has shortened the disposition time for deciding cases, greater certainty exists regarding the effect the BAP has had on the number of appeals to the district and circuit courts. For example, in 1987 the BAP considered 901 appeals. We might assume that the effect was to reduce by that number the appeals that would otherwise have been lodged in the district court, but the validity of that assumption depends on how the BAP affected each petitioner's choice to seek review in the first instance. It is, of course, conceivable that some cases would not have been appealed at all were it not for the BAP. In other words, in addition to diverting the flow of business from the district court to the BAP, the BAP may have encouraged judicial review of bankruptcy rulings. However, a comparison of bankruptcy appeals in 1979, a period that covered the pre-BAP era, with appeals in 1980 and 1981, when the BAP was in full force in selected districts, does not reveal that the BAP had any appreciable effect on the rate of appeal.[28] Furthermore, the FJC concluded from its review of initial bankruptcy appeals that the Ninth Circuit "does not have an anomalous rate of initial bankruptcy appellate activity."

The clerk of the BAP has reported favorably on the effect of the BAP on the frequency of bankruptcy appeals in the Ninth Circuit:

> During 1987, of the 409 bankruptcy cases that opted-out of the BAP to the district courts, 101 cases or 25% were appealed to the Ninth Circuit. At the same time, of the 901 cases remaining with the BAP, 87 cases or 10% were appealed to the Ninth Circuit.[29] Had the BAP's cases gone to the district courts, it is conceivable that the Ninth Circuit Court of Appeals would have received 225 additional bankruptcy appeals ($901 \times 25\% = 225$).[30]

Actually, the volume of bankruptcy appeals would have increased by 140, that is, the difference between the number of appeals actually filed (188) and the number that would have been received if the 25 percent rate had been applied to all cases (328). This increment of 140 cases represents approximately 2.5 percent of the appeals filed in the Ninth Circuit in 1987, a slight reduction in workload for the court of appeals.[31]

Review of BAP Decisions: The Record on Appeal

Any judicial reviewing authority performs two separate but interrelated functions: an error-correcting function, which is of prime signifi-

---

[28]Initially, I had some doubts about the validity of this proposition in view of the FJC's statement that BAP filings increased from 56 in 1980 to 397 in 1981 and 615 in 1982. However, the extension of the BAP to all districts within the Ninth Circuit over the three-year period may account in large part for this increase. In addition, the enactment of the Bankruptcy Code (1978) appears to have caused an increase in appeals from bankruptcy courts throughout the nation during this period.

[29]These 87 appeals from BAP dispositions in 1987 represent a substantial increase from 1986, when the number was only 53. On the other hand, the 101 appeals from district court dispositions in 1987 closely parallel the 85 appeals from district court dispositions in 1986. Overall, it remains clear that the volume of appeals to the court of appeals in bankruptcy matters increased from 1986 to 1987.

Calendar year 1988 witnessed another increase in overall bankruptcy appeals despite a reduction in appeals from the BAP: 141 from the district court and 76 from the BAP.

[30]This proposition assumes that the same rate of appeal would occur for those cases that would otherwise have remained in the BAP.

[31]During calendar year 1988, bankruptcy cases accounted for 3.2 percent of the appeals in the Ninth Circuit.

cance to the litigants, and a law-deciding function, which is of prime concern to the public.[32] From either perspective, one way of evaluating the BAP's performance is to discover how BAP cases have fared on review in the court of appeals, especially in comparison with review of district court bankruptcy cases and with other kinds of cases. Research has supplied some information, although further investigation is warranted.[33] As of December 31, 1988, the Ninth Circuit had decided ninety appeals from BAP decisions.[34] Eight appeals were dismissed on various procedural and technical grounds such as mootness, lack of standing, and lack of jurisdiction. Of the remaining number, forty-nine were affirmed. Of these forty-nine affirmances, twenty-seven were on grounds generally advanced by the BAP opinion and nineteen were by unpublished opinions. In three instances the court disagreed with the reasoning of the BAP.[35]

This leaves thirty-three cases that were reversed or vacated (including five cases that were affirmed in part and reversed in part), for a nonaffirmance rate of 37 percent.[36] Great caution must be exercised, however, in drawing conclusions from that figure because of the wide variations from year to year. In 1987, of twenty BAP cases decided by the court of appeals, only three were reversed; another two were vacated. Yet 1988 witnessed twelve reversals in a group of thirty appellate decisions. This reversal rate might well encourage appeals to the court of appeals; if so, a principal factor supporting the BAP would be undermined.[37]

Comparing the BAP's reversal rate with reversal rates for other kinds of cases reinforces these concerns. In 1987 the Ninth Circuit's reversal rate for private civil appeals (excluding prisoner petitions)

---

[32]See Shirley M. Hufstedler, "New Blocks for Old Pyramids: Reshaping the Judicial System," 44 *S. Cal. L. Rev.* 901 (1971).

[33]Comparative investigation is made more difficult by the fact that the BAP keeps its own records on a calendar-year basis, whereas the Administrative Office uses a July 1– June 30 statistical year for national data.

[34]This figure is based on a LEXIS search augmented by data from the Ninth Circuit's ARMS database. See Chapter 4 for a description of the database.

[35]In re Torrez, 827 F.2d 1299 (9th Cir. 1987); In re Dill, 731 F.2d 629 (9th Cir. 1984); In re Madrid, 725 F.2d 1197 (9th Cir. 1984).

[36]Nonaffirmance is defined in accordance with the criteria delineated by Oakley and Thompson. See Chapter 4, note 49. If dismissals are excluded from the calculation, as is done in the Oakley-Thompson study, the nonaffirmance rate is 40 percent.

[37]The 1988 reversal rate may be purely idiosyncratic. The Ninth Circuit's ARMS database for the six-month period January 1, 1989, through June 30, 1989, reveals a reversal rate of 22 percent for appeals from the BAP.

was 16.5 percent; in 1988 the figure was 19.7 percent.[38] Ninth Circuit reversal rates for all first-level bankruptcy appeals were 18.4 percent and 22.9 percent, respectively. During 1987 the courts of appeals throughout the nation reversed 13.5 percent of all appeals terminated on the merits, 16 percent of private civil appeals (excluding prisoner petitions), and 17.7 percent of all bankruptcy appeals (88/498). The bulk of the 498 bankruptcy reviews emanated from the district courts. Separate statistics indicate that the Ninth Circuit reversal rate for district court bankruptcy decisions was somewhat lower than the reversal rate for BAP rulings during the period January 1, 1986, through December 31, 1988.[39]

Although conclusions drawn from these statistics must be provisional, it does seem that the BAP decisions have not fared as well on review as other types of cases, including district court bankruptcy decisions. Several factors may account for this discrepancy. BAP cases may in fact be more carefully scrutinized because of the constitutional overtones of *Marathon*.[40] Because the court of appeals presents the initial Article III review, it may examine more closely the BAP decisions. On the other hand, the specialized nature of the BAP should militate in favor of some deference to its expertise in bankruptcy law.[41] The factors that should inform the process of review of BAP decisions have not been fully articulated. In any event, the tentative conclusions drawn from the raw numbers should not end the inquiry.[42] More

[38]The data in this paragraph are taken from Table B-5 of the 1987 and 1988 Annual Reports of the Director of the Administrative Office of the United States Courts.

[39]For statistical year 1987, the reversal rate in the other regional courts of appeals of first-level bankruptcy appeals ranged from 3 percent in the Second Circuit to 25 percent in the Eleventh Circuit. The Ninth Circuit's reversal rate is definitely on the high side, but the number of cases in each circuit is small enough that the reversal rates for any one year might well be anomalous.

[40]See In re Burley, 738 F.2d 981 (9th Cir. 1984) ("Article III judges may . . . overturn appellate decisions of a BAP more freely than they may overturn trial decisions of a bankruptcy judge"). The Ninth Circuit reviews BAP decision under a *de novo* standard. Id. at 985–86.

[41]In one instance in which there was a disagreement between the BAP and the United States District Court on a bankruptcy-related issue, the Ninth Circuit sided with the Article III court. See In re Windmill Farms, Inc., 841 F.2d 1467, 1469 (9th Cir. 1988). If the district courts are not encouraged to follow the BAP on bankruptcy law, a major reason for the BAP's existence—establishing a uniform body of case law—will be undermined, and litigants will opt out when it is in their best interest to do so. For further discussion of this phenomenon, see Chapter 8.

[42]I am reminded of Justice Jackson's oft-repeated assertion in commenting on the

significant than the raw reversal/affirmance data is an investigation of the reasons for the reviewing court's disposition.

An examination of all the published opinions through the year 1988 in which the court of appeals reversed the BAP reveals some interesting patterns. The BAP opinions did not display any evidence of bias or a rigidly unacceptable vision of bankruptcy law. Indeed, the decisions that were reversed were nearly equally divided between pro-debtor and pro-creditor, and many of the opinions found in favor of secured creditors[43]—a finding that proved somewhat counterintuitive.[44] Most of the court of appeals decisions reversing the BAP opinions expressly recognized either the novelty of the issues or a split of authority. Approximately a quarter of the decisions involved admittedly close questions of state law, matters over which the BAP has no particular expertise.[45] The ultimate resolution of these issues will, of course, have to await state court resolution.

On the one occasion when the Supreme Court has resolved a controversy between the BAP and the Ninth Circuit, it sided with the BAP. In *In re American Mariner Industries*,[46] the Ninth Circuit reversed the BAP and held that an undersecured creditor that was stayed by the bankruptcy petition from repossessing its collateral was entitled to compensation for delay in enforcing its rights against the collateral. The Ninth Circuit's decision was severely criticized, and the Fifth Circuit, sitting en banc, refused to follow it.[47] The Supreme Court granted certiorari to resolve the conflict and unanimously adopted the position originally taken by the BAP.[48] The Ninth Circuit acknowl-

---

Supreme Court: "We are not final because we are infallible, but we are infallible only because we are final." Brown v. Allen, 344 U.S. 443, 540 (1953) (concurring opinion).

[43]See In re Cimarron Investors, 848 F.2d 974 (9th Cir. 1988); In re Mills, 841 F.2d 902 (9th Cir. 1988); In re Mellor, 734 F.2d 1396 (9th Cir. 1984); In re Matthews, 724 F.2d 798 (9th Cir. 1984); In re Bialac, 712 F.2d 426 (9th Cir. 1983).

[44]In responding to the Federal Judicial Center's open-ended question about the reasons for opting out, several lawyers perceived the BAP as "pro-debtor"; none asserted that the BAP was "pro-creditor."

[45]See In re Windmill Farms, Inc., 841 F.2d 1467, 1468 (9th Cir. 1988) (California landlord/tenant law); In re Mills, 841 F.2d 902, 903 (9th Cir. 1988) (California antideficiency statute); In re Bloom, 839 F.2d 1376 (9th Cir. 1988) (exemptions of retirement plans under California law); In re Probasco, 839 F.2d 1352 (9th Cir. 1988) (rights of a bona fide purchaser under California law); In re Wegner, 839 F.2d 533, 536 (9th Cir. 1988) (Montana contract law).

[46]734 F.2d 426 (9th Cir. 1984).

[47]In re Timbers of Inwood Forest Assocs. Ltd., 808 F.2d 363 (5th Cir. 1987).

[48]United Sav. Ass'n v. Timbers of Inwood Forest Assocs. Ltd., 108 S. Ct. 626 (1988).

edged the overruling of *American Mariner* in reversing a BAP opinion that, in the interim, had relied on *American Mariner* in allowing interest payments to undersecured creditors.[49]

A handful of the court of appeals reversals of BAP decisions in nonbankruptcy areas deserve consideration. On occasion the court has scolded the BAP for opining about constitutional principles and discussing areas of federal law beyond its expertise in bankruptcy.[50] For example, in reversing a BAP decision enjoining a state court from enforcing an order for restitution in a criminal case, the court reminded the BAP of the principles of *Younger v. Harris*,[51] which preclude such injunctive relief except in extraordinary circumstances.[52] In one case in which the BAP attempted to legitimate a state court judgment in favor of a secured creditor, the court of appeals denounced the attempt to legitimate retroactively a void judgment and stated that the BAP opinion should not have any precedential effect.[53] When the BAP dismissed a proceeding under Rule 37 of the Federal Rules of Civil

---

[49]In re Cimarron Investors, 848 F.2d 974 (9th Cir. 1988). The Supreme Court's decision in *Timbers of Inwood*, although not citing the BAP as authority, agreed with the BAP's reasoning that it was the value of the collateral, not the interest in the earning power of the collateral, which was the focus of congressional protection in Sections 361 and 362 of the Bankruptcy Code. Compare *Timbers of Inwood*, 108 S. Ct. at 629–31, with In re American Mariner Industries, 27 Bankr. 1004, 1010 (Bankr. 9th Cir. 1983).

[50]See, e.g., In re Kelly, 841 F.2d 908, 915 (9th Cir. 1988) ("Although the BAP found it unnecessary to address [the constitutional] claims, it nonetheless opined that [debtor's] due process arguments are troublesome. . . . We do not find them so"); In re Lara, 731 F.2d 1455, 1460 (9th Cir. 1984) (holding that the legislative classification at issue easily withstood review under the rational basis test, rejecting BAP's equal protection argument).

[51]401 U.S. 37, 43–49 (1971).

[52]See In re Heincy, 858 F.2d 548 (9th Cir. 1988), reversing 78 Bankr. 246 (Bankr. 9th Cir. 1987). Even though the BAP majority did not mention *Younger* in its opinion, Chief Bankruptcy Judge Volinn (who also authored the BAP's *Mariner* opinion vindicated by the United States Supreme Court) argued in a strong dissent that "the principle of federalism was overriding," citing *Younger*. 78 Bankr. at 251. The BAP majority considered and distinguished a recent federalism case, Kelly v. Robinson, 479 U.S. 36 (1986). The BAP held that "equal consideration should be given to the concept of separation of powers which does not provide the judiciary with the power to legislate." Id. at 249. The argument was that the BAP was not free to consider "our federalism" since Congress had clearly articulated in the Bankruptcy Code its intent that criminal restitution is a dischargeable debt. Id.

[53]In re Mellor, 734 F.2d 1396, 1402 (9th Cir. 1984). The court found that the BAP's attempt to avoid the rule of Kalb v. Feuerstein, 308 U.S. 433, 443 (1949), which held that a postbankruptcy petition state-court judgment affecting estate property is void, was based on a faulty factual and legal premise.

Procedure for failure to respond to discovery requests, the court of appeals reversed, holding that such draconian measures should be reserved for extreme cases and admonishing the BAP to weigh other alternatives.[54]

These cases sound the cautionary note that the BAP may encounter difficulties when considering matters beyond its special competence. This should hardly take anyone by surprise. The BAP is a specialized court that does not have the generalized perspective or broad knowledge of an Article III court. It may occasionally go astray in novel areas of law and in matters beyond its special expertise. Specialist panels within the court of appeals are unlikely to commit these kinds of errors.

The court of appeals, too, must be wary lest it exacerbate the BAP's difficulties. The BAP has received conflicting messages from the court of appeals in the critical area of statutory construction. In one case the court of appeals instructed the BAP not to stray from the plain meaning of the statute;[55] yet in another the BAP was reversed for adhering to a literal construction of a statute.[56] Such conflicting messages serve only to confuse the BAP and to encourage appellate review. Moreover, the court of appeals should defer somewhat to BAP expertise in the bankruptcy law field, lest a principal benefit of the BAP—establishing a uniform body of case law—be undermined.

BAP and the Law-Deciding Function

Litigants ordinarily are concerned with the result in their case, not with the precedential value of the decision. Yet an essential aspect of evaluating the BAP relates to how well the system performs its law-

---

[54]In re Rubin, 769 F.2d 611, 618 (9th Cir. 1985). In this case the debtor filed his disputed claims statement and his answer to the second set of interrogatories fifteen days late and refused to make his offices available for the deposition of his custodian of records until ordered a second time.

[55]In In re Kelly, 841 F.2d 908, 913 n. 4 (9th Cir. 1988), the court said, "Bankruptcy judges have no more power than any others to ignore the plain language of a statute in order to reach a result more in keeping with their notions of equity."

[56]In re Hudson, 859 F.2d 1418, 1420 (9th Cir. 1988). In this case the Ninth Circuit extended the coverage of section 523(a)(9) of the Code, denying a discharge to postpetition judgments, even though the statute's plain meaning denied a discharge only "to the extent that such debt arises from a judgment or consent decree." A dissenting opinion would have affirmed BAP on the basis of the plain meaning of the statute.

deciding function.[57] This assessment requires an examination not only of the soundness of its opinions, but also of its ability to infuse doctrinal stability into the law. Predictability is essential to guide future behavior, to assure evenhanded administration of the law, and to limit litigation strategies such as forum shopping.

Whether BAP decisions provide the desired stability in bankruptcy law cannot yet be determined. A 1987 BAP decision, *In re Windmill Farms, Inc.*,[58] held that BAP decisions are binding on all the bankruptcy courts within the circuit.[59] In contrast, district court opinions bind only the bankruptcy courts within the district. Assuming that *Windmill Farms* is good law on this point, an interesting question arises whether the bankruptcy court must follow the BAP or whether the bankruptcy court is bound by an inconsistent district court opinion within its district. The social and administrative desirability of uniformity throughout the circuit may outweigh the incongruity of subordinating decisions of an Article III court to those of an Article I court, even one that possesses expertise in the area. On the other hand, because district courts are not bound by BAP decisions, inconsistent adjudications will doubtlessly encourage forum shopping through the opt-out procedure. Finally, the circuit may need to create en banc procedures to resolve intra-BAP conflicts.[60]

I must sound a cautionary note. The opt-out rule itself frustrates the goal of a uniform law of bankruptcy in the circuit, a principal reason

[57]An appellate court need not necessarily perform a law-deciding function. In fact, the Evarts Act, which created regional courts of appeals with three judges in each circuit, rejected the law-deciding function for the new tribunals and left it to the Supreme Court. See Chapter 1. Some scholars favoring an appellate division of the district court would not give the division any law-deciding function. The BAP, however, was specifically created "to provide a uniform body of quality decisional law for the Ninth Circuit." This indicates that the Ninth Circuit intended the BAP to furnish precedents as well as to correct error.

[58]70 Bankr. 618 (1987).

[59]The BAP explained: "One of the reasons for establishing the BAP was to provide a uniform and consistent body of bankruptcy law throughout the entire Circuit. In order to achieve this desired uniformity, the decision of the Bankruptcy Appellate Panel must be binding on all of the bankruptcy courts from which review may be sought, i.e., each district in the Ninth Circuit. Any decisions to the contrary . . . are in error." Id. at 622. On appeal to the Ninth Circuit, the court of appeals reversed without addressing the precedential status of BAP decisions. 841 F.2d 1467 (9th Cir. 1988). At least one bankruptcy judge has rejected the BAP's assertion of authority. See In re Junes, 76 Bankr. 795, 797 n. 1 (Bankr. D. Or. 1987).

[60]This step would apparently require congressional action; the law now in force provides that a BAP panel "*shall* consist of three bankruptcy judges." 28 U.S.C. § 158(b)(3) (emphasis added).

for the establishment of the BAP. If district courts are free to take an independent view of bankruptcy issues, the problem is exacerbated. Bankruptcy judges in districts that have differing BAP and district court opinions on a particular point of bankruptcy law will face, in the absence of a court of appeals directive, the dilemma of which rule to follow. Because litigants have the right to choose the reviewing panel, the bankruptcy judge probably would choose the district court rule.[61] Thus, unless the BAP retreats from its own view and adopts the district court's position—a possibility that seems remote in view of the BAP's expertise and the fact that there may be inconsistent district court opinions—the goal of uniformity within the circuit cannot be achieved. Indeed, as Carrington points out in Chapter 8, these differing rules would actually encourage appeals. Moreover, unless the court of appeals gives a strong message to the lower courts reaffirming the BAP's expertise in bankruptcy law, matters will only worsen. A specialist bankruptcy panel of the court of appeals could bring some certainty out of what may otherwise soon become chaos.

That BAP decisions would articulate and develop the law in the specialized area of bankruptcy would be expected from the background of the judges who compose the panel. The available evidence suggests that this development has indeed occurred. Bankruptcy courts, district courts, and regional courts of appeals frequently cite BAP decisions as persuasive authority. In the eight-year period from 1980 to April 1, 1988, 335 BAP decisions were published, 47 from the First Circuit and 288 from the Ninth Circuit.[62] During that period courts of appeals have cited BAP opinions as persuasive authority on numerous occasions.[63] In several cases BAP decisions have been fol-

---

[61]But see In re Kao, 52 Bankr. 452 (Bankr. D. Or. 1985) (following BAP notwithstanding district court's contrary view).

[62]This number appears to represent a significant percentage of all BAP opinions, thus providing practitioners with substantial guidance in the bankruptcy field. In contrast, district court opinions in bankruptcy cases are rarely published, thus offering little guidance to the bench and bar.

[63]Prior to the Ninth Circuit's reversal of the BAP decision in In re Cecchini, 780 F.2d 1440 (9th Cir. 1986), reasoning that the BAP's interpretation of "willful and malicious" was too strict a standard for determining dischargeability of debts, the BAP's strict interpretation was cited by both the Eighth and Tenth circuits as the correct standard. See In re Long, 774 F.2d 875, 880 (8th Cir. 1985); In re Compos, 768 F.2d 1155, 1158 (10th Cir. 1985). The Tenth Circuit, citing cases on both sides of the "willful and malicious" issue, did not mention a Ninth Circuit Court of Appeals opinion that had been issued only two months prior to *Compos*.

The Eighth Circuit Court of Appeals also followed BAP's *Mariner* reasoning that undersecured creditors are not entitled to postpetition interest, even though that posi-

lowed without extended analysis. Given the controversial status of the BAP after *Marathon*, the widespread antipathy to specialized courts, and the short time span of the BAP's existence, this acceptance seems quite remarkable.

BAP in the Balance

Whether the BAP has been a success can perhaps best be measured by the opinion of its consumers, the bankruptcy bar. This bar has been polled on two occasions, by the Ninth Circuit in 1982 and by the Federal Judicial Center in 1987. In significant respects the polls contain similar results. As stated by the FJC in its report:

> When asked to show the strength of their agreement with the state-ment that the BAP should continue, almost 70 percent agreed or agreed strongly. Seven percent disagreed or disagreed strongly,[64] and the re-mainder did not respond to the item.
> When asked whether they would prefer the BAP or the district court to decide their bankruptcy appeal, approximately twice as many preferred the BAP to the district court than vice-versa, with approximately 35 percent expressing no preference.

These studies, as well as my own interviews of bankruptcy practi-tioners, demonstrate that in its short existence the BAP has gained the respect and recognition of the Ninth Circuit bar. A principal reason for its success relates to its expertise and understanding of bankruptcy law, discussed in the preceding section.

We have already examined the BAP's impact on the workload of the district courts and the Ninth Circuit and have concluded that the number of bankruptcy cases filed in the district courts and, with less certainty, in the court of appeals has decreased. But these gains are not cost-free. The increased appellate workload of the BAP reduces the

---

tion had already been rejected by the Ninth Circuit Court of Appeals in *Mariner*. See In re Briggs Transp. Co., 780 F.2d 1339, 1347 (8th Cir. 1985). In *Timbers of Inwood*, the United States Supreme Court cited a BAP decision as authority for determining when a creditor may recover postpetition proceeds of her collateral. 108 S. Ct. at 631 (citing In re Johnson, 62 Bankr. 24, 28–30 (Bankr. 9th Cir. 1986)).

[64]Just why anyone would disagree in view of the opt-out provision is difficult to comprehend. It should be noted that the Ninth Circuit survey occurred at a period when there was no opt out. The favorable responses indicate enthusiastic support of the BAP as an exclusive alternative to district court review.

time the BAP judges otherwise devote to original proceedings. Other bankruptcy judges may be required to work harder to handle these cases. Nevertheless, while recognizing the increased burdens, the non-BAP judges enthusiastically endorse the BAP. To alleviate the increased workload, the Ninth Circuit recently approved an additional judgeship for the BAP, bringing the total to seven judges. Of course, an increase in the number of BAP judges may have the same undesirable consequences in the bankruptcy area as an increase in the number of judges in the courts of appeals.[65]

On balance, then, the BAP can be regarded as a successful experiment. Even opponents of specialist courts do not desire to return to exclusive district court review. Indeed, the major criticism of the present structure relates to the opt-out device. Abolishing the right to opt out would help streamline initial bankruptcy review and eradicate forum shopping by litigants. Perhaps the handful of cases that eventually are appealed to the court of appeals can be reduced even further by providing for discretionary review by the court of appeals.[66]

The most troublesome finding revealed in this study is the high reversal rate of BAP decisions in the court of appeals, in particular the twelve reversals in 1988.[67] The flow of cases to the court of appeals can be expected to increase if this trend continues.[68] Yet even if the reversal rate of BAP decisions proves to be higher than for district court bankruptcy decisions, this would not necessarily negate the utility of the BAP model in bankruptcy or in other areas of the law. The discrepancy may have more to do with the practical scope of review of BAP decisions than with a systemic problem with specialist courts or with the manner in which the BAP decides cases. The comparison may also be

---

[65]This statement assumes that the BAP performs a law-deciding function. See note 57. A court composed of seven judges has more three-panel units. The increase in decisional units increases the greater potential for intra-BAP conflicts and creates a greater need for some type of en banc procedure to eliminate any inconsistencies that do arise.

[66]Several factors militate against discretionary review of BAP decisions. First, many believe (whether or not on constitutional grounds) that a litigant should have one appeal as of right to an Article III court. The right to opt out, however, does ensure one opportunity for access to an Article III court. Second, the procedures that the court of appeals would adopt to implement discretionary review in the bankruptcy area would not save much judge time; or, alternatively, such saving might be gained by vesting too much discretionary power in the professional staff.

[67]As noted earlier, the 1988 rate may be an anomaly.

[68]During 1988 the number of BAP decisions appealed to the Ninth Circuit actually decreased. The effect of the reversal rate, however, would not have been felt until 1989 at the earliest.

skewed by differences in the types of cases that are appealed from the two systems, a factor that should be considered in any future study of the BAP.

Specialized Panels in the Courts of Appeals

The success of the BAP suggests at least two approaches for relieving the beleaguered court system. If the BAP's success stems primarily from the expertise of its judges, the circuits should consider establishing specialist panels in the courts of appeals. On the other hand, if the success of the BAP is due to the fact that its judges are selected from the trial bench and also perform trial functions, Congress may wish to consider creating an appellate division of district judges. In Chapter 5 Jerry Goldman discusses the possibility of establishing an appellate division within the trial court. This chapter examines the desirability of specialist panels within the court of appeals.

Although I cannot be certain of the reason for the success of the BAP, several indicators point to its special expertise as the key. Article III judges—even after appointment to the bench—can certainly acquire this kind of expertise. And experience with the limited use of specialists in other judicial systems justifies consideration of structures that will enable the federal courts of appeals to develop and use the expertise of their judges.

To place this proposal in perspective, it is necessary to distinguish among several alternate ways of organizing intermediate appellate courts by subject matter. These include:

1. Creating specialized courts staffed by specialized judges. The BAP provides an example of this model. So, too, does the now-defunct and largely discredited Commerce Court.
2. Creating specialized courts staffed by generalist judges. The Temporary Emergency Court of Appeals and the Court of Appeals for the Federal Circuit exemplify this model.
3. Granting generalized courts exclusive jurisdiction over cases arising under particular statutes. The Court of Appeals for the District of Columbia, for example, has exclusive jurisdiction over certain administrative appeals.
4. Creating specialist panels within generalized courts. The Fifth Circuit Court of Appeals has a de facto energy panel of five to seven judges.[69]

---

[69]The court created the panel because strict disqualification rules required most of the judges to recuse themselves in oil and gas cases.

> The Arizona Court of Appeals, too, until recently assigned all work-
> ers' compensation cases to a particular division within the court.

Before analyzing the specialist panels, I should briefly note some of
the disadvantages associated with the first three organizational forms.
Specialized courts[70] suffer from charges that they become captives of
the system and do not exercise independent judgment, that the appointments process does not ensure quality representation, that the
dialogue among different courts is either terminated or restricted, and
that an erroneous decision may remain uncorrected indefinitely. A
higher court exercising discretionary review may not have sufficient
familiarity with the specialty to recognize possible errors or to appreciate their significance. Another problem associated with specialized
courts relates to jurisdiction. If jurisdiction is exclusive, forum selection becomes risky business. If jurisdiction is nonexclusive, the dangers of forum shopping emerge.

Whatever the merits of these arguments against specialized courts,[71]
they have little applicability to specialist panels. For example, much of
the concern about specialized courts centers on the appointment process. Specialized bar associations and other interest groups often play a
central role in recommending and reviewing nominees for specialized
positions. The process vests in these groups, who may represent a very
narrow range of interests, the capability of "capturing" a nominee. In
the selection of generalist judges, however, the chances that a particular constituency would capture any nominee are significantly reduced.[72] Even assuming that a nominee is recognized as having strong
views about a particular issue or area of the law, supporters would not
know whether the individual would be placed on a specialized panel at
any time in the immediate future. Any benefit that might accrue to a
special interest group from the capture of a nominee would be so
remote as not to be worth the effort. Overall, it is hard to believe that the
appointment process would be altered in any substantial way simply
because a nominee may be placed on a specialist panel.

Critics also express concern that courts performing only specialized

---

[70]In this context, specialized courts include generalized courts that have as a major
part of their business a specialized subject area.

[71]Distinguished scholars have suggested that the dangers even of specialized courts
have been greatly exaggerated. See, e.g., Symposium, The Federal Courts: The Next 100
Years, 38 *S.C. L. Rev.* 363, 452 (1987) (remarks of Professor Bator).

[72]This is not the place to question the soundness of the appointments process for court
of appeals judges. Whatever may be the problem with the process, few would contend
that the nominees are captured by special interest groups.

tasks do not attract the highest-caliber judges. They fear, too, that lawyers who might otherwise aspire to these positions often find career paths leading them from the judiciary to more lucrative positions in the private sector or to high-level appointments in government. These apprehensions, even if generally well founded, cannot be carried over to specialist panels in the courts of appeals.

Another fear is that specialized courts may become biased in the way they approach their judicial tasks. An oft-cited example is the now-defunct Commerce Court. Rather than regulating and overseeing the industry, it became a partner of the regulated.[73] Specialized courts may lose the generalist perspective and, because they become isolated and fail to engage in dialogue with judges having differing perspectives, may develop tunnel vision. Jargon may take the place of reason; narrow focus may replace broad perspective. Indeed, some believe that the workers' compensation panel of the Arizona Court of Appeals became technocratic and lost sight of its mission to further the goals of the law embodied in the Arizona Constitution. According to this view, the specialist panel's narrow focus accounted for the high reversal rate of its decisions in its waning days. Yet it is noteworthy that Arizona is once again in the forefront in experimenting with specialist panels. It recently created a specialist tax panel in the state court of appeals.[74]

In this respect, too, specialist panels differ from specialized courts. The dialogue between the specialist panel and panels of the other regional courts of appeals should still occur, with all the attendant benefits to the system in correctly solving legal problems through dialogue. Perhaps the generalist panels in other regional courts of appeals would accord some deference to decisions rendered by a specialist panel. This course would save judicial energy that could be devoted to other tasks. But even if this does not occur, there is small risk that the judges on the specialist panel would develop tunnel vision, especially under the carefully limited plan suggested below.

While avoiding the disadvantages of the specialized court, specialist panels in a generalist court retain many of the benefits. One of these is the early identification of the reviewing panel. Knowing who will sit on the panel can have a salutary effect on the way litigation is handled in the lower courts and even on the decision whether to appeal. In the Ninth Circuit, as elsewhere, litigants today sometimes file appeals

[73]The classic account of the demise of the Commerce Court is found in Felix Frankfurter and James M. Landis, *The Business of the Supreme Court* 162–74 (Macmillan Co., 1928).

[74]In reviewing BAP opinions, I found no evidence of bias on bankruptcy issues.

hoping for a favorable panel. But the luck of the draw should not be a factor in the decision to appeal. It encourages a gambler's instinct in litigation and corrodes the justice system.

The Ninth Circuit Court of Appeals considers identification of the panel sufficiently relevant to appellate strategy to have changed its practice from one of not identifying the judges until the day of argument to one that identifies the panel seven days in advance. Yet in some respects the seven-day notice simply reinforces the lottery aspects of the present system. Although the briefs will already have been submitted, counsel will certainly be tempted to shape their oral arguments to fit the perceived views of the particular judges on the panel. To the extent that the judges respond, the decisions may veer even more unpredictably from one approach to another.

The specialist panel system avoids these consequences by giving the notice months or even years in advance. More important, rather than merely affecting appellate argument strategy, it should influence the conduct of the trial as well as the decision whether to appeal, and perhaps even the counseling that underlies the primary activity. In 1960 Karl Llewellyn listed "a known bench" as one of the "steadying factors" fostering a "gain in reckonability" and heightened predictability.[75] Specialist panels would serve that purpose far more effectively than the present system.

Specialist panels would provide another benefit. At the 1988 Ninth Circuit Judicial Conference, Justice Anthony M. Kennedy remarked on his experience regarding the differences in reviewing cases in the court of appeals and in the Supreme Court. He commented that the lawyers appearing before the Supreme Court present the issues more sharply than do their counterparts in the court of appeals. A generalist panel may be led astray by the advocates' failure to crystalize the issues and pinpoint the legal arguments. Panel decisions become the law of the circuit—even those decisions based on poorly briefed and argued cases. On the other hand, a specialist panel may not so easily err.

The benefits that may accrue from the use of specialist panels include greater consistency in the development of law in the area of specialty and increased judicial efficiency. With respect to uniformity of decisions, we are, of course, talking about a matter of degree. As Judge Browning has pointed out, the Supreme Court demonstrates that perfect predictability is not possible even if the same judges sit on

[75]Karl N. Llewellyn, *The Common Law Tradition: Deciding Appeals* 30–35 (Little, Brown, 1960). See also Chapter 8.

all the cases.[76] Yet it can hardly be doubted that reducing the number of judges who hear cases involving a particular subject matter will reduce conflicts in the law. There are other advantages as well. The number of appeals may decrease if the litigants know in advance the identity of the reviewing panel. That in turn may reduce the pressure for increasing the number of judges on the court. Further, specialist panels may develop a strong sense of collegiality because the judges will sit together more frequently.[77]

The disadvantages of boredom and of the development of tunnel vision can be surmounted. No more than a quarter of the judge's caseload should be from the specialty, even if accommodating that limitation requires the creation of other panels to hear the remainder of the cases. Development of tunnel vision has not occurred in the BAP, a judicial body chosen because of its expertise in bankruptcy law. It seems even more unlikely to develop in a randomly selected group of generalist judges. As an additional precaution, however, a judge's participation on a specialist panel could be restricted to no more than five years.

In a limited sense, specialist panels already exist in the Ninth Circuit. Staff attorneys review the briefs in advance of scheduling for oral argument so as to identify and classify the issues in each case. The information is programmed into a computer that sends all cases involving the same issue to the same panel, which thus becomes a limited specialist panel overseeing the decision of related issues. The computer also advises each panel if a similar issue has been submitted to another panel within the preceding six-month period. This process gives the later panel a chance to confer with the earlier one to avoid conflicts. The proposal suggested in this chapter is to some degree an extension of a procedure already in existence.[78]

Assuming the desirability of specialist panels in the large courts of appeals, we must address the types of cases that should be referred to

---

[76]Annual Judicial Conference, Second Judicial Circuit of the United States, 106 F.R.D. 103, 162–63 (1984) (remarks of Judge Browning).

[77]Conversely, one possible danger is that the junior-most member of a specialist panel may unnecessarily defer to the expertise of senior members. This situation may have actually developed in the specialist workers' compensation panel of the Arizona Court of Appeals. It is, however, highly unlikely that any Article III judge would defer to a colleague simply because he or she had more experience.

[78]Note a major difference: the same issue may appear in two different kinds of cases. For example, a particular state-law question may occur in a bankruptcy case as well as in a diversity suit. A specialist panel hearing bankruptcy appeals would not, under the proposal advocated in this chapter, necessarily hear the diversity case presenting the same issue.

the panels and the method for selecting the judges for the panels. Several years ago, Daniel Meador offered a solution to these problems. He proposed dividing the Ninth Circuit Court of Appeals into five divisions of five judges each and organizing the workload of the divisions into discrete subject matters.[79] Once the start-up period had passed, the judges would be regularly rotated to other subject areas on a five-year basis. Meador's solution is drastic medicine for the judiciary. This chapter advocates a more modest proposal, one that could alleviate many of the problems of the large circuits without causing such a radical disruption of the system: creation of a few specialist panels within the court of appeals. Judges would be randomly assigned to panels. Subject matters for these panels could include tax, bankruptcy, Social Security, and labor law. Tax cases, a highly complex specialty, accounted for approximately thirty cases in 1987. As matters now stand, a judge of the Ninth Circuit can expect to hear only a few tax cases within a lifetime. What a waste of judicial talent! Even if particular issues contained in a given tax case do not often recur, experience with the tax code might place all the issues in proper perspective. Such perspective cannot easily be gained under the present system.

It is important that these panels be given other types of cases as well. If they are not, the judges' work may become dull and repetitive.[80] After a few years of experimentation, a study should be undertaken to determine the success of the panels and the desirability of further expansion of specialist panels.

Conclusion

The time is ripe for a modest experiment with specialist panels in the large circuits. The BAP demonstrates the effectiveness of specialists to decide cases in highly specialized areas. Even if the conclusions drawn from the BAP are tentative, other indicators point to the desirability of specialist panels. There is little to lose from the experiment and much to gain—the preservation of the system of regional courts that so many have struggled for so long to save.

[79]See Meador, supra note 10.

[80]Repetitive work appears to have been a problem for the specialist panel that handled all workers' compensation cases in the Arizona Court of Appeals. Those cases constituted a large portion of the business of the special panel. It has been reported that the work became tedious, and this factor contributed significantly to the panel's demise.

PART IV

Adjudication: Alternative Perspectives

7

Struggling against the Tower of Babel

DANIEL J. MEADOR

The extraordinary magnitude of the appellate enterprise with which this book is concerned is underscored by a glance back at the federal appellate scene a century ago. In 1890, on the eve of the creation of the courts of appeals, the United States Supreme Court with nine justices exercised nationwide appellate jurisdiction over seventy-seven federal trial judges. The Court was receiving about eighteen hundred appeals annually. Currently, the United States Court of Appeals for the Ninth Circuit is exercising appellate jurisdiction over eighty-four federal district judges spread from Tucson to Anchorage and from Missoula to Honolulu.[1] The court is receiving more than fifty-six hundred appeals annually. The court today has twenty-eight active judges, plus ten senior judges and the assistance of numerous judges sitting with it temporarily. In other words, compared with the Supreme Court of a century ago, this regional appellate court has more trial judges under its jurisdiction, more than three times as many appeals, and more than four times as many judges. An appellate court of this size would have been unimaginable to American lawyers and judges only two decades ago; it would have been considered unmanageable and to be inevitably a judicial Tower of Babel.[2] Indeed, as recently as 1975 the Hruska

---

[1]The figure in the text substantially understates the number of judicial personnel at the trial level over whom the court exercises appellate jurisdiction, because it does not include federal magistrates, bankruptcy judges, and senior district judges who still sit actively.

[2]This metaphor, as applied to the contemporary appellate scene, appears to have been first employed by Geoffrey C. Hazard in "After the Trial Court—the Realities of Appel-

Commission laid it down that an appellate court could not function effectively with more than nine judges.

Apprehensions about the potential cacophony of judicial pronouncements in an appellate court of some three dozen judges are not unfounded. The system of deciding appeals through frequently rotating three-judge panels means that a court of this size is speaking through hundreds of differently composed decisional units. The risk of differing pronouncements on the same rules of law and of subtle differences of approach to the same legal problems is quite high. That this risk is not altogether imaginary is evidenced by a 1987 survey of Ninth Circuit district judges and lawyers. Fifty-nine percent of the attorneys and 68 percent of the district judges disagreed with the proposition, "There is consistency between [court of appeals] panels considering the same issue."[3]

Three of the chapters in this book address the problem in varying ways: Rosenberg's study of standards of review (Chapter 2), Hellman's study of intracircuit conflict (Chapter 3), and Berch's study of the Bankruptcy Appellate Panel (Chapter 6). These chapters together portray a court conscious of the threat to the uniformity of law, and they reveal an array of efforts to ward it off. The relative success of these efforts is, I submit, the ultimate test of the viability of a large appellate court. Quantitative, administrative, and logistical problems can all be solved. But in the end, if an appellate court cannot speak harmoniously and maintain a coherent body of legal doctrine, it fails of its mission in a regime of law.

These chapters reveal five major developments within the Ninth Circuit aimed at maintaining doctrinal consistency. They can be recapitulated as follows:

Central staff attorneys. Although this court was not the first to employ central staff attorneys, today it has the largest staff of any appellate court in the United States. The staff is well organized and provides a thoroughgoing support system for the judges. The staff's inventory of issues in each appeal filed is an especially important device in enabling cases involving the same issues to be scheduled before the

late Review," in *The Courts, the Public and the Law Explosion* 61, 81 (Harry W. Jones ed., 1965). The original source is, of course, Genesis 11:1–9.

[3]Ninth Circuit Judicial Council, Survey of District Court Judges and Attorneys (July 1987) at 19. Curiously, majorities in both groups *agreed* with the statement, "Ninth Circuit opinions generally adhere to law announced in earlier decisions," although substantial minorities disagreed. Id.

same panel and in providing for priority of decisions among panels having the same issues under consideration. Staff review of opinions immediately after their issuance to check for inconsistencies with other panel decisions can be an important protective device, although this process does not seem to be as fully developed as it could be.

Circulation of opinions to nonpanel judges. Prompt circulation of panel opinions to all other judges of the court with an opportunity afforded them to make suggestions and comments is a useful check. Internal harmony of decision would be served more effectively, however, if opinions could be circulated to all judges of the court in draft form before their issuance. But as Hellman points out, with some seventy-five opinions monthly coming out of the court, it would be impracticable for each judge to read every opinion in draft form.

At one time it was said that an appellate court is too large if its judges cannot read all of their own court's opinions. That seemed to be a useful and commonsense rule of thumb to define the maximum size of an appellate court. But that rule may have been disproven by the Ninth Circuit experience. Whether that is so is one of the ultimate questions on which these studies do not provide a conclusive answer.

Limited en banc. The Ninth Circuit is the only federal appellate court to exercise the option provided by Congress to hold an en banc with fewer than all the judges of the court. Hellman's description of the debates within the court over the appropriate size of a limited en banc and the method of choosing its judges will be helpful to other courts and may save them from reinventing the wheel when they come to considering this device—as any appellate court with more than fifteen judges should do. The limited en banc has worked well in the Ninth Circuit, at least in the sense that no judge has ever requested rehearing by the full court of a limited en banc decision. But the extent to which this device has actually eliminated internal inconsistencies is less clear from the data generated by this study.

Clearly articulated standards of review. The premise here is that standards of appellate review, if precisely defined and clearly communicated, will help ensure uniformity of outcomes at the appellate level, as well as retard the filing of hopeless appeals. Conversely, if appellate judges differ among themselves as to the degree of deference to be accorded particular kinds of trial court rulings, appellate outcomes will differ, and losing litigants will more readily seek review on the chance

197

that a nondeferential approach will be taken by the judges on the panel drawn for the appeal. Rosenberg's study discloses that the court has been aware of the importance of this matter. The court requires counsel to state the applicable standards of review at the outset of the brief, and the court itself has recited these standards of review in some three-quarters of its published opinions. As Rosenberg points out, however, there is room for improvement.

The court's use of the words *de novo* in this context is ambiguous and not especially helpful. As Rosenberg suggests, more meaningful formulations are available. As he also notes, more precise explanations for reversals for abuse of discretion would be helpful, as would recognition by the court of the various degrees of discretion. The court's formulation of standards for reviewing Rule 11 sanctions seems especially good; nonetheless, there is room to wonder about the court's pattern of decisions in Rule 11 cases. The high rate of reversal of the district court's imposition of sanctions, along with the even higher rate of affirmance of a refusal to impose sanctions, suggests a bias against the invocation of Rule 11. Surely this is a counterproductive stance in a jurisdiction beset with an extraordinary number of appeals and in circumstances that create a strong systemic interest in discouraging unfounded, poorly prepared, or harassing litigation. As to the various review standards, what remains to be investigated is the extent to which the court's formulations affect decisions of lawyers to appeal.

Bankruptcy appellate panels. Like the limited en banc, the Bankruptcy Appellate Panel (BAP) was pioneered in the Ninth Circuit. It serves to heighten circuit-wide coherence in bankruptcy law, at least to the extent that BAP decisions are binding on all bankruptcy courts throughout the circuit.[4] Moreover, it fosters uniformity without adding to the burdens of the court of appeals. During 1987 only 10 percent of BAP decisions were taken to the court of appeals, whereas 25 percent of the district court's decisions in bankruptcy cases went to the court of appeals.

The BAP is the only example we have in the federal judiciary of the use of trial judges to sit periodically as an appeals tribunal (not including occasional designations of district judges to sit with a court of appeals), but there is much to be said for that idea. Trial judges bring a special feel for the problems confronted in the conduct of litigation and

[4]As Berch points out, the court of appeals has not yet taken a position on the binding effect of BAP decisions. See p. 182.

can provide ready-at-hand, error-correcting review. In England trial judges are used regularly in criminal appeals, to the apparent satisfaction of all concerned. Inspired by the BAP experience, appellate panels of district judges might be employed to provide a first level of review for at least some district court cases. A proposal of that sort has been put forward by Paul Carrington.[5] Whether district-judge review panels would work well in the overall federal appellate structure can only be determined after some experience. Congress should authorize circuits to experiment with that arrangement without necessarily making a permanent, long-range commitment to it.

But with all these innovative efforts on the part of the Ninth Circuit to maintain doctrinal coherence, the question remains as to the extent to which the court has been successful. That is the ultimate issue addressed in Hellman's study in Chapter 3. His three-step test to determine intracircuit inconsistency and his application of that test to a sample of Ninth Circuit published opinions represent the most thoroughgoing, scholarly attempt that has yet been made to answer this vexing and much-debated question. The research carried out along this line reveals relatively few genuine intracircuit conflicts, as determined by his use of the three-step test. That is a significant finding. It goes far toward rebutting the assumption that such a large appellate court, sitting in randomly assigned three-judge panels, will inevitably generate an uneven body of case law. Although the finding is not that there are no intracircuit inconsistencies, it nevertheless provides important support for the view that large federal circuits are viable.

This conclusion, however, may be surprising to lawyers and trial judges, because they may perceive a conflict between the tone and tenor and thrust of opinions where the Hellman analysis would say there is no genuine inconsistency. Although Hellman is sound in principle in saying that a conflict with dicta should not be considered a conflict of holdings, in the rough-and-tumble of law practice and litigation those who must use the opinions of the court may not see it quite that way. Survey evidence and opinions voiced at the 1988 Judicial Conference reveal a discrepancy in perception between lawyers and district judges on the one hand and the court of appeals judges on the other as to the inconsistency problem. The latter are much less likely than the former to perceive inconsistencies. Hellman's "fifteen-minute rule" is an approach that practitioners will likely

---

[5]Paul D. Carrington, "The Function of the Civil Appeal: A Late-Century View," 38 *S.C. L. Rev.* 411, 433–34 (1987).

appreciate. There is another rough-and-ready test that I have found useful in determining whether two appellate opinions are inconsistent with each other: would the same judges on the same day have handed down both opinions? If the answer is either "no" or "probably not," then for practical purposes we have a decisional disharmony, which might range along a spectrum from a square conflict of holdings to a relatively mild discordance.

The studies bring to light at least two situations in which users of the court's products are likely to perceive inconsistencies and in which indeed there are likely to be inconsistencies. One of these, revealed in the Rosenberg study, concerns decisions reversing district courts for "abuse of discretion." The appellate opinions apparently fail to take into account—or to articulate clearly—the different gradations of discretion, that is, the degree of leeway permitted the trial judge. Rosenberg classifies these from grade A (maximum deference to the trial judge's choice) down to grade D (minimum deference to the trial judge's choice). An appellate decision holding that a trial judge has or has not abused his discretion, without identifying the "grade" of discretion involved, can easily generate confusion as to the consistency of the court's work. This may be no small matter, in that some 20 percent of the court's published opinions involve an issue of trial court discretion.

The other situation is identified in the Hellman study. It involves areas of the law in which there are multiple precedents pointing in different directions. Illustrations are provided by opinions construing and applying concepts such as "extreme hardship" in the immigration laws, defining the weight and credibility of testimony concerning levels of pain in Social Security disability cases, and deciding whether an allegedly infringing work was "substantially similar" to a copyrighted work. The common characteristics of these types of cases, Hellman explains, are that they are numerous and fact-specific, the governing law does not provide clear guidance, and the issues involve deeply held views about competing social values. He suggests that there is probably no way to avoid such inconsistencies where the cases are not being decided by the same group of decision makers.

This last point is the key to the next major innovation that challenges the Ninth Circuit judges. It is what I would describe as an internal appellate court organization based on stabilized panels with subject-matter assignments of cases. Indeed, this innovation may well be a matter of necessity to suppress the Tower of Babel effect as the number of appellate judges continues to grow. This innovation is suggested in the Berch study, drawing from the BAP experience. Its advantages are well explained there. However, the word *specialized* is misleading in this connection, as the main point of such an arrangement is to provide for continuity of decision makers, not to create specialists. "Drastic medicine" is the way Berch refers to a proposal I made several years ago for an internal reorganization of the Ninth Circuit Court of Appeals along these lines.[6] His characterization is probably accurate, if the step is to be taken comprehensively all at once. There is much wisdom in his suggestion that the idea be experimented with modestly for a while, taking a few categories of cases and assigning them to designated panels that would remain intact over a substantial period of time, but whose judges would also sit on other panels dealing with the court's entire docket. This suggestion is quite similar to a proposal developed by the Ninth Circuit's central staff in 1987 and circulated among the judges.[7]

That staff memorandum undertook to translate the concept of subject-matter panels into operational detail. The specific suggestion was that for this purpose two panels of five judges each be established. To panel 1 would be assigned all appeals in admiralty, public lands, and tax cases. To panel 2 would be assigned all appeals in copyright, trademark, securities, and Indian law cases. The judges on these two panels would sit in three-judge groupings, the five on each panel rotating with each other. Each judge would also sit with judges not on these panels for about two-thirds of the time during the year, dealing with all types of cases on the docket. If the judges on these two panels are designated A through J, their sittings to decide the specially designated categories of appeals would be as follows:

[6]For a detailed explanation of this proposal, see Daniel J. Meador, "An Appellate Court Dilemma and a Solution through Subject Matter Organization," 16 *U. Mich. J.L. Reform* 471 (1983).

[7]Memorandum to Chief Judge Browning from Dinah Shelton, Office of Staff Attorneys (Nov. 16, 1987). Experimentation with this concept has also been endorsed in a recent ABA committee report. American Bar Association Standing Committee on Federal Judicial Improvements, "The United States Courts of Appeals: Reexamining Structure and Process after a Century of Growth," 125 F.R.D. 523 (1989). The concept was originally put forward in Paul D. Carrington, "Crowded Dockets and the Courts of Appeals: The Threat to the Function of Review and the National Law," 82 *Harv. L. Rev.* 542 (1969). For other discussions of the concept, see Robert L. Stern, *Appellate Practice in the United States* 26–28 (BNA, 2d ed., 1989); Paul D. Carrington, Daniel J. Meador, and Maurice Rosenberg, *Justice on Appeal* 174–84, 204–7 (West Publishing Co., 1975).

Month	Panel 1	Panel 2
January	ABC	FGH
February	BCD	GHI
March	CDE	HIJ
April	DEA	IJF
May	EAB	JFG
July	ACD	FHI
August	BDE	GIJ
September	ABD	FGI
October	ACE	FHJ
November	BCE	GHJ

Five-judge pools provide a wider range of judicial participation in the decisions of these specially assigned cases than would three-judge groupings. At the same time, the group is small enough to enable it to maintain the kinds of working relationships and collegiality that are difficult, if not impossible, to maintain among twenty-eight judges who sit with each other only infrequently.

If we use the 1986 filings in the case types assigned to these panels, the volume of cases would be as follows:

Panel 1		Panel 2	
Admiralty	32	Copyright	5
Public lands	12	Trademark	7
Tax	30	Securities	31
		Indian law	9
Annual totals	74		52

The staff memorandum suggests that other likely candidates for such panel assignments would be military, bankruptcy, and Social Security cases. The latter two, as well as tax and labor cases, are also suggested by Berch. All of these are good prospects for subject-matter panel assignments, especially in an initial, experimental phase.

During each monthly sitting of the court, the judges assigned to these two panels would spend one to two days on these cases and the remainder of the hearing week on panels with other judges hearing other types of cases. This arrangement would provide the advantage of continuity of decision makers in the designated fields while also involving the judges in a wide variety of adjudicated business, shared with all the other judges on the court.

The crucial point here is continuity of decision makers. That factor more than anything else is likely to ensure a higher degree of uniformity in the doctrines being articulated and to heighten the predictability in appellate adjudication. The latter in turn is important in enabling district judges to make decisions unlikely to be reversed and enabling lawyers to make better-informed and more realistic judgments about the likelihood of success on appeal. Hellman is right in observing that doctrinal uniformity and predictability of decisions are not the same. Nonetheless, the former fosters the latter. Although predictability can never be altogether achieved in our common-law style of adjudication, it has important values, as suggested above, and we should favor an appellate organization that promotes it rather than one that undermines it.

The fields suggested by Berch and by the staff proposal for assignment to these subject-matter panels are generally not of the sort identified by Hellman as those most likely to generate inconsistencies. It is well, however, to begin with relatively noncontroversial types of cases to test the administrative and logistical feasibility of a plan of this sort. If the wrinkles can be ironed out of the process and judges become comfortable working in this type of internal organization in a few subjects, the likelihood of success in other fields will be heightened. After a year or two of experimentation, the court should then consider similar arrangements with appeals under the immigration laws, Social Security laws, and perhaps others—areas in which continuity of decision makers will likely have the greatest payoff and will hold perhaps the ultimate key to uniformity and doctrinal harmony in an unusually large appellate court. Indeed, one could imagine an appellate court twice the size of the present Ninth Circuit functioning without significant inconsistencies in the law if the entire court were organized into stabilized (but gradually rotating) panels on a subject-matter basis. That is the system employed with success in the extraordinarily large German appellate courts, the average size of the intermediate appellate courts there being seventy-two judges, all organized into subject-matter divisions.[8] An attractive feature of this style of appellate organization is that it becomes more feasible as the court grows larger.

A comprehensive subject-matter plan of organization within the Ninth Circuit will still not get at the kinds of problems identified in Rosenberg's study. Standards of review come into play in all fields. Questions of the trial court's discretion can arise in any type of litiga-

---

[8]For a detailed description of the German scheme, see Daniel J. Meador, "Appellate Subject Matter Organization—The German Design from an American Perspective," 5 *Hastings Int'l & Comp. L. Rev.* 27 (1981).

tion. Thus even the most thoroughgoing, carefully designed subject-matter plan of organization will not eliminate actual and apparent inconsistencies in dealing with those sorts of questions. The best hope there lies in adopting the suggestions made by Rosenberg for more precise and unambiguous articulation of the standards being employed.

Despite the potential gains in circuit-wide doctrinal coherence that an internal subject-matter plan might bring, most Ninth Circuit judges show little interest in testing it, even on an experimental basis. For a court that has been at the forefront of judicial innovation in its adoption of the limited en banc, its establishment of bankruptcy appellate panels, and its creative use of staff attorneys, this reluctance seems curious. Two possible explanations come to mind. One may be that these appellate judges genuinely do not perceive any significant problem concerning internal inconsistencies in their decisions, despite the perception to the contrary among many lawyers and district judges. This difference of perception is itself a perplexing matter, one on which these studies do not shed much light. The other explanation may be that these judges are aware of inconsistencies but do not consider them to be troublesome. That attitude, if it really exists, raises some disquieting questions about contemporary notions of law and the role of courts. It is disturbing because a judicial system that produces legal doctrine differing because of the happenstance of the particular judges sitting on the case—and thus treats similarly positioned litigants differently—does not foster the reign of law.

There are at least three possible explanations as to why judges would not be seriously concerned about decisional disharmonies in their court. One is that a growing proportion of today's judges came on the bench at a time when a noticeable degree of incoherence in federal decisional law had already begun to appear; thus, they have never known the system to be otherwise and are less likely to see such discrepancies as abnormalities. Another explanation may lie in the legal realism movement taken to its extremes, as in "Critical Legal Studies." Those enamored with that view have little belief in law as a known and predictable set of conduct-governing principles and rules and therefore do not expect the judiciary to produce a tidy, coherent array of doctrinal decisions. Still another explanation may reside in a vague distrust of judges among judges themselves. Such an attitude leads to the view that it is undesirable for one group of judges to be the exclusive decision makers as to any given type of case; rather, it is better to have random groups of judges deciding the same questions.

This view may rest in part on professional ego and a desire to have an opportunity, at least occasionally, to address any and all types of questions that may be generated in federal litigation.

It is unlikely that any appellate court of the Ninth Circuit's size during the Browning years could have functioned more effectively than this court. But circumstances continue to change. It is highly probable that more judges will be added to the court and that its docket will continue to grow. However successful the court may have been in warding off decisional inconsistencies, the measures taken in the past are unlikely to be adequate as the court gets even larger. With ever-growing numbers of judges deciding an ever-swelling number of cases, through constantly shifting three-judge panels with randomly assigned dockets, subject only to the remote possibility of Supreme Court review, the Tower of Babel may not be avoidable unless the court moves toward a subject-matter style of organization. This is a natural, and perhaps the most promising, next step in the evolution of American appellate structures. No court is in a better position to pioneer experimentally in this development, as it has done so effectively with other procedures, than the United States Court of Appeals for the Ninth Circuit.

8

An Unknown Court:
Appellate Caseload and the
"Reckonability" of the Law of the Circuit

PAUL D. CARRINGTON

We cannot explain the enormous increase in the caseloads of the United States courts of appeals. The possible causes are far too many and too interlocking to allow us to comprehend the data recorded in the annual reports of the Administrative Office of the United States Courts. We do know that the increase has no obvious cause, being out of all proportion to the growth in caseloads of district courts or the Supreme Court or any other judicial institutions in America.[1]

Illustrative of the mystery is the steep increase in the volume of civil appellate litigation to which the United States is a party. This body of data is of special interest because it is subject to fewer influences of changes in the governing substantive law, and because the United States as an appellant is seldom influenced by economic factors, but is constrained to behave more rationally than most other civil litigants.[2]

A generation ago, in the biennium 1957–58, there were 666 appeals a year terminated on the merits in civil cases to which the United States was a party.[3] There had been an annual average of 20,654 such cases

---

[1]For a brief discussion of possible causes, see Paul D. Carrington, "U.S. Courts of Appeals and U.S. District Courts: Relationships in the Future," in Cynthia Harrison and Russell Wheeler, eds., *The Federal Appellate Judiciary in the Twenty-first Century* 69–89 (Federal Judicial Center, 1989).

[2]See generally Paul D. Carrington, "United States Appeals in Civil Cases: A Field and Statistical Study," 11 *Houston L. Rev.* 1101 (1975). Of course, the data discussed in the text also include—and indeed are dominated by—cases in which the United States is the appellee.

[3]There were 646 appeals disposed of after hearing or submission in 1957, and 687 in 1958. (In this and the following paragraphs, data on appeals are taken from Table B-1 of

filed in all districts in the biennium 1956–57.[4] Thus, in cases of this kind the ratio of trial court filings to appeals terminated on the merits a year later was 31 to 1.

Thirty years later, during the 1987–88 biennium, 2,931 appeals in United States civil cases (prisoner litigation excluded) were terminated per year by consolidation or on the merits.[5] In the 1986–87 biennium the average of annual filings of such matters in the district court was 77,450.[6] The ratio of filings to appeals terminated on the merits a year later was thus about 26.5 to 1.

These data reflect a 16 percent increase in the durability of civil cases in which the United States is a party. Put another way, the settlement rate of United States civil cases decreased from 96.8 percent in 1957–58 to 96.2 percent in 1987–88. More concretely, if the settlement rate had remained constant over the thirty-year period, the judges of the late 1980s would have had to consider almost five hundred fewer appeals per year in such cases. Although no conclusion can be justified with such crude data, one can perhaps say that the government's civil cases are harder to settle than they used to be.

One possible reason could be a steady decline over the last thirty years in the predictability of appellate outcomes. This hypothesis assumes that adversaries making divergent estimates of the probable outcomes of appeals are less likely to settle their disputes; this has not been demonstrated to be so, but it seems plausible.[7] The hypothesis also assumes that appellate outcomes in federal courts of appeals are less easy to forecast than they used to be. This, too, has not been demonstrated, but few knowledgeable lawyers would doubt that it is so.

One cause for believing that appellate outcomes are harder to fore-

---

the Annual Reports of the Administrative Office of U.S. Courts for the particular year or years. Data on district court filings are taken from Table C-1 of the reports.)

[4]There were 21,393 such cases filed in all districts in 1956, and 19,914 in 1957.

[5]In 1987 the number was 3,000; in 1988 it was 2,862. Prisoner litigation constituted such a negligible proportion of the caseload in the 1950s that it was not recorded separately.

[6]In 1986 there were 87,398 such cases filed in all United States district courts. This number reflects an extraordinary number of contract actions. In 1987 the number was 67,503.

[7]Although I have found no studies that test the proposition empirically, the assumption is widely held that legal uncertainty discourages settlement and encourages litigation, especially at the appellate level. See, e.g., Richard A. Posner, *Economic Analysis of Law* 511 (Little, Brown, 3d ed. 1986); George L. Priest, "Selective Characteristics of Litigation," 9 *J. Leg. Stud.* 399, 405 (1980).

cast is the number and organization of the judges participating in decisions made by the courts of appeals. Most lawyers would intuitively accept the observation of Karl Llewellyn that important keys to forecasting appellate outcomes are the lawyer's knowledge of the persons who will decide an appeal and the lawyers' expectation of effective participation in the decision. Llewellyn summarized his learning about legal decision making and listed some "steadying factors" that made it possible for American lawyers to "reckon" the ultimate outcome of most cases.[8] Many of those "steadying factors" are eroded by the accommodations made in the Ninth Circuit and elsewhere to the growth in caseload. They include such procedural amenities as oral argument, published opinions, conferences of the judges, and, most prominently, a "known bench."[9]

There seems to be a persistent cleavage between lawyers and judges in their estimates of the importance of these amenities. Judges often discount them in the belief that their own decisions and those of their colleagues are controlled by law and but slightly affected by judicial idiosyncrasy. Lawyers have a professional predisposition to believe otherwise, as Ninth Circuit survey findings confirm.[10] Even if the lawyers are mistaken in their assessment, it is the perception, not the reality, of predictability that influences the appeal rate.

Thus, if Llewellyn was right in his analysis of the sources of *perceived* predictability, the accommodations under discussion make outcomes in the Ninth Circuit less perceptibly predictable. If, moreover, settlement is a function of perceived predictability, the accommodations, by reducing predictability, are decreasing the settlement rate and serving as a cause of the rising caseload.

Central to this analysis is the bar's knowledge of the ways of the appellate court, the phenomenon Llewellyn describes as "the known bench." His point was that words gain much of their meaning from our knowledge of the speaker or writer. Familiar speakers can transmit much meaning with a few words or even a gesture that coming from a stranger would be meaningless. Lawyers and trial judges who know the judges who will decide an appeal are in a fair way to predicting its outcome. Llewellyn, of course, does not suggest that legal texts are not

[8]Karl N. Llewellyn, *The Common Law Tradition: Deciding Appeals* 30–51 (Little, Brown, 1960).

[9]Id. at 34–35.

[10]For example, in a December 1988 survey of lawyer members of the Ninth Circuit Judicial Conference, more than three-quarters of the respondents said that the different philosophies or approaches of different judges are "very important" as a cause of intracircuit conflict.

an important influence on judges striving to obey them; he is saying, rather, that the words are, as Holmes had it, "but the skin of living thoughts" which will be read through the minds of individual judges. Different minds in characterizing facts for legal purposes will produce different results even though using the same legal texts or "living thoughts" to decide cases.

The larger the appellate court, the less well known to the bar and the trial court are its individual members. A larger group sitting together may more than compensate for the decline in personal familiarity by submerging the idiosyncratic impulses of its members. A very large court, while almost faceless, might be relatively predictable in the way that large juries are predictable, for it is then a stable community that is making decisions.

But this is not so when the large court sits in randomly selected panels of three. The individuality of the members of so small a body will materially influence the decision on reasonably close questions of characterization and interpretation. The district judges and the law-yers attempting to predict the outcome of appeals in such a context must take account of the importance of these individualities without knowing the identities of the individuals involved. This adds mea-surably to the difficulty of comprehending the texts. Thus it seems inevitable that the law of the Ninth Circuit will grow ever less clear even though it may be proclaimed in words of the utmost precision by judges who are striving with the greatest self-discipline to adhere to the same body of legal rules.

The difficulty of reckoning is compounded if the text of the law to be interpreted is either too loose or too tight. Loose text may result from a contemporary taste for "balancing tests" that ask the lawyer to esti-mate the relative value to be assigned to multiple factors by a court to be assembled from among a large and unknown group.[11] Too tight a text may result from overdevelopment of case law that occasions multiplication of fine distinctions.

The latter point is elaborated by the most subtle American legal writer of the nineteenth century, Francis Lieber, in emphasizing the wisdom of legal principles

> drawing general outlines in a clear and easily understood language . . . rather than . . . giving minute details, which, in whatever degree we may augment the enumeration of minutiae, have a tendency to contract

---

[11]See generally Richard A. Posner, *The Federal Courts: Crisis and Reform* 245–47 (Har-vard University Press, 1985).

Paul D. Carrington

rather than to extend.* It is far easier to act upon laws . . . when they are brief and clear . . . than when the details embarrass every step and prevent the application of the general principle. . . .[12]

Lieber's footnote adds: "I found on the wall of a humble tailor's shop in Warwickshire, these words in large letters: 'TIGHT WILL TEAR; WIDE WILL WEAR.' That sartorial wisdom made an impression upon me that now . . . recurs to my mind."

At the 1988 Ninth Circuit Judicial Conference, Daniel J. Meador observed that a lawyer or trial judge looking at the court might reasonably conclude that almost anything could happen on appeal. This was, I am sure, not a comment on the professionalism of the judges. It was a reaction to an appellate structure that conceals the identities of those who are in authority to make decisions interpreting a body of law that is at once too loose and too tight. This was likewise, I assume, what was in the mind of one lawyer, who, in response to Meador's assertion, muttered that "Las Vegas is the capital of the Ninth Circuit." Indeed, what the present system dictates is that at the very end of almost every case, there is a final roll of dice to see whose mind will be applied to the subtle tasks of characterizing the facts and applying an often opaque legal text to those facts.

The stakes and odds in this game of chance are elevated by the procedural accommodations described in the chapters by Oakley and Thompson, Goldman, and Berch. These studies chronicle the earnest efforts of Chief Judge Browning and his colleagues to fashion a system of deciding a very large number of appeals with an insufficient number of judges, but without sacrificing important values. At each step, these devices have enhanced the mystery of the process as viewed from below and have thus magnified the uncertainty and indeterminacy of the law. They may, therefore, have impeded settlement of civil disputes and contributed a cause to the rapidly growing caseload.

It would be nice to confirm this observation with published data

---

[12]Francis Lieber, *Legal and Political Hermeneutics* 195 (3d ed., 1880; work originally published 1839). Lieber's point is illustrated by a recent Ninth Circuit decision involving a claim for Social Security disability benefits based on pain. The court acknowledged that "[t]he growth in the number of excess pain cases may be a self-perpetuating phenomenon. As we decide more cases involving pain, the law regarding pain acquires more and finer refinements. . . . The likelihood that an excess pain claimant will win reversal on appeal because the [administrative law judge] applied the wrong law accordingly increases, causing a corresponding increase in the number of excess pain cases appealed. And so on." Fair v. Bowen, 885 F.2d 597, 602 n.3 (9th Cir. 1989).

210

bearing on the appeal rate in the Ninth Circuit. If that court is materially less predictable than other federal courts, the consequences might be expected to show up in the appeal rates. Maybe they do, but maybe they don't.

Thus, the increase in tax and administrative appeals in the Ninth Circuit is out of all proportion to the national data. In the Ninth Circuit, tax appeals per year increased from 32 to 114 over the thirty-year period, an increase of 256 percent, compared to the national increase of 87 percent.[13] With respect to other administrative appeals and enforcement proceedings, the Ninth Circuit docket jumped from 25 to 300, an increase of 1,100 percent, twice the national growth rate.[14]

On the other hand, the data on apparent appeal rates in United States civil litigation not involving prisoners seem to point the other way. For the earlier biennium in the Ninth Circuit, the ratio of United States civil cases filed to appeals terminated on the merits a year later was 27 to 1.[15] In the later biennium the ratio was about 41 to 1.[16] This represents a material increase in the settlement rate and is contrary to the national trend. We would, however, have to know much more than we can know about the mix of cases to evaluate these data with any confidence.

Making the Bankruptcy Law of the Circuit

The challenge of maintaining a coherent law of the circuit takes on special difficulties in the field of bankruptcy. In particular, although in its present form the Bankruptcy Appellate Panel (BAP) is not intended to provide relief for the workload of the court of appeals, it might actually serve to stimulate the nonsettlement of bankruptcy disputes. As Berch reminds us, the BAP was initiated for the convenience of the

---

[13]Compare 1958 Annual Report, Table B-3, with 1988 Annual Report at 152. Nationwide, tax appeals increased from an annual average of 254 in 1957–58 to 474 in 1987–88.

[14]The annual average for all courts of appeals increased from 369 in 1957–58 to 2,409 in 1987–88.

[15]There were 122 appeals in United States civil cases that were disposed of after hearing and submission in 1957 and 106 in 1958, for an annual average of 114. In 1956 and 1957 the average number of such cases commenced in the district courts of the Ninth Circuit was 3,071 (3,371 in 1956 and 2,771 in 1957).

[16]The number of appeals terminated by consolidation or on the merits was 427 in 1987 and 480 in 1987, for an annual average of 453. Filings in the district courts in cases of this kind averaged 18,545 in the 1986–87 biennium (19,758 in 1986 and 17,331 in 1987).

parties, to permit greater procedural amenity in bankruptcy appeals, and also to provide "a uniform body of quality decisional law for the Ninth Circuit."

The BAP seems to be well received by the bar, presumably because it does achieve the stated aims of convenience, economy, expedition, and the procedural amenity of permitting "argument in an appellate setting." It is, however, unlikely that the BAP in its present form provides a uniform body of circuit law. Indeed, it is possible that the BAP is an unsettling force that makes outcomes less predictable and the law less coherent than it would be if the BAP did not exist.

This is so for several reasons. The central problem is suggested by Berch in adverting to the issue of whether a bankruptcy judge should follow the "law of the district" embodied in the decisions of the district court rendered in bankruptcy appeals in which a party "opts out" of the BAP review system, or whether the bankruptcy judge should adhere to decisions of the BAP as it strives to make bankruptcy law for the larger territory, in circumstances in which those bodies of law point in different directions. There is no good answer.[17] If a party would benefit by the application of the law of the district, that party must be expected to opt out of the BAP to secure enforcement of the law of the district by the district court that made it. For this reason, if bankruptcy judges try to give superior weight to the "law of the circuit" as articulated by the BAP, the BAP will be effectively ousted from its jurisdiction by opters-out. On the other hand, if bankruptcy judges adhere to the law of the district as articulated by the district court, the disparities undermine the circuit-wide uniformity of the BAP's law. The same court is assigned the task of applying competing interpretations of the same rule, an awkward task, to say the least.

The central problem thus revealed is that the present system confounds hierarchical control over the decisions of bankruptcy judges by providing two channels or tracks of appellate review. There are, in short, two commanders. The bankruptcy judge and lawyers involved in bankruptcy proceedings cannot know in any given case who is the authority to whom that judge is subject—the district judge or the

---

[17]The problem is not entirely hypothetical. As Berch points out, in at least one instance the BAP and the district court reached opposite conclusions in reviewing decisions of the same bankruptcy judge on the same point of law. See In re Kao, 52 Bankr. 452 (Bankr. D. Or. 1985). More recently, another district court has rejected the reasoning of a BAP opinion, although finding the case distinguishable. See In re Nelson, 91 Bankr. 904, 905 (E.D. Cal. 1988).

BAP? That will be revealed to the judge and lawyers only after the decision is made and the opt-out period is activated.

The problem is not unique in the federal system. A similar difficulty confronts the Tax Court of the United States, which is subject to an "inverted pyramid" of review.[18] That arrangement has long prevented the Tax Court from serving as a "steadying" factor with respect to the tax laws of the United States. The Bankruptcy Appellate Panel is crippled in exactly the same way.

The effect of the two-track appeal system can also be viewed from the perspective of the litigant engaged in a bankruptcy dispute. A disappointed litigant may find the necessary encouragement to take an appeal in reading two available sets of signs rather than one; instead of one uncertainty about appellate outcome, there are two. The lawyer's inability to know to whom an appeal might be taken may, as I have observed above, make it harder for adversaries to agree on the settlement values of claims and thus hardens disputes that might have been settled early if there had been one clearly marked appellate track from the outset.

There may be an impression in some parts that the resulting increase in the number of bankruptcy appeals will sooner rather than later produce enough appellate law that many matters will be settled and appellate caseloads in bankruptcy will decline. In this vein, casual examination of the Annual Reports of the Administrative Office of the United States Courts suggests that new statutes generate for a time more appellate litigation, but that such a period is generally followed by a declining appellate caseload as the statute "matures." But this process of maturation presumes that there is a single hierarchy responsible for making those interpretations, so that when interpretations are made, they can be used to predict the behavior of lower courts that will adhere to them. A two-track appeal system makes it more difficult for lawyers to have confidence in prediction. Accordingly, there seems little prospect that the Bankruptcy Appellate Panel as presently constituted will lead to an accelerated maturity for the bankruptcy law of the Ninth Circuit.

Indeed, it is possible that a resulting increase in the number of

---

[18]Thus, the Tax Court follows its own precedents in cases appealable to circuits that agree with its view or have not passed on the question, but it defers to contrary court of appeals decisions in cases that are appealable to circuits in which its view has been rejected. See, e.g., Indianapolis Power & Light Co. v. Commissioner, 857 F.2d 1162, 1165 & n.5 (7th Cir. 1988).

bankruptcy appeals may be self-magnifying. More frequent testing of the law of the circuit is likely to produce more doctrinal elaboration, but this may serve only to call attention to additional opportunities for conflicting interpretations of judge-made bankruptcy doctrine. As Francis Lieber put it, "tight will tear." The recent history of all the courts of appeals tends to confirm that more appeals tend to beget still more appeals.

For these reasons, to the extent that the circuit council in creating the Bankruptcy Appellate Panel sought uniformity and predictability of outcomes in bankruptcy cases in the circuit, the plan is likely to fail. The council may wish to consider some of Berch's prescriptions in that light. Given that the courts cannot eliminate the opt-out provision that is imposed by statute (and perhaps by the Constitution), the hope for uniformity requires that some other method be found to reconcile the two competing tracks of appeal from bankruptcy decisions.

One possible response to the problem would be to confirm the power of the BAP to establish the law of the circuit. This approach would require that the court of appeals express its intent to be bound by the interpretations of the Bankruptcy Act made by the BAP and affirm its own role as a policeman to see that the district courts in opt-out cases followed the law established by the BAP. This would be a role reversal that would in a sense subordinate the Article III judges to the bankruptcy judges, much as they are subordinated to state court judges in diversity litigation, and is perhaps objectionable on that ground. But it would enable the BAP effectively to perform its role of stabilizing the law of the circuit.

The other possible response would entail close hierarchical control by the court of appeals over the intermediate appeals taken either to district courts or to the BAP to give assurance that those appeals are not materially influenced by the individualities of district judges and members of the BAP. This solution has the disadvantage of increasing the burden on the court of appeals. Close scrutiny of all bankruptcy cases would be required, and the court would need to manifest a readiness to go en banc to secure substantial consistency among its own panels reviewing those decisions. Even then, it is not clear that the effort could succeed.

Whichever course is chosen, the court ought to give very close attention to Berch's suggestion that a special panel of the court of appeals be established to hear bankruptcy cases. If the task of the court of appeals is to ensure a role reversal and adhere to doctrine established by the BAP, it will be a great advantage to develop a bit of expertise on that doctrine, and it would also be rather a misallocation of energy to have every member of the court obliged to master that subject whenever called by the random method to decide a bankruptcy case. On the other hand, if the task is to retain the responsibility for the bankruptcy law of the circuit in the hands of circuit judges, and therefore to give especially close scrutiny to all bankruptcy cases, the special panel even more strongly recommends itself. Only a small group of circuit judges well known to the bench and bar could effectively perform that role.

As both Berch and Meador have pointed out, such a panel should not be thought of as a specialized court. Its members would not be commissioned as specialists; they would not serve full time on bankruptcy matters; and they would not be consigned to bankruptcy for a career. Bankruptcy would merely be a part of their workload for a sufficient period that the bar and the courts would have an opportunity to know the court well enough to predict appellate outcomes in bankruptcy cases. If that end could be achieved, a relative reduction in caseload might accrue.

Screening—and an Alternative Plan

One must admire the earnest effort put forth by the judges of the Ninth Circuit to overcome the various obstacles to coherence. But at yet another point it seems likely that the effort is misdirected. As the Goldman and Oakley-Thompson chapters describe, the court of appeals is investing heavily in systems to track its cases to ensure both that cases receive no greater attention than their merit justifies and that the law of the circuit is abundantly articulated and enforced. The system is so elaborate that I am now moved to wonder whether it can withstand reasonable cost-benefit analysis. In particular, the system sacrifices the procedural amenities that contribute so substantially to the "reckonability" of appellate outcomes in order to invest more judicial time and energy in the task of articulating a corpus of law that is diminishingly useful. It seems to me to be an increasingly unwise misallocation of resources. I urge the judges to spend more time listening to and responding to the bar, and less time expostulating on the law of the circuit.

Not with any thought that I have solved the complex problem facing the court, but merely to suggest a somewhat different line of attack, I set forth an alternative scheme, having the following features.

215

First, regular panel assignments would be stabilized over significant periods of time. Each nonrotating panel would then be assigned to oversee the work of particular district courts or even particular district judges. The purpose of this feature would be to disclose to the lower court and the bar from the earliest stage in the proceeding the identity of the appellate judges likely to decide any appeal that might be taken in the case.

Second, there would be no screening in advance of argument. Argument would be scheduled in every case; if counsel chose not to argue, the event would be held anyway as an open conference of the judges. Such arguments might, on request of counsel, be conducted by telephone, video, or even computer; all would be in some appropriate way recorded. The important attribute of the argument would be dialogue among counsel and appellate judges. The panel hearing the argument would come as a "hot bench," using the occasion to ask questions confirming the judges' own preparation and awareness of the contentions of the parties. Only secondarily, if at all, would it be the aim of argument to ventilate policy considerations underlying the development of the law of the circuit. The purpose of this feature would be to make the individual judges and their work visible to the trial court and to counsel, to eliminate the facelessness of the court of appeals: Goldman's litigants would know that they had been heard.

Third, in about nine cases out of ten, the court would make its decision on the spot, each judge briefly explaining his or her vote, but without an opinion of the court. In this way each panel would in effect do its own screening. Each judge's opinion would be brief, addressed to the parties only, and assume a knowledge of the facts at hand. In abandoning the official opinion of the court, this procedure would resemble that of all common-law courts prior to John Marshall's invention of the present tradition in 1801, and it would also resemble the practice of many appellate courts in other systems. The primary purpose of this feature would be to achieve the massive economies in the use of judge-time, and of staff time, necessary to ensure that time is available for the procedure described in the preceding paragraph.

This feature would secondarily serve to reduce materially the burdens on the lawyers' bookshelves and relax concern about intracircuit conflicts on issues of law so fine that it is uneconomic to eliminate them. The actions of the court taken orally at the argument or conference would be of record, and perhaps scholars and publishers could discern in them predictive indicators worthy of reportage, but that would be no concern of the judges, and the volume of such reportage could not be great. In this way the proposal addresses the difficulty that law too tight keeps tearing.

Fourth, in the tenth case not decided orally from the bench, the judges might take the matter under submission for the purpose of preparing a written opinion of the court. Additional briefing might be invited. The size of the deciding court might be enlarged to five or seven or nine to give additional weight and stability to the opinion. The additional judges might be selected on a subject-matter basis in order to ensure substantial continuity in the membership of the enlarged panels writing the law of the circuit with respect to any particular topic of federal statutory law. Each member of the court of appeals would write many fewer opinions than required by the present system, but those written would indeed establish the law of the circuit, and each would be a genuinely significant contribution to the professional literature in the territory of the circuit.

Fifth, the task of the central staff in such a system would be to prepare bench memoranda. These memoranda would be grounded in part on a close scrutiny of the record on appeal in order to give emphasis to arguments of counsel that are soundly supported by factual considerations, such as a well-based argument that an important finding of fact is "clearly erroneous."[19] The central staff memorandum might also suggest that a case seems ripe for plenary treatment and an opinion of the court; this suggestion would be made on the basis of an independent evaluation of the law and the possible need for a precedential opinion. One starting point for such an evaluation would be a computer-assisted examination of other like cases pending in the district courts of the circuit.

Sixth, because the circuit judges would be writing fewer opinions and would have the central staff bench memoranda, they might be able to function with a lighter "elbow" staff. A reduction in staff is likely to improve the efficiency of most circuit judges' chambers, restore the intimacy to elbow relationships, increase the interdependence of members of the court, and enable Congress to raise judicial salaries without violence to the principle of Gramm-Rudman.

The comprehensive purpose of this contrasting approach to the screening enterprise is to reveal as fully as possible the identities and individualities of the circuit judges to those who are expected to ad-

---

[19]See pp. 131–32.

here to their guidance. It is a plan rooted in Llewellyn's insight that such knowledge is an important basis for those kinds of predictions that are the essence of effective lawyering. And it is a plan that would hope to reduce the self-reinforcing pressure on the caseload which may result from the frustrations of lawyers unable to make those predictions because the Ninth Circuit Court of Appeals is, in an important sense, an unknown court.

PART V

Governance and Administration

Introduction

Fifty years ago, a book about the large circuit (had anyone seen the need for one) would have stopped with the preceding chapter, for judicial administration was still in its infancy. Indeed, the entire notion of "administering" a court or creating structures of governance other than those implicit in the system of appellate review was regarded with great suspicion by some of the nation's most distinguished judges. Today, everyone recognizes that if courts are to serve their constituencies effectively they must take on a variety of nonadjudicative responsibilities. Some of these involve routine managerial tasks common to any enterprise; others implicate the unique characteristics of judicial decision making.

Governance and administration take on even greater importance— and greater complexity—in the large court, and particularly in the large circuit. Matters that might be handled informally or ad hoc in a smaller institution require structure and established processes. A larger number of constituencies, with a greater variety of interests, must be taken into account. Competing demands for coordination and for independence must be reconciled vertically, through the establishment of hierarchies, and horizontally, in delineating the boundaries between central and regional authority.

In this light, it is not surprising that the Ninth Circuit's innovations have been bolder and more pervasive in the realm of governance and administration than in the sphere of adjudication. Existing structures—the circuit council and the circuit conference—have been reorganized; new structures—administrative units and an executive committee of the court of appeals—have been established. The studies in Parts V and VI examine the innovations, place them in perspective, and evaluate their implications for the workability of the large circuit and the continuing vitality of the circuit system.

One caveat is in order at the outset. The Ninth Circuit is not, of course, an autonomous entity. The circuit operates as part of the federal judicial system, and within that system, authority is heavily concentrated at the national level. On most important matters (and some of lesser importance), policy is made by the Judicial Conference of the United States. For example, no federal court in the Ninth Circuit could permit television cameras to record its proceedings as long as the Judicial Conference forbids the practice. Moreover, the Administrative Office of the United States Courts, nominally the ministerial arm of the Judicial Conference, in reality exercises wide power over the internal operations of the federal judiciary. The A.O. makes decisions about budgeting, equipment, and, above all, personnel which severely constrain the freedom of the Ninth Circuit's courts to innovate or even to take measures to meet day-to-day needs. One experienced judge has gone so far as to say, "Until the circuit councils and the court of appeals are given some autonomy in resource allocation, it is probably a benign form of fraud to label courts as carrying policy-making authority." As will be seen, that is something of an overstatement; nevertheless, it serves as a reminder of the context in which the Ninth Circuit's reforms were carried out.

The inquiry begins at the appellate level. In Chapter 9, Thomas W. Church, Jr., examines the administrative and managerial structure of the Ninth Circuit Court of Appeals, with particular attention to the court's efforts to decentralize its administrative machinery. When Congress expanded the court of appeals from thirteen to twenty-three judgeships, it also authorized the court "to constitute itself into administrative units." The legislation itself gave no clues as to what functions the administrative units might serve, but the plan adopted by the court articulated the goal of "achiev[ing] the managerial advantages that would have arisen from smaller circuits if the Ninth Circuit had actually been split."

Creation of administrative units and related innovations raise a number of questions. What purposes are served by dividing a large appellate court into geographically organized subdivisions for administration or management but not adjudication? To what extent has decentralization actually taken place? Above all, can administrative functions be decentralized to any substantial degree while preserving the adjudicative unity that is the justification for maintaining large circuits in the first place? Church addresses these issues; he also considers the other major innovation in the realm of governance, the establishment of an executive committee with wide powers to shape the court's administrative agenda and narrower powers to act on behalf of the court.

Church finds that the administrative units plan has had little real effect on the court's operation or organization, but that, ironically, its lack of impact may well have helped to hold the Ninth Circuit together. At the same time, increased authority has flowed to the executive committee, a development that involves the concentration of power. Church concludes that effective administration in a large appellate court may require centralization, not decentralization.

In Chapter 10, authored by Doris Marie Provine, attention shifts from the court of appeals to the circuit of which it is a part. As Provine points out, governance at the circuit level has traditionally been a low-profile activity. The circuit occupies a middle position between self-reliant districts and a Judicial Conference that speaks for the entire body of the judiciary. Without a system of representation that gives voice to the various constituencies within the circuit, it is difficult to justify much more than a caretaker role at the intermediate level.

Judge Browning, however, had a different vision of the circuit. He saw it as a democratic polity, a community with a responsibility to govern itself and a corresponding right to speak as an entity to the outside world. Turning this vision into reality required reshaping the structures of governance to bring about both democratization and representation. Provine describes the changes and assesses their consequences.

The particular focus of the chapter is on the primary governing body within the circuit, the circuit council. Provine explains how a congressional mandate applicable nationwide, reinforced by concerns about size unique to the Ninth Circuit, provided the opportunity for Browning to implement his vision. The combination of these forces led to a dramatic shift in the locus of power. District judges became partners in governance, and their participation on the council soon pointed the way to further changes. Trimmed down and more representative, the council could take a more active role in managing the affairs of the circuit.

Provine's study traces the radiating effects of these reforms. Drawing on interviews with key participants, she assesses the impact of innovation from the standpoint of the objectives sought: enhancing

the legitimacy of the council, increasing its effectiveness as a deliberative body, and strengthening the position of the circuit as an independent decision maker in a decentralized system. She analyzes the reorganized council's performance of the responsibilities assigned to it by
statute and considers the prospects for the future.

The vision of the circuit as a purposive institution within the federal
judiciary encompasses more than the judges and their staffs. In Chapter 11, Stephen L. Wasby examines the Ninth Circuit's efforts to reach
out to its primary constituency, the bar of the circuit, to communicate
more effectively with it, and to involve it in the process of governance.
He devotes particular attention to the circuit conference, which underwent substantial reorganization during Browning's tenure, and to
lawyer participation in committees—committees of the court of appeals and the circuit council as well as of the conference.

A key question is whether the structures and processes adopted by
the circuit have more than symbolic importance. What difference does
it make that lawyers now participate in governance? Are lawyers
brought in early enough in the decisional process? Wasby also addresses issues more directly related to the management of the large
circuit. Can communication be hindered by structure, or is structure
necessary when a circuit reaches a certain size? To what extent are
there differences—different constituencies—within "the bar" of a
large and diverse circuit?

The implications of the Ninth Circuit's reforms are further explored
in Part VI. In Chapter 12, Judith Resnik addresses the "interdependencies" of the Ninth Circuit and the federal judiciary as a whole. She
points to unanswered questions about the mission and the voice of the
Ninth Circuit: on what issues should "the circuit" speak? Through
what instruments should its voice be heard? Resnik finds that confusion about the definition and mission of the Ninth Circuit reflects a
larger struggle to define the domain of the judiciary and the special
role of Article III courts.

In Chapter 13, A. Leo Levin assesses the Ninth Circuit's experience
in light of the ambitious goal articulated by Judge Browning in 1984:
"to test whether a large circuit, and particularly a large court of appeals, can function effectively." Looking first at the circuit and its
innovations in the realm of governance, Levin finds much to admire,
including a receptivity to experimentation, a commitment to openness, and a pattern of widespread involvement by the people affected.
In the court of appeals, on the other hand, there have been continuing
problems, problems that appear to be the result of size.

These problems, however, do not necessarily call for change. Before adopting any "solution," it is necessary to consider possible negative consequences. Levin examines one alternative that has been proposed to Congress with impressive political support: circuit realignment. He finds that the issues are more complex than is sometimes supposed and that further exploration is warranted. He suggests that any geographical restructuring of the federal judicial system must take into account the potentially competing values of diversity and regionalism; it must also acknowledge the force of circuit loyalty and give appropriate weight to the "federalizing function" of the courts of appeals.

9

Administration of an Appellate Leviathan: Court Management in the Ninth Circuit Court of Appeals

THOMAS W. CHURCH, JR.

Appellate courts are in the business of deciding cases, ideally through procedures that are efficient and expeditious, but more importantly through enunciation of law that is consistent within the circuit and congruent with standards announced by the United States Supreme Court. The mechanisms through which a court maintains doctrinal consistency and case-processing efficiency are a central concern of judicial administration, and the contribution of the Ninth Circuit Court of Appeals to these areas is substantial. Indeed, analysis of these reforms dominates the first two-thirds of this volume. But innovation in decisional practices requires more than the creative implementation of case-processing innovations; *court* management as well as case management is necessary to the effective functioning of any court. It is all the more necessary in an appellate court the size of the Ninth Circuit's.

In this chapter I assess the administrative structures that provided the framework both for the court's innovations and for its performance of the day-to-day tasks of deciding cases and articulating the law. The chapter is premised on the assumption that how a court is managed—how it organizes its governance, administration, and support services—can have an important impact on the efficiency and fairness of its procedures and on the consistency of its decisions. Further, it

This chapter is based on interviews with judges of the Ninth Circuit Court of Appeals; interviews with court staff in the clerk's, staff attorneys', and circuit executive's offices; and review of various files, primarily those of former Chief Judge Browning. For their time and help, I am grateful to the judges and staff who agreed to be interviewed, often more than once. Special thanks to Judge Browning, Mary Schleier, and Cathy Catterson.

assumes that as federal and state appellate courts continue their seem-ingly inexorable increases in size, something may be learned from the administrative experiences of a court that appears to have flourished, although its twenty-eight judges are flung across fifteen cities in nine states and its cases arise out of disputes occurring from northern Montana to the Northern Mariana Islands.

I examine court management in the Ninth Circuit Court of Appeals in terms of both administrative services and governance. In this con-text I discuss the offices providing decisional and clerical support: the Clerk of Court and the central legal staff. I also explore two innova-tions in governance within the court: the establishment of three ad-ministrative chief judge positions and the institution of a powerful executive committee. These elements are viewed through a particular lens, that of the continuum between decentralization and centraliza-tion.

Decentralized administration was first proposed in the court's Ad-ministrative Units Plan of 1980, instituted after the court received a specific invitation (if not the proverbial "offer it could not refuse") from Congress to move toward more decentralization in organization. The evidence suggests that neither Congress nor the judiciary had a very clear idea of what decentralized administration would look like in an appellate court or even of what values it would serve. Yet it is widely believed that one of the distinctive contributions of the Ninth Circuit Court of Appeals lies in its move toward decentralized administration. This chapter tests the accuracy of that perception.

Decentralization and the Administrative Units Plan

Decentralization in the Ninth Circuit is difficult to understand with-out some background concerning the origins of the court's Admin-istrative Units Plan. Ultimately, the press toward decentralization came not from within the court or even the circuit, but from a complex political environment in Washington that resulted in congressional passage of the Omnibus Judgeship Act of 1978. A full discussion of the political maneuverings that brought about the relevant provisions of that act is beyond the scope of this chapter. But a brief review of the highlights sets the stage for the analysis that follows.[1]

[1]For a comprehensive discussion of the political origins of the Omnibus Judgeship Act of 1978, written in the context of a study of the ultimate split of the Fifth Circuit, see Deborah J. Barrow and Thomas G. Walker, *A Court Divided: The Fifth Circuit Court of Appeals and the Politics of Judicial Reform* 171–218 (Yale University Press, 1988). See also

Spurred by unprecedented growth in federal appellate caseloads and frustrated by an increasingly acrimonious and seemingly unresolvable debate concerning proposals to split the Fifth and Ninth circuits, the Judicial Conference of the United States recommended in 1971 that Congress establish a blue-ribbon, independent commission to investigate the boundaries and organization of the existing federal circuits.[2] Although it might appear that the issues to be investigated by this commission would be arcane and politically uninteresting, in fact the topic of "circuit splitting" aroused considerable political passion.

Intense political pressures on Congress over the circuit-splitting controversy were provoked by several factors. Civil rights advocates feared that a "dismembered" Fifth Circuit would result in less favorable treatment of black claimants in the Deep South, where the Fifth Circuit Court of Appeals had been a major force in eliminating governmental race discrimination. Bar associations in both circuits weighed in on different sides of the issue, with worries over how particular geographic configurations of the new circuits would affect the practice of law in their regions. Meanwhile, the judiciary was clamoring for a substantial infusion of new judgeships—an increase that would put the courts of appeals in the Fifth and the Ninth circuits at more than twenty judges each. These pressures, together with uncertainty concerning the doctrinal and administrative implications of the various proposals, led Congress to take the path of least resistance: a Commission on Revision of the Federal Court Appellate System was established by statute in 1972.[3]

The commission was chaired by Senator Roman Hruska of Nebraska, who gave his name to the shorthand appellation of the body: the Hruska Commission. Its stated mission was to study not only "geographic realignment of the circuits, or circuit splitting," but also the "structure and internal procedures of the [United States] courts of appeals."[4] After hearings in the South and the West, the commission

---

Judicial Council and United States Court of Appeals for the Ninth Circuit, "Report to Congress on the Ninth Circuit's Implementation of Section 6 of the Omnibus Judgeship Act of 1978 and Other Measures to Improve the Administration of Justice within the Ninth Circuit," ch. II (June 1982) (hereafter cited as Section 6 Report, 1982).

[2] The recommendation was not universally applauded, even within the judiciary. In congressional hearings one critic, Chief Judge Henry J. Friendly of the Second Circuit, likened the proposal to using a "steamroller to crack a nut," since the only real issue was how to realign the states of the Fifth and Ninth circuits, which hardly needed such a cumbersome and expensive forum to resolve. Barrow and Walker, supra note 1, at 157.

[3] See Barrow and Walker, supra note 1, ch. 6.

[4] Section 6 Report, 1982, supra note 1, at 11–12 (quoting Senate committee report).

concluded in its first report in 1973 that an appellate court of more than fifteen judges "inevitably" gives rise to "[s]erious problems of administration and of internal operation." The commission urged that the Fifth and Ninth should each be divided into two separate circuits. In particular, it recommended a three-three split of the six-state Fifth Circuit and expressed a strong preference for a realignment of the Ninth that would have placed two of California's districts in one circuit and two in another.[5]

Throughout 1974 and 1975 Congress considered various bills aimed at addressing the caseload problems of the federal courts; these bills were inevitably linked to realignment of states in the two largest circuits and thus to the commission's recommendations. Several bills were introduced in early 1974 that embodied the Hruska Commission's division of the Fifth and Ninth circuits. Opposition developed from the same groups that opposed earlier efforts to split the circuits, most notably southern civil rights advocates who opposed splitting the Fifth Circuit and California congressmen (and Governor Ronald Reagan) who opposed splitting their state between two circuits.[6]

Further politicking ensued. Senator Quentin Burdick, another member of the Hruska Commission, introduced a bill that would have reorganized the Fifth and Ninth circuits into "divisions" rather than separate circuits, each with its own judicial council, chief judge, and circuit executive. This hybrid plan was designed to address some of the alleged administrative difficulties of retaining the two large circuits, but presumably would not have brought on the political heat associated with creating new circuits. This notion of a "half-way house" between retaining large courts of appeals and physical division of the circuits was supported by a majority of the active circuit judges in both the Fifth and Ninth circuits; it was to emerge several years later as the basis of the compromise that allowed passage of the Omnibus Judgeship Act of 1978. Because of the controversy engendered by splitting California even into separate divisions, however, the Senate Judiciary Committee reported out a proposal to reorganize only the

[5]Commission on Revision of the Federal Court Appellate System, "The Geographical Boundaries of the Several Judicial Circuits: Recommendations for Change," 62 F.R.D. 223, 227, 232, 235 (1973). The commission's second and last report focused more on administrative issues but retained the same perspective on the optimal size of an appellate court. See Commission on Revision of the Federal Court Appellate System, "Structure and Internal Procedures: Recommendations for Change," 67 F.R.D. 195, 264–66 (1975).

[6]See S. Rep. No. 1227, 94th Cong., 2d Sess. 10–11 (1976); 121 Cong. Rec. 3283, 3284 (1975).

Fifth Circuit. Nevertheless, no action was taken by the Senate prior to adjournment at the end of the session.[7]

In 1977 the Senate Judiciary Committee responded to pleas by Chief Judge Browning and the eighteen senators from the nine states in the Ninth Circuit by reporting out a bill that added ten judges to the court. The committee also noted its expectation that the court "would make an effort to resolve the problem of managing a court of 23 judges."[8] The bill that was ultimately passed by the Senate, somewhat hurriedly, provided for twenty-four new federal appellate judges (ten for the Ninth Circuit), division of the Fifth Circuit into two separate circuits, and a "report back" provision that required the Ninth Circuit to "submit to the Congress recommendations for such rulemaking authority or for such statutory amendments as may be necessary to provide for the effective and expeditious administration and disposition of the business of the court."[9]

A year later the House of Representatives passed a bill that also provided for additional district and circuit court judges, but that specifically omitted any realignment of the states in the Fifth or the Ninth Circuit. Congressman Peter Rodino, chairman of the House Judiciary Committee, wanted no division of the Fifth Circuit to take place without a full airing of the concerns of civil rights groups; yet he wished to provide new judgeships to deal with what was widely perceived as a caseload crisis in the federal courts.

The conference committee established to reconcile the substantial differences between the House and Senate bills was under considerable pressure, particularly with respect to the issue of splitting the Fifth Circuit. As the committee met during the waning days of the 95th Congress, the prospect that the omnibus judgeship bill would die with the Congress became increasingly real. The committee was able to dispose of many of the differences between versions of the legislation rapidly: conferees agreed to add eleven circuit judges to the Fifth Circuit and ten to the Ninth. They also agreed to include the report-back provisions of the Senate version.

The most contentious issue—how to deal with the Fifth Circuit (a

---

[7]No action was taken on the Ninth Circuit because "further study" was deemed necessary to determine how and whether to split California. Section 6 Report, 1982, supra note 1, at 15.

[8]S. Rep. No. 117, 95th Cong., 1st Sess. 36 (1977). For an account of Judge Browning's role in securing the support of the eighteen senators for the immediate addition of ten new judgeships, see Chapter 14.

[9]123 Cong. Rec. 16397, 16405–7 (1977).

division of the Ninth was not in either version of the bill)—was ultimately resolved by language drafted by Attorney General Griffin Bell and a staff of luminaries assigned to the problem.[10] The compromise, embodied in Section 6 of the act, consisted of a single sentence:

> Any court of appeals having more than 15 active judges may constitute itself into administrative units complete with such facilities and staff as may be prescribed by the Administrative Office of the United States Courts, and may perform its en banc function by such number of members of its en banc courts as may be prescribed by rule of the court of appeals.

This provision broke the political deadlock because it finessed the key issue of Fifth Circuit division. In the words of one account of this legislation:

> Bell's proposal was successful because it allowed the warring factions to avoid confrontation on key issues. First, because it applied to all circuits with more than fifteen judges, the provisions could be used by both the Fifth and Ninth circuits. Second, whether the circuits wanted to use administrative units was left up to them. Third, Congress would not be forced to decide the question of geographical boundaries; that, too, was left to the courts. And fourth, the question of en banc procedures was left to circuit discretion. . . . In other words, it was a compromise that allowed both sides to claim victory.[11]

The conference bill was passed as the Omnibus Judgeship Act of 1978. The "administrative units" provision of the act, the basis of the Ninth Circuit's Administrative Units Plan, was a political compromise that enabled Congress to authorize a record number of new judgeships while avoiding the political minefield involved in splitting the Fifth Circuit. Accompanying passage of the act was congressional rhetoric suggesting that Section 6 provided "additional administrative remedies . . . and new tools" that allowed "the circuits to experiment by rule with a whole new problem, . . . the administrative problem of circuits containing more than 15 judges."[12] There is little indication,

---

[10]The staff ultimately assigned to the issue included Patricia Wald, Michael Egan, and Daniel J. Meador. Barrow and Walker, supra note 1, at 215.

[11]Id. at 215–16.

[12]Statement of Rep. (now Judge) Charles E. Wiggins, 124 Cong. Rec. 33510 (1978). Notwithstanding the earlier agreement by the conferees, the final version of the bill omitted, as unnecessary, any requirement that the Ninth Circuit report back on recom-

however, that either the bill's supporters or those representatives of the judiciary who embraced the proposal had thought very much about the benefits or liabilities that might accompany a decentralized circuit court. A court divided administratively into units simply appeared to be a compromise between a unitary (and, allegedly, unmanageable) judicial leviathan and a set of new autonomous circuits of smaller size. More important, this expedient ensured that necessary judicial resources were not denied to the federal courts because of the political heat generated by the Fifth Circuit controversy.

The Section 6 compromise was directed primarily at the problems of the Fifth Circuit, but pressure for division of the Ninth Circuit was never very far from the surface, particularly after the Fifth Circuit was statutorily split into two circuits in 1980, just two years later. Although the congressional authorization to divide a large circuit court into administrative units was (at least formally) permissive rather than mandatory, discussion of how the court should respond to Congress's invitation regarding administrative units (as well as the limited en banc authorization discussed in Chapter 3) began immediately upon passage of the Omnibus Judgeship Act.

The first version of the Administrative Units Plan, prepared by court staff and presented to the court in late 1978, contemplated very limited decentralization. Emphasizing the importance of the court's functioning "as a unified entity for adjudicative purposes" and fostering "collegiality and interpersonal relationships among the judges essential to maintaining a reasonably integrated and consistent law of the circuit," the document proposed creation of three geographically defined administrative units in the court.[13] It suggested that the clerk's office be organized into "teams" based on those units, but it argued that even

---

mendations for statutory change. However, the conference committee report suggested that within one year of the appointment of the last of the new judges, the judicial council of the circuit should report to Congress on the implementation of the act and the need for further legislation. H.R. Rep. No. 95-1643, 95th Cong., 2d Sess. 9 (1978). In 1982, a year after the twenty-third judge "assume[d] full calendar responsibilities," the Ninth Circuit Court of Appeals and the circuit council submitted a detailed report in response to the committee suggestion. See Section 6 Report, 1982, supra note 1, at 2. Although neither Congress nor the conference committee required or requested follow-up reports, the court and council issued "biennial" Section 6 reports in 1984, 1986, and 1989. The 1984 and 1989 reports were used as vehicles to respond to proposals for dividing the circuit. See Chapter 14.

[13]"Implementing Section 6 of the Omnibus Judgeship Bill: Preliminary Outline," at 1 (n.d.). This outline was considered at the same meeting at which the judges began discussing various proposals for the limited en banc court. See Chapter 3.

that degree of organizational decentralization in the staff attorneys' office "would be incompatible with a recently adopted program to secure for the court some of the benefits of staff specialization."[14] Little else in the court's operations would have been changed.

The plan ultimately adopted by the court in May 1980 embodied the essentials of the draft proposal as "Phase I" but promised a far more substantial move toward decentralized administration in "Phase II," to take effect at an unspecified time in the future. Phase I embodied minor alterations in the way the court conducted its business. Administrative centers were established in Seattle, San Francisco, and Los Angeles/Pasadena;[15] geographical boundaries for each unit were delineated;[16] and case management operations in the clerk's office, while remaining physically in San Francisco, were subdivided into three teams that processed cases arising from each of the units. The major administrative support units of the court—the clerk's office, the circuit executive and his staff, the staff attorneys' office, and the library— remained together in San Francisco. This limited step toward decentralization allegedly "simulated" the operation of administrative units "with only a limited physical dispersion of personnel."[17]

In Phase II this simulation would presumably become reality, with a major geographical reallocation of staff in the court's administrative support units from San Francisco to Seattle and southern California. The specific outlines of this redeployment of staff were left vague,[18] but the clear implication was that the court was moving toward a more extensive administrative decentralization that would provide "flexible, decentralized administrative mechanisms, [while permitting] the

[14]Id. at 4–5.

[15]The court was then beginning a heated internal and external debate that was to culminate in the establishment of a southern California base of operations in a new courthouse in Pasadena. Judges' chambers and limited staff were located in both Los Angeles and Pasadena, with an accelerating shift toward Pasadena after the courthouse was completed in 1986.

[16]The original plan placed the districts of Alaska, Eastern and Western Washington, Oregon, Montana, and Idaho in the Northern Unit. Northern California, Eastern California, Nevada (Reno only), Hawaii, and Guam were in the Middle Unit; Arizona, Nevada (Las Vegas), and the Central and Southern districts of California were in the Southern Unit. The court subsequently moved the District of Arizona and the southern part of the District of Nevada to the Middle Unit. See note 23.

[17]Section 6 Report, 1982, supra note 1, at 57.

[18]"Based on the experience gained in Phase I, the court will decide the degree of physical decentralization, beyond that of Phase I, to be undertaken in Phase II." Administrative Units Plan at 3. The Administrative Units Plan is reprinted in Section 6 Report, 1982, supra note 1, as Appendix P.

Court of Appeals to discharge its judicial responsibilities effectively on a uniform, circuit-wide basis." The goal was "to realize the managerial advantages of smaller circuits without actually splitting the Circuit."[19]

The postponement of any substantial decentralization of its support services allowed the court to adopt the plan unanimously, while putting off the hard policy decisions involved in actual implementation of the decentralization promised in Phase II. Nevertheless, it is puzzling that the court chose to commit itself to such extensive physical decentralization even at some indefinite time to come. Decentralization was viewed with misgivings by several judges on the court from the very outset.[20] These misgivings multiplied as the court came to debate—in the context of a 1988 long-range planning document—the establishment of a "full service" clerk's office in Pasadena.

The explanation for the court's adoption of a plan that promised more administrative decentralization than many of the judges wanted may lie in a concern that the plan appear responsive to Congress's invitation regarding administrative units. A scheme that seemed to accomplish only cosmetic decentralization might provide a weapon for those in Congress who wished to split the circuit. The two-phase plan had the advantage of appearing to establish meaningful administrative units while allowing for a more or less indefinite postponement of any real decentralization of staff operations. Not incidentally, it also provided a rationale to justify requests for substantial additional staff resources.[21]

The decentralization contemplated in Phase II of the Administrative

[19]Section 6 Report, 1982, supra note 1, at 56, 57.

[20]In fact, I was able to find very little evidence of court support for anything more than cosmetic administrative decentralization, while there is ample evidence of opposition to the physical dispersal of court staff, particularly the central staff attorneys. This opposition was voiced whenever proposals were made to move staff away from the San Francisco headquarters. As early as 1981, the year after the Administrative Units Plan was adopted, one judge suggested that the court reconsider decentralization of the staff. In his view, decentralization was neither cost-efficient nor productive. The judge also argued that decentralization was not consistent with the court's practice of having all judges sit throughout the circuit as part of a common pool, a system he favored. A year later another judge quoted these views and expressed agreement with them.

[21]From its inception, the plan was used by the court in that way. The original plan contained requests for a total of twenty-five new positions "required to implement Phase I of the administrative units' [sic] program." Section 6 Report, 1982, supra note 1, at P-10. Although not all these positions were subsequently approved, the plan provided a continuing justification for additional staff positions for the court beyond the numbers indicated by the Administrative Office's staffing formulas. The plan was also used as a partial justification for construction of the new courthouse in Pasadena.

Units Plan held implications both for the operation of the court's critical administrative and legal support services and for governance of the court. Many of the responses of the court to increased size could have taken place in the absence of a move toward decentralization, but the rhetoric, at least, of the Administrative Units Plan affected nearly every change in court management that occurred in the decade that followed the plan's approval.

Court Support Services:
Clerk of Court and Staff Attorneys

After adoption of the Administrative Units Plan and the limited changes undertaken pursuant to Phase I, little movement took place toward Phase II. There was much discussion of decentralization in the court's biennial "Section 6" reports to Congress and in subsequent planning for the new courthouse in Pasadena. Yet one of the more striking facts about the operation of the clerk's office, staff attorneys' office, and circuit executive's office is the abundance of discussion of decentralization—both within the court and especially in communications with the outside world—and its virtual absence in operation.[22]

At this writing, the clerk's office has skeletal staff in Seattle (one deputy) and Pasadena (six deputies), but all the major functions of the office are performed centrally in San Francisco. The entire central legal staff of the court is based in San Francisco. And although the court approved in 1988 a long-range planning document that recommended further decentralization in both of these offices, implementation of the proposal—after nearly a decade of "simulation"—was postponed indefinitely.

The continued centralization of court staff and administrative opera-

---

[22]I do not discuss the circuit executive's office at length because of a recent change in the responsibilities of the circuit executive vis-à-vis the court of appeals. Most "line" management responsibility of the circuit executive over the staff and activities of the court of appeals has been transferred to the Clerk of Court, who has assumed the added title of "court of appeals executive." The court executive concept implies that the circuit executive will have the same "staff" relationship to the court of appeals that he or she has with the district and bankruptcy courts of the circuit. It should be noted, however, that the effect of the Administrative Units Plan on the circuit executive's office has been similar to that on the clerk's and staff attorneys' offices. The plan called for assignment of an assistant circuit executive to each administrative unit, but that assignment never took place. Instead, assistant circuit executives were allocated to specialized circuit-wide functions such as education and training or personnel.

tions in San Francisco not only has been maintained in the face of an Administrative Units Plan that promised substantial geographical dispersion of support services; it also runs counter to a long-term change in the center of gravity of the court's business and the home bases of its judges. This southward shift was most dramatically manifested by the completion in 1986, after more than a decade of internal debate, of an impressive and spacious new courthouse in Pasadena. This courthouse was designed and justified, at least in part, as the headquarters of the southern unit of the court, and space was allocated for the staff necessary to carry out the requisite administrative functions. At the end of 1988 it housed a clerk's office staff of six and served as home chambers for four active judges. Four other active judges retained chambers in downtown Los Angeles.[23]

What are we to make of this rhetoric of decentralization in the face of the reality of centralized staff support in the Ninth Circuit's clerk's and staff attorneys' offices? My assessment, after spending a good deal of time talking with judges and staff in the court and thinking about its operation, is that the failure of the court to accomplish meaningful decentralization in its support services may be the good news rather than the bad news concerning court management in the Ninth Circuit. In my view, whatever administrative lessons the Ninth Circuit experience holds for appellate courts elsewhere, they do *not* lie in the realm of decentralization. Rather, I believe, the essential elements of administrative support that have allowed the court to function effectively over the past decade tend more toward centralization than its opposite. This pattern can be seen in the work of both the staff attorneys' and the clerk's offices.

The Ninth Circuit staff attorneys perform a number of functions that support the adjudicative activities of the court. These activities were put forward by several judges with whom I spoke as a major factor in allowing the Ninth Circuit to function as a single court as the number of cases and judges increased. When cases are filed, they are assessed by attorneys in the prebriefing conference unit to determine if they would benefit from early intervention for purposes of issue clarifica-

---

[23]The southward shift was somewhat mitigated by the court's decision to move the District of Arizona and the southern part of the District of Nevada from the Southern to the Middle Unit. The change was made in part because the caseload in the Southern Unit was so high, but also because lawyers in Arizona preferred to travel to San Francisco rather than Los Angeles for oral argument. See Conference on Empirical Research in Judicial Administration, 21 *Ariz. St. L.J.* 33, 97, 98–99 (1989) (remarks of Judge Bilby and Judge Schroeder).

tion, agreement on brief and record length, or (sometimes) discussion of settlement. Substantive motions in all cases are first directed to staff attorneys in the motions section.[24] When cases are ready for submission to a panel of judges, they are evaluated by another unit responsible for "inventory," a process that involves assessing the complexity (or "weight") of the cases, selecting "light" cases for a special track that avoids oral argument, and preparing memoranda for judicial screening panels in those cases chosen for the special track. The legal issues raised in the cases are coded and added to a computerized database so that cases involving similar issues can be assigned to the same panel, and so that judges can be informed of relevant cases pending before other panels.[25]

In carrying out these functions, a primary goal of the staff attorneys' office has been to bring about unity and consistency in the treatment of the court's expanding caseload. The case-inventory process, for example, is meant to ensure that every case before the court, no matter where it originates or before whom it will be argued, can be reliably compared to every other case in terms of complexity and the legal issues raised. Consistency of output has obviously been promoted by the centralized structure of the case-inventory unit, in which norms and standards are taught to new attorneys and the staff receives extensive supervision. The same can be said for the motions unit of the office: a major concern is the maintenance of uniformity in motions practice across the circuit, an effort promoted by the socialization, supervision, and specialization made possible by a staff that works collegially in one central location.

The clerk's office in a court of appeals performs functions that are essential both to the bar and to the judges. Some of these activities are linked directly to the court's adjudicative role; others are of a more generalized administrative nature. Examples of the former include accepting and keeping track of a vast flow of case-related filings, monitoring presubmission progress of appeals, assignment and scheduling of the three-judge panels, and distribution of briefs and other submissions to the judges prior to oral argument. Nonadjudicative support consists of such tasks as the procurement and mainte-

[24]Under a procedure adopted by the court in 1988, most routine procedural motions (such as requests for extensions of time to file briefs or for somewhat longer briefs than those allowed in the court's rules) are handled by specially trained personnel in the clerk's office.

[25]For further discussion of screening and the staff attorney role, see Chapters 4 and 5. For more about issue identification and the use the court makes of it, see Chapter 3.

nance of space, equipment, and supplies, and operation of the court's personnel system.

The clerk's office has taken limited steps toward decentralization of its nonadjudicative activities. For example, the satellite clerk's office in Pasadena has gradually assumed responsibilities for the space needs of the southern unit, particularly (but not exclusively) in the new courthouse in Pasadena. Building maintenance and procurement of equipment and supplies are similarly handled by staff situated in the southern unit.

In contrast to this limited delegation of general administrative functions, little progress has been made toward the Phase II goal of decentralizing the adjudicative support services in the clerk's office. The computers of the court's management information system, New-AIMS, are located and programmed in San Francisco, as are the computers of the court's sophisticated electronic mail system. Case docketing and scheduling is done centrally. Physical case files for all cases in the circuit are maintained in San Francisco. Routine procedural motions (most involving requests for extensions of time or waivers of limitations on brief length) are similarly handled by clerk's staff in San Francisco. With the exception of the original case opening, which can be executed on computer terminals by staff in Pasadena, all filing of documents must be done in San Francisco.

The court's 1988 long-range planning report contained recommendations to establish a full-service clerk's office in the Pasadena courthouse, with southern unit files to be physically located in Pasadena and with case-management functions to be performed there by the southern unit team currently located in San Francisco. It also contemplated a more limited dispersal of lawyers from the court's central staff. This proposal precipitated one of the first court-wide discussions of decentralization since the Administrative Units Plan was adopted in 1980. The strongest supporters of decentralizing the clerk's office tended to be judges in the southern unit, several of whom felt that the concentration of support services in San Francisco neither reflected the growing southern concentration of the court's judges and business nor provided an appropriate level of administrative support for southern unit judges. Managers in both the clerk's office and the office of staff attorneys argued against these proposals, as did several judges on the court. As a result, in an action reminiscent of the court's first approval of the Administrative Units Plan, the court adopted the plan "in principle" but postponed its implementation indefinitely.

Staff memoranda opposing decentralization pointed to logistical barriers to decentralizing adjudicative support functions. Many of these barriers resulted from the need of staff attorneys to have access to files and records in order to inventory cases and prepare memoranda on pending motions and in screening track cases—functions that nearly all on the court concede should remain centralized in San Francisco. Through expanded use of the court's electronic mail and docketing systems and increased use of express mail services, these difficulties are probably surmountable. Yet it is not clear what objective such a shift would serve. Indeed, several judges and staff members suggested to me that lack of a clear rationale for further decentralization of the clerk's office led several judges on the court to oppose any additional steps to implement Phase II of the Administrative Units Plan.

More significant than the tentative moves toward dispersion of functions in the clerk's office are changes that appear to go in precisely the opposite direction. The most obvious manifestation of increased centralization in the clerk's office has come in the two computer systems that have changed the face of the court: the NewAIMS case-docketing and record-keeping system and the court-wide electronic mail system. NewAIMS terminals in Pasadena, San Francisco, and Seattle allow staff to inquire as to the current status of any case filed in the court. "Electronic dockets" hold all information that was contained on the old paper dockets maintained previously in San Francisco. With added terminals and telecommunications lines, judges, court staff, and attorneys anywhere in the circuit will be able to "look" at a case docket containing information on case status and progress which was previously available only to clerks in San Francisco. I spoke to no one on the court who did not agree that NewAIMS (at least when fully "debugged" and operational) has made the substantial growth of caseload in the court more manageable.

NewAIMS is a unitary, centralized computer system with hardware and staff support located in San Francisco. Although the existence of the system permits some decentralization, in that "satellite" offices can perform many of the clerical and record-keeping functions previously done entirely in San Francisco, the fact remains that the increasingly critical component of data-processing operations for the court—and the equipment, staff, support services, and policy-making authority that go with it—is located in the San Francisco headquarters. It is hard to imagine how a system could provide the same level of consistent, timely, court-wide information in a decentralized configuration. The same can be said, albeit to a somewhat lesser degree, with regard to the court's electronic mail system.

I suspect that some of the disjuncture between the rhetoric and the reality of decentralization in the Ninth Circuit has come about because of an implicit confusion, present from the start in the administrative units provisions of Section 6 of the Omnibus Judgeship Act, over the function of a court of appeals. In the limited congressional debates over this provision, and even more prominently in the more recent discussions within the Ninth Circuit concerning the staffing and functions to be performed by the clerk's office in Pasadena, decentralization was put forward as a way of improving the "services" of the court to the bar and the public across the circuit. Realistically, however, the size of the Ninth Circuit precludes "home town" service to any but those attorneys and litigants who happen to be located within easy access of one of the court's few existing places of business. Thus, under any conceivable degree of decentralization, the vast majority of the court's dealings with its "clients" will continue to be by mail and over the telephone.[26]

The problem with a focus on service, however, goes deeper. Appellate courts are not primarily—or even peripherally—service-oriented institutions. It may be that governmental agencies that provide client services are best organized in a decentralized fashion, so that offices delivering services, whether welfare benefits or crop subsidies, are in close proximity to recipients. Trial courts, as the judiciary's first-line dispute-resolution agencies, arguably fall into this category. But whether the primary function of the circuit courts is viewed as one of correcting errors or as one of enunciating law, it is clear that the endeavor requires the application of consistent legal standards. Federal circuit courts are not in the business of encouraging "a hundred [doctrinal] flowers" to bloom. Quite the contrary. I would thus argue that those aspects of an appellate court's administrative structure which support its *adjudicative* functions are best organized to encourage the maintenance of the unifying, centralizing function of the court. The experience in the Ninth Circuit in the 1980s suggests that, in the absence of a compelling rationale supporting dispersal of personnel, this function is most effectively served by strong, centralized support services.[27]

---

[26]My interviews with clerk's office staff in San Francisco indicate that most attorneys in the city of San Francisco, despite easy access to the court, conduct almost all their business with the court by telephone, mail, and courier.

[27]At the same time, *nonadjudicative* administrative support, such as space acquisition and maintenance, personnel, and procurement, may well be more appropriately decentralized. As indicated previously, the clerk's office has already taken limited steps in this direction in Pasadena. I suspect that the interest among some judges of the court for decentralization in the clerk's and staff attorneys' offices may be grounded in part on

Governance

Governance of the federal courts of appeals is vested in the judges themselves, led by the "first among equals," the chief judge.[28] Although it is true that administrative decisions affecting the courts of appeals are often made elsewhere—in the Administrative Office of the United States Courts, the Judicial Conference of the United States, and the circuit judicial councils—on most matters of internal policy the decisions of the assembled judges of the court hold sway.

Two aspects of governance in the Ninth Circuit Court of Appeals are worthy of discussion in a chapter focusing on the special problems of administration in large appellate courts. Both are related to the tension between centralization and decentralization embodied in the Administrative Units Plan. The first is the designation of an administrative chief judge for each of the administrative units. The second, and to date much more significant, is the establishment and expansion in the role of the executive committee of the court of appeals.

Adoption of the Administrative Units Plan was accompanied from the beginning by a decision of the court to establish a more decentralized governance structure. While the chief judge retained his important administrative responsibilities for the court and circuit as a whole, the senior active circuit judge in each geographical unit was given a supervisory role and various duties in the unit.

From the very first, the court experienced difficulty in specifying the duties, or even the title, of the judges who supervised each unit.[29]

---

frustration over perceived inequities in the level of these nonadjudicative support services available to judges in the different administrative units.

[28]It is difficult to speak of governance in the Ninth Circuit Court of Appeals without an extended treatment of the stewardship of Chief Judge James R. Browning. Almost every interview I conducted began and ended with a discussion of the distinctive contribution of "the Chief" to the administration of the court over the years of his tenure. He was perhaps the ultimate centralizing force in administration of the court, so clear was his influence in nearly every aspect of its operation. Yet a Great Man theory of judicial administration teaches few general lessons for other courts. I trust that my focus in the following pages on general structure and process is not read as deprecating the enormous contribution that Browning made to all the issues involved. A more extended account of the role of the chief judge is found in Chapter 14.

[29]Various alternative titles were debated for what they allegedly implied concerning the functions and responsibilities of the position. Suggestions included "coordinating judge," "head judge," "head," "administrative judge," and "lead judge." One judge advised Browning that " 'Coordinating Judge' is unsatisfactory. 'Head Judge' is no better because it sounds like something out of the Navy." He added, however, "By all means, don't put this to a vote of 23 active and numerous senior judges because we would never decide it."

Ultimately, the court agreed to the title of "administrative chief judge" and to a set of formal duties that more or less ensured that the significance of the role would vary with the energy and interests of its occupant. Many of the duties are ceremonial or involve nominations to various boards and committees of the court. Substantive duties include overseeing the clerk's office in the unit and reviewing support services (including space needs and improvement of facilities). The administrative chief judge serves as a liaison between the court of appeals and the district courts and bar associations in the unit and "maintain[s] contact with Court of Appeals judges within the unit and report[s] on their needs." He or she reviews reports of cases under submission with the judges in the unit and may, at the chief judge's direction, review judicial discipline matters arising within the unit. Finally, the three administrative chief judges serve on the executive committee of the court and rotate through one position on the circuit judicial council.

My interviews with present and prior occupants of the administrative chief judge position suggest that it is at best an ambiguous one. Even with twenty-eight judges, the court of appeals is small enough that a circuit judge with a pressing concern will communicate it directly to the chief judge, without going through an intermediary. The limited clerk's office facilities and staff in the northern and southern units require minimal judicial supervision. Though the administrative chief judge of the middle unit has formal supervisory authority over the clerk's office in the San Francisco headquarters, that role remained undeveloped while the chambers of the chief judge were located in San Francisco.[30] One administrative chief judge held monthly meetings attended by staff and judges; this practice has not been emulated by other occupants of the position. For a time, the three administrative chief judges met with the chief judge after the court executive committee meeting, but the sessions were discontinued when the length of executive committee meetings, together with the press of travel plans of judges wishing to return home, squeezed them out. The overall result is that, despite efforts by Chief Judge Browning to breathe substance into the position of administrative chief judge, the position remains largely honorific.

The same cannot be said for the executive committee of the court of

[30]This situation may change under Chief Judge Goodwin, since his chambers are in Pasadena and Judge Browning has become administrative chief judge for the middle unit.

appeals. Several judges and staff members to whom I spoke indicated their belief that the evolution of the current executive committee was one of the critical elements which has allowed the court to function as its size grew from thirteen to twenty-eight judges. An executive committee was authorized by the court shortly after Browning became chief judge. Its duties, as described in the court's minutes, were to deal with emergencies that presented themselves between regular court meetings and to act on the court's behalf on "routine matters not requiring decisions as to [court] policy."[31] In 1981 the duties of the committee were expanded to include authorization to act on "[m]atters that, in the unanimous opinion of the Executive Committee, are of insufficient importance to require action by the full Court." A year later the committee was given two additional responsibilities:

> Review and make recommendations on other proposals regarding the operation of the Court prior to their submission to the Court; and

> Advise the Chief Judge as he may request, and perform such tasks as he may delegate to the Committee.

These two new duties, particularly the former, have proved especially important in the evolution of the executive committee of the court to an influential position in managing the court's administrative business. Indeed, Browning testified before a Senate committee in 1984 that "[m]ost of the Court's administrative problems are handled by an Executive Committee," adding that "[u]se of the Executive Committee produces better decisions, reduces travel, and results in fewer and better Court meetings."[32]

The present organization of the executive committee is the result of the confluence of several developments in the early 1980s. Congress authorized the circuit judicial councils to include district judges, thereby separating the court of appeals as a decision-making body from the judicial council.[33] The court adopted the Administrative Units Plan described earlier and used the opportunity to tie the executive commit-

---

[31]Technically, the executive committee was initially authorized as a committee of the circuit council, although it addressed "court" matters as well. When the circuit council was reorganized and made independent of the court, the existing committee was redesignated as the executive committee of the court. See Section 6 Report, 1982, at 59.

[32]Oversight on the Federal Court of Appeals and U.S. Claims Court Workload and a Hearing on S. 386, S. 677, and S. 1156 before the Subcomm. on Courts of the Senate Judiciary Comm., 98th Cong., 2d Sess. 81 (1984).

[33]For a detailed account of this change, see Chapter 10.

tee to the new organizational structure by making the three administrative chief judges permanent members of the committee. (Other members are the chief judge and five other judges chosen by lot on a yearly basis from the group of active circuit judges who put their names forward.)[34] Finally, the court had grown from thirteen to twenty-three judges, making the full court meeting an increasingly cumbersome body for dealing with the number of decisions regularly thrust upon it.

The executive committee meets monthly; the court, at most bimonthly. Since the 1981 addition to committee duties, virtually every item requiring a decision by the full court has been presented first to the executive committee. Executive committee members debate, revise, and often return staff and committee reports and proposals for reworking. On the vast majority of items, the committee arrives at a consensus before submitting the issue to the full court for a formal and final decision. When executive committee matters reach court meetings, they are presented by one of the members of the committee, not by staff or by the chief judge. Not surprisingly, given the current size of the full court meeting and the amount of "predigesting," revision, and consensus building that goes on in the committee, most executive committee proposals are approved without a great deal of discussion by the full court. Of course, matters of substantial interest and controversy produce the lively debates at court meetings that one would expect on a court of twenty-eight strong-minded individuals.

The executive committee is not integrally related to the Administrative Units Plan, despite the fact that three of its permanent members are the administrative chief judges from each of the administrative units. The configuration of the executive committee has proved to be an effective one, ensuring that the three geographical regions are represented by judges with substantial seniority, while allowing more junior judges with an administrative bent to participate as well. But an equally effective executive committee could certainly exist in the absence of the decentralization implied in the Administrative Units Plan. Indeed, the increasing influence of the executive committee has actually resulted in a concentration of power within the court; the committee is therefore most appropriately viewed as a centralizing influence. When this fact is combined with the minimal importance of the administrative units, symbolized by the somewhat peripheral nature of the

[34]The executive committee initially consisted of seven judges; the membership was increased to nine in 1985.

position of administrative chief judge, the lesson of governance in the Ninth Circuit Court of Appeals is complementary to that of the previous section on administrative support: effective administration in a large appellate court may require centralization, not decentralization.

Conclusion

In the preceding pages I have assessed administration and management of the Ninth Circuit Court of Appeals, with a particular focus on the issues of support services and governance. I have not discussed how the court has handled its adjudicative role, most particularly its efforts to maintain consistent law as the court has grown in size. To a degree, however, it is not possible to discuss judicial administration apart from judicial decision making. Nearly every management determination by an appellate court affects the nature, quality, and consistency of the decisions made by its judges. This truism is all the more valid when the administrative issues concern the overall organization of a court's administrative support structure and its governance.

It is in this context of the substantive implications of administrative arrangements that the preceding discussion of centralization and decentralization should be placed. The Administrative Units Plan almost certainly would have had more vitality had it not been accompanied by another decision by the court that ran in the opposite direction: the determination that to the extent practicable each judge would sit an equal number of times with each other judge on the court, regardless of the judges' "home bases," and that each judge would sit an equal number of times in each of the three administrative units. This decision relates more to the judicial than to the administrative organization of the court and, as such, is somewhat outside my remit. But I do not believe it is possible to understand the fate of the Administrative Units Plan without reference to this decision.

Geographically defined units in which the same judges routinely sat together, heard cases arising exclusively from that region, and had only limited contact with judges in other parts of the circuit necessarily would have developed into more meaningful administrative entities than the ones that now exist in the Ninth Circuit.[35] Demands for "full

[35]The Fifth Circuit proposal for implementation of administrative units, although never carried out because of the intervening agreement on the court and in Congress to split the circuit, was closer to this decentralized decisional model than the path ultimately taken by the Ninth Circuit. See Barrow and Walker, supra note 1, at 227–30.

service" clerk's and staff attorneys' offices would certainly have been more compelling if cases, judges, lawyers, and litigants were all located in the same courthouse, or at least in the same region. As the units attained more individual identity and cohesion, and as significant staff resources were allocated to them, the position of administrative chief judge would necessarily have become more significant as well.

The Ninth Circuit experimented with "regional sittings" in the late 1970s, when there were only thirteen judges on the court: judges from the north, the central, and the southern parts of the circuit sat almost exclusively in their own areas and heard only local cases. In fairly short order the court concluded that its decisional unity, to say nothing of its internal cohesion, required judges to sit throughout the circuit rather than just in their own regions.[36] One can only speculate about the long-term impact of a different resolution to this issue. In light of a doubling in the number of judges on the court and the degree of administrative decentralization implied in the Administrative Units Plan, I suspect that a doctrinal and managerial balkanization would have occurred, with a de facto—if not de jure—split of the circuit its likely result.

But the court determined not to pursue a regionalization of the circuit, at least in the allocation of judges to cases and panels. It is against this crucial decision that decentralization in administration must be evaluated. If I am correct in the preceding analysis, if it has been the trend toward increasingly centralized support services and governance which has most characterized the recent history of the Ninth Circuit, the ironic administrative lesson is that the court's success in staying together—both doctrinally and institutionally—can be attributed in no small measure to the *failure* of the Administrative Units Plan to have any substantial impact on the court's operation or organization.

---

[36]See Conference on Empirical Research, supra note 23, at 43–44 (remarks of Judge Browning).

10

Governing the Ungovernable: The Theory and Practice of Governance in the Ninth Circuit

DORIS MARIE PROVINE

Much of the day-to-day life in any federal circuit revolves around the requirements of decision and review. The organization of these activities is strictly hierarchical, with the court of appeals identifying errors in district court judgments under appeal and enunciating the law of the circuit, and district judges correcting and supervising non-Article III decision making. Important as this division of labor is in resolving appeals, the principle of hierarchy offers only limited guidance in suggesting how the circuit should deal with breakdowns in administration, with disputes over circuit practice or policy, or with demands that the circuit supervise its activities, discipline its judges, and plan its future. These are the tasks of governance.[1]

The federal judiciary has always been libertarian in its stance toward government within the judiciary. In the organization of their own work, judges value decentralization, local autonomy, and ample room for individual initiative. The institutions that Congress has established to facilitate communication and policy making within the federal courts—chief judgeships, circuit councils, circuit conferences, and the Judicial Conference of the United States—reflect this individualistic bias; they are active in communicating the needs of the judiciary to others, but they are reluctant to exercise power over judges. A tradi-

---

[1]This is not to suggest that appellate review plays no role in matters of administrative policy, but only that this role is sharply constrained by the case-specific format of review. See, for example, Dunbar v. Triangle Lumber Co., 816 F.2d 126 (3d Cir. 1987), in which the Third Circuit Court of Appeals set forth standards for dismissals for failure to prosecute.

tion of concern for preservation of the sovereignty of judges circumscribes policy initiatives at each level. In our country judicial independence means not just freedom from control by the other branches of government, but freedom from control by other judges. This ideal of autonomous judges, with roots deep in American legal culture, powerfully influences contemporary debates about efficiency and accountability within the judicial branch.

Concern that governance not go too far is particularly manifest at the level of the regional circuits, where arguments for coordinated action and centralized oversight can be challenged by the district courts that make up each circuit as well as by individual judges. Joint action beyond what is clearly required by law, emergency, or the mandate of the Judicial Conference of the United States is inevitably controversial.[2] The makeup of the circuit councils, the bodies authorized to establish and implement policy at this level, also encourages reticence: only court of appeals judges could be members until 1981, and even now district judges are a distinct minority on most councils.[3] Magistrates, bankruptcy judges, and other non-Article III personnel who share responsibility for adjudication are ineligible for seats on the council. Squeezed into an uncomfortable middle seat between self-reliant districts and a Judicial Conference that speaks for the whole system, and lacking a system of representation reflecting the makeup of the circuit, circuit governance not surprisingly tends to be a low-profile activity.

The Ninth Circuit deviates from the norm in its approach to governance. The circuit reorganized its council in 1980 to create seats for four district judges (on a nine-member council), and the council includes nonvoting representatives from every stratum within the Ninth Circuit judicial community. Committees and task forces reporting to the council include members from all segments of the bench, the bar, and the professional staff. The circuit has also developed a network of specialized bodies, such as the Conference of Chief District Judges, that provide opportunities for various constituencies within the circuit to share ideas and information. The annual circuit conference has been

[2]The capacity of the circuit council to act as nerve center for a circuit that perceives itself under attack is explored in Deborah J. Barrow and Thomas G. Walker, *A Court Divided: The Fifth Circuit Court of Appeals and the Politics of Judicial Reform* (Yale University Press, 1988).

[3]The Judicial Councils Reform and Judicial Conduct and Disability Act of 1980 mandated representation of district judges. The requirement and implementation by the circuits is discussed later in this chapter.

reorganized several times, as will be seen in Chapter 11, to give more voice to lawyers and to make it more functional. The circuit has also been innovative in using its executive staff to assist and extend the work of its council, committees, and specialized fora. The annual action plan, another Ninth Circuit invention, is designed to focus the energies of the circuit toward specific reforms.

The Ninth Circuit has clearly departed from the usual pattern of passive circuit governance by court of appeals judges in favor of a multilayered, broadly based system organized to promote consensus and permit decisive action. The structure suggests a vision of the circuit as a democratic polity, a community with a responsibility to govern itself. This model casts the circuit as an independent decision maker in a decentralized system, positioned to assist the Supreme Court and the chief justice of the United States, acting through the Judicial Conference, in its efforts to maintain order across a system of far-flung trial and appeals courts, yet prepared also to keep its own house in order and to make its views known in Washington.

These departures from the national norm raise several questions. How does this model articulate with a tradition of administrative individualism? How much governing does the Ninth Circuit actually do? How much governing *should* a circuit do, and who should participate in this process? How much autonomy, for example, is appropriate for district courts (or individuals within these courts) in tailoring procedures to local needs and personal preference? Who should define the relationship between Article III and non-Article III judges? This chapter is concerned with how the Ninth Circuit came to adopt its unique approach to governance and with what this commitment means in practice. At stake is the long-term survival of the Ninth as a single circuit and, perhaps, the survival of the system of regional decentralization established by Congress half a century ago.

The language of governance invoked above and throughout this chapter suggests a set of concerns derived from experience in more familiar political settings. This terminology encourages the reader to think in terms of policy making by duly selected agents, mechanisms for enforcing these choices, a community linked by common concerns, and citizenship within that community. Accountability, access, and participation are relevant values in assessing governing institutions, and the Ninth Circuit has taken these values into account in designing its governing institutions.

The circuit has not, however, embraced those aspects of democratic governance associated with mobilizing citizen interest and defining political issues: campaigning, partisanship, and the development of political platforms. These activities, so familiar in less constrained political settings, seem anomalous in a judicial polity. The Ninth Circuit's version of organizational democracy, however robust against the backdrop of the judiciary, inevitably seems bloodless against the backdrop of political life in the larger community. The very imagery that justifies the circuit's movement toward democracy thus points to certain tensions in the concept when it is applied to a judicial setting.

The first part of this chapter explores the concept of regional self-government enacted by Congress in 1939 and implemented by the federal judiciary in the decades that followed. The second section is concerned with debates and innovations in the Ninth Circuit related to governance, particularly those associated with democratizing the process. The theme of the third section is evaluation; interviews with members of the Ninth Circuit community suggest the strengths and weaknesses of the circuit's experiment and, more generally, the problems that can be expected to arise when a circuit undertakes to govern itself.[4]

Institutional Accountability: Finding a Role for the Circuit

The current system of governance within the federal courts took shape with the adoption of the Administrative Office Act of 1939.[5] The impulse for broad institutional reform came from many sources, including President Roosevelt, who had an agenda for improving the administration of the federal courts.[6] The 1939 legislation provided the

[4]In addition to interviews, the chapter draws on internal court documents made available to the author. Statements not otherwise attributed are based on these materials. For further details of the interviews, see note 71 infra.

[5]Pub. L. No. 76–299, 53 Stat. 1223 (1939) (codified as amended at 28 U.S.C. §§ 332–33).

[6]Peter Graham Fish, *The Politics of Federal Judicial Administration* 112–16 (Princeton University Press, 1973). The president's plan for increasing the membership of the Supreme Court is better known, but his ideas for improving the courts extended to the rest of the federal court system as well. He recommended the establishment of a "proctor" who would help the Supreme Court play an active role in administering the system. Judges would be made available for service wherever needed, for example. This plan was unpopular at every level in the federal judiciary, including the Supreme Court. The justices, particularly Chief Justice Hughes, did not want the Court to become embroiled in problems of administration. Id. at 119–21, 137–38.

federal court system with its own agency, the Administrative Office of the United States Courts, which assumed administrative functions previously performed by the Department of Justice. The Administrative Office was to take its direction from the Judicial Conference of the United States, a body at that time headed by the chief justice of the United States and made up of the senior judges from each circuit. (In 1948 the position of "senior circuit judge" was renamed "chief judge of the circuit.")

The framers of the new law envisioned a significant regional dimension in the overall scheme of government.[7] Problems arising in the districts would be resolved at the circuit level, and grass-roots ideas for reform would be debated in the circuits first.[8] The senior judge of each circuit would communicate the region's concerns and ideas to institutions at the national level and assist the circuit in implementing national policy. Giving the circuits a significant role in governance was a strategy for satisfying demands for a more accountable system while avoiding centralized control based in the United States Supreme Court or a Washington bureaucracy.

The legislation set up two fora for communicating, clarifying, and resolving administrative problems at the circuit level: an annual conference of bench and bar and a council composed of members of the court of appeals and headed by the senior judge of that court. Some of the circuits had already instituted such conferences on an informal and irregular basis.[9] In an effort to ensure that these gatherings were more than purely social events, the 1939 law specified that the conferences be devoted to "considering the state of the business of the courts and advising ways and means of improving the administration of justice within the circuit."[10]

Actual policy making was to occur in the circuit councils. Several specific duties were mandated, as well as the general purpose of ensuring that "the work of the district courts shall be effectively and expeditiously transacted."[11] District judges were required to "promptly . . .

[7]See pp. 14–15.
[8]See 53 Stat. 1224–25.
[9]Fish, supra note 6, at 145–52.
[10]53 Stat. 1225. This language, in modified form, is now at 28 U.S.C. § 333.
[11]53 Stat. 1224. The 1948 revision of the Judicial Code strengthened this language somewhat, as did a 1980 amendment. The provision now reads: "Each judicial council shall make all necessary and appropriate orders for the effective and expeditious administration of justice within its circuit." 28 U.S.C. § 332(d)(1).

carry out the directions of the council as to the administration of the business of their respective courts."[12]

With the encouragement of the Judicial Conference, Congress built on this foundation in subsequent legislation, adding tasks for the councils beyond those outlined in the 1939 law. The Federal Magistrates Act of 1968, for example, requires the circuit councils to recommend when full- and part-time magistrates are needed. The Judicial Conference relies on these evaluations in its own recommendations to Congress.[13] The clear intent, in the words of the leading historian of these developments, was to make the councils "the cornerstone of the federal judiciary's administrative institution."[14]

Ambiguities in Regional Authority

The activities of the councils were the subject of congressional reconsideration in 1979. In a statement prepared for Senate hearings, Circuit Judge J. Clifford Wallace provided a useful summary of the council's responsibilities as of that time:

> [First, the councils] approve plans of the district courts for jury selection, for the appointment of counsel under the Criminal Justice Act, and for speedy trial compliance. . . . [Second,] they approve certain housekeeping details, such as the repository for records, court quarters, designation of residences of district judges, pretermission of regular sessions of court, and staffs of senior judges. [Third,] they approve the selection and salaries of public defenders. [Fourth,] they recommend the numbers and salaries of magistrates and bankruptcy judges. [Fifth,] they certify the physical and mental disability of judges. And, [sixth,] they make deci-

[12]53 Stat. 1224. This provision, too, was amended in 1980; it now reads: "All judicial officers and employees of the circuit shall promptly carry into effect all orders of the judicial council." 28 U.S.C. § 332(d)(2).

[13]See 28 U.S.C. § 633(b). Other responsibilities are vested in the councils by the provisions of the Criminal Justice Act of 1964 dealing with district court procedures for ensuring representation of indigent defendants and by the section of the Jury Selection and Service Act of 1968 providing for the selection of grand and petit jurors by the district courts. In each case the council reviews the district court's plans for conformity with statutory requirements. These specific grants may be redundant in light of the broad grant of authority over district court administration provided in 28 U.S.C. § 332. For discussion, see Fish, supra note 6, at 397–98.

[14]Id. at 165. Elsewhere Fish states that "the framers of the 1939 Act intended the councils as the administrative linchpin of the federal judiciary." Id. at 387.

sions when district judges cannot agree on rules, magistrates to be selected, or salary.[15]

This summary suggests considerable council authority to affect the conditions of adjudication within the circuit, but no orientation toward planning, mobilizing for change, or mandating improvements in the way judges administer their courts. It is unclear how far the drafters of the 1939 legislation expected the councils to go in these directions. The Federal Rules of Civil Procedure, first promulgated in 1938, were also silent on just how the new national policy of uniform rules was to coexist with the tradition of localism and personal idiosyncrasy in federal court administration.[16] The federal rules allow (but do not require) rule making at the district level, and they permit individual judges considerable latitude to experiment with procedures. Rule 16 exemplifies the approach; it offers a catalog of options for district judges who seek to streamline trials or facilitate settlements.[17]

Still, circuit governance must have disappointed some of its earliest proponents. In the 1940s and 1950s some circuits did not even convene the required conferences, or held pro forma gatherings.[18] The councils likewise failed to do more than the minimum required. Conceived without power to subpoena witnesses, without significant staff support, and without clear-cut sanctioning authority, the councils appear to have been unprepared to move forcefully against errant judges or to take on other difficult regulatory tasks.[19]

---

[15]Judge Wallace's statement appears in somewhat different form in Judicial Discipline and Tenure: Hearings on S. 295, S. 222, and S. 678 before the Subcomms. on Judicial Machinery and the Constitution of the Senate Judiciary Comm., 96th Cong., 1st Sess. 37 (1979). Subsequent legislation has added to these responsibilities. See discussion infra.

[16]The Federal Rules of Civil Procedure represented a truly radical break with tradition and prior law, which had prescribed that the federal courts should model their local rules to conform to court rules in their own localities. See Carroll Seron, "The Limitations of Standardizing Judges' Practices" (unpublished manuscript, on file with the author).

[17]The tendency has been to interpret these sections expansively and to find in the common law additional rationales for leaving district judges to their own administrative devices.

[18]Russell R. Wheeler, "Federal Circuit Judicial Conferences: Changing Format and Changing Role" at 6 (unpublished manuscript, March 15, 1982, on file at the Federal Judicial Center). The problems associated with making the circuit conference a meaningful forum for the discussion of administrative business are detailed in Chapter 11.

[19]Fish suggests that the framers expected judges to behave appropriately because

Some of these deficiencies were remedied over the course of years, but there have been no dramatic changes in the character of council activity. The councils gained the power to require the attendance of witnesses with the adoption of the Judicial Councils Reform and Judicial Conduct and Disability Act of 1980.[20] This act was designed to encourage circuit councils to deal more vigorously with the problem of judicial misconduct.[21] By that time, the circuit councils had also acquired more staff support. In 1971 Congress created the position of circuit executive and authorized the executive, subject to council guidance, to arrange for and attend council meetings, to conduct studies, and to prepare reports for the council.[22]

More important than lack of enforcement power or staff support in explaining council passivity has been confusion and continuing disagreement over the degree to which appellate judges should oversee the administration of justice in the district courts. Even before the adoption of the stronger 1980 legislation, many judges worried that

---

they had internalized professional norms and dreaded rejection by professional peers. Fish, supra note 6, at 161–62. Flanders and McDermott found that this approach was working "fairly well" in 1978 when they interviewed judges and court personnel in every circuit. Steven Flanders and John T. McDermott, *Operation of the Federal Judicial Councils* 52 (Federal Judicial Center, 1978). They concluded that the initial powers delegated to the councils were adequate; the problem was that judges were sometimes unwilling to use them. Id. at 46–52.

[20]Pub. L. No. 96–458, 94 Stat. 2035 (1980) (effective Oct. 1, 1981). The misconduct and disability procedures are codified at 28 U.S.C. § 372(c). For an argument that these new provisions have done very little to encourage more vigorous enforcement, see Carol T. Rieger, "The Judicial Councils Reform and Judicial Conduct and Disability Act: Will Judges Judge Judges?" 37 *Emory L.J.* 45 (1988).

[21]For a detailed discussion of the act's legislative history, see Stephen Burbank, "Procedural Rulemaking under the Judicial Councils Reform and Judicial Conduct and Disability Act of 1980," 131 *U. Pa. L. Rev.* 283, 291–308 (1982).

[22]Circuit Executive Act, Pub. L. No. 91–647, 84 Stat. 1907 (1971), codified at 28 U.S.C. § 332(e). The first decade of experience with circuit executives is discussed in John W. Macy, Jr., *The First Decade of the Circuit Court Executive: An Evaluation* (Federal Judicial Center, 1985).

In 1981 Congress established executive positions in the five largest districts on an experimental basis; the Central District of California (Los Angeles) was the only district in the Ninth Circuit to qualify. Perhaps because the relationship between the district executive and the Clerk of Court was never made clear, the concept of a district executive never gained a sure foothold. The Senate refused to approve funds for these positions in the 1989 budget, and the Judicial Conference did not appeal the decision. William B. Eldridge evaluated the role of these officials in *The District Court Executive Pilot Program* (Federal Judicial Center, 1984).

the councils had too much power. Writing in 1978, Flanders and McDermott concluded:

> The supervisory powers of judicial councils make many judges uncomfortable, whether they serve on a district court or a court of appeals. Many judges feel that section 332 lacks effective enforcement power, or that it is unconstitutional, or both. Many circuit judges also feel that, whatever their powers under section 332 might be, the unpleasant duties associated with council responsibilities are "not really part of the job" or are not truly part of the judicial system.[23]

The question of council power to discipline judges remains controversial. Congress has never spelled out how council oversight of circuit activities is to be justified in constitutional terms, probably because the leadership within the judicial branch has always been divided on this issue.[24] Nor has the Judicial Conference come to terms with its own authority to supervise and demand action from the councils.[25]

The makeup of the councils has also discouraged active governance. The court of appeals judges who sit on the councils have little day-to-day contact with the type of administrative problems that district judges experience, though some can draw on earlier experience as district judges. The organization of work at each level is very different, with appellate judges enjoying considerable insulation from the management problems district judges confront as they struggle to cope with attorneys, litigants, jurors, and the general public in their daily work. The problem of differences in administrative experience is exacerbated by the appellate process, which creates tensions between reviewers and the reviewed.[26] Friendships between some district and

[23]Flanders and McDermott, supra note 19, at 46. See also id. at 15, 26, 47–49.

[24]Perhaps the best-known example of dissension in the judicial ranks is Chandler v. Judicial Council of the Tenth Circuit, 398 U.S. 74 (1970). The majority never reached the constitutional issue, but it did approve in a general way of the exercise of council authority; Justices Black and Douglas, in a vigorous dissent, challenged that authority. Id. at 137. District Judge Frank J. Battisti recorded a similar opinion of the potential for council overreaching in "An Independent Judiciary or an Evanescent Dream," 25 *Case W. Res. L. Rev.* 711, 745 (1975). For a description of Battisti's recent battles with his own circuit council, see "Battisti Battling Bench Brethren," *National Law Journal*, April 3, 1989, at 12.

[25]For a discussion of the problem in the context of procedures the circuits have developed to deal with complaints about judicial disability and misconduct, see Stephen B. Burbank, "Politics and Progress in Implementing the Federal Judicial Discipline Act," 71 *Judicature* 13, 14–16 (1987).

[26]"The problem," as one district judge remarked, "is that they grade our papers." See

appeals judges also complicate circuit governance. Reticence in second-guessing the district courts in the administrative realm has therefore seemed the wisest course in the circuit councils.[27]

Evidence of the administrative independence federal district judges enjoy is everywhere. No two judges, it seems, do anything in precisely the same way. Litigators ignore these local idiosyncrasies at their peril. Federal litigators in one California district, for example, recently compiled a manual documenting differences among district judges in such matters as scheduling procedures, motion practice, alternative dispute-resolution programs, and voir dire.[28] The local federal bar, which marketed the volume to finance its activities, reports brisk sales. Lawyers, this California example suggests, have learned to cope with administrative diversity within a supposedly national system of court rules.

The Demands of Contemporary Conditions

Governance at the district, circuit, and national levels has thus never really challenged the federal tradition of administrative individualism. The circuit councils and other institutions of governance have had some success in dealing with sharp deviations from acceptable practice and in communicating good ideas, but they are not inclined to mandate consistency across administrative units. The Judicial Conference of the United States, often working through the Administrative Office, has moved into the administrative breach to a limited extent, but it too treads softly in dealing with Article III judges.

This approach to governance is solicitous of the independence of judges, but it offers the judiciary as a whole little protection against charges that it is inefficient and unaccountable for its actions. These concerns take on greater weight in the current environment. The federal caseload is increasing in size and complexity. The makeup of the federal court work force is also changing, with managerial and Article I personnel taking over some of the tasks formerly performed by Article III judges, who are in ever-shorter supply relative to the

---

generally Robert Carp and Russell Wheeler, "Sink or Swim: The Socialization of a Federal District Judge," 21 *Journal of Public Law* 359, 378 (1972).

[27]See Fish, supra note 6, at 406.

[28]The District Judges Association first tried to negotiate uniform rules, but gave up after six years. The Lawyer Representative Committee of the Eastern District then interviewed each judge in the district and compiled a manual. See the discussion of current efforts to achieve greater uniformity in local rules infra this chapter.

caseload. The federal courts, in short, are being asked to manage larger caseloads with fewer resources in a more complex organizational environment.

These increasing demands on courts have created unprecedented pressures to rationalize and streamline the process of adjudication without neglecting individual rights. Coordination, accountability, cost savings, and efficiency have become the watchwords of the new judicial administration.

With pressure to improve administration has come pressure to improve the processes and structures associated with the development of administrative policy. Chief judges, for example, can no longer rely as much on the informal methods they used for resolving problems within the circuit when the organization was smaller and slower. As Wheeler and Nihan report in their 1982 study of administration in the federal circuits:

> Courts of appeal are in transition from one era to another. . . . The chief judge's personal attention to detail took root when the circuits were smaller and the responsibility for overall supervision was less onerous. Increasingly, chief judges wish to avoid detailed personal involvement in all aspects of circuit business and thus are seeking to delegate much of this responsibility to the circuit executive and to committees of judges. . . . Perhaps the most important impression we have gained from this inquiry is that chief circuit judges are facing a double bind created by the growth in the size of the judiciary, on the one hand, and the desire to maintain traditions of close personal relations with their colleagues, on the other.[29]

Nowhere has the pressure to rethink administrative processes and revamp governing institutions been felt more keenly than in the Ninth Circuit. Unprecedented numbers—of cases, of district courts, of judges and support personnel—have created pressure to split the circuit, which has in turn forced leaders in the Ninth Circuit to take seriously the problems of coordinating a massive judicial enterprise and rendering it accountable to its attentive publics.

Strong circuit governance represents one solution to the problem of mediating between the varied constituencies that make up the circuit. During the Browning years, when the circuit grew rapidly and the pressure to improve its performance was great, innovation in matters

---

[29]Russell Wheeler and Charles W. Nihan, *Administering the Federal Judicial Circuits: A Survey of Chief Judges' Approaches and Procedures* 9–10 (Federal Judicial Center, 1982).

of governance became a key strategy for accommodating the burden of numbers and accountability to the reality of independent, nearly autonomous judges.

Democratizing Circuit Governance

The exclusion of district judges from membership on the circuit councils and the Judicial Conference of the United States never sat well with district judges.[30] The conference did welcome district judges on its committees from the beginning. Chief Justice Hughes initiated this policy and it quickly became institutionalized, but there was significant opposition to the idea of extending membership on the conference itself to district judges.[31]

The effort to achieve representation at both levels began early, with Ninth Circuit district judges playing a leading role in lobbying the Judicial Conference.[32] With Chief Justice Warren's active support, Congress in 1957 finally expanded the membership of the Judicial Conference to include one district judge from each circuit.[33] Selection of the circuit's district judge representative occurs during the annual circuit conference.[34] In most circuits, including the Ninth, the position is elective, an exception to the usual rule in the federal courts. These elections also elicit atypical judicial behavior, with district judges campaigning for the post, sometimes with the help of a campaign manager and a platform of issues.

Court of appeals judges were no more anxious to relinquish their monopoly on the circuit councils than they had been to give up full control of the Judicial Conference. No one objected to allowing district judges to attend an occasional meeting as a guest of the council, when their input would be helpful, but there was strong resistance to the idea that district judges should be on an equal footing with appeals

[30]Fish, supra note 6, at 248–54, 380–84. See also Flanders and McDermott, supra note 19, at 50–51.

[31]Fish, supra note 6, at 274–75.

[32]Id. at 253.

[33]Pub. L. No. 85–202, 71 Stat. 476 (1957).

[34]"The district judge to be summoned from each judicial circuit shall be chosen by the circuit and district judges of the circuit at the annual judicial conference of the circuit . . . and shall serve as a member of the conference for three successive years. . . ." 28 U.S.C. § 331. The statute envisions participation by both court of appeals and district judges. In the Ninth Circuit the district judges elect a candidate and the appellate judges affirm the selection by an automatic unanimous consent.

judges in setting circuit policy, particularly if that policy might involve changes in the procedures or resources of the court of appeals. Again, a few district judges in the Ninth Circuit were active in the effort to achieve representation, but they were opposed by appeals judges in their own circuit.[35]

District Judge Representation, by Invitation Only

During the 1970s the Ninth Circuit, like most others, experimented with various compromises short of full representation for district judges on the council.[36] In 1972 members of the circuit's District Judges Association were invited to attend in an "advisory capacity" when the chief judge deemed their presence appropriate. They were generally invited to sit in on part of one or two of the council's eight annual meetings, which occurred in conjunction with meetings of the court of appeals, but a whole year might pass without a district judge observer's attendance at a single council meeting.[37]

Shortly after he assumed the chief judgeship, Browning took steps to give the district judges more voice in circuit affairs. In 1976 he instituted a separate organization for the airing of issues of concern to the district courts, the Conference of Chief Judges of District Courts.[38] In May 1977, in anticipation of eventual district judge participation on the council, he proposed to divide the day-long court/council meetings into a morning session that would consider problems specific to the court of appeals, such as discussion of the need for additional appellate judges, and an afternoon session concerned with circuit-wide or district-level issues, such as retirement provisions and circuit conference matters. Two district judge representatives, the president of the District Judges Association and the chairman of the executive

---

[35]See Fish, supra note 6, at 382. See also Chapter 14.

[36]Wheeler and Nihan, supra note 29, at 3–4.

[37]Council minutes for 1977, for example, indicate no district judge attendance. Browning discussed the pattern in a letter to Chief Judge Bailey Brown of the Sixth Circuit, August 30, 1978.

[38]By-Laws of the Ninth Circuit Conference of Chief Judges, no date, Browning papers. This conference became the model for biannual gatherings of the magistrates and chief bankruptcy judges and their clerks. Materials distributed for each conference are similar: information on matters pending before Congress, the courts, and the U.S. Judicial Conference, and updates from the Administrative Office, the circuit executive, and relevant committees of the council. The agenda features reports from committees, from the chief judge, and from the circuit executive.

committee of the Conference of Chief (District) Judges, would be invited to the afternoon session as nonvoting members.[39]

This proposal met with strong opposition from a few court of appeals judges, although others supported the move. One judge reported that he was "very much opposed to the idea of permitting district judges to participate in Council sessions" because the presence of the two district judges "would destroy both the efficiency and the collegiality of our Council sessions." Another judge responded with "strong reservations" about regular participation by district judges. Ultimately the council agreed to divide its agenda but not to invite the district judges to attend the afternoon sessions on a regular basis.

In an effort to strengthen the circuit as an institution, even at a risk to collegiality within his own court, Browning issued the invitation himself, relying on the authority of the council's 1972 resolution, which left the matter of district judge attendance to the discretion of the chief judge.[40] From that point on, District Judge Spencer Williams began to attend council meetings regularly as a nonvoting observer.

Full membership on the circuit councils was not available to the district judges until 1981, when the Judicial Councils Reform and Judicial Conduct and Disability Act took effect.[41] The act required councils to include two to three district judge representatives, depending on the number of appeals judges on the council.[42] To appease those concerned that the reconstituted council might be inclined toward too active a role, the legislation specified that "unless an impediment to the administration of justice is involved, regular business of the courts need not be referred to the council."[43] The language was Congressman Robert W. Kastenmeier's, and it was designed to satisfy constituencies in the courts and Congress who had pressed hard for changes in the orientation and organization of the circuit councils.

The district and appeals judges did not generally see eye to eye on the issue of council membership, but the real prospect that Congress

[39]The concept of a dual agenda, with court of appeals business differentiated clearly from council business, was later incorporated into the 1980 legislation.

[40]James R. Browning to Bailey Brown, August 30, 1978. The liaison committee elected to accept Browning's invitation by sending only one of their number to council meetings. Id.

[41]Pub. L. No. 96-458, 94 Stat. 2035 (1981), amending 28 U.S.C. § 332.

[42]The law required at least two district judges on a council consisting of up to five appeals judges, and three district judge representatives in councils with more than six appeals court members. See 28 U.S.C. § 332(a)(1)(C).

[43]See 28 U.S.C. § 332(d)(3). For a discussion of the legislative history of the act, see Burbank, supra note 21, at 291–308.

might take jurisdiction over judicial misconduct away from the circuits and centralize it in Washington discouraged vigorous opposition to more modest changes. Judicial lobbying for district judge representation began with a May 1977 resolution by the Fifth Circuit District Judges Association calling for equal representation on the councils and requesting action by the Judicial Conference. Judge Elmo Hunter, chair of the conference committee on court administration, ordered a study of council activities, which revealed that two-thirds of those affected by council decisions were district judges. Yet most appellate judges opposed any representation for district judges on the councils. According to a poll conducted in November 1978 for the conference, the sentiment on the courts of appeals was more than two to one against inclusion, with 81 judges opposed and 39 in favor. The district judges, on the other hand, were overwhelmingly of the opposite persuasion, with only 16 opposed and 377 in favor.[44]

Meanwhile, some appeals judges, prompted by the fear that Congress might divest the circuits of power to resolve misconduct complaints, had begun to work actively for district judge membership on the councils. Congress at that time was considering two bills that would eliminate council jurisdiction over misconduct, one sponsored by Senator Sam Nunn, the other by Senator Dennis DeConcini. Judge Wallace argued for equal numbers of district and appeals judges on councils and election of all representatives in a May 1978 article revealingly entitled, "The Nunn Bill: An Unneeded Compromise of Judicial Independence," and he testified before Congress in support of equal representation in May 1979.[45] Browning also testified in favor of maintaining council authority over discipline, though he did not take a position at that time on election of representatives or the precise makeup of the councils.[46] His decision to include district judge observers on the Ninth Circuit council, however, apparently impressed Kastenmeier and encouraged him to believe that the circuits could operate effectively if council membership were extended to district judges.[47]

---

[44]Telephone interview with Judge Elmo Hunter, March 9, 1989.

[45]See J. Clifford Wallace, "The Nunn Bill: An Unneeded Compromise of Judicial Independence," 61 *Judicature* 476, 480 (1978). See also Hearings before the Subcomm. on Courts, Civil Liberties and the Administration of Justice of the House Judiciary Comm., 96th Cong., 1st & 2d Sess. 72 (1979) (statement of Judge Wallace).

[46]See id. at 85 (testimony of Chief Judge Browning).

[47]March 9, 1989, telephone interview with Judge Elmo Hunter.

The Implications of Equality

The Ninth Circuit responded to the new law by drastically reorganizing its council, a move encouraged by a roughly contemporaneous growth in the already numerous ranks of appeals court judges. In most of the other circuits, where the number of appeals court judges was much smaller, the councils simply added district court judges to their membership.[48] In the Ninth Circuit, however, if the mandated three district judges had simply been added to a council made up of the court of appeals judges, the council would have numbered an ungainly twenty-six.

Equal representation emerged as the unanimous recommendation of the Ninth Circuit Court of Appeals, a surprising result considering the earlier opposition on that court to *any* representation for district judges.[49] Browning defused opposition by appointing a committee to advise the council on district judge representation and including on it the circuit judge who was most opposed to the idea.[50] Browning himself chaired the committee and urged it to include any protections it thought necessary to ensure acceptance by the circuit judges of district judges on the council.

The committee moved quickly to draft a rule that included equal representation, but also the proviso that "the Council will not intervene in the internal functions of the Court of Appeals or of any district court unless it is determined by a majority of the judges of the particular court or two-thirds of the members of the Council that intervention is appropriate and necessary because an impediment to the administration of justice is involved."[51] That stipulation alone, however, did not sufficiently assuage the concerns of the circuit judges about potential overreaching. When the committee's draft rule was presented to

[48]Eric Neisser, "The New Federal Judicial Discipline Act: Some Questions Congress Didn't Answer," 65 *Judicature* 143, 144 (1981).

[49]The unanimous vote was announced in Browning's June 29, 1981, Report to the 1981 Circuit Conference.

[50]The committee was appointed on November 20, 1980. In addition to Browning, it was made up of Judges Wallace, Sneed, and Skopil from the court of appeals and Judges Ray McNichols, Robert Peckham, and Robert Belloni of the district courts. Sneed was a leader in arguing for maintaining exclusivity.

[51]Rule Governing the Restructuring of the Judicial Council of the Ninth Circuit, Dec. 23, 1980, Provision #1 (hereafter cited as Council Rule). The circuit thus made mandatory what the legislation left optional. See 28 U.S.C. § 332(d)(3), discussed earlier. The rule was amended March 6, 1981, to include only active judges in the tallying of affected judges.

the court of appeals, the judges instructed the committee to redraft section 2, the provision delineating the council's membership, to include a definition of a quorum of the council. In response, the committee prepared a new draft requiring a quorum of five, two of whom had to be district judges and two of whom had to be circuit judges other than the chief judge. The revised rule also provided that action on most matters would require a majority of those present, including at least one district judge and one circuit judge other than the chief judge.[52]

The plan, with minor revisions, was submitted to all active Article III judges and was approved 76–3. The final, and unanimous, court of appeals vote took place April 17, 1981, and the new rule took effect the following October.

The decision to go beyond congressional requirements and equalize the representation of district and appeals court judges had profound implications for governance in the Ninth Circuit. The appellate judges forsook their preeminent role in governing the circuit and became simply one of the two levels represented on the circuit council, a loss of power that some court of appeals judges predicted would cause serious problems in the governance of the circuit.

Circuit Judge Joseph T. Sneed, who argued against the inclusion of district judges when the matter was before Congress, cast the issue in terms of effectiveness.[53] A council that equalized representation of district and court of appeals judges, he speculated, would please neither group and would stimulate "oligarchic" tendencies in the council. Emboldened by its district judge representatives, the council would take up issues it had treated as off-limits before. Courts would try to deflect the intrusion of the council into their affairs by declaring as many issues as possible "court business," thereby avoiding council action. The result would be an ineffective council.

Judge Sneed appears to have been wrong in anticipating that the presence of district judges on the council would come to be regarded as a mistake, but he was clearly right in identifying their inclusion as a turning point in circuit governance. District judges not only became

[52]Council Rule, supra note 51, Provision #2. The rule required that action on complaints against judges or magistrates be supported by a majority of all members of the council other than the chief judge.

[53]Sneed presented the arguments against altering the existing structure of the councils in a memorandum circulated to the court of appeals judges in the summer of 1979. The memorandum was drafted for submission at a congressional hearing, but it was not made part of the record of the 1980 legislation.

partners in governance, but their participation on the council pointed the way to further changes. Soon magistrates and bankruptcy judges had joined the council as observers. Senior judges noted their lack of representation and gained observer status. The once-heretical idea that those with a stake in the deliberations of the council deserve a chance to participate in those deliberations had within a few years become orthodoxy in the Ninth Circuit.

The reorganization of the council to serve circuit-wide needs encouraged the court of appeals to develop its own institutions for handling issues arising at that level. Browning had laid the groundwork for this development in 1977 when he divided the council's agenda into matters of primary concern to the court of appeals and matters of circuit-wide interest. With the reorganization of the council, the court of appeals began meeting separately. In part because of its size, but also because many judges showed no particular interest in administration, the court came to rely on a seven-member executive committee to make both routine and emergency decisions and to evaluate proposals and recommend action to the court.[54]

Splitting the council from the court of appeals also had an impact on the organization of administrative support in the circuit. As the circuit executive's office came to be identified more closely with the council, the circuit executive's relationship with the clerk of the court of appeals began to change. In a sequence of steps typical of the process of institutional reform in the Ninth Circuit, the circuit first experimented with an arrangement by which the clerk took over appeals-related supervisory and procurement functions formerly within the circuit executive's jurisdiction; then, after discussion in the court of appeals executive committee, the court voted to create a new position, "court of appeals executive," "to be responsible for the day-to-day operations of the Court of Appeals."[55]

The effort to define a more active role for the trimmed-down, more representative circuit council began shortly after the 1981 reorganization. Browning, relying on the management skills of his circuit executive of the time, William E. Davis, initiated many changes in the

[54]The makeup and operations of the court of appeals executive committee are described in Chapter 9.

[55]Ninth Circuit Judicial Council minutes, November 17, 1987, p. 2. See Memorandum from Cathy A. Catterson (Clerk, Court of Appeals) to Chief Judge Browning, Sept. 28, 1987, and Fiscal Year 1990 Position Requirements, outlining the new court of appeals executive's needs for increased staff.

council.[56] Davis suggested, and the council implemented, quarterly meetings organized around a written agenda that began with a report by the chief judge on the state of the circuit and included reports of committees and a report from the circuit executive on progress toward objectives outlined in an annual action plan.[57] In developing and implementing these reforms, both men were motivated by the specter of a divided circuit. "If the circuit splits," Browning laughingly told Davis one day, "it's your fault."

For Browning, the objective of enhancing the council's effectiveness involved broadening as much as possible the base from which the council could draw ideas and suggestions. This meant developing criteria for council membership that would allow for the representation of diverse interests. Arbitrary appointments and politicking for office, however, were to be avoided. The solution was to create a council of delegates, with members coming onto the council by virtue of their status or seniority in some separate realm. Thus three of the circuit judges serve by virtue of their seniority in the administrative units; the fourth circuit judge member represents the court's executive committee. District judge members are two members of the Conference of District Court Chief Judges selected by seniority as chief judges, the Ninth Circuit's district judge representative to the Judicial Conference of the United States, and the president of the District Judges' Association.

Observers also represent organized constituencies, as do the liaison committees the council created to maintain close contact with key nonjudicial officers, such as district court clerks and probation officers. With Browning's encouragement, these constituencies were organized to meet regularly to share ideas and discuss common problems. There has been no effort, though, to make such meetings the only source of information about the council; minutes of council meetings are distributed to all judges and available to any member of the Ninth Circuit community. The circuit even has a newsletter, *9th Circuit News*.

The council's work is conducted through an executive committee and a combination of standing and ad hoc committees; the executive committee handles routine and emergency issues arising between

---

[56]Davis, who left the Ninth Circuit in 1986, won awards for his earlier work as court administrator for the state of Kentucky. Los Angeles Daily Journal, April 6, 1987, p. 1, col. 3. He now serves as director of the Administrative Office of the Courts for California.

[57]Davis outlined most of these ideas in a 1981 memorandum to Browning. He offered a similar series of organizational proposals to the court of appeals.

meetings. The committees have been encouraged to take their mandates seriously by the requirement that they report regularly to the council. The precaution of regular reporting was necessary, Browning reasoned, because on a council made up of full-time judges "everybody's engaged in just what they've got to do today."

In staffing council committees, Browning and the circuit executive's office made an effort to include as many members of the Ninth Circuit community as possible, but especially new judges who could thus become oriented to thinking in terms of the business of the circuit.[58] The development of a wide-ranging, well-populated committee system on the council was also intended to legitimate the council in the eyes of its constituents and to inspire judges, lawyers, and professional staff to think in terms of their circuit and its interests at the national level. Committee jurisdictions and membership were organized to parallel those of the Judicial Conference of the United States, thereby to ensure that the interests of the circuit would be effectively represented at that level.[59]

Were the council an executive body in a bureaucratic organization, attention to the creation of opportunities for discussion within and across organizational segments might be desirable, but it would hardly be perceived as essential to efficient operations. In a court system there are no other options. Orders from a body of legislator-judges, no matter how representative, will be resented by many judges and resisted by a few. Circuit councils have avoided the embarrassment of defiance by issuing orders infrequently.[60]

The leader's task in such a setting is to create opportunities for

---

[58]In a 1987 report to chief circuit judges and circuit executives in other circuits, Circuit Executive Francis Bremson outlined three types of committees on the council: circuit conference committees; conference and liaison committees (reporting on the concerns of the conferences of chief district judges, chief bankruptcy judges, and U.S. magistrates and the committees of bankruptcy clerks, district clerks, federal public defenders, and probation officers); and advisory committees and task forces set up to address particular issues of wide concern in the circuit, such as alternative dispute resolution and evaluation of local rules. Bremson noted that "committee members come from every district within the circuit."

[59]Browning and the circuit executive also made an effort to have a Ninth Circuit representative on every Judicial Conference committee, and anyone in the circuit who was invited to serve on such a committee automatically became a member of the relevant circuit committee. The Judicial Conference of the United States alters its committee structure occasionally. When it does, as in 1988, council committees are adjusted accordingly.

[60]Fish, supra note 6, at 406–26.

collegial exchange, to provide information that will be helpful in choosing among alternatives, to engage in "friendly persuasion" to point out the advantages of change or create embarrassment about failure to conform with expectations, and to protect the institutional interests of the organization. Browning nurtured institutions that would assist him in these endeavors, including even a historical society to help provide the circuit with a sense of its past[61] and a regional research center (an idea that is still in its early stages). The obvious question is whether his effort to define a meaningful, albeit circumscribed, role for circuit governance has been successful.

Ninth Circuit Government in Action

Judge Browning saw circuit government as a challenge to his skills in persuasion. Judges and other members of the Ninth Circuit community had to be persuaded that the institutions that made decisions on their behalf were legitimate. Skeptics in Washington also had to be persuaded to take circuit government seriously. In their reluctance to undertake necessary but unpleasant regulatory tasks, the circuits had allowed themselves to become almost supernumeraries in the administrative process. As Browning noted in his 1982 report to the Ninth Circuit:

> For forty years the judicial councils of the circuits failed to discharge the responsibilities imposed on them by Congress. . . . But life moves on. The administrative functions left unperformed by the judicial councils were necessarily assumed by others. Over the last forty years administrative authority gradually concentrated in the Judicial Conference of the United States, the Administrative Office, and the Federal Judicial Center.[62]

It would not be easy, Browning warned, to reclaim this authority from Washington.

Has the Ninth Circuit fashioned a meaningful role for itself in an administrative system in which power tends to be concentrated in the periphery and the center, but not in the middle? The remarkable

---

[61]The Ninth Circuit Historical Society solicits members and invites them to participate in historical scholarship. It also publishes a journal, *Western Legal History*.

[62]Office of the Circuit Executive, *1982 Annual Report of the Ninth Circuit* at 15. The Federal Judicial Center was founded in 1967 to serve as the Washington-based research and planning arm of the federal court system. Its authority is outlined in 28 U.S.C. § 620.

energy and imagination Browning devoted to the task, along with his unusually long tenure as chief judge, suggests that the Ninth should be considered a "best case" example of circuit governance. Are the innovations of the Browning period viewed as legitimate and desirable by members of the Ninth Circuit community? What can be learned from this struggle to create a regional polity?

The Circuit's Agenda

Governance is a process with no single, easily definable product. At the level of the federal judicial circuits, however, it is at least possible to discern the tasks of government as defined by Congress and the Judicial Conference and to evaluate how the circuit discharges its mandate. The activities of the circuit council offer a useful starting point for this analysis because it is to the councils that Congress and the Judicial Conference have spoken most clearly. The duties of the councils, contained in a variety of statutory and regulatory provisions, are a product of legislative accretion. They can be summarized as follows:

- Resolution of complaints of judicial misconduct and certification of judicial disability;
- intracircuit dispute resolution;
- scrutiny and approval of certain administrative proposals emanating from the district courts, including designation of schedules and staff allocations;
- supervision of the condition of dockets, criminal adjudication, and the use of jurors throughout the circuit, including responsibility to take action to assist a judge who has a large backload of pending cases; and
- evaluation and recommendation of personnel and equipment needs.

Most of these duties consume relatively little of the Ninth Circuit's collective attention. Judicial misconduct and disability issues, following the pattern elsewhere, are most often handled by the chief judge and court staff and seldom come before the council for action.[63] The dispute-resolution function of the council has almost never come into play in the Ninth Circuit, although on one of the few occasions when it did, the issue split the council in half. The four district judge represen-

[63]Rieger, supra note 20, at 58–59. In 1986, for example, 277 complaints were concluded, 86 percent by the chief judges. The remaining 39 were dismissed by the judicial councils. Id. at 59.

268

tatives voted unanimously in opposition to the appeals court representatives, rendering the vote invalid according to the council's charter, which was designed to short-circuit just such divisions.[64] The council spends more time with required approvals of district plans and proposals (for juror utilization, appointment of assigned counsel, judicial assignments, etc.) and local rules, but these activities are generally uncontroversial and elicit little discussion.

The council, through its committees, spends much more time on caseload management and personnel issues. Some committees (task force on alternative dispute resolution, space committee, and jury management and utilization committee) are designed to address specific management issues directly; others deal with the organizational prerequisites of an effective system (intracircuit assignment committee, liaison committees with magistrates, bankruptcy courts, and clerks); and others are concerned with the circuit's resource and information base (statistics committee, automation and technology committee). The circuit executive conducts research designed to improve caseload, and the chief judge and council have not hesitated to ask the Federal Judicial Center to conduct additional studies.

The circuit executive also drafts the annual action plan, which Browning instituted in 1982 to focus the energies of the circuit on problems in the system. The plan, made up of ideas solicited from members of the Ninth Circuit community and, to an even greater extent, ideas contributed by the professional staff, is designed to encourage the council to become a policy-making, priority-setting body, not just a regulator of functions required by central authorities.

The attention the circuit devotes to studying its caseload helps support the effort to make its needs for personnel and resources known to the Judicial Conference and Congress. Lobbying for additional personnel and equipment has become an art form in the Ninth Circuit. The council is sometimes the nerve center for operations, but other governing institutions within the circuit are also involved in these matters. When the issue of enhanced retirement benefits for magistrates was before Congress, for example, Ninth Circuit magistrates invited the director of the Administrative Office to address them

---

[64]At issue was the allocation of space in the Central District of California. A circuit judge had taken space the district judges thought they were entitled to use. The district judges in that district brought the matter to the council repeatedly and in June 1987 sought an order. It was not until after the vote that Browning and the circuit executive realized the vote was in violation of the council's charter. By the next meeting the problem had been resolved.

on the subject at their annual magistrates' conference. He gave them details on the leanings of various members of Congress and urged them to contact their representatives directly. The magistrates also went on record in favor of hiring a professional lobbyist to pursue the matter further.[65]

Externally inflicted threats to the circuit's well-being are also likely to evoke aggressive action from a variety of governing resources. Browning became personally involved in the effort to keep the bankruptcy courts operating after the Supreme Court's decision in the *Marathon* case, and he worked equally hard to keep the Bankruptcy Appellate Panel in its present form. His style, according to one observer, was to "grab problems by the throat and not let go."[66]

The circuit treads much more lightly when it focuses on the management problems of specific Article III judges. When the council learns that a judge has a backlog problem, the chief judge generally contacts the judge and offers assistance. Sometimes, however, the council's statistics committee or a friend on the council may call the judge in question to express concern; often such contacts are made through the appropriate chief judge. The council has never found it necessary formally to request changes in management practices that allow judges to become seriously in arrears in their work, though the statistics committee has on a few occasions sent a visiting judge to assist in revamping procedures. Intracircuit assignment policy also encourages timeliness: if a judge has five or more cases under advisement for sixty days or more, he or she is not available for assignment.

Just getting some judges to report their case-disposition statistics is a delicate matter. Many judges ignored reporting requirements until the 1980s, when the chief judge and the council's statistics committee began to press for compliance. Now only a few refuse outright to cooperate, though there are persistent rumors that some judges manipulate their statistics by last-minute assignments of long-pending cases and other devices. At this writing, the council is on the verge of taking a more active role in prodding judges to comply with reporting requirements, and the circuit executive's office is exploring the possibilities of installing a computer-generated reporting system.

Judges on the Ninth Circuit clearly give each other wide berth to

---

[65]The magistrates and bankruptcy judges were ultimately successful in their efforts to get enhanced benefits in the 100th Session of Congress.

[66]This style was not limited to matters of governance. It can also be seen, for example, in Browning's effort to persuade the initially resistant court of appeals judges to adopt a screening program. See Chapter 5.

make their own administrative decisions in their own courts. Judicial government works around this major constraint on its activities by emphasizing its role in education, planning, lobbying, and consensus building, and by handling its regulatory duties with extreme circumspection. That most delicate of regulatory duties, controlling judicial misconduct, is handled informally and in person whenever possible, with the chief judge acting as emissary of the council.

The potentially controversial matter of approving changes in the local rules of constituent courts is also handled with care. Until the late 1980s the council treated approvals as a purely procedural matter of ensuring adequate notice and comment, even though "inter-district uniformity" is stated as a goal in the advisory committee notes that accompany the relevant section of the Federal Rules.[67] "Uniformity in the federal system," according to one Ninth Circuit judge interviewed in connection with this project, "is the biggest joke going." Congress finally mandated a more thorough review of local rule changes in November 1988.[68]

Commitment to a model of regional government that is primarily facilitative is also evident in the Ninth Circuit's efforts to decentralize the budgetary process. Spending for courts traditionally has been handled almost entirely from Washington through the Administrative Office, which negotiates with Congress, sets priorities, and administers the budget. The Administrative Office makes no effort to include the circuits in these decisions. Each circuit executive submits a budget to assist in the process of assessing needs, but these budgets are not used in channeling funds to the circuits, nor is the circuit executive involved in allocations to constituent courts within the circuit. Thus judges contact the Administrative Office if they need extra office supplies or new furniture, an arrangement that some judges find quite advantageous, because the Administrative Office turns down few requests. Several judges likened the agency to a sugar daddy who

[67]Fed. R. Civ. P. 83. The Notes of the Advisory Committee on Rules to the 1985 Amendment state: "The expectation is that the judicial council will examine all local rules, including those currently in effect, with an eye toward determining whether they are valid and consistent with the Federal Rules, *promote inter-district uniformity and efficiency,* and do not undermine the basic objectives of the Federal Rules." (Emphasis added.)

[68]Judicial Improvements and Access to Justice Act § 403(a)(2), Pub. L. No. 100–702, 102 Stat. 4642, 4651 (1988). This new section specifies that the council shall periodically review the circuit's local rules for conformity to the requirements of the Federal Rules of Civil Procedure. The new law became effective December 1, 1988.

dispenses money from an unseen pocket of unknown depth; another called the agency a cow.

Browning and his circuit executive worked hard to change this system, which they considered inefficient, unreliable, and wasteful.[69] In 1982 the circuit executive proposed a decentralization plan that would place authority for approval of requests in the circuit council, and decentralized budgeting became an item in the 1983 and subsequent annual action plans. The once-explosive idea of decentralizing budgeting has gained ground in the Administrative Office and Judicial Conference as Congress has become less generous in its allotments.

It now appears likely that both the districts and the circuit councils will be loci of distributive authority and that the Judicial Conference will supervise the process. Just how this will be accomplished remains unclear, for districts and circuits vary in the capacity to ensure their needs are met. The role of professional administrators in the distributive process also remains uncertain, and judges are sharply divided on this issue. "Decisions about who gets what," one judge remarked to me, "should be made by judges." The Administrative Office is currently experimenting with several plans for decentralizing authority over controllable items in the budget, and three Ninth Circuit districts are involved in this experiment.[70]

From the campaign to decentralize budgeting and other circuit activities described here, it is possible to discern the pattern of government during the Browning years. When the circuit's autonomy or resources were threatened, Browning moved decisively to protect local interests. The threat might be long-term, like centralized control over the budget process, or immediate, like the Nunn bill. Browning and other leaders worked through the circuit's governing institutions, but it was the energy and talents of a few individuals that lent coherence to the effort.

---

[69]"Eventually this reform will have its way; it must if the growing judicial establishment is to operate efficiently." Chief Judge James R. Browning, "State of the Ninth Circuit" at 18 (address delivered in Seattle, Wash., Aug. 13, 1984).

[70]The experiment began in November 1987 and was to run for three years. In the Ninth Circuit it involves the Northern District of California, the Western District of Washington, and the District of Arizona. Outside the Ninth Circuit, the participants are the Second Circuit Court of Appeals, the District Court for the Southern District of New York, and the council of the Eleventh Circuit. The Administrative Office is also decentralizing some building projects, permitting clerks of court to make decisions involving amounts up to $5000, delegating to staff in the circuit executive's office with some council oversight decisions involving between $5000 and $25,000, and requiring full council review of decisions in the $25,000–$500,000 range.

The approach was much different when the issue was self-regulation. Here Browning's persuasive powers were directed at the Ninth Circuit community, not Washington, and the problem was to improve performance, not to precipitate decisive action. In such instances government takes on a more institutional, less personal cast, and information sharing, example, exhortation, and embarrassment become the levers for change.

The Consent of the Governed

There is every evidence that the judicial rank and file strongly supports the current approach to governance and would resist more activist circuit government. In conducting this research, I interviewed most of the circuit's chief district judges, as well as an assortment of rank-and-file district judges, bankruptcy judges, magistrates, members of the circuit executive's office, and other professional personnel.[71] The circuit membership at large, including litigators, was asked to discuss the issue of governance in a series of break-out sessions during the 1988 circuit conference, and notes on each of those sessions were made available to me.

A survey of each constituency within the circuit would have added a scientific gloss to this rather unsystematic-sounding data-gathering procedure, but in estimating what might be learned from such an undertaking, one should take into account the sentiment that predominated in the break-out sessions: that governance is a low-salience, generally benign activity in the Ninth Circuit, despite the elaborate institutional transformation that has occurred there. "The council," as one district judge remarked, "just doesn't seem to influence my life." A chief district judge expressed the same sentiment in a

[71]Each of the ten chief district judges I interviewed had either sat on the council in the past or was currently serving. Each could thus speak from two vantage points: as a circuit legislator with inside knowledge of the council's work and as a circuit citizen with district-wide administrative responsibility. These interviews were conducted by telephone in September and October 1988.

Nonjudicial personnel interviewed include a member of the staff attorney's office, the clerk of the court of appeals (now the court executive), a public defender, the current and former circuit executive, and two members of the current circuit executive's staff. These interviews were conducted in an October 14–15, 1987, visit to the court of appeals and the District Court for the Northern District of California.

Interviews with non-Article III personnel have been in person (chief bankruptcy judge and a second bankruptcy judge, October 15, 1987) and by telephone (a magistrate, in December 1988). I also interviewed a senior judge (October 15, 1987, San Francisco).

personal interview: "District judges don't worry about administration—until six months before they become chief judge." Fish describes this attitude in his 1973 analysis of administration in the federal courts: "Lower court judges thus may identify generally with the system of which they are a part. Specifically, they relate to their own courts, not to more remote national and regional agencies such as the Judicial Conference, its committees, the Administrative Office, or the circuit judicial councils."[72]

The decision to add district judges to the council appears to have satisfied any concern at the district level about the legitimacy of the council as a governing body. Every chief district judge I interviewed stressed the significance of the decision to give district judges four slots on the council, but none detected any pressure for more representation, despite what several described as the "natural enmity" between trial and appellate judges.[73] At the break-out sessions the only criticism of the system voiced by district judges was that the one-year term for district judge representatives was too brief. (Three of the four district judge positions are defined as one-year terms; court of appeals representatives serve for two years.)

Judges on the court of appeals also accept the council as legitimate, in part perhaps because it has little impact on their day-to-day lives. As one circuit judge observed, "The cautiousness of the council in approaching issues of governance of the respective courts ensures its tranquility and survival."

Ninth Circuit judges display more enthusiasm for the committees of the council, despite the demands committee work places on judicial time. Not long after the end of the Browning era, the judges demonstrated their commitment to this form of participation by rejecting a staff proposal to cut back sharply the number of circuit standing committees. Apparently, the committee system serves social and educational functions that judges appreciate.

---

[72]Fish, supra note 6, at 429–30.

[73]A recent survey conducted under the auspices of the Ninth Circuit Judicial Council substantiates this observation. When district judges were asked about their views of the court of appeals, 95 percent responded that circuit judges should show greater deference to the trial judge's evaluation of the facts in an appeal; 80 percent agreed with the suggestion that a circuit judge should sit as a trial judge at least once a year; and 44 percent noted a lack of collegiality between circuit and district judges. Ninth Circuit Judicial Council, "Survey of District Court Judges and Attorneys Regarding the U.S. Court of Appeals for the Ninth Circuit" at 18, 27 (Office of the Circuit Executive, July 1987).

If the attitude toward circuit government among Ninth Circuit district and appeals judges can be described as satisfaction bordering on complacency, the viewpoint among non-Article III judicial officers must be set forth in more affirmative terms. The bankruptcy judges and magistrates I interviewed were openly enthusiastic about Browning-era innovations. Browning recognized the significance of these constituencies in the circuit community to a much greater extent than has Congress, which authorized these positions but failed to provide for the full participation of these judicial officers in circuit affairs. Browning offered these groups observer status on the circuit council and membership on council and conference committees. He helped organize specialized conferences for magistrates and bankruptcy judges, provided administrative support, and attended their meetings.

The warmth of his welcome can be discerned in an incident that Circuit Judge Warren J. Ferguson recalled at a ceremony commemorating Browning's service as chief judge:

> [At a Circuit Conference gathering] I was the escort to a young bankruptcy judge who had just been appointed. . . . I made my way through the crowd with this little bankruptcy judge and introduced her to Jim Browning. And he immediately sensed what he had to do. He knew that he had to devote at least five minutes of his entire attention to that judge. That this was a moment of her life that would always be remembered. And he did. He did it seriously and truthfully, telling her how proud he was of the bankruptcy courts in the Ninth Circuit. How proud he was of their achievements. How proud he was that she was appointed through a very elaborate program that picked the best. And he was most happy because women were achieving some of their status in the judiciary. With that we walked away and she grabbed my arm and stopped. And she said, you know, I have fallen in love with him.[74]

This difference in perspectives between district judges and other judicial officers suggests the importance of Article III status in defining roles in the circuit. With that status, a judge need not be particularly concerned about how the circuit as a whole operates (though some are). Without it, a judicial officer may have to depend on the organization of the circuit and the leadership of its chief executive officer to

---

[74]Reporter's Transcript of Proceedings, Special Session of U.S. District Court, Central District of California in Tribute to Chief Judge Emeritus James R. Browning at 37 (Dec. 8, 1988).

overcome the indifference or hostility of Article III judges and find a satisfying and effective role.[75]

Ninth Circuit Government: An Assessment

Apart from judging, one of my informants observed, judges care only about their space, their personnel, and their creature comforts. If circuit government can help them with these needs, fine. If it purports to tell judges how to judge, on the other hand, it will be universally resented. The judicial and administrative leadership in the Ninth Circuit, it seems clear, sets its course with this standard in mind. There is real reluctance to interfere in the administrative decisions of judges, but there is also unabashed activism when the issue is more resources for the circuit.

The activities involved in lobbying for more resources and in administering courts cannot, however, be so easily separated. The Ninth Circuit has developed a habit of self-study that serves not just to pinpoint needs, but to create incentives for better practice. The court of appeals, for example, recently commissioned a study to determine how its rule regarding unpublished opinions is working.[76] The council's Task Force on Death Penalty Habeas Corpus likewise works from an impressive empirical base that includes information about the number of inmates on death row and the point at which their state remedies will be exhausted.[77]

The Browning legacy of studies and information sharing also has implications for the distribution of power within and beyond the circuit. The information that can form the basis of persuasive arguments for change is available to all members of the Ninth Circuit community, not just the leadership. Such information is a by-product of automation in any large organization: "The same systems that make it possible to automate office transactions," sociologist Shoshana Zuboff has observed, "also create a vast overview of an organization's

---

[75]An indication of the fragility of this status occurred in the 1988 circuit conference when bankruptcy judges complained that Article III judges were given preference in hotel accommodations.

[76]The judges asked Lauren K. Robel of Indiana University at Bloomington School of Law to conduct the study. Her results were published as "The Myth of the Disposable Opinion: Unpublished Opinions and Government Litigants in the United States Courts of Appeals," 87 *Mich. L. Rev.* 940 (1989).

[77]Report of the Task Force on Death Penalty Habeas Corpus, included with materials for the August 1988 meeting of the Ninth Circuit Judicial Council.

operations, with many levels of data coordinated and accessible for a variety of analytical efforts."[78] The capacity the Ninth Circuit has developed to gather and disseminate information also has a bearing on the contemporary debate over central versus regional control of resources. The Ninth Circuit is in a better position than many circuits to take over tasks that until now have been within the ambit of the Administrative Office.

The approach to governance which Browning attempted to institutionalize, however, exacts a high price in the time and effort required of staff and participating judicial officers. The numerous court, council, and conference committees involve considerable staff work. For judicial officers, too, active involvement in governance reduces time available for the day-to-day tasks associated with managing court business, the tasks judges identify as their fundamental professional obligation.

There will be pressure to increase the commitment of resources to governance if decentralization of budgeting and associated administration goes further, as seems likely. It is unclear at this writing, however, what role current circuit-wide institutions will play in the process. It is difficult to imagine thoroughgoing decentralization without a significant role for the circuit council, the closest approximation the circuit has to a legislature. Yet if hard resource-allocation and enforcement decisions are to be made at this level—and especially if those decisions infringe on traditional judicial prerogatives in administration—it can be safely predicted that many judges will resist circuit authority. The Ninth Circuit experience suggests that representation for all constituencies, broad-based participation, and openness in decision making do help make circuit-level guidance and information sharing palatable, but they do not legitimize authoritative action, except where misconduct is egregious. Even within the district courts, any exercise of power by a chief district judge beyond what is strictly necessary for day-to-day operations is unacceptable to some judges.

The issue for the future is whether judicial independence as traditionally understood can survive pressure for more accountability within the third branch. The threat of a split forced the Ninth Circuit to face this issue earlier than its counterparts. Browning responded with changes designed to improve communications within the circuit and to encourage judges to take administrative concerns seriously. It is

[78]Shoshana Zuboff, *In the Age of the Smart Machine: The Future of Work and Power* 11 (Basic Books, 1988).

impossible to determine how much these innovations in governance contributed to the circuit's improved performance during the Browning period, but it is clear that the Ninth Circuit is better organized than its counterparts to discuss its problems and to plan for its future.

Conclusion

The 1939 reformers who created circuit councils and conferences envisioned circuit governance as a bulwark against excessive centralization—and against excessive decentralization—in a national system of justice. Circuit governance has not proven much of a bulwark against either the growth of the Administrative Office or the individualism of judges, even in the Ninth Circuit, where circuit institutions are strongest. Should circuit governance be stronger? Or would the system be better if reform went in the other direction and circuit-level adjudication and administration were decoupled? Each level of courts could manage its own affairs, with the districts organizing into statewide associations and hiring their own administrative personnel.

Eliminating the circuits as a significant element in the governance and administration of the federal courts would ease certain tensions in the current system. The logistics of gathering the administrative unit under one roof would be much simpler. The problem of mistrust between circuit and district judges would be resolved, or at least deferred to national-level institutions. Some administrative problems might be easier to attack in a system in which trial and appellate judges met separately and meetings were limited to judicial officers within a single state.

Abolition of circuit-wide institutions would do little, however, to remedy the deficiencies for which the federal courts are criticized most often: costly, slow litigation; toleration for inefficient, irascible, and unfair judges; and failure to confront current problems or plan for the future. When the circuit councils were made up entirely of circuit judges, they demonstrated little interest in these issues in their own courts. There is no reason to expect the situation to be different in associations of district-level judicial officers.

The current system of regional governance also offers certain important advantages. The large regional units are well positioned to make their views heard in Washington—in Congress, the Administrative Office, and the Judicial Conference. The interests of non-Article III judicial officers are likely to be better protected in a regional system in which these officers can associate by specialty; the chief circuit judge and the circuit executive's office are resources that these newly arrived professionals may be able to use in defining a position for themselves in their districts. A mix of appellate and trial-level personnel in a circuit council and at annual gatherings may also promote understanding between levels in the system and may promote better decisions when the issue is misconduct and disability in the judicial ranks. In sum, the heterogeneity of the circuit is an argument for its preservation as a unit of governance.

The basic problem, crudely put, is that judges don't want to govern themselves, but they don't want anyone else to do it either. In this respect, judges resemble other professionals in contemporary American society. Judicial reluctance either to discipline colleagues or to assign the task to others is a theme in debates over the role of managerial staff and in the controversy over whether budgeting should be centralized, regionalized, or carried out at the district level. The inertial tendencies in such a system are formidable. Many of the ideas implemented in the 1970s and 1980s, and some still under discussion, were raised by articulate spokesmen in the 1930s, 1940s, and 1950s. The concept of a circuit executive, decentralized budgeting, and representation of all judges in circuit governance are examples.[79]

The mechanisms through which judges communicate and deliberate are relevant to the performance dilemma even though these institutions are in no position to mandate across-the-board change. The Constitution vests Congress with the responsibility to make the law for the federal courts, and our tendency has been to see any change in the litigation process as a matter of constitutional moment. Efforts to keep down costs or speed up adjudication, for example, are bound to be challenged as infringing on due-process guarantees and judicial independence. Yet although Congress is the locus of final authority in federal court reform, it is individual judges who typically initiate the process and keep it in motion.

Reform initiatives can be encouraged or discouraged by the organization of governance within the courts. It is helpful, for example, to be able to discuss ideas in a forum in which the varied constituencies that make up the court system are represented. The dissemination of ideas is easier if the governing system within the courts is perceived as legitimate. Here lies the importance of the Browning legacy. The system of circuit governance the Ninth Circuit created—however limited

[79]Fish, supra note 6, at 155.

in its ability to coerce judges—provides a healthy environment for considering the implications of administrative changes. And the Ninth Circuit is good at making its voice heard in Washington. Committed to the concept of decentralized authority and sensitized to the fierce independence of judges, the Ninth Circuit is bound to star in the drama in which the classic issues of judicial self-governance are debated and transformed.

11

The Bar's Role in Circuit Governance

STEPHEN L. WASBY

A major development during Chief Judge Browning's tenure was a sustained effort to reach out to the court's primary constituency, the bar of the circuit, to communicate more effectively with it, and to involve it in the circuit's governance. The most important element in that endeavor was the reconceptualizing of the circuit conference. This chapter examines the structures and processes developed in that effort; it also includes a brief survey of lawyer participation on committees of the circuit council and of the court of appeals. Its fundamental premise is that lawyers should be involved in circuit governance activities on a systematic basis, with the corollary that they should participate with judges in all the circuit's policy-making entities rather than only in separate groups of lawyers that can do no more than develop policies for judges' disposition.

Developments concerning the conference prompt several questions. In addition to the basic empirical question of what lawyer participation has taken place, within what structures, there is the analytical question of what the goals are in involving lawyers in the administration of justice in the Ninth Circuit and the evaluative question of the extent to

I gratefully acknowledge the assistance of the lawyers and judges who submitted interviews, responded to surveys, and were supportive of my efforts; the help of those who reacted to an earlier version of this chapter presented at the Ninth Circuit Judicial Conference at Coeur d'Alene, Idaho; and the assistance of Mary Schleier and the circuit's staff. I dedicate this chapter to the memory of the late Judge J. Blaine Anderson, simply for the person he was and also for his generosity in helping with this and other research projects.

which those goals been accomplished. In keeping with a major theme of this volume, we must also ask whether, and in what ways, these matters are affected by the circuit's size. Whether the structures and processes that have been adopted have made a difference in circuit policy is problematic. Both judges and lawyers may believe that mechanisms like the circuit conference are absolutely essential for lawyers' input into governance. Yet we need to ask whether, given the asymmetry in the relationship between lawyers and judges, these mechanisms can be more than symbols of judicial concern. Thus we must treat as an open matter whether substantive contributions have been made.

Criteria and Methods

Because no single standard of evaluation is likely to capture all important effects of any institution or process, multiple measures are preferable. One appropriate basis for judgment is formal provisions in statutory mandates or other formal documents, including committee reports. Carrying almost the same cachet are statements by principal actors in establishing and maintaining an institution, particularly the chief judge. One is likely to miss much by relying solely on such statements, however; it is also necessary to look for functions not explicitly discussed in the creation of institutions, but which they regularly perform, such as educating lawyers about the circuit.

In developing standards for evaluation, the distinction between substance and process is important. The substantive accomplishments of any institution provide a basis for evaluation, yet determining who or what causes them is quite difficult. If the Judicial Conference of the United States takes action requested in a Ninth Circuit judicial conference resolution, how does one know whether, and to what extent, the resolution played a part? Likewise, how can one attribute a judge's change in trial procedures to lawyers' suggestions? Drawing the causal link may be reasonable if lawyers persistently raise a problem and the judge then changes procedures, but in their absence the judge might have developed the idea independently. Determining what might have resulted from a particular structure is even more difficult—for example, whether the Advisory Committee on Rules of Practice and Procedure would have produced a different set of rules if it had no judges or a different mix of lawyers and judges.

The obvious fact that institutions are dynamic and do not stand still to facilitate examination poses another difficulty in measuring effects.

282

Just as one begins measuring effects of a particular change, another is added. Since its 1970s restructuring, the circuit judicial conference has been fine-tuned, and it was again reexamined in the mid-1980s, with new recommendations being implemented incrementally. Evaluating it is thus like shooting at a moving target. People inhabiting an institution also change, making it difficult to decide whether identifiable effects result from structural changes, changed personnel, or a combination, with structural changes at times not fully taking hold *until* personnel change.

Especially if one lacks a metric against which to measure substantive accomplishments, attention to process is important, although it is also important in its own right, because *how* an institution functions may be at least as important to those involved as *what* it accomplishes. When process is the focus, participants' perceptions may be a useful measure of effects, probably more valuable than official views of the institution's accomplishments.

Data for this chapter come from court and committee documents, observation of several circuit conferences, and particularly from interviews and surveys.[1] Documents and correspondence provide some comparative information on activities in other circuits. Forty-seven individuals were interviewed about the circuit conference, and nine completed shorter mail surveys; many were especially active in the conference, and some served on its executive committee.[2] Four judges and eighteen lawyers were interviewed or surveyed about committee service, primarily about the court of appeals' advisory rules committee and the council's Senior Advisory Board. We have quite properly been warned not to rely too heavily on interviews and questionnaires to learn how policy makers make decisions.[3] Nonetheless, these sources are appropriate if one wants to learn people's reactions, and comparison of responses from differently situated individuals (triangulation) can provide a reasonably accurate portrayal of how an institution functions.

---

[1]For a more detailed account of the study, see Stephen L. Wasby, "The Bar's Role in Governance of the Ninth Circuit," 25 *Willamette L. Rev.* 471 (1989).

[2]Included were ten district and seven circuit judges, six court staff, and thirty-three lawyers—six U.S. attorneys, nine federal defenders, and eighteen private practitioners who were lawyer representatives at different times from the mid-1970s to the present.

[3]See Vladimir J. Konecni and Ebbe B. Ebbesen, "The Mythology of Legal Decision Making," 7 *Journal of Law and Psychiatry* 17 (1984). I am indebted to Gordon Bermant for calling this article and the basic argument to my attention.

Stephen L. Wasby

The Circuit Judicial Conference

Prior to 1939, some circuits held informal conferences, meetings of district judges alone or, more commonly, of both district and circuit judges, with lawyers also present; these gatherings provided a forum for discussing docket backlogs, sentence disparity, and many other problems of judicial administration.[4] Formalizing the circuit conferences at the same time it established circuit judicial councils in 1939, Congress made the judgment that the conferences could play an essential deliberative and advisory role within each circuit, but that circuit councils, given the sole power to order, were to be the focal point of action.[5]

The reorganization of the Ninth Circuit conference toward a more direct focus on its statutory purposes, "considering the business of the courts and advising means of improving the administration of justice in the circuit" (28 U.S.C. § 333), began in 1974, when Chief Judge Chambers appointed a committee of two circuit and two district judges and three lawyers to examine the conference's structure and functioning. No particular events seem to have prompted this action, although people remember that the conference "lacked shape and function" and was "not productive from an institutional point of view."[6] Circuit Judge J. Clifford Wallace was appointed to chair the committee; Judge James R. Browning, because he was to succeed Chambers as chief judge, was the other circuit judge. Both became strongly identified with the "new" conference that resulted from the committee's report, which was adopted by the circuit council in October 1976. The committee's recommendations were put into effect at the 1977 conference, the first after Browning, their strong supporter and implementer, became chief judge.

The Wallace Committee formulated specific goals for the Ninth Circuit conference:

1. to involve more people in the conference and to increase the diversity of the lawyers who attended;
2. to strengthen the role of lawyer participants so that it would fit the

---

[4]Peter Graham Fish, *The Politics of Federal Judicial Administration* 146–49 (Princeton University Press, 1973).

[5]See pp. 251–52.

[6]Material in quotations but not attributed is drawn from interviews in which respondents were promised anonymity.

conference's statutory functions, with a particular goal to increase lawyers' speaking out;

3. to limit the size of the conference;
4. to restructure the conference organization, in part to increase lawyer involvement; and
5. to have the conference assist the circuit council.

Later, another goal was developed:

6. to turn the conference, through regular meetings of judges and lawyer representatives in the districts, into a year-long process, not only an annual event.

Browning has also spoken of conference goals that stem from lawyers' participation, which is to benefit not only lawyers but also the courts. He recently told the Fourth Circuit that lawyers' "understanding of the problems facing the court" will allow them to help judges solve problems, "directly by organizing the cooperation of the bar in projects to assist the administration of our courts" and "indirectly in such ways as working for the passage of legislation necessary for the improvement of the functioning of the courts."

The goals enunciated by the Wallace Committee are interrelated and to some extent potentially competing; for example, involving more people through turnover may limit lawyer representatives' effectiveness. Likewise, the conferences' general purposes may conflict somewhat. In several days it is difficult to accommodate reports on the courts' business, substantive programs, discussion of issues, *and* social exchange, even if the social function is seen "as a method of continuing a stimulating program."[7] Nor is there consensus as to the conference's purpose; one critic observed, "I haven't found out what the function really is—social or business."

The Ninth Circuit judicial conference of the late 1980s was quite different from the pre-reorganization conference. For Browning, the conference "now has a conscious sense of purpose," entailing "a conscious process of self-examination" of the courts; Judge Wallace earlier said that "we now do a far better job of meeting our statutory responsibility."[8] Without doubt, much that is positive has occurred, and the circuit has gone a long way to meet the goals established in 1976,

[7] J. Clifford Wallace, "Remarks to Second Circuit Judicial Conference," 93 F.R.D. 683, 800 (1981) (hereafter cited as Wallace Remarks).
[8] Id. at 800.

although talk of conference goals may create expectations that, when not met, lead to disappointment. In addition to the positive, much remains to be done. A certain amount of self-congratulation is not only deserved but is also necessary to get conference participants to move forward in their endeavors; however, too much is counterproductive because it obscures areas where participants could do better. Also, if those outside the circuit are to learn from the Ninth Circuit's experience and its extensive effort to integrate lawyers into its governance, they need to see realistically the Ninth Circuit's difficulties so they can take them into account. For these reasons, the "negative" may appear to be emphasized in this chapter.

The conference's accomplishments have been primarily in the area of process for those who participate, not substance. Even those most heavily involved cannot remember any substantive accomplishments, perhaps because "the work of the conference is largely reactive." There are, however, some substantive outcomes to which people point. Substance, in the form of a program, is necessary to bring people together so the benefits of process can occur, but process is crucial, making participants' satisfaction from their involvement particularly important for the conference's success. The conference leads to a "feeling of goodwill that carries over and helps each side do little things that make the other side's job easier," and it helps produce cohesion among those from different districts. Participants from many districts repeatedly stress the usefulness of informal judge-lawyer exchanges and the opportunity to communicate. Yet the conference's usefulness can be diminished if participants experience only talk and do not see outcomes, so one does, after all, need actual results. Nonetheless, a positive answer to the question, *Are* there any effects? is more important than any particular effects.

An important element of process is that many now see the conference as a joint enterprise in which judges and lawyers have equal status, a view reinforced by repeated statements reminding lawyers that, like judges, they are there "as of right." Yet the circuit conference remains a *judicial* conference, with lawyers participating in an event belonging predominantly to others. It provides the judiciary the opportunity to cultivate the friends that it, like any organization, needs to provide support in the community. The bar provides that support because, as one judge put it, "bench and bar have the same object: to be trustees for the public in the operation of the system."

In 1986 a reevaluation of the conference was undertaken by a committee chaired by Chief District Judge Owen Panner of Oregon. Other committee members were three circuit judges (including Wallace), another chief district judge, a bankruptcy judge, a magistrate, and two former chairs of the Lawyer Representatives Coordinating Committee (LRCC). Although there was concern about particular aspects of the judicial conference, the Panner Committee was created not out of substantial criticism of the conference, but for a variety of other reasons: ten years had elapsed since the Wallace Committee report; relations between the conference and the restructured circuit council (see Chapter 10) needed to be "smoothed out" because the two bodies "were seen as wandering around as to who was doing what"; and the Gramm-Rudman-Hollings Act mandated budget reductions, adding to a rising concern about the conference's expense. This third factor reinforced Browning's positive response to a shortened, business-only Second Circuit judicial conference.

The Panner Committee's twenty-six recommendations touched on conference length and frequency, lawyer representatives' selection and service, and the conference program. The process following the completion of the committee's report was drawn out to avoid foreclosing a new chief judge's action. After an ad hoc subcommittee (Judges Goodwin and Wallace, a district judge, and the LRCC chair) made recommendations on each element, all but a few were adopted by the circuit council in 1988. Because these actions came shortly before the end of Browning's tenure as chief judge, the committee's recommendations provide a useful marker of conference accomplishments during the Browning years and of what remains to be done. Of particular note, the committee rejected the idea for a conference restructured along the lines of the Second Circuit's experiment, so that on the major point of contention the chief judge's wishes did not govern. That may, however, have resulted in part from a "lame duck" effect because the chief judge's tenure was about to end.

Conference Organization

Conference structure appears not to be a matter of major controversy and is not well known except by those involved in it. Many lawyer representatives seem not to care, perhaps because they are generally satisfied with how the conference operates: comments on organizational structure range from "generally good" to "excellent."

The Wallace Committee, finding the existing committee system "unsatisfactory," with most committees not meeting and many not submitting reports,[9] recommended that standing committees be discontinued and that an executive committee be established. The recommendation was adopted, and the executive committee is now seen as a forum in which "ideas would continue to develop and the program could have continuity where necessary." The committee has nineteen members: ten judicial officers—the circuit's chief judge (or a designee), three other circuit judges, four district judges, one bankruptcy judge, and one magistrate; eight attorneys—six lawyers chosen for staggered three-year terms by lawyer representatives (including either a U.S. attorney or federal defender) and the LRCC chair and chair-elect; and the spouses committee chair.

The executive committee has been called "a sovereign nation, an arm of the chief judge," and Wallace, as Browning's designee, was "put on the program committee permanently" to be sure it did not wander too far from the chief judge's wishes. This raises the question of the chief judge's role in the conference. Historically, circuit conferences were the chief judges' conferences, bearing their imprint. The chief judge's effect now is likely to extend beyond the format and contours of the conference program to the substance of discussion and the results. Although one can easily see evidence of Browning's imprint, it is important to distinguish between ideas originating with him and those initiated by others but which he adopted. And although his writ did not reach to all corners of the conference, if the chief judge "disliked something or someone, it was difficult to counter his wishes."

The executive committee forms several joint lawyer-judge subcommittees: program, budget and finance, activities, resolutions, site selection, and special studies. Principal is the program committee, whose chair—in successive years a circuit judge, district judge, and lawyer—has, as a matter of practice, chaired the conference the next year. From time to time there are also ad hoc committees or task forces, which include lawyers drawn from outside the executive committee and perhaps outside the conference. These committees are often suggested by the special studies subcommittee to examine particular substantive issues, and their reports sometimes serve as the basis for conference program topics. The conference appears to use committees

---

[9]A part of the problem may have been that committee members attended the conference regardless of committee productivity.

instead of staff work, but there are committees *and* staff because committees rely on the circuit executive's office for assistance to a considerable extent. This reliance, reinforced by the presence for an extended period of a person considered highly competent, may mean staff direction.

The Lawyer Representatives Coordinating Committee, composed of the heads of all lawyer district delegations, is important because it links conference governance and the focus on lawyer participation. Its tasks have included coordinating lawyer activities and serving as liaison between both the executive committee and the circuit council and lawyer representatives. Still an evolving and "not fully established" entity and not yet a central player in the conference, it has become "primarily a communication link and policy board" that "serves to translate and fine-tune general material into local concerns." Efforts have been made to increase its functions further; it now helps orient new lawyer representatives at the conference and raises lawyers' concerns with the chief district judges when it meets annually with them.

The circuit conference is tied organizationally to the circuit council, which must consider conference actions on the administration of justice. Judge Browning, one of whose purposes has been "to integrate the conference, particularly as a year-long process, into the circuit's governance," finds the conference "not tied in well enough," with close interaction between conference and council necessary. Making the conference officially a council committee, a formal organizational relationship clarified in 1988, does not, however, mean clear or well-developed working relationships. For example, when the special studies committee's chair takes an "activist" role, there is likely to be an overlap between matters examined by the conference (or its adjuncts) and those the council considers its "turf." The council is now asked for reactions to circuit conference executive committee proposals. The conference could also help carry out the circuit's annual action plan, which could be the conference's primary planning document now that the reconstituted council deals with a wider range of problems concerning the administration of justice.

The Size of the Conference

The conference's ability to fulfill its functions is affected by the number of people eligible to attend. The Wallace Committee stated the general principle: "Attendance which exceeds acceptable limits inhibits individual communication and participation, making exchanges of ideas and interaction of personalities difficult."[10] The optimal number for effective participation is also related to the type of conference one prefers. The number attending a day-and-a-half working conference without social events (and thus without spouses) will be much smaller than the numbers attending the present self-contained function, which combines business and social purposes, with spouses included.

In 1976, before reorganization, there were 94 judges and 335 lawyers, a ratio of 1:3⅓. A conference of 409 participants was thought too large, so that it "inhibited individual communication. It was more difficult to interact and to exchange ideas."[11] The *appearance* of a large number of lawyers may have stemmed from the presence of many not in federal practice or interested in discussing the administration of justice. If lawyers interested in federal practice attend, the size issue takes on a different focus, and judges might actually want more lawyers present.

The Wallace Committee felt the number of lawyers could be reduced and still be large enough so "judges would be exposed as much as practicable to a wide variety of views and experiences."[12] The principal changes were a shift in the manner of selection and a reduction in the number of lawyers. Although state bar associations retain a major role in selection of lawyer representatives, their direct representation was ended because state bar presidents were "too busy" to serve as effective representatives, conference leaders wanted lawyer representatives to be federal practitioners (the bar president might never have been in federal court), and the bar associations were "very blunt instruments" for representing and communicating with federal practitioners. The decision seems fully justified, as there is relatively little federal court-related activity by either state or local bar associations.[13] Law schools' presence at the circuit conference was also ended, although this step was viewed with ambivalence. When a desire (but no serious pressure) to have some law school connection and to restore

[10]Committee on Reorganization of the Ninth Circuit Conference and Conference Committees, Report, 75 F.R.D. 553, 558 (1976) (hereafter cited as Wallace Committee).

[11]Wallace Remarks, supra note 7, at 696.

[12]Wallace Committee, supra note 10, at 558.

[13]Because few states have institutionalized settings in which judges and lawyers meet, bench-bar relations, although a concern of many state and local bar association leaders, is not a topic about which federal courts can learn much from the states.

the schools' representation resurfaced in the mid-1980s, nothing was done about it.

Along with a reduction in the number of lawyers came an increase in judicial officers. The number of circuit and district judgeships was increased; bankruptcy judges were added to the conference by act of Congress; and all full-time magistrates were added by the circuit's own decision. At the 1987 conference there were 243 judicial officers and 119 lawyers (U.S. attorneys, federal defenders, and lawyer representatives), for a 2:1 ratio. However, the full roster showed roughly 430 people, including members of the liaison committees of district court clerks and bankruptcy court clerks, the senior advisory board (9), and 23 official guests, including Justice O'Connor (the circuit justice) and the Ninth Judicial Circuit Historical Society's board. With spouses and friends, there were 700 to 800 people.

Not surprisingly, no judge or lawyer who was asked whether the conference size was now appropriate said it was too small. Roughly twice as many agreed the size was appropriate as felt it was too large.[14] The views of some were a function of their experience, with "younger, new people" more likely to see it as too large in their first year; for others, preferences about circuit size affected perceptions of appropriate conference size. That the conference's size was "imperfect but a workable compromise" in relation to circuit size or the conference's goals best captured the general tone. The circuit's present size means that a large number of people will be at the conference if all judges are to be present and there is to be representation from other groups. Indeed, the only way to make the conference smaller may be to divide the circuit.

Growth of the conference stemmed both from the increased number of judges and from pressure to add new categories of people, for each of which there is a plausible reason for inclusion. For example, we are now told that district court and bankruptcy court clerks should attend because they could provide "valuable insight as to the practical clerical impact upon the court and parties in relation to topics discussed, and . . . a further contact between the court and lawyers in the district."[15] Additions, however, have not resulted from overall consid-

[14]A survey at the 1988 conference provides confirmation that the conference was about the right size. A plurality (57 of 126, or 45 percent) thought the conference the right size, but surprisingly, more respondents (46, or 37 percent) felt the conference could be bigger than thought it too big (26, only 21 percent).

[15]Terence H. Dunn, Clerk, U.S. Bankruptcy Court, District of Oregon, to Chief Judge Alfred T. Goodwin, August 31, 1988.

eration of conference numbers or a balancing of the particular groups' relative merits, but have occurred on an ad hoc basis, with no systematically applied rationale for inclusion or exclusion of groups. For example, although there is discussion at the conference of court of appeals rules that could provide the grist for rules changes, the court's advisory rules committee does not attend. Despite the view, stated acerbically by a district judge, that one "should not cut down on any category—except guests, staff, staff of guests, and guests of guests," there are no guidelines for "just saying 'no'." People "don't see any way you can cut down the size" and "can't figure out how to do it politely." Nor is there a policy to keep overall numbers stable by ensuring that any proposed change was "revenue-neutral," with any addition accompanied by an equivalent deletion.

Concern about conference size is not simply about numbers but about who is present. Key are the interrelated issues of judge-lawyer balance and whether all judicial officers should attend. The shift to including all bankruptcy judges and full-time magistrates led to questions about whether, if lawyers are present as representatives, the same should be true for those judicial officers. There is a specific dispute over the presence of bankruptcy judges, despite their inclusion in the statutory mandate that judicial officers be present, because of concern about how to integrate them and their specialized work into the conference. Indeed, some circuit and district judges seem to give higher priority to the presence of lawyer representatives because they feel bankruptcy judges' presence impairs effective lawyer communication with judges.

The issue of judge-lawyer balance is seen in the comment that, "as a practical matter, the conference is a judges' meeting attended by a few lawyers." The question is how many lawyers (really: what proportion) are necessary to make the conference function effectively, with a "critical mass" absent below a certain level. The number of lawyers is also closely related to several other matters, such as selection of lawyer representatives (an increase might facilitate having a reasonable cross-section of federal practitioners), the number of different individuals to attend the conference over time, and lawyer participation (hindered by the ratio of fourteen judges to six lawyers in "break-out" sessions). At the end of his tenure, Judge Browning, noting that the Ninth Circuit had the lowest ratio of lawyers to judicial officers of any conference, urged a substantial increase in the number of lawyers, and in 1988 a committee was appointed to consider conference size. One of the proposals under examination called for a ratio of one lawyer for each active judge, including magistrates and bankruptcy judges. Such an increase does not receive uniform support from either lawyers or judges, however. Some lawyers even argue that "being outnumbered by judicial officers actually facilitated judge-lawyer communication."

Lawyer Selection

Not until 1948 was it mandated that each court of appeals "shall provide by its rules for representation and active participation at such conference by members of the bar of such circuit" (28 U.S.C. § 333). How to choose lawyers was left up to the circuits. Generally, judges or bar associations selected lawyers, or lawyers attended by virtue of holding designated positions. Rotation among the lawyers was the exception, with conference memberships often permanent, or "static."[16] The Ninth Circuit was much like other circuits, although unlike some, it had no lifetime or honorary positions. Each judge selected several lawyer *delegates*, usually close friends ("drinking buddies"), former law partners, or even relatives. Many of those invited were not in federal practice or were no longer in active practice, and were not interested in conference business. Nor were lawyer delegates expected to perform meaningful tasks.

The Wallace Committee made a significant change in how lawyers were selected—the change at the center of the conference reorganization—by developing mechanisms for selecting lawyer *representatives* in which lawyers played a part and by establishing selection criteria. The size of the practicing bar in the Ninth Circuit, and even the size of the federal bar, made it necessary to develop a system of lawyer representation rather than having a "you-all come" system like that used earlier in the Eighth Circuit and still used in the Seventh and Tenth circuits, in the former through the Seventh Circuit Bar Association.[17]

Lawyer representatives are to "constitute a fair cross section of practitioners before the federal courts of the district." The lawyers are expected to be "actively involved in federal practice," "interested in the purposes and work of the conference," "willing and able to contribute actively to the purposes and work of the conference," and

---

[16]Fish, supra note 4, at 343.

[17]The committee evaluating the Seventh Circuit's conference found that this process of lawyer self-selection had not produced too large a conference and was better than invitations, inevitably based on social considerations. Report of the Special Committee to Evaluate the Judicial Conference of the Seventh Federal Circuit, 86 F.R.D. 579, 589 (1979).

"willing to assist in implementing conference programs with the local bar."[18] A list of nominees three times the number of lawyer positions is developed by either the bar or judges in each district, with the other making the final selection.

"The bar" may not be a group created only to select lawyer representatives and must be "representative of the attorneys practicing in the federal courts of that district."[19] This prescription poses a problem, because federal practitioners are a very small portion of the membership of state and local bar associations. The Federal Bar Association's chapters supplement or complement other bar associations' limited federal court-related activity, and in one district the chapter now selects lawyer representatives. That organization is not a fully satisfactory option, however, because there are no FBA chapters in several Ninth Circuit states, and the organization does not necessarily represent the full range of federal practitioners (government attorneys are overrepresented); thus it does not perform the functions of a separate circuit-wide bar association of federal court practitioners. Alternative mechanisms that "adhere[] to the principle that the lawyer representatives shall represent the attorneys rather than the judges"[20] can be used if approved by the conference executive committee. For example, lawyer representative delegations, which in theory represent all bar associations, have been allowed to nominate or select new lawyer representatives.

The changes, initially used for the 1977 conference, were met "with much gnashing of teeth," and at first some judges invited special guests despite a requirement that judges certify such invitations to the chief judge. This outcome perhaps indicates the limits of a chief judge's authority. The new method then took hold, although full implementation of its spirit was unlikely until a significant portion of judges accustomed to the "old boy" arrangement were replaced by those who had not known it; greater commitment came as some of the latter became chief district judges.

In some districts the actual selection has followed the mandated rules, but there are departures and a definite disjuncture between what some lawyer representatives report as their districts' selection mechanisms and what court staff believe to be operating; inadequate monitoring of district selection processes leads to such situations.

[18]Order [for circuit conference], 2.c(1)–(5).
[19]Order, 2.b(1)(d).
[20]Order, 2.b(1)(c).

Selection also appears to be concentrated in fewer hands than intended: instead of being made by a resident circuit judge and two district judges, selections become the chief district judge's province, and the state bar president, rather than the board of governors, appears to make choices.

Interaction over selection is often a three-stage process in which lawyers informally suggest names to judges, who then prepare a list to submit to the lawyers who select; or judges informally indicate names to the bar for inclusion on the formal list for the judges' final selection. Nor do judges restrict themselves to submitted names, turning either to social acquaintances or those who appear frequently before them. Perhaps surprisingly, lawyers selected in these ways have with limited exceptions satisfied the official selection criteria, but the choice of some lawyer representatives seems almost a foregone conclusion, with the use of existing networks definitely limiting the range of those considered. It also has the effect that those who "look at the function of the conference to 'hob nob' with the judges in a vacation atmosphere" are overrepresented.

Cross-section.   The Wallace Committee report spoke of the need for an "effort . . . to secure an appropriate race, sex and age representation within the lawyer representative contingent," at least without undercutting the need for a cross-section of federal practitioners or conference purposes.[21] "Product follows process" in having produced lawyer representatives from federal practice and increased lawyer diversity, but achieving diversity has not been easy. Roughly two-thirds of the lawyers and judges commenting said that the selection mechanism does produce a reasonable cross-section of federal practitioners, yet as measured by the ideal sought, "we could do better," because "judges' selection doesn't get good enough even among those who applied." Both lawyers and judges bear responsibility, because prior and present lawyer representatives are frequent initiators of getting lawyer names on the lists for final selection.

Many lawyers feel that certain types of lawyers are over- or underrepresented in the conference. Most frequently mentioned as overrepresented is "the large, financially well-established, downtown civil firm," a result of the law firms' desire to have a presence "reflective of their prestige and credibility in the federal process" and of judges selecting on the basis of reputation. Overrepresentation of these firms

[21]Wallace Committee, supra note 10, at 560.

produces a disproportionate number of "white male fortyish attorneys." Perhaps surprisingly, the median age has decreased, and the most senior lawyers became underrepresented. The latter result was the reason for creation of the senior advisory board. The number of women has increased along with "modestly greater acceptance of women participants," and women have been on the conference executive committee; one of those women was chair of the conference, following two women judges. However, some note judges' reluctance to choose women from nominee lists. Blacks and Hispanics are "few and far between," and no one seems to know how to alter that situation.

Certain types of lawyers are scarce or absent despite their frequent presence in court: criminal defense attorneys, public interest lawyers, labor union attorneys, those filing § 1983 civil rights actions, and bankruptcy wage-earner lawyers. Apart from some "white-collar" criminal defense attorneys from larger firms, there are few lawyers from private criminal practice, perhaps because such lawyers come from small firms and thus are less able to afford the expense. Indeed, some lawyers' inability to spend the time or money required throughout the year is a significant "preselection mechanism." Despite the argument that lawyers from small firms cannot attend without financial support, proposals to provide a subsidy for them have been rejected;[22] however, at least one state bar association helps diversify its delegation by providing funds toward expenses.

Lawyer representatives are supposed to be spread throughout each district, but lawyers outside a district's principal city are underrepresented. Efforts to seek out lawyers from outside the central city are not strong in some districts, and some large-firm lawyers who are the core of a delegation are self-congratulatory about their efforts or say that the process is reasonable on the basis of selection of who applied instead of focusing on the range of applicants. Indeed, less populous districts, with fewer representatives, do a good job of distributing lawyer representative positions throughout the district.

To speak of over- and underrepresentation of various segments of the bar is to recognize constituencies in the bar. Constant reference to *the* conference may lead to a view of it as internally undifferentiated.

[22]A resolution presented to the 1989 conference would have directed the Administrative Office of U.S. Courts to reimburse lawyer representatives for the expenses of attending the conference. Attorneys supported the resolution by a vote of 52 to 27, but the judges disagreed by the narrowest of margins (63–65); thus, under the conference rules (see p. 302), the resolution was defeated.

Common concerns, however, have not fully displaced particularized interests, which may require varying the means of communication, as must also be done depending on whether lawyers are inside or outside "the system" and whether they are from highly urbanized or less populated districts. Most obvious among lawyer groupings are U.S. attorneys and federal public defenders, both of whom attend the conference because of their positions; each group meets to exchange ideas and adopt positions on conference matters. The less "cohesive" U.S. attorneys took a negative view of the conference in earlier days, when they saw "antigovernment" resolutions going against them, but by the mid-1980s they viewed it more positively because of the presence of judges appointed by the Reagan administration, who were "much more deferential and respectful of the other branches of government."

Constituency can also mean those whom lawyer representatives purportedly represent, supposedly the remainder of the federal bar in their districts. Because most bar associations lack mechanisms for dealing with federal practitioners' separate concerns, lawyers do not participate in the conference as representatives of the institutionalized bar, nor is there much representation in the sense of interacting with an identifiable group from which lawyer representatives' bring ideas to the conference and to which they report. The Panner Committee recommendation that lawyer representatives be reminded "of their responsibility to communicate the concerns of the federal courts to the remaining federal practitioners" is evidence that more needs to be done on this point, as in the comment that "lawyers are representatives but don't have a constituency and don't have formal mechanisms to gather opinion."

Length of service.   Apart from any deficiencies in representation at a specific conference, turnover leads to a more representative conference over time. The Wallace Committee had argued that lawyers' attendance at the conference be rotated "to avoid the vices of inbreeding and stagnation which result from choosing the same representatives for long periods of time."[23] Judges may believe that lawyers, once having learned about the circuit through conference attendance, should be sent out to carry the message to the larger legal community, with their departure allowing education of another set of lawyers. Three-year terms for lawyer representatives have provided turnover.

[23]Wallace Committee, supra note 10, at 560.

Continuity is achieved not only by the presence of judges, federal defenders, and U.S. attorneys, but also by staggering lawyer representatives' terms, having terms overlap with those of newly selected lawyer representatives, and, after their terms expire, having lawyers remain ex officio delegation members in the district for two years. Nonetheless, complete lawyer delegation turnover every three years leaves very little institutional memory, although those selected to the executive committee remain beyond their terms as lawyer representatives.

Roughly three-fourths of those responding said the appropriate length for lawyers' terms was three years, a length of time the Panner Committee recommended retaining. (Were there to be a biennial conference, terms should be four years so all lawyer representatives could attend two conferences.) For some, three years was the "result of a trade-off between experience and maximizing diversity." No one wanted a term shorter than three years, because a three-year term meant that "just as you understand, you leave." Those who believed the three-year term too short said that, because two conferences were often necessary for some to learn, a three-year term allowed only one effective year, so a four-year term would provide two effective years.

Age or experience, personality, and the district represented affect how long it takes to feel fully participant. Some lawyers felt comfortable and able to be full participants "from the beginning," but others never became full participants. One who had "grown up in the courthouse" was comfortable far more quickly than "outsiders who didn't know very many people," just as lawyers from districts where the "delegation was more close-knit" were more likely to participate earlier. Conversely, those from districts with "more friction" and "more distance" between lawyers and judges "take longer to get acclimated."

Discomfort was a frequent first-year feeling, often continuing into the second year as well, because the conference is "intimidating." Some think this reaction might be alleviated by paying more attention to the selection process and by providing more effective orientation. The latter is thought necessary, as in other circuits, because of "uncertainties about the role of lawyer representative within the framework of the conference" and because few new members know much about the conference. Although each lawyer representative is supposed to receive a set of written materials about the circuit and the conference, until recently little regular orientation was provided. Orientation sessions can give those in charge of the conference an opportunity to "imprint" new representatives with the conference's purposes, but conference leaders appear not to use the situation effectively. Districts vary in the additional orientation they provide. Informal contacts from lawyer representatives—"two hours over a pitcher of beer about what I was going to get into"—and judges can be especially significant.

The Program

Starting in 1977, the Ninth Circuit made a serious effort to move the conference from its earlier social focus to a more "businesslike" one, but the present conference format did not take form immediately. At first, although lawyer representatives, circuit judges, and district judges each had separate sessions, and there were meetings of judges and lawyer representatives by district, the conference was a set of meetings for all attendees.[24] After having too many educational sessions about the law and too many reports, which left inadequate time for questions or discussion, more effective program formats were produced. Particularly noteworthy are (1) small (twenty-person) "break-out" sessions of judicial officers and lawyer representatives from different districts, cochaired by a judge and a lawyer, with lawyers also serving as reporters,[25] to discuss topics from large meetings, and (2) use of a theme throughout each conference, to "make people more likely to participate because things build on each other." Now accepted but without many advocates, themes may reduce continuity between conferences as they are rarely related to each other. New large sessions include those with a member of Congress, the attorney general, and a member of the Supreme Court, often the circuit justice.

The program still has a large social component, with "at least one extremely informal event to bring people together," and ending each day's program in early afternoon allows social activities before more formally organized evening social events. Even with social components viewed as part of conference work, they necessitate having the conference in a resort setting, because "everyone went away at the end of the day" when conferences were in San Francisco and Seattle, seriously reducing interchange. Although many see social interchange as essential to holding people's attention, others feel the present ar-

---

[24]An alternate model is the Seventh Circuit arrangement in which judges and attorneys meet separately for a day, then meet together for a day.

[25]In the Fourth Circuit, attorneys have presided over break-out sessions, and law deans and professors have been reporters.

rangement traps people into "a 'forced' vacation" and wastes precious time, interfering with courts' ability to process cases.

Lawyer concerns. If lawyers are to be an integral part of the conference, more must be done than talking to them. When circuit conferences first began to meet and to have lawyers present, the lawyers were not immediately involved in conference planning, a necessary condition if their concerns are to be met.[26] For some, the conference program is not meant to meet lawyers' concerns (as one lawyer put it, "It's not my conference, it's the judges' conference"), but many do feel it should, at least in part, do so. On this score, participants give the program mixed reviews. Like much else about the conference, reactions touch on both process and substance. Most obvious is that breakout sessions receive high marks from virtually everyone, although there are cautions about avoiding the inclusion of judges and lawyers from the same district "so that the lawyers can use examples of good and bad practice without angering the judges they have to live with."

One aspect of the program that arouses objection is a perceived tilt toward the circuit level and away from the district level; many lawyers "down in the trenches" see the circuit as distant and not related to their immediate concerns. This tilt occurs despite a balanced program committee, a rotating chairmanship, and the presence of circuit judges who are former district judges and who could serve as an effective link between the two levels if such a role were made more explicit. Emphasis on circuit-wide concerns is, however, an important aspect of the conference's integrative function, at least if not overdone. Lawyers' cynicism makes more than a small amount of "cheerleading" about holding the circuit together a risky business, especially among those already unhappy about the conference's size and expense. Browning has been criticized for placing too much emphasis on "demonstrating we've staved off the critics" and for limiting discussion of contrary views, something directly conflicting with the goal of openness.

A greater concern of lawyers is the absence of topics directly related to their practice needs, such as sentencing guidelines, motions practice, and sanctions. Perhaps for fear of returning to a series of sessions

---

[26]There were, however, instances, like that in the Second Circuit under Chief Judge Charles E. Clark, when a lawyer-dominated planning and program committee was established. Yet even here judges retained—and exercised—a veto power over topics proposed by lawyers for conference agendas. Fish, supra note 4, at 344–45.

on legal developments, others, particularly judges, often hastily dismiss such concerns as a desire for "CLE" (continuing legal education). One judge argued that lawyers should come to the conference not to work for CLE units but to educate judges about the administration of justice; lawyers' needs for "nuts and bolts" are to be met in the districts. Yet failure to address lawyers' practical concerns at the conference may interfere with its success, because "to have interaction, one must choose topics of interest to lawyers." One solution to the problem of meeting the diverse needs of the many different types of disparate constituencies present would be to hold simultaneous panels on specialized topics.

The program is seen as "designed by the program chairman and maybe a small support staff," with "topics the pet projects of judges" and "very little consultation" about the conference theme despite its pervasive effects on the program. Nonetheless, almost all lawyer representatives active in the conference who were asked said that there was adequate consultation of lawyers about the program, but not beyond program or executive committee lawyers, whom most representatives are willing to have act for them. Despite occasional suggestions of a broad canvass of lawyers about program topics and isolated instances of consultation, as well as comments that the program committee "was trying to find, not ward off, topics," consultation devices seem not to be used systematically. (Lawyers may also have input into the conference through solicitation of their views on substantive matters considered there, particularly through surveys of attorneys practicing in the various courts.[27])

The resolutions process. A conference resolutions process, even if not producing specific results, is valuable if it "furnishes the opportunity to ventilate and a forum to place questions before the conference." Even "when you think a matter is open and shut," said one judge, "it is good to hear others' views and realize it isn't so." As this comment indicates, judges' "consciousness" can be raised by conference discussion. Despite these favorable responses, however, the resolutions process has stood out as the least satisfactory part of the program. By the late 1980s, it had come to be thought "meaningless," "toothless," "a big fat zero," and "pointless," and the Panner Commit-

---

[27]Federal Judicial Center studies presenting lawyer responses by circuit provide further direct information about Ninth Circuit lawyers' views.

tee acknowledged that some conference members "believed that the resolutions process was futile."

In the restructured conference's early years, intense debate took place over controversial resolutions—on lawyer participation in voir dire, extended criminal discovery, and peremptory challenges of judges. When the last of these topics was initially raised, the lawyers came close to prevailing. That conflict brought to a head concerns that the process was too "acrimonious." Although such views are in part a function of lack of tolerance for conflict, with some finding the debates relatively mild (a "tea party compared with political conventions") or necessary to the democratic process, the view that "if the process is inflammatory, it colors the entire conference, so you don't get any-where" carried the day.

The result was a series of changes that "severely downplayed" the process, including requirements for advanced submission of resolutions, screening by the resolutions committee, and separate judge and lawyer majorities. Ironically, although under the old rule obtaining a majority for any resolution without substantial judge support would have been difficult, the new rule allows lawyers to thwart the much larger number of judicial officers; therefore, lawyers now wish to retain it because it serves to protect their small numbers.

The changes were effective: they eliminated controversy. However, they also went too far, eliminating most of the resolutions process's usefulness. Only "pro forma and cosmetic" resolutions, like those supporting salary increases for judges, were left, and the number of resolutions was seriously decreased, so that at times people were "casting about" for some. These results ran directly counter to the efforts, which lay at the heart of the restructuring, to make the conference more open. Shutting off lawyer participation when it seemed to succeed confirmed for many that the stated goal was largely symbolic, with judges desiring only the appearance of lawyer participation; at least under the "buddy system" no such expectation existed. Because the changes so thoroughly "sanitized" the process that either a meaningful resolutions process had to be restored or it had to be dropped completely, action has begun to restore some of its effectiveness.

Also troubling lawyers have been problems with implementation of resolutions, which are advisory and nonbinding; the process is viewed as flawed if no results are seen from adopted resolutions. The Panner Committee thought that adopted resolutions "were neither implemented nor even adequately communicated to the relevant authority," consonant with the basic perception "that resolutions had no follow-through." Some lawyers believed that Ninth Circuit resolutions "just sit" at the Judicial Conference of the United States, although those who had served on national committees said that resolutions had some legislative effect, even when recognized to be the circuit chief judge's view; in particular, because the Ninth was a large circuit, conference resolutions "carried a lot of weight" if they concerned proposed rules.

A basic problem was that people did not know what had transpired. Even when action was taken or committees were appointed to pursue a matter, lawyer representatives were not informed. Here action to correct the situation was prompt. Now the circuit executive has been directed to place resolutions on the agenda for the council, which will decide if they are "council business" or should be forwarded, and Judge Browning, "sensitive" to frequent comments that "we pass something and nothing happened," instituted reports to the subsequent conference about resolutions. The LRCC chair also used the *9th Circuit News* to write about action on resolutions by bar associations and the circuit council. (In addition, the Administrative Office of the United States Courts agreed to keep tabs on resolutions submitted to it or to the Judicial Conference.)

District meetings at the conference. An important part of the conference, particularly for lawyer representatives, is the relatively short (one and one-half hours) district meeting the lawyers have with judicial officers, ostensibly to apply "conference topics to the problems and individual characteristics of each district, . . . develop an annual action plan for resolving problems that have been identified,"[28] and review the district report prepared by the chief district judge and the chair of the lawyer delegation. Reactions to these meetings are very positive. Usefulness does vary among districts, with these sessions at the conference not as crucial when lawyers and judges meet regularly during the year.

Chief judges are thought responsible for the success of these meetings; those who took them seriously produced highly effective meetings, whereas those who "didn't take it seriously" came up with "singularly uneventful" sessions. Planning and an agenda for a "well-structured" meeting are necessary for the sessions to work effectively, but lawyers have in mind an agenda the chief district judge—and,

[28]Office of the Circuit Executive, *1986 Annual Report of the Ninth Circuit*, at 44.

often, lawyer representatives—develops, not what the circuit executive provides. Some think district meetings are effective almost to the extent that the circuit executive's "directives" are ignored, illustrating that some of what the conference accomplishes is done despite or outside its formal framework.

District meetings are felt to accomplish something; the achievements can be divided into substance and process. On the substantive side, "judges and lawyers get resolutions of some problems" and lawyer-suggested rules have been implemented. The meetings' process values are helping to bring judges and lawyers together, producing "cross-pollination," and "furnishing a good social bond" with "collegiality and increased understanding" a result. This is important, said a judge, because "lawyers understanding judges is more a problem than the reverse—because judges were lawyers." Although the meetings create the opportunity for such exchange, it does not happen in all districts. If lawyer representatives "do not develop the issues, the tendency is for the judges to take control," and even in relatively "open" districts the meetings may not be "the best forum for hard issues" because it is "embarrassing and impolitic" to discuss certain topics when "all are there."

The official view is that these meetings should follow the conference theme, but the emphasis tends to be more on "the problems . . . of each district," and there is much feeling that the theme should not control, in part because in the break-out sessions small groups discuss conference themes. Lawyers would probably be happier if districts were allowed to follow the theme only to the extent they feel it relevant to district concerns.

Lawyer Participation

A principal goal of those in charge of the circuit conference is to have lawyer representatives speak out. When the conference was solely a social event, there was little likelihood that lawyers would raise their concerns to judges. Moreover, although those who know judges may be more willing to speak frankly to them, under the "buddy system" lawyers' dependence on judges for being at the conference also chilled their frankness.

Changing the selection method, assuring lawyers of their official status, and urging them to speak out did not immediately change their posture toward judges: they generally were reticent about expressing criticism. (Participants generally feel that "no selection process will alter the reality" of lawyers' hesitancy to be candid in front of judges.) Because "lawyers are reluctant to take positions that may offend judges" and even "lawyers aggressive with other lawyers are not necessarily so in the presence of judges," a conducive program structure is especially necessary to produce greater lawyer participation, for "simmering bar feelings [that] bubble just beneath the surface . . . require a special occasion for explicit expression."

The Wallace Committee spoke of programs in which "judges and lawyers confront each other in a constructive way" and of "spit and growl" sessions with judges and lawyers "express[ing] their feelings in a frank but cordial atmosphere."[29] Lawyer participation has increased since 1977, but the picture is mixed as to whether lawyers have spoken out as much as was sought. Important in this evaluation are expectations about a reasonable level of lawyer participation and about what participation can achieve. Although it is recognized that the conference cannot be "a full-scale debating house," there is a tendency to measure participation in terms of lawyers "speaking up" in large, formal sessions, and to expect that problems will be resolved instead of simply accepting the value of providing participants a more realistic picture of lawyers or judges.

Over four-fifths of those responding thought the opportunity for "give-and-take" at the conference was adequate. However, against the quite positive view that "the kind of lawyers at the conference aren't wallflowers" must be set the perception that "judge domination" meant insufficient opportunity for participation unless a lawyer was a "strong person." And opportunities for participation do not always translate into actual participation. In 1981 Judge Wallace told the Second Circuit, "We have, to some extent, broken down the barrier so that lawyers . . . do not seem to feel as reticent to discuss problems that they might otherwise not talk about."[30] The general view in 1988 was that there had been some increase in lawyer frankness but "no material difference." Some views are quite positive. "Some discussions get quite intense" and "quite candid," with "judges told things they don't want to hear." There is also the contrary view that frankness "doesn't occur very often," that "plenty more needed to be done," and that "diplomacy" was necessary at a judges' conference, which was "not the time to rake them over the coals."

The extent of lawyer participation is largely situational. The con-

---

[29]Wallace Committee, supra note 10, at 567.
[30]Wallace Remarks, supra note 7, at 700.

sensus is that plenary sessions do not produce participation, which is more likely in district meetings and break-out sessions. Discussions in those meetings may in turn establish the basis for further informal communication, "particularly in the saloons." "At times [lawyers] are incredibly frank" at break-out sessions because they "don't know to whom they are speaking"; by comparison, at district meetings the presence of judges before whom the lawyers practice may depress participation.

Factors accounting for differences in lawyer participation are age, experience, and type of practice. Younger lawyers are thought "more timorous"; lawyer representatives with seniority at the bar gain judges' acceptance most readily. "Institutional members" such as federal public defenders are more likely to be "gadflies," because, as one of their own put it, they are "not as concerned with being unpopular" as lawyers in private practice. In general, although one circuit judge said that outspoken attorneys were no longer "viewed as troublesome" and were "less and less out there by themselves," both "establishment types" and "outsiders" suggested that no "heretics" or "outsiders" were selected, with "those who surface as lawyer representatives Sanforized; the lawyer representative today is a person with a mission selected carefully" from among "those who work up through the bar."

If lawyers are to be frank, they must believe judges want to hear them. Some feel that judges are "responsive," at least "when relevant issues are raised," and that "over the years, there has been a process where judges who felt put upon by [lawyer participation] have become more receptive." Judges' tolerance varies, however, "all the way from total arrogance and closed-mindedness" to "what amounts to almost undue deference" to lawyers. "Some of the newer judges who didn't know the old boy conference" come to the conference more committed to its goals and "might be more willing to listen."

Having judges act on what they hear is a different matter. Judges may be "perfectly prepared to listen" but show "lots of inflexibility"; others, however, will do "a 180-degree change in five days" because "they didn't realize their practice was causing a problem for litigants until the lawyers told them." Judges may be more willing to receive proposals for change at the conference, where they "can take off their institutional hats," than in the district, where they might see suggestions as more of a challenge. Even so, "policy-permeable" judges (those to whom a lawyer can make a pitch and affect the outcome) may not indicate being affected by discussion. How lawyers approach judges is important, because it may take judges time to realize that lawyers are not going to discuss pending cases. One lawyer said that a larger proportion of federal judges than of state judges were willing to listen but that state judges were "more likely to act," because the former, even with "a sympathetic ear," "feel the frustration of a bureaucratic system not willing to deal with their concerns."

During the Year: Meetings in the District

One of Judge Browning's purposes was to turn the "one-shot" annual circuit conference into "an ongoing process, consisting of a year-long continuing dialogue among all segments of the legal community," with the annual meeting as its culmination.[31] A serious effort has been made to carry out this goal, with considerable activity in the districts. Nonetheless, the conference remains primarily an annual event, and even Browning has said that "clearly not enough" has been done about making it year-long. There is also a great deal of variation among districts. In some, lawyers control the agenda and make formal, well-researched presentations, whereas in others activity is negligible, with the meeting being nothing more than a lunch for one district judge and three attorneys. An effective device for monitoring district activities appears to be lacking, even though the need has been pointed out.

In most districts lawyer representatives hold some meetings by themselves, with "pretty good" attendance. Viewed as necessary but "less interesting" than those with judges, these meetings focus on selecting the next lawyer representatives, preparing resolutions for the conference, determining agendas for meetings with judges, and perhaps resolving the lawyers' own concerns before those meetings. Most lawyer delegations have at least two, and a few have as many as four, meetings with district judges. "Generally district judges will not spearhead setting up meetings in the districts," instead "generally reacting to lawyer representatives setting them up." Although some meetings deal with substantive matters, in some districts not only is the number of meetings minimal but there is little discussion of the administration of justice. District meetings may be particularly difficult to carry out effectively precisely where they are needed most because lawyers are having problems with the district court. Differences between districts reveal the imprint of chief judges, as do differ-

[31]Office of the Circuit Executive, *1987 Annual Report of the Ninth Circuit*, at 6.

ences within a district from one chief judge to a successor, but the chief judge must act within expectations that lawyers help create.

Attendance at lawyer-judge meetings is generally good, especially on the lawyer side, perhaps because lawyers are expected to attend to remain representatives. Except in smaller districts, a lower proportion of judges attend even when meetings are held at four o'clock in the afternoon in the courthouse, because of lack of interest and because in large districts judges are insulated from lawyers. However, "communicative" and "interested" judges attend and constitute a "sufficient number to make the meetings worthwhile." (Circuit judges are invited to attend and some do participate.) The fact that districts are small does not preclude activity, such as a meeting of the district judge, a few attorneys, and court clerks to discuss practical issues.

With limited exceptions, lawyers other than lawyer representatives, the U.S. attorney, and the federal defender are not present at these meetings.[32] Inclusion of other lawyers besides the past lawyer representatives invited for two post-term years helps produce an understanding of the conference. Seminars and miniconferences are a major way of including other lawyers.[33] Particularly important are extended meetings, initiated by Eastern California, which holds a two-day district meeting with about one hundred lawyers attending by judge and lawyer invitation. Other districts picked up the idea, including Arizona, which holds a "seminar" for judges and lawyer representatives; Central California, which held a "retreat" in 1988; and Oregon, where lawyers and judges have for several years held a January "Saturday Session," also including other federal practitioners, to discuss a wide range of topics, including local rules, discovery procedures, the district's settlement program, and sanctions. (Setting aside Saturday is important to get adequate time.) Lawyer representatives are also involved in "overlapping" meetings not officially part of the circuit conference but at which they "will be a large part of the group."

[32]In some districts, U.S. attorneys and federal defenders are not seen as "lawyer representatives" and have not been invited to between-conference meetings, but that is the result of oversight, and they want to be included as special constituencies in the federal bar.

[33]The Panner Committee advocated mini-intradistrict conferences and suggested that they identify problems, issues in administration of courts, and the bar activities affecting the federal courts. The special executive committee subcommittee urged flexible application of this idea, saying that such meetings could implement business from the last conference, work on problems relating to the district court or court of appeals, recommend programs for the judicial conference, and consider and help develop conference resolutions.

Lawyer-judge district meetings are generally thought to be useful, with a combination of process effects and actual substantive outcomes to which the former sometimes lead. Some judges and lawyers unable to recall substantive outcomes from the conference point to such results from district meetings. In addition to educational programs, there are judges' changes in trial procedures, lawyer proposals considered by the court's local rules committee, and adoption of rules. The process category includes lawyers' "seeing what's on judicial officers' minds," which assists in "creating a rapport and relationship" that over several years may "give you freedom to sit down with judges or a judge to state your concerns." Regular district meetings also give lawyers a "forum so they can raise questions that affect them and their practice that would not otherwise come to judges' attention" because of the daunting task of arranging a special meeting with a judge to deal with a particular problem or complaint.

Consensus is lacking as to whether local district meetings are more useful than conference district meetings; roughly equal numbers think the local meetings more useful than, less useful than, or as useful as those at the conference. For some, conference district sessions are more valuable because of a less formal atmosphere ("people never relate as well in ties and jackets") and better judges' attendance. The two types of meetings, with differing climates, serve different purposes and thus complement each other. Each can also function as an extension of the other. When conference district meetings do not deal adequately with lawyers' practical concerns, meetings in the district can satisfy those unmet needs.

There is some carryover, or a "continuum," between the two sets of district meetings, although "we have not got to the ideal yet." One reason is that, although the circuit executive's office provides a liaison function and some prodding, more effective mechanisms are necessary to reinforce the conference's executive committee's exhortations; here the LRCC could be of assistance. A slightly higher proportion felt that carryover took place from conference to local meetings than saw carryover in the reverse direction. Adopted resolutions can be the basis for further activity in the district, and some delegations identify topics for further discussion in the district; some districts make conscious efforts to have at least the first local meeting deal with conference follow-up. Achieving this type of carryover is difficult, however, because one leaves three days of intensive discussion to turn to other matters.

Carryover from local district meetings to the conference occurs because much district activity is aimed toward the following conference, and because one function of the conference district meeting is "to apprise others (including judges) who had not been there" of what had occurred during the year, a use of time detracting from dealing with new business. Local district projects can lead to resolutions proposed at the annual conference, and orienting new lawyer representatives helps them function effectively in their first annual conference. There is the feeling, however, that "the conference is a place to start anew [and] to move to new issues," and use of a conference theme makes carryover of discussion of important issues from the district to the conference unlikely except for "some topics that are always around."

Lawyers on Committees

Lawyer participation in the circuit's work through participation at the circuit conference, on conference committees, and in district activities during the year is important. For effective continuing lawyer input into circuit policy development between annual conference meetings, however, it is extremely important that lawyers participate on committees of the circuit council and of the court of appeals. Any limits to effective lawyer participation in the conference can be offset to some extent through such committee work.

Lawyers' presence on committees other than the one advising the court of appeals on rules, on which their presence is statutorily mandated, varies among the circuits, with several circuits having none. The Ninth Circuit is unusual in the range of council committees on which lawyers serve, although they do not serve on all. In contrast to the deliberate effort to integrate lawyers into all aspects of the conference, similar efforts were not made with respect to committees of the circuit council or of the court of appeals. (There are not many committees of the court of appeals, as most of what would otherwise be committee work is done by the court's executive committee and staff, although the court may appoint ad hoc committees.)

Lawyer participation on council committees is sought ostensibly to obtain their views—and to educate them further about circuit operations—but the utility of such membership is not assumed. Because few committees develop lawyer input on their own, absence of lawyers means that committees are likely to develop policy without the benefit of lawyers' views. One cannot, however, easily determine

whether lawyers' presence on committees has had any effect: committees often reach consensus, and lawyers or judges could "win" only
when disagreements were along lawyer-judge lines, which apparently
is not often the case.

Another purpose of lawyer service may be to blend lawyers' and
judges' views before making recommendations, so that if there is
disagreement, compromises will be worked out early and the council
will not have to contend directly with as many disputes. Judges on
committees may persuade lawyers that judicial colleagues would not
accept a proposal, and lawyers on committees are necessary "to have
someone say, 'That's not going to fly.'" Committee discussion thus
"provides an interesting, informal method of communicating the reservations of practitioners to the committee members who are judges,
and thus to the entire court."

When the circuit council was restructured in the early 1980s, committees were reorganized to add "new blood," but there was no
change in the number of committees with lawyers. A 1988 reorganization also produced no essential change. Nonetheless, a new eleven-
member sentencing guidelines task force has among its members a
federal defender, a U.S. attorney, and one private criminal defense
attorney, and greater lawyer membership is contemplated for some
possible new committees. Thus lawyers continue to serve on several
committees, but not all, a situation for which there appears to be no
rationale.[34] It was not a matter of a "conscious decision" not to have
lawyers on particular committees; it simply "never occurred" to anyone to have lawyers on, for example, the jury instructions committee,
where their potential contribution is obvious. Although at least some
all-judge committees have later considered adding lawyers, the
"purely ad hoc" decision to include lawyers occurs at a committee's
creation, which invariably comes on judges' initiative rather than in
response to lawyer demand. This and the absence of lawyers from the
council, which creates committees, may explain why lawyer membership is "likely to be overlooked," although the LRCC chair's presence
might attune the council more to placing lawyers on committees.

Before 1988 there was "no system" for selecting lawyers for council

[34]Committees on which lawyers serve are defender services (formerly criminal justice
act) (4—a panel attorney, 2 federal defenders, and 1 U.S. attorney); evaluation of judges
and lawyers (6 of 13, explained by its origins as a conference committee); bankruptcy
courts advisory (1); automation and technology (2); the committee to revise district court
local rules (2 of 7); and the task force on alternate dispute resolution (7).

committees beyond the chief judge's seeking input from the circuit executive and the chair of the committee; there was no committee on committees, nor was the LRCC used to supply names. In addition to limiting committee members' terms to three years, with a second three-year term possible, the 1988 committee realignment brought an important change: the council created a committee on committees, but one composed solely of judicial officers. Failure to use the LRCC means that there is no mechanism for lawyers on committees to serve as representatives unless they create links to the larger federal bar themselves.

Committees vary in their levels of activity, from one to another and over time. Some have high levels of activity and productivity. However, after an initial period of activity in response to the currency of the issue that prompted their creation, over the longer run they tend to move into lower levels of activity, with some kept alive despite inaction. For some, the activity level seems to be a function of the committee chair's activity, with a chairperson's poor health at times seriously decreasing committee activity. Committees also vary in the extent of lawyer input. For example, the task force on alternative dispute resolution had heavy lawyer involvement stemming from its Northern District of California origins; the goal of the judge who led it was "to get a range of types of firms" involved "so the big firms can't dominate access." In contrast, the bankruptcy courts advisory committee represents a situation of little judge-lawyer exchange (not meeting as a body, with members responding individually to memoranda) and relatively little lawyer input, although it played a major role in obtaining such input about the bankruptcy courts by helping oversee the bankruptcy management study.

Examples of active committees are the Senior Advisory Board and the Committee on Evaluation of Lawyers and Judges. The former, the sole lawyer-only committee, has a charter giving it a broad, virtually open-ended charge to advise the circuit council, the conference, and the courts "regarding proposed changes in practice and procedure" and to "formulate recommendations for improvement of any aspect of judicial administration." It meets roughly three times a year, but there seems to be relatively little other interaction apart from correspondence from the chairperson to committee members. This relatively self-contained committee also has little contact with lawyers outside the committee, although it occasionally circulates proposals to selected members of the bar. The Committee on Evaluation of Lawyers and Judges was active from its inception as a conference committee on

evaluation of lawyers, with that activity continuing through its transformation into a council committee focusing on judicial self-evalua-
tion. It meets regularly, although no more than twice a year, with
active discussion at its meetings but little contact outside the committee.

The committee to which people point as a model of effective participation, substantial activity (as many as six meetings per year), and
accomplishments on a major project is a committee not of the council
but of the court of appeals. It is the fifteen-member (three judges,
twelve lawyers) Ninth Circuit Advisory Committee on Rules of Practice and Procedure, whose co-chairs have been lawyers, not judges.
Lawyers have regularly been involved in writing rules, at least lo-
cally,[35] but such involvement in court of appeals rules is now mandated by 28 U.S.C. § 2077. This requirement resulted in part from the
work of the Hruska Commission, whose survey of lawyers suggested
"that attorneys may be able to bring to the court's attention considerations and values that might otherwise be slighted in the rule-making
process"; moreover, their presence would contribute to the rules' legitimacy.[36]

In the Ninth Circuit the committee initially dealt with suggestions
from judges, council committees, or, at times, members of the bar that
specific rules be revised. When this agenda did not provide substantial
work, the committee on its own initiative moved to its major project:
using the Fifth Circuit's manual as the model, it prepared a volume
integrating the Ninth Circuit Rules with the Federal Rules of Appellate
Procedure (FRAP). As the committee moved on to integrate the court's
General Orders and Internal Operating Procedures with the rules, the
court began to treat it "more like a standing committee"—for example,
by asking it to consider the "hot" issue of sanctions against lawyers.

A large part of the positive reaction the committee receives from its
own members can be explained by its extremely effective working
arrangement for carrying out its major projects: division into geographically organized subcommittees that work on segments of the
Rules before the whole committee meets. Although committee members, said one, "were put there because of our broad contacts and

---

[35]See Steven Flanders, "In Praise of Local Rules," 62 *Judicature* 28 (1978). On lawyer
involvement in rule making at the state level, see Charles W. Grau, "Who Rules the
Courts? The Issue of Access to the Rulemaking Process," 62 *Judicature* 428 (1979).

[36]Commission on Revision of the Federal Court Appellate System, "Structure and
Internal Procedures: Recommendations for Change," 67 F.R.D. 195, 251–53 (1975).

experience—we would speak for more than ourselves when we spoke," they "haven't done a good job" in making other lawyers aware of their existence and do not function as representatives. Prior to completion of the proposals, there was "no outside input on an institutionalized basis," although individual members made some informal contacts with other lawyers and one "sent a letter to all U.S. attorneys about their practice on particular criminal matters" in order "to get a broader perspective to help the committee." Once a full document was developed, however, systematic input was sought using the publication process and sending the document to judicial officers and the circuit conference's lawyer representatives, a "very broad circulation to constituencies widely construed."

Conclusions and Implications for a Large Circuit

This chapter has undertaken an evaluation of lawyers' participation in circuit governance, with particular attention to the circuit conference and brief examination of council and court committees. Examination of the circuit conference is especially important in a volume seeking to offer lessons for other courts. The Ninth Circuit's restructuring of its circuit conference has already had extraterritorial effects. The Third Circuit was the first to make use of it, and other circuits then drew either directly on the Ninth Circuit experience or indirectly on it through the Third Circuit's work. For example, the Second Circuit, which examined the Ninth Circuit report and listened to both Judge Wallace and the Third Circuit's Judge Leonard Garth, found that it could make use of the work of both. The 1979 Seventh Circuit report also showed familiarity with the Ninth Circuit's experience, but that circuit did not follow the same path.

In a way, this chapter has been a reevaluation of the circuit conference itself, drawing on and extending the work of the Wallace and Panner committees. Such an exercise raises the question about how and how often the circuit conference should be evaluated. The frequency of and stimulus for an evaluation help determine its thoroughness. The Wallace Committee "model" was undoubtedly needed for the shift to a systematically run circuit conference focused on fulfilling its statutory responsibilities. As the circuit conference has become institutionalized, with a better institutional memory, the thorough set of studies, including visits to other circuits and hearings, that characterized the Wallace Committee's work may be less necessary. New ideas can now be obtained on a continuing basis. If evaluation is undertaken regularly, like the decennial census, independent of dissatisfactions, it is more likely to be an across-the-board assessment than if stimulated by perceived shortcomings, on which it is then more likely to be focused.

The internal evaluation being undertaken at the time of this writing was prompted by a concern about the conference's size, but its scope soon widened. The initial sense that the conference was too large turned into a realization that more lawyer representatives were needed; ultimately, the new chief judge charged the committee undertaking the evaluation to examine other matters related to the conference as well.

One aspect of the circuit conference perhaps not given sufficient attention in the official evaluations already made is the relation of the conference to the circuit's size or, rather, the implications of the latter for the conference—a matter central to this volume. The extent to which the present circuit conference is a reflection of a large circuit and whether it has helped keep the circuit together are important issues. Having a circuit conference is mandated by statute, which likewise spells out the conference's basic purposes. People wanted to reform the Ninth Circuit judicial conference before circuit splitting became a serious issue, and they did not link reexamination of the conference to that issue. Thus restructuring of the circuit conference appears not to have had its genesis in the politics of circuit division. And it must also be stressed that the circuit conference's usefulness in producing greater cohesion across districts or states in the circuit, so that lawyers and judges feel part of a larger entity, has little to do with the circuit's size: a three-state circuit like the Seventh also has to get people to look beyond district boundaries.

Nevertheless, a large circuit requires greater attention to the circuit conference's structure and to its size. Were there two circuits where there is now one, a smaller conference might remove much impetus to think carefully about conference size, operation, and procedures for selecting those who attend. Because the large number of lawyers in the Ninth Circuit prevents attendance of all or even most of those in federal practice, the circuit was required to develop methods of representation. These were at the core of the mid-1970s conference structuring. It may turn out, however—and the current reevaluation of conference size is a possible indication—that once the conference reaches a certain size, the concern about its size will diminish. "After all," some will say, "we have functioned reasonably well as we are; adding a few won't matter much—particularly if we can meet some of our goals in doing so." Given prior concerns about the dysfunctional effect of large numbers while the conference was continuing to function effectively, one can suggest that, where the addition of lawyer representatives serves an important purpose, the conference will not be "brought to its knees" and that it will function well as adjustments are made to the newcomers' presence.

Circuit size has also affected committee activity. One member active both in court committees in his district and on a circuit council commit- tee has suggested that the latter is affected by the circuit's size. Because of the circuit's "dispersion," most work is done by phone. That does not preclude "thoughtful discussion," which takes place often, but since people tend to feel during a conference call that someone is anxious to get off, it is advantageous when committees meet, because then people have their other work cancelled. As suggested earlier, lawyer participation on committees is important to provide input into circuit policy, and the court of appeals' advisory rules body is a model of what can be done. However, much of the group's success can be attributed to the committee members' own initiative, rather than to the court. Moreover, the circuit's middling record with respect to the committees of the council, even after more than one restructuring presented the opportunity for increasing lawyer membership (and thus input), should make one hesitant about placing much faith on committees either to increase lawyers' participation or to improve circuit governance.

Drawing the causal link from the conference to the large circuit— that is, determining whether the conference has helped keep the circuit together—is very difficult. Some who believe the circuit should be split have said that the conference has served to "perpetuate the myth a large circuit could function effectively and that the circuit conference was an integral part of that functioning." The conference brings judicial officers and lawyer representatives into a larger whole by breaking down people's quite natural tendency to spend their time with others from their own districts. Break-out meetings with people from different districts help considerably in this regard; so do con- ference themes with a circuit-wide focus. Thus the circuit conference is an integrative device that does assist in keeping the circuit together, and one might hypothesize that lawyers and judges, through par-

316

ticipation in the conference, are more likely to resist efforts to divide the circuit.[37]

Certainly making the circuit conference into a serious working body, not only a social event for judges' "buddies," became linked for some with Judge Browning's goals for the circuit. Such a connection may have had distinct benefits for lawyers, to the extent that the chief judge, because of his desire to keep the circuit intact, worked more actively to pull lawyers into administration of justice matters in the circuit. And some say that the conference became "more educational" in part "as a defensive measure" because of the chief judge's concern about the movement to split the circuit. Put differently, the desire by some for circuit cohesion may have provided motivation to work harder to make the conference a success, apart from an effort, independent of holding the circuit together, to have an effective conference.

Where does all this leave us with respect to the lawyers' role in circuit governance in the contemporary Ninth Circuit? Serious efforts have been made, and continue to be made, to involve the bar in circuit governance and to facilitate lawyers' participation so that their place in the circuit conference will be a meaningful, not merely a symbolic, one. Compared to the situation prior to the Wallace Committee's ground-breaking work, the change has been substantial. More lawyers in federal practice concerned about administration of justice in the circuit have become involved. Yet some districts still do not score well, and having lawyer representatives has not yet resulted in effective mechanisms of representation. Given these factors, as well as lawyers' reluctance to speak out and the ways in which actions taken at the conference—often not of great substantive weight—become diffused after the conference adjourns, it cannot really be said that the Ninth Circuit has yet succeeded in securing genuine participation by the bar in circuit governance. Some of the obstacles are those normally associated with any social institution, such as a lack of monitoring by even those most committed to the new mechanisms. These difficulties are

---

[37]Lawyers and district judges responding to a survey conducted for the judicial council in 1987 were asked to indicate agreement or disagreement with the statement, "In spite of its size, the Ninth Circuit works satisfactorily." Lawyers were more positive (82 percent agreeing somewhat or strongly) than judges (67 percent), but more judges (33 percent) agreed strongly than did lawyers (26 percent). With one-sixth of the judges disagreeing strongly with the statement, more of them also felt the circuit did not work; only 4 percent of the lawyer respondents so answered.

perhaps magnified by the fact that the circuit conference and council committees are peripheral activities for most who do participate.

Yet, all this having been said, increased lawyer presence in Ninth Circuit governance means much. Whatever the apparent paucity of substantive outcomes, the presence of lawyers at the conference and, to a lesser extent, on committees is part of a most significant process that serves to bind the circuit together and to integrate members of one of its most important constituencies into the system in which they work.

PART VI

Beyond Governance: Reflections on the Ninth Circuit Experience

12

Independent and Interdependent: The Ninth Circuit and the Federal Judiciary

JUDITH RESNIK

The focus of the preceding section of this book is on the governance and structure of the Ninth Circuit. This chapter attempts to place that discussion in the context of contemporary concerns about the governance, structure, and mission of the federal judiciary as a whole.

The chapters by Thomas Church, Doris Marie Provine, and Stephen Wasby provide some immediate and important lessons. The first is to avoid an easy but inaccurate equation—of the Court of Appeals for the Ninth Circuit with the Ninth Circuit itself. Given current nomenclature,[1] it is easy to slip into an assumption that the "Ninth Circuit" is an appellate court—and, we are constantly reminded, the largest appellate court in the United States. But as the text of these chapters makes plain, the Ninth Circuit includes not only an appellate court but also district courts, magistrates, bankruptcy courts, and a host of administrative personnel.

Furthermore, as Provine explains in Chapter 10, the Ninth Circuit is distinctive in an emphasis on its multiple constituencies. Many federal circuits are run by a council composed primarily of appellate judges.[2]

My thanks to Donna Murphy for comments on this essay.

[1] For example, one of the thirteen judicial "circuits" is the Federal Circuit, which has nationwide appellate jurisdiction over a specified set of cases from all the district courts. See 28 U.S.C. §§ 41, 1295. The other "circuits" include trial and appellate courts within a certain geographical area.

[2] As Provine discusses, under the Judicial Councils Reform and Judicial Conduct and Disability Act of 1980, some representation of district judges on a circuit council is mandatory.

In contrast, the Judicial Council of the Ninth Circuit consists of five appellate judges and four district court judges. The innovation of the Ninth Circuit is to come close to equalizing the participation of trial and appellate court judges on its council—as well as to include observers to represent the distinct concerns of magistrates, bankruptcy judges, and senior judges. This structure accurately reflects and helps to create the fact that the Ninth Circuit is not to be equated with the appellate court. As Provine aptly describes it, the Ninth Circuit is "a community linked by common concerns" and "with a responsibility to govern itself."[3]

A second lesson comes from Wasby's essay (Chapter 11). Even if one avoids equating the Ninth Circuit with the appellate court, one might still be tempted to assume that the relevant members of the Ninth Circuit "community" are the judges of the trial and appellate courts, magistrates, and bankruptcy judges. But as Wasby reminds us, there are other essential members of the "community": lawyers. Wasby's chapter outlines the self-conscious efforts of the judges within the Ninth Circuit to reach out to those members of the community. These efforts demonstrate that judges are keenly aware of their own dependence—of the need for cooperation from and support of the lawyers who appear in the courts of the Ninth Circuit.

A third lesson comes from Church's comments (Chapter 9), which teach us that the work of the Ninth Circuit in the last years of the twentieth century is not limited to deciding some fifty-six hundred appellate cases, forty-six thousand civil and criminal district court cases, and one hundred fifty thousand bankruptcy proceedings. More than adjudication is going on. There is the immense task of running the circuit, which extends over nine states, has a budget projected as more than $200 million, and has a staff of more than three thousand.[4]

In short, these three chapters document the interdependencies that exist in the Ninth Circuit and in the federal judiciary as a whole. Although United States jurisprudence is laden with rhetoric about the "independence" of the federal courts, and although Article III judges do in fact have substantial protections by virtue of the constitutional grants of life tenure and salary protection, an important but not often acknowledged aspect of judging is its *dependent* quality. Judges rely on a variety of other actors—lawyers, staff, and the parties—to enable the process of adjudication to occur. Legal discourse might well be helped

[3]See p. 249.
[4]Office of the Circuit Executive, *1988 Annual Report of the Ninth Circuit* at 71, 78, 82, 90, 4.

by an acknowledgment of and an appreciation for judicial connectedness and dependence, which need not be understood as negating the structural protections afforded federal judges.[5]

In addition to providing valuable insights into the workings of the largest circuit, these chapters on governance also identify questions that need to be addressed when evaluating current structures and when considering whether to reshape the federal adjudicatory system in the future.[6] As I learned about this entity called the "Ninth Circuit," I found myself unclear about its mission and its voice. What falls appropriately within its competence? Are there instances in which we might describe the Ninth Circuit as doing something it should not? Who speaks for the circuit?

Sources for defining the work of the Ninth Circuit include federal statutes and rules. For example, Rule 83 of the Federal Rules of Civil Procedure requires that all "local rules" (those promulgated by district courts) be sent to the judicial council of the circuit in which a particular federal district court is located. The councils have the authority to abrogate local rules that are inconsistent with the general federal rules or otherwise illegal.[7] The Federal Judicial Center has sponsored a study of local rule making; from preliminary reports we know that there are more than five thousand local rules at the trial level around the country and that the topics addressed in these rules range from setting the time for filing reply briefs to requiring prosecutors to seek prior judicial approval before subpoenaing attorneys to testify about clients before grand juries.[8]

In the Ninth Circuit, several local rules have been the subject of

[5]See generally Judith Resnik, "On the Bias: Feminist Reconsiderations of the Aspirations for our Judges," 61 *S. Cal. L. Rev.* 1877 (1988).

[6]In 1988 Congress directed the chief justice to appoint the Federal Courts Study Committee to develop plans for the future of the federal judiciary.

[7]Fed. R. Civ. P. 83. The provision authorizing council abrogation of local rules was not adopted until 1985. Legislation in 1988 further strengthened the powers of the councils: Congress amended the Rules Enabling Act to explicitly require the councils to "periodically review" all local rules within a circuit; it also authorized the councils to "modify or abrogate any such rule found inconsistent" with the federal rules. The amendment has been codified at 28 U.S.C. § 332(d)(4). In 1987 the Supreme Court restricted local rulemaking power by invoking its own supervisory authority to strike down a local rule. Frazier v. Heebe, 482 U.S. 641, 645 (1987).

[8]See generally Stephen N. Subrin, "Federal Rules, Local Rules, and State Rules: Uniformity, Divergence, and Emerging Procedural Patterns," 137 *U. Pa. L. Rev.* 1999 (1989); Robert E. Keeton, "The Function of Local Rules and the Tension with Uniformity," 50 *U. Pitt. L. Rev.* 853 (1989). See also United States v. Klubock, 832 F. 2d 664 (1st Cir. 1987) (en banc) (local rules governing prosecutors' authority to subpoena attorneys to appear before grand juries).

litigation. Cases have raised questions about the propriety of rules that authorize a wide range of judicial action: suspending attorneys from practice, imposing monetary sanctions on attorneys and litigants who fail to comply with local mandates, dismissing cases for failure to comply with local rules, waiving requirements of the general federal rules, and allowing magistrates to conduct jury voir dire.[9] In short, some local rules involve significant political and social issues. Moreover, there is reason to believe that some local rules within the Ninth Circuit are not consistent with the governing general federal rules. Nonetheless, according to Provine, "[c]ircuit councils have avoided the embarrassment of defiance by issuing orders infrequently." Further, council review of local rules is "generally uncontroversial and elicit[s] little discussion."[10] Similarly, Provine reports that other statutory duties of the Ninth Circuit council have been delegated to the chief judge (as in the case of complaints against individual judges),[11] are handled by staff, or involve minimal attention from the judicial council.

In contrast, the Ninth Circuit (or some portion thereof) does, on occasion, take controversial stances. For example, in 1987 the Judicial Council of the Ninth Circuit forwarded recommendations to the Judicial Conference of the United States. Included was a proposal to "initiate a study of the . . . desirability of legislation explicitly authorizing [the federal courts of appeals to] exercise discretionary jurisdiction."[12] As is familiar, in the federal system today litigants who lose at

---

[9]See, e.g., United States v. Stoneberger, 805 F.2d 1391 (9th Cir. 1986) (attorney suspension); Matter of Yagman, 796 F.2d 1165, opinion modified, 803 F.2d 1085 (9th Cir. 1986) (monetary sanctions imposed on attorney); Toombs v. Leone, 777 F.2d 465 (9th Cir. 1985) (monetary sanctions); Carey v. King, 856 F.2d 1439 (9th Cir. 1988) (dismissal of pro se complaint); Henderson v. Duncan, 779 F.2d 1421 (9th Cir. 1986) (dismissal); Alaska Limestone Corp. v. Hodel, 799 F.2d 1409 (9th Cir. 1986) (court discretion to dispense with requirements of federal rules); United States v. Bezold, 760 F.2d 999 (9th Cir. 1985) (magistrates' authority to conduct voir dire). The practice permitted in *Bezold* was disallowed in Gomez v. United States, 109 S. Ct. 2237 (1989).

[10]See pp. 266 and 269; see also p. 271.

[11]The statute itself gives substantial responsibility to the chief judge, see 28 U.S.C. § 372(c)(3), but Provine reports that the chief judge also acts as the "emissary" of the council. See p. 271.

[12]See Judicial Council of the Ninth Circuit, "Studies and Long-Range Planning by the Federal Judiciary" (1987) with cover letter to the Administrative Office of the United States Courts (Dec. 28, 1987) (hereafter cited as Judicial Council Studies), and the response from the Director of the Administrative Office of the United States Courts, in which the "recommendations of the Judicial Council of the Ninth Circuit" were referred to the subcommittee on federal-state relations of the Judicial Conference (Jan. 19, 1988).

the trial level have an appeal as of right from final decisions of the district court.[13] A report accompanying the judicial council recommendations asked whether appeal as of right is "something every case is born with."[14] The report detailed criticism of such appellate rights and seemed to argue that such a right should be constricted, presumably by congressional legislation.

My purpose here is not to explore the pros and cons of the preservation of appellate rights.[15] Rather, my interest lies in the process through which this particular issue was raised. The recommendation originated with the Ninth Circuit's Senior Advisory Board,[16] which as Wasby tells us is a relatively self-contained body that has little institutional contact with lawyers outside the committee.[17] The proposal was not presented to the circuit conference, nor was it submitted to the court of appeals. However, after the council had forwarded the recommendation to the Judicial Conference of the United States, concern was expressed by some members of the appeals court. The controversy ultimately prompted a clarifying letter emphasizing that the council had not approved any of the specific proposals mentioned in the letter of transmittal, such as the proposal to limit access to the courts of appeals by making some appeals discretionary.

This episode, which may or may not be representative of circuit practices, raises several questions—about how issues become part of the agenda of the council, about whether the council should speak for the circuit on such issues, or whether the voice of the Ninth Circuit should be heard only through the process of voting on resolutions at its annual conference.[18] Should the council or the conference, on

[13]28 U.S.C. § 1291. See p. 97.
[14]Judicial Council Studies, supra note 12, at 6 (Tab 2).
[15]See generally Paul D. Carrington, "The Function of the Civil Appeal: A Late-Century View," 38 *S.C. L. Rev.* 411 (1987); Judith Resnik, "Precluding Appeals," 70 *Cornell L. Rev.* 603 (1985); and Donald P. Lay, "A Proposal for Discretionary Review in Federal Courts of Appeal," 34 *Southwestern L.J.* 1151 (1981).
[16]See Stephen L. Wasby, "The Bar's Role in Governance of the Ninth Circuit," 25 *Willamette L. Rev.* 471, 560 (1989).
[17]See p. 312. Elsewhere Wasby observes that the members of the board are "unrepresentative not only in . . . age and experience but also in . . . the relative frequency with which most of [their firms] appear before the federal courts, perhaps giving their members a skewed view of appropriate practices." Wasby, supra note 16, at 559. It does appear that the "concept paper" that preceded the discretionary review proposal received some circulation among "selected members of the legal community." See id. at 560.
[18]See, e.g., the Ninth Circuit Judicial Conference's 1988 Resolutions, which begin with the following explanation: "It is the statutory function and purpose of the Ninth

behalf of the circuit, engage in lobbying? Should the council draft proposed legislation? At what point would one say that some issues are either not properly within the domain of the council or conference, or indeed within the circuit itself? Further, why should researchers find relatively little council activity in the area of local rule making, when a statutory mandate exists for control, yet more activity when the charge to action is less specific?

The answers to these questions come, I believe, not from the particular story of the Ninth Circuit, but from general aspects of the federal judicial system. Because the Ninth Circuit is both distinctive from yet reflective of the federal courts as a whole, its experiences are relevant to all who care about the federal judiciary. One finds a proliferation of local rules but little supervision of them—because of longstanding traditions of judicial independence that make Article III judges chary of telling other Article III judges how to run their courts. At the same time that a remarkable degree of what Provine calls "libertarian"[19] administration exists, there is also a proposal as radical as abolition of the right of appeal—because of a growing sense of work overload and a willingness to cut back on adjudication whenever one can.

The confusion about the definition and mission of the Ninth Circuit stems from a more generalized confusion—about the definition and mission of the federal courts. As noted above, in 1988 Congress created a committee to study just that problem. The committee was given fifteen months in which to report to Congress on what, if any, restructuring of the federal adjudicatory system is needed. Of course, the possibility of revamping aspects of the federal judicial apparatus has been with us for some time. As Hellman describes in his introductory chapter, the impetus to study the Ninth Circuit comes, in part, from questions about the capacity of multijudge courts and multidistrict circuits to function effectively.

Although issues concerning court governance are not novel, some of the contemporary commentary is. For example, during earlier parts of this century, the creation of adjudicatory structures in administrative agencies was a response, in part, to concerns about the federal

---

Circuit Judicial Conference . . . to *consider* the business of the Ninth Circuit, to *advise* [on] means of improving the administration of justice, and to *assist* in implementing decisions made by the Judicial Council as to administration of the business of the courts of the Ninth Circuit." Ninth Circuit Judicial Conference, 1988 Resolutions at 3 (emphasis in original). The resolutions process is discussed in Chapter 11.

[19]See p. 247.

judiciary. Yet in the 1930s, when considering the legality of the assignment of longshore workers' claims to the United States Employees' Compensation Commission, the Supreme Court spoke of the "essential attributes of judicial power" that could not be vested elsewhere.[20] Some concept of the quintessentially "judicial" existed. In contrast, in the middle of the 1980s, when the Court considered the legality of the assignment of claims to the Commodity Futures Trading Commission and the Environmental Protection Agency, the Court spoke of balancing the perceived needs of economical dispute resolution against the fear of encroachment on the federal judiciary.[21]

"Essential attributes of judicial power" are words that, in this decade, have little force, because most aspects of judging can be found in a variety of institutions: military courts, territorial courts, bankruptcy courts, and federal agencies. Much of the adjudicatory work of the federal system occurs outside the boundaries of Article III.[22] And, within the boundaries of Article III courts, one finds a host of judicial personnel, such as magistrates, staff attorneys, and law clerks, all of whom lack life tenure but play important roles in case disposition. Further, one finds Article III judges themselves engaged in a variety of activities: negotiating settlements, managing cases, urging parties to avoid adjudication. Just as the social scientists who look at the Ninth Circuit find it difficult to define its parameters, so do many judges and commentators find it difficult to describe the federal courts' distinctive aspects that must not be altered.

All of us who are concerned about adjudication face two, interrelated, sets of problems. The first involves the structure of the federal judicial system; the central issue is whether the formal relationships among the existing federal courts should be changed by altering the tiers of decision making. The second issue is what kind of cases should be heard by Article III judges. The Ninth Circuit's experience is relevant to both problems. As for the first, the circuit provides an example of a large regional structure that might be a model for redrawing existing circuit boundaries so as to increase the reliance on divisions that cross many state lines but are not purely national institutions.

---

[20]Crowell v. Benson, 285 U.S. 22, 51 (1932).

[21]See Commodity Futures Trading Comm'n v. Schor, 478 U.S. 833 (1986), and Thomas v. Union Carbide Agricultural Products Co., 473 U.S. 568 (1985). Compare Northern Pipeline Constr. Co. v. Marathon Pipe Line Co., 458 U.S. 50 (1982).

[22]For example, administrative law judges far outnumber Article III trial judges, and the Social Security Administration alone disposes of more cases in a year than does the federal judiciary.

Within the Ninth Circuit, several districts have experimented with court-annexed arbitration and other alternative dispute-resolution techniques.

When considering possible revisions of federal adjudication, we must be self-conscious about the perspective from which we work. Currently, there is failing faith in adjudicatory procedure, a general unhappiness about adjudication, and a general enthusiasm to have less of it, wherever it is found. Today's conferences on adjudication are typically filled with discussions of alternatives to adjudication, which are advertised as preferable to trials, judges, and litigation. In some cases, lower-court judges are responding by mandating that parties appear for settlement conferences, by requiring participation in summary jury trials, or by ordering the entry of settlements. Some appellate courts have also instituted settlement programs, and even federal agencies (the very places Congress created as alternatives to the federal courts) are sending some of their work away—to yet another forum for alternative dispute resolution.

As we approach the end of the twentieth century, I find a decreasing interest in paying attention to individual problems, to the adjudication of small disputes and individual cases. There is a tension between processes based on individuals and those predicated on groups. The jurisprudence of England and the United States has espoused individuality as a central premise. The rhetoric speaks of a specific injured plaintiff suing an identified defendant, with a third party, judge or jury, imposing a resolution. But in today's reality the pressures to aggregate are everywhere. More than 170,000 asbestos injuries. Some 200,000 Dalkon Shield claims. The shareholders of a company, the children in a school, the inhabitants of a prison. Whether by administrative processing, class action, liberal rules of joinder, interpleader, or bankruptcy, increasingly the unit of a case is not a single plaintiff, a single defendant, but groups, entities, conglomerates, and governments on both sides.

Increasingly, there is an unwillingness to accord the resources of the federal courts to respond to individual problems. Multiparty, multi-claim cases have begun to seem "more" important, and individual cases, those involving a lone Social Security claimant, a lone tort victim, have begun to seem "less" important. Despite this trend, there remains the appeal as of right, a rule that enables a single unhappy litigant (with resources) to compel three state-empowered, high-prestige individuals (to wit, federal appellate judges) to attend to her or his claim of illegality. But recall the recommendation of the Judicial Council of the Ninth Circuit: to have the United States Judicial Conference study the abolition of appeal as of right, to let an appellate court choose which cases are worthy of consideration and which cases should be finally decided by a lone federal district judge.

How can one appraise the validity of suggestions like a limitation on the possibility of appeal? One aspect of such a proposal is that it concentrates substantial power in the first tier of decision making, in a federal district court judge. Similarly, efforts to divest the federal courts of some parts of their jurisdiction give power to other actors, often those who sit in federal agencies. Before becoming enthusiastic about sending categories of cases elsewhere or limiting access to review of particular kinds of decisions, one must have a high level of confidence in the adequacy of the decision makers whose powers will increase.

Further, one must ask what will remain for the federal courts to do. If one were to adopt the view that individual cases arising under a host of federal statutes are too "ordinary," too "trivial," too "unimportant" for federal courts,[23] if one were to send all these litigants to "other" courts, to agencies, to the state system, to alternative dispute resolution, then left to the federal judiciary are the "big" cases and those raising constitutional claims and challenging the legality of federal statutes. It is in this decision making en masse and in constitutional and statutory interpretation that a general truism about adjudication becomes all the more plain: application of rules of law to given cases is law-generative, and courts are (of course) lawmakers. Lawmaking on the basis of large sprawling records is vulnerable to criticism, and such cases generate additional pressures to have the parties find solutions, to obtain settlements, to avoid adjudication. A standard principle of federal adjudication is to avoid constitutional issues, to decide on a narrow rather than a broad ground. But if the only cases left to the federal courts are the "big" ones, narrow grounds will be all the more difficult to find.

For me, the lessons of this book are not only lessons about how to cope with the size of this particular circuit, with its large number of judges, its many lawyers, its thousands of cases. The lessons are that we are watching a struggle about the definition of the task, the domain, and the nature of the work of the federal courts. Questions about the governance, structure, and mission of the Ninth Circuit are

---

[23]See, e.g., Robert Bork, "Dealing with the Overload in Article III Courts," 70 F.R.D. 231 (1976).

inevitably part of questions about the governance, structure, and mission of the entire system of which it is a part. That discussion necessarily entails consideration of what the caseload should embrace and what the tasks of judging should entail. Addressing those issues is the work of all of us concerned about the federal courts in the twenty-first century, and the experience of the Ninth Circuit is tremendously important in exploring the utility of one possible approach, the development of large regional divisions. But one needs not only to describe and define structures of governance; one needs also to understand what problems one wants the courts to consider.

13

Lessons for Smaller Circuits, Caution for Larger Ones

A. LEO LEVIN

The context has been the country's largest circuit, and the focus of attention has been on size. How has the Ninth managed to cope with a circuit that extends from Guam to Montana and from Arizona to Alaska, a circuit that includes well over one hundred fifty Article III judges and a commensurate number of magistrates, bankruptcy judges, and supporting personnel? That the center of interest should be size is hardly surprising; that it should give primacy to the question of how the Ninth has been able to cope is certainly understandable.

In examining the Browning years, however, it is important to avoid too narrow a focus. There have been exciting successes widely applicable to other circuits without regard to size. There have also been problems, problems that likely are a function of size. And, more recently, there have been legislative developments which invite renewed reflection on the factors that deserve consideration in the alignment, or realignment, of tomorrow's federal court system. This chapter will consider each of these points in turn.

Some of the innovations that most clearly reflect Judge Browning's philosophy of administration deserve serious consideration by other circuits, small as well as large. A good example is the presence of magistrates, bankruptcy judges, and even senior judges at meetings of the circuit council, albeit as observers. Their inclusion, reminiscent of the decision to invite representatives of the district judges to attend council sessions even before the governing statute was amended, reflects a deeply rooted belief in the value of making those likely to be affected by the deliberations part of the process or, stated more generally, a belief in participatory democracy.

The intensive effort to involve members of the bar in the operation of the circuit, to have lawyer members of judicial conference committees active on a year-round basis, may well be worthy of emulation in other circuits. The significant role of the lawyer members of the circuit conference is dramatized by the requirement that for a resolution to be adopted by the conference it must command a majority of the lawyer representatives as well as a majority of the judges.

For another example of innovation unrelated to the size of the circuit, consider the practice instituted by Browning in connection with the semiannual meetings of the Judicial Conference of the United States. Both the chief judge and the circuit executive scheduled meetings with various officials of judicial-branch agencies in Washington (the director and deputy director of the Federal Judicial Center, for example), not so much to go over a predetermined agenda of problems to be solved, but rather to consider whether there were areas that offered the potential for more cooperative effort or for better procedures on the part of the circuit.

There can be no doubt that size and the threat of division were powerful catalysts for many of the changes that occurred in the Ninth Circuit, especially those assessed in the chapters by Church, Provine, and Wasby. Some of the innovations were size-driven in a very direct way. A good illustration is the meetings of the chief judges. In the other circuits the usual practice is for all Article III judges to meet in executive session during the annual circuit conference. Sometimes non–Article III judicial officers—the magistrates and bankruptcy judges—are also included. In the Ninth Circuit, however, a meaningful session of this type, even if limited to district and circuit judges, would hardly be feasible. Instead, there developed a breakfast session of the chief judges of the district courts of the circuit and, understandably enough, a similar session of the chief judges of the bankruptcy courts. In addition, various other groups of judges hold separate meetings. It is difficult to compare the value of such sessions with a large but manageable plenary meeting of all judicial officers.[1] Yet these gatherings need not be mutually exclusive, and the example of the Ninth's meetings, instituted as an added means of communication, deserves thoughtful consideration.

[1]The circuit and district judges do gather each year at a three-day midwinter workshop, but the sessions are primarily educational.

Many judges enjoy administration. The challenge of making a system work, of facilitating adjudication, which is after all the mission of the courts at every level, of creating and maintaining an environment that is both pleasant and conducive to efficiency, has its attractions. For other judges, however, administrative obligations are anathema, and it is virtually impossible to attend any sizable gathering of judges in which there will not be a substantial number eager to be free of such "chores." In this context three steps taken by the Ninth Circuit deserve attention. First is the relatively small size of the judicial council: the chief judge aside, only four judges of the court of appeals and four from the district courts compose the entire council. Second, despite the relatively small size of the council—certainly the number of appellate judges is quite small—there is an executive committee empowered to deal with the more mundane matters that arise, a committee charged with ensuring efficient operation of the council itself. Third, the council is assisted by an array of task forces, liaison committees, and advisory committees whose members are drawn from courts and other constituencies throughout the circuit. The overall pattern is unmistakable and deserving of thought and emulation: widespread involvement through committee work of those affected by the processes of governance; widespread dissemination of information concerning issues under discussion; and, at the same time, a small but efficient mechanism for taking action.

None of what has been said thus far is intended to deny that the imperatives and constraints of size had a direct impact on many facets of circuit life. The circuit conference, for example, was structured and restructured critically and creatively; the limited en banc was designed and made to function. In the long term, however, the indirect benefits of the circuit's reforms may prove of even greater significance. The willingness to innovate, the receptivity to experimentation, to new ideas, became part of the climate of the circuit.

Climate alone, however, does not produce change in a judicial system. To give reality to inchoate aspirations, several subsidiary factors came into play. There was a recognition of the importance of planning (manifested, for example, in the circuit's annual action plan), and also an awareness of the need to evaluate and assess newly adopted procedures. There was a commitment to openness in the process of administrative decision making, an approach that did not always obtain elsewhere in the federal judicial system. We find, too, a belief in the value of decentralization and a corresponding recognition of the role of the region. Finally, the circuit's leaders demonstrated an ability to articulate persuasively the needs of the circuit and of the system as a whole, as well as a willingness to draw on the resources of the Judicial Conference, the Washington agencies, and the Congress to meet those needs. These qualities reflect Browning values; they exemplify attitudes that are relevant to other courts regardless of size.

Success—and Problems That Persist

The Ninth Circuit is not, however, without its problems. The particular focus of concern is the court of appeals. We begin with the median time from filing a notice of appeal to final disposition in cases adjudicated on the merits. Since 1984 the figure has increased every year, and in 1988, the last year for which published statistics are available, the figure was 14.5 months, ranking the Ninth eleventh among the twelve regional circuits.[2] Less than a month separated the Ninth from the cellar, and the median for the Ninth was more than twice as long as that for each of the two fastest circuits. To lawyers and litigants fourteen and one-half months elapsed time may seem long enough, but it bears emphasis that this is only a median figure: half the cases took longer.

In 1985 the Federal Judicial Center published *Administration of Justice in a Large Appellate Court: The Ninth Circuit Innovations Project*, by Joe S. Cecil. The study described the steps taken by the court starting in 1980 to expedite the handling of appeals; it noted that the program "included a commitment by each of the judges of the circuit to accept a substantially increased workload." The foreword to the monograph characterized the results as "dramatic." Indeed they were. The 1984 statistics, the latest then available, showed that the median time from the filing of the record to disposition had been reduced to 9.5 months from a 1980 high of 17.4 months. Nonetheless, as the foreword pointed out, this was "longer than the median time for the twelve regional circuits and more than twice as long as the time for the leading circuit."[3] It may be noted parenthetically that the 9.5 months translated in 1984 to a median of 12.1 months elapsed time from notice of appeal to disposition, and the latter figure—the one currently re-

---

[2] Preliminary data for 1989 show that the median time increased once again, to 15.3 months, and again the Ninth was eleventh out of the twelve circuits.

[3] Joe S. Cecil, *The Administration of Justice in a Large Appellate Court* at v (Federal Judicial Center, 1985) (Foreword by A. Leo Levin).

ported in the Administrative Office's Management Statistics—rose by slightly more than 20 percent over the next four years.

Other figures offer little comfort. In total number of appeals terminated on the merits per panel, the Ninth Circuit ranks tenth out of the twelve circuits. If the data are analyzed in terms of actions per active judge, where only judges active during the entire 12 month period are included, and if one excludes the District of Columbia Circuit with its idiosyncratic mix of cases, the Ninth has the poorest record: 257 cases compared with 492 in the circuit with the largest number. Nor is this the result of too high a proportion of signed opinions. With 30 per active judge, the Ninth Circuit is among the lower circuits; the highest figure is 71. Data on number of senior judges who sit, number of months of judicial vacancies compared to the number of authorized judgeships, and volume of petitions for rehearing yield no obvious explanation. The Ninth Circuit does rank high in procedural terminations per active judge, although the significance of this datum is not clear.

Perhaps clues can be found in some of the studies in this volume. In Chapter 10, Provine refers to the heavy obligations of time and effort imposed on participating judicial officers by the Ninth Circuit's approach to governance. In Chapter 3, Hellman comments on the time and effort required to achieve uniformity in so large a circuit. These factors are difficult to quantify.

A more promising clue is found in Church's analysis, in the conclusion to Chapter 9, of the implications of the court's decision that "to the extent practicable each judge would sit an equal number of times with each other judge on the court, regardless of the judges' 'home bases,' and that each judge would sit an equal number of times in each of the three administrative units." It is counterintuitive to suggest that this travel has no impact on judicial time or energy, although elaborate explanations supporting that conclusion have been offered. Careful analysis of detailed data on time away from chambers and how it is spent would be required to assess the proposition in terms of present practice.[4] Of course, the question concerns not only the time consumed by each trip in order to effectuate the stated policy, but the number of trips necessary to ensure the rotation.[5]

---

[4] See p. 142.

[5] If a northwestern circuit were to be created, as discussed later in this chapter, the judges residing in Portland and Seattle could be expected to cut their travel quite substantially.

The costs of this dispersion cannot necessarily be measured by judge-time alone. There is good reason to believe that the intellectual give-and-take among judges who have frequent contact in conference and in the decision-making process is simply of a different quality from that which obtains when contact is relatively rare.[6] Under current calendaring practices, an active judge of the Ninth Circuit Court of Appeals could expect to sit on a regular panel with each of twenty-seven colleagues at intervals of eighteen months.[7]

Finally, the foreword to the 1985 Federal Judicial Center report made the following suggestion concerning the locus of the delay: "Some of the difficulty appears to be in the time it took from filing until availability for argument or submission, and this may well result in an improved statistical profile in the future."[8] That improvement has not occurred. On the contrary, analysis of the 1988 data in the circuit's Fourth Biennial Report to the Congress suggests that delays in these early stages remain troublesome. Of course, it is the responsibility of the court to monitor undue delay at any stage.[9]

Whatever the causes, the contrast between the success story reported in the Federal Judicial Center monograph and the statistics that emerge a few years later raises once again the perplexing problem of what makes innovations in judicial administration work, what makes a beneficent effect last. The question is as important as it is difficult to answer, at least with any measure of confidence.

It may well be that any innovation, any program of reform, has a high probability of initial success if it is adopted with commitment, with a zeal on the part of its proponents to make it work. Whether that zeal is born of a sense of crisis resulting from existing conditions, as so often happens, or whether it is motivated simply by the desire to excel, it can do much to yield success. Thus we find that the case-management data for 1984, three years after the judges of the court of appeals agreed to accept "a substantially increased workload," present a

[6]See Deborah J. Barrow and Thomas G. Walker, *A Court Divided: The Fifth Circuit Court of Appeals and the Politics of Judicial Reform* 234 (Yale University Press, 1988); Stephen L. Wasby, "Communication in the Ninth Circuit: A Concern for Collegiality," 11 *U. Puget Sound L. Rev.* 73, 131 (1987).

[7]The judges sit on nine monthly calendars a year, and active judges generally remain together for a full calendar. Of course, the judges also sit with one another on en bancs, screening panels, and motions panels.

[8]Cecil, supra note 3, at vi.

[9]It should be noted that the Ninth Circuit has one of the better records in median time from hearing or submission to final disposition.

greatly improved picture from that of 1979. Again, this suggests no more than what might have been expected: effort above and beyond the call of duty can result, for a time, in increased productivity, where productivity is measured by the objective data of the type typically included in annual reports. But sustaining that effort is another matter. From 1984 through 1988, the number of terminations on the merits per active judge remained virtually unchanged, while the number of pending appeals per panel increased substantially.[10]

In any event, speed of adjudication can hardly be the most important consideration in evaluating an administrative arrangement; clearly, it is not the exclusive one. At some point, sustained overload may be unfair or even begin to affect the quality of justice. Certainly, we can agree that there are limits beyond which it would be undesirable to go.

Intracircuit uniformity of decisions is another factor, one of particular importance in evaluating an intermediate appellate court. As Hellman points out, two-thirds of the district judges disagreed with the statement, "When intracircuit conflicts do arise, the Court of Appeals generally resolves them through modification of opinions or en banc rehearings." And as Hellman adds, "among lawyer members [of the circuit conference] the disagreement was even higher."[11]

It is clear that the judges are expending a great deal of effort in the attempt to achieve uniformity. As Hellman notes, "Members of the court acknowledge that they spend a substantial amount of time reviewing opinions and exchanging memoranda in order to iron out apparent inconsistencies" without resorting to an en banc. Indeed, some members of the court have suggested that it would be appropriate, if not politically acceptable, to reduce the workload of the judges to accommodate this extra burden.[12]

In sum, the evidence can be read as portraying a court that has devoted tremendous time and effort to maintaining uniformity, with-

---

[10]Whatever difficulties the court may have had in keeping up with its docket did not come about because filings outpaced judgepower. From 1984 to 1988, filings increased by 21.7 percent, but the number of judgeships increased by an identical figure. And although the court lost some judgepower through unfilled vacancies, the number of sitting senior judges increased.

Preliminary figures for 1989 show dramatic improvement in the data on terminations per active judge; however, recent history suggests caution, at the least, in assuming that this pace can be maintained.

[11]P. 56.

[12]See Chapter 3 at note 69.

out changing the perception of the "consumers"—the district judges and lawyers—that inconsistencies persist. Perhaps it is a matter of perspective; to borrow a phrase from Daniel Meador, distinctions that are viewed as significant and indeed persuasive by appellate judges may appear otherwise when the cases are read in "the rough-and-tumble of law practice" and in the chambers of hard-pressed trial judges.

Regionalism and Realignment

Does any of this call for significant change? The question is not rhetorical. First, it is far from clear that any available alternative is preferable. Second, in addressing alternatives, one must always be mindful of potential side effects. Solutions all too often prove to be the source of new problems. In the case of the Ninth Circuit, however, the need at least to consider alternatives cannot be avoided. Once again the question of circuit realignment is before the Congress, this time as a result of the action of seven senators, representing "most of the states forming the Ninth Circuit," in introducing a bill calling for the creation of a Twelfth Circuit.[13]

The issues are complex, and it would be inappropriate, within the compass of this chapter, to attempt a detailed analysis. Nor would it be useful, without such analysis, to state and explicate a position. It may not be inappropriate, however, to deal briefly with at least some aspects of the concepts of regionalism and circuit loyalty as they apply to circuit realignment.

A priori, one might have thought that realignment of all the regional circuits, on a national basis, should be seriously explored. Not only is the Ninth Circuit so much larger, by any measure, than any other circuit, but there is serious lack of uniformity in size among the remaining circuits. The Seventh, for example, has a caseload almost twice that of the First and roughly half that of the Fifth. The Second Circuit encompasses three states; the Tenth, six. The First Circuit has six judgeships; the Fifth, sixteen. Nevertheless, when the Hruska Commission announced its intention to explore the possibility of moving a single state from one circuit to another in the interest of a more rational and more efficient system, there was near-unanimous opposition on the part of those most immediately concerned. To a certain

[13]S. 948, 101st Cong., 1st Sess. (1989); see 135 Cong. Rec. S 5026 (daily ed. May 9, 1989) (remarks of Sen. Gorton).

extent this reaction can be explained by the desire for stability; circuit law and circuit practice would change for those affected. This was not merely a reflection of the conservatism of lawyers when it comes to certain aspects of lawyering, but rather the product of a deep-seated doubt that anyone had demonstrated the likelihood of a net gain. Change exacts a price, and it was not clear that the benefits warranted the expenditure. But this explanation does not account for the vigorous opposition of lawyers and judges who would not be directly affected.

At the root of the opposition, it seems clear, was a basic loyalty to the circuit as circuit. Circuit conferences engender that type of loyalty; so do relationships between bench and bar. Wasby's analysis in Chapter 11 of the role of the bar in the Ninth Circuit amply demonstrates how significant the contribution of the bar can be. When the possibility of a realignment of existing circuits, as distinguished from circuit splitting, arose again at the time the judges of the old Fifth Circuit were considering whether to favor or oppose division of that circuit, serious consideration of this alternative was short-lived. Circuit loyalty remains a significant force today, and as has already been suggested, there are reasons to applaud rather than to deprecate its existence.

Although circuit loyalty may render it impractical or impolitic to attempt a *de novo* redrawing of circuit lines, it has not prevented the division of a circuit and the creation of new circuits. This was true in the case of the division of the old Eighth to create the Tenth and the division of the old Fifth to create the Eleventh. It is interesting that, for many years after the old Eighth Circuit was divided, the Eighth and Tenth held joint circuit conferences at regular intervals. In addition, the annual workshop for district judges sponsored by the Federal Judicial Center was typically a joint enterprise for the two circuits. Similarly, the year after creation of the Eleventh Circuit, the workshop for district judges was, on their initiative, a joint one for the Fifth and Eleventh Circuits.

The great challenge in circuit realignment is developing and applying the principles that should govern. There is virtual unanimity in the recognition that a one-state circuit is unthinkable. The courts of appeals are national courts; a single-state circuit would create the danger of excessive parochialism.[14] In addition, the nature of the appointment process needlessly increases the risk of undesirable homogeneity on the bench. Wherever practicable, the Hruska Commission urged, cir-

[14]Judge John Minor Wisdom has eloquently emphasized the federalizing function of the courts of appeals. See Barrow and Walker, supra note 6, at 77–78.

cuits should be composed of at least three states "with a diversity of population, legal business and socio-economic interests."[15]

Is there a point, however, at which diversity in abundance becomes too much of a good thing? Senator Slade Gorton, in introducing the legislation that would create a Twelfth Circuit, argued on behalf of his constituents for greater regionalism in circuit composition. "We in the Northwest," he said, "have developed our own interests in every aspect of the law from natural resources to international trade. Our interests cannot be fully addressed from a California perspective."[16] But if we look to the experience of other circuits, we find substantial diversity and strong feelings about the desirability of maintaining that diversity. Arkansas and North Dakota in the Eighth are not commonly thought of as part of the same region, nor are Tennessee and Michigan, yet there is widespread recognition of the advantage of having such different perspectives reflected on a national court. At the same time, the "sense of community [that is] shared by lawyers and judges within the present circuits,"[17] engendering respect and loyalty as well as providing stimulus and challenge, can be achieved even in the presence of very substantial diversity.

On closer analysis, the primary thrust of Gorton's statement concerns the perceived dominance of a single state within the circuit. What is meant by dominance, whether it exists, and, if so, precisely why it should be avoided are questions that need careful consideration. It is important, however, not to be too quick to cry "parochialism" or to read Gorton as espousing a narrow homogeneity. Certainly, Hawaii and Idaho would not be regarded as part of the same region, and yet both would be included in Gorton's Twelfth. Admittedly, without Hawaii, a five-state northwestern circuit would have a timber-oriented economy that calls to mind the concerns that underlay much of the opposition to creating an "oil and gas circuit" out of the two western states of the old Fifth.[18] But the five northwestern states differ in many other ways, and even without Hawaii there is no reason to believe that the judges of the Twelfth Circuit would be any more homogeneous in their attitudes or decisions than the judges of, for

[15]Commission on Revision of the Federal Court Appellate System, "The Geographical Boundaries of the Several Judicial Circuits: Recommendations for Change," 62 F.R.D. 223, 231–32 (1973).

[16]135 Cong. Rec. S 5026 (daily ed. May 9, 1989).

[17]Commission on Revision, supra note 15, at 228.

[18]See Barrow and Walker, supra note 6, at 201, 235. In July 1989 the Hawaii State Bar Association expressed opposition to any effort to divide the Ninth Circuit; it also opposed "any . . . effort to separate Hawaii from California for purposes of federal appeals." If a new Twelfth Circuit is created, it is unlikely to include Hawaii.

example, the Third Circuit, composed of three mid-Atlantic states with economies that are similar in many respects.

Conclusion

The federal judicial system, and therefore the country at large, owes an enormous debt to Chief Judge Browning and his colleagues for the innovations in judicial administration introduced during what has come to be known as the Browning era. Perhaps of greater significance than any individual innovation or combination of them is the impact the Ninth has had on the climate of judicial administration nation-wide. The core values of openness, of consultation, of widespread participation in the decision-making process have achieved a new level of recognition.

To be sure, these were hardly revolutionary ideas when Browning became chief judge. Only a year earlier the Hruska Commission had recommended notice-and-comment rule making "as the normal in-strument of procedural change," publication of the court's internal operating procedures, and "creation of an advisory committee to pro-vide input from the bar and others who may be affected by procedural change."[19] The specific recommendations were bottomed on the premise that those concerned with the operation of rules and pro-cedures had a "creative and constructive" role to play in developing those procedures. But it is a far cry from a commission report to wholehearted implementation by a court system.

Perhaps most remarkable, and least remarked, is the fact that so many of the Browning era innovations are applicable to circuits of any size, and indeed to the courts of different judicial systems. From that perspective, it would be shortsighted to concentrate overmuch on the fact that not all of the circuit's problems were solved. Nor should we discount the possibility that the zeal, the dedication, the willingness to experiment that accomplished so much in the realms of governance and administration will yet enable the court of appeals to achieve the goals in the sphere of adjudication that have thus far eluded it. The court, like the circuit of which it is a part, remains a living organism, adjusting, advancing, succeeding, occasionally falling short. It should occasion no surprise that when Browning passed on his office there were still challenges to be met, opportunities for creativity. How could it be otherwise?

[19]Commission on Revision of the Federal Court Appellate System, "Structure and Internal Procedures: Recommendations for Change," 67 F.R.D. 195, 251 (1975).

Part VII

The Dynamics of Institutional Change

14

Judge Browning and the Remaking of the Ninth Circuit's Institutions

JOHN R. SCHMIDHAUSER

In 1985 the Federal Judicial Center published Joe S. Cecil's description of the significant administrative reforms developed and implemented by the Ninth Circuit Court of Appeals. His study, entitled *Administration of Justice in a Large Appellate Court: the Ninth Circuit Innovations Project*, assessed the dramatic and apparently successful innovations adopted by a court that for many years had been a target of numerous criticisms. Analysis of the Ninth Circuit's transformation from an ungainly and uncooperative resister of change to a national leader in judicial innovation is the central purpose of this chapter. The main thrust of the investigation is the modern interaction between two significant external influences, congressional imperatives and caseload pressures, and one crucial internal factor, circuit leadership in the period from the New Deal to the late 1980s. Attention focuses primarily on the court of appeals, although developments involving the circuit as a whole are treated where relevant.

The chapter begins by sketching the historical background: the origins of the Ninth Circuit in the nineteenth century, the evolution of the congressional role from the 1930s through the 1950s, and the developments in the years immediately antedating Judge Browning's accession to leadership in 1961.[1] Next, Browning's precourt career is outlined, with emphasis on the qualities that prefigured his accom-

---

[1]These sections draw on the more extended treatment in John R. Schmidhauser, "The Browning Era in the Context of the Ninth Circuit's Tradition of 'Rugged Individualism,'" 21 *Ariz. St. L.J.* 17 (1989).

plishments as chief judge. The chapter then examines Browning's manner of leadership in the context of the court's response to proposals for dividing the circuit. The final sections analyze Browning's approach to governance in the effectuation of internal reforms.

Federalism, Separation of Powers, and the Rugged Individualism of the Ninth Circuit

The Constitution itself, especially Article III, Section 1, provides the basis for continuous interaction between Congress and the federal judicial circuits. In the first Judiciary Act, that of 1789, Congress took up the option offered by the Constitution and established national tribunals below the Supreme Court. Although the new system included circuit courts, each with jurisdiction over two or more states, Congress chose, for economic and political reasons, not to give those courts judges of their own, a decision that would prove important to the internal organization of the West Coast circuit created on the eve of the Civil War.[2]

The first Congress also established the principle of sectional or regional-cultural representation in the geographic organization of the circuits. Thus the Federalist goal of a federal judiciary that would play a nation-unifying role was partly contradicted. As a consequence, federal circuits, though primarily oriented toward uniform application of national law and decisions, often reflected fundamental regional differences, such as the South's militant defense of slavery prior to the 1860s.

No less important than federalism as an institutional influence on the federal courts is the concomitant principle of separation of powers. When a competitive two-party system emerged with the critical election of 1800, the stage was set for periodic confrontations between members of the federal judiciary, who were provided life tenure on good behavior, and presidents and members of Congress, whose terms were renewed every two, four, or six years. For example, the geographic size and remoteness from the East Coast of newly created circuits were occasionally used as instruments of partisan punishment

---

[2]Each member of the Supreme Court was assigned duties as a circuit justice. Because California was not included in a circuit in its earliest statehood years, Congress initially created a special circuit judgeship for the state. In 1863 a new circuit comprising California and Oregon was established, and Associate Justice Stephen J. Field, a Lincoln appointee, became its circuit justice.

by majorities in the House and Senate against some justices chosen by a party that had lost the presidency and majority control in the Congress.[3]

The West Coast circuit itself was created out of economic and political necessity. In its early institutional development this circuit was subjected to a good deal of congressional modification from its initial temporary organizational status before the Civil War to its immediate postwar status as a regular circuit in the national system. For a short time the circuit was designated the Tenth to reflect the addition of a tenth justice to the Supreme Court. When the size of the Court was reduced to nine, the westernmost circuit became the Ninth Circuit.[4] It has retained that designation ever since.

From its origins in the 1850s to the present, the western circuit has been characterized by vast geographic expanse, portions of which were, until modern times, quite isolated. Of greater importance, it has been regarded by both admirers and critics as a circuit manned by judges who tended to reflect a judicial and institutional philosophy of rugged individualism and (in an earlier era) economic laissez-faire considered typical of the region itself. It is perhaps not coincidental that the two men who served as circuit justices for the Ninth Circuit from 1940 to 1986 were William O. Douglas and William H. Rehnquist, two of the most individualistic justices ever to serve on the Supreme Court.

Associate Justice Stephen J. Field of California, the first circuit justice, dominated circuit decision making and was aggressively retaliatory against those judges he deemed unsound or uncooperative.[5] Field's influence held sway for the first three decades after the Civil War and did not provide a very auspicious start for trust and cooperation within the circuit. His successors were more temperate and col-

---

[3]Floyd E. McCaffree, "The Nomination and Confirmation of Justices of the Supreme Court of the United States, 1789–1849" (Ann Arbor: Ph.D. Dissertation, University of Michigan, 1938). McCaffree reports that early nineteenth-century justices were sometimes given onerous circuit assignments by antagonistic congressional majorities to encourage their resignation.

[4]The Act of July 23, 1866, provided that the districts of California, Oregon, and Nevada would constitute the Ninth Circuit. Over the years, six states—Washington, Idaho, Montana, Hawaii (initially as a territory), Arizona, and finally Alaska—were added to the original three. The circuit today also includes Guam and the Northern Mariana Islands.

[5]Christian G. Fritz, "San Francisco's First Federal Court: Ogden Hoffman and the Northern District of California, 1851–1891" at 292 (Berkeley: Ph.D. Dissertation, University of California, 1986).

legial in their relationships with circuit colleagues, but in any event the opportunities for dominance by the circuit justice diminished after 1869, with the appointment of the first judge designated as a circuit judge, and even more after 1891, when the now-familiar three-tier system came into existence.

Congress and the Federal Courts: The Twentieth-Century Background

The modern history of the Ninth Circuit begins with the Evarts Act of 1891, which increased the number of circuit judges to two and for the first time established an intermediate court with a significant appellate responsibility.[6] No legislation of comparable importance has been enacted in the century since the Evarts Act, but a series of incremental reforms has created the framework for both adjudication and governance within which the circuit operates today.

Recognition of the role that Congress plays as the constitutionally ordained, major external influence on the organization and administration of the federal courts does not detract from the significance of the initatives taken by Judge Browning and his colleagues. To be sure, even the internally generated innovations were often developed in the context of congressional pressures that many of the judges considered disruptive of their own efforts at internal reform. Indeed, the severe criticisms of the circuits after World War II underscore the fact that judicial leadership in the federal system involves not only internal administrative direction, sensitive exchanges of ideas with judicial colleagues, and day-to-day management of a growing administrative staff, but considerable skill in dealing with powerful and occasionally antagonistic members of Congress and their staffs. These complex leadership requirements became increasingly evident as Congress enacted laws affecting not only the organization and workload of the circuits, but the characteristics of judicial leadership in the circuits as well. Thus, to put the Ninth Circuit's innovations of the 1980s in proper perspective, it is necessary to examine the basic framework of twentieth-century congressional initiatives.

The most important developments of the prewar era, largely influenced by recommendations of Chief Justices William Howard Taft in the 1920s and Charles Evans Hughes in the 1930s, were the establish-

[6]See pp. 12–13.

ment of the Judicial Conference of the United States and the creation of the judicial councils of the circuits and the Administrative Office of the United States Courts.[7] These structural innovations were stimulated in part by sheer increases in the work of the federal courts, by resultant increases in the number of circuit and district judges in each circuit, and by intensified interest in the work and internal management of the federal courts by the Congress.

Of the three reforms, the creation of judicial councils within the circuits had the greatest potential for change. The Judicial Conference of the United States, composed initially of the chief justice and the chief judges of the circuits, could make recommendations but lacked power to issue orders. The Administrative Office of the United States Courts was given centralized administrative, budgetary, and statistical responsibilities, but it too was allowed no direct authority over individual judges or their staffs.

In contrast, the judicial councils of the circuits were not only authorized but directed to "make all necessary orders for the effective and expeditious administration of the business of the courts within [their circuits]." The statute further mandated that district judges "promptly . . . carry out the directions of the Council as to the administration of the business of their respective courts."[8] From 1789 to 1939, the district judge had enjoyed almost total independence within his own court. Now that regime came to an end, de jure if not always de facto. At the same time, the councils satisfied Hughes's desire to decentralize the administration of the judiciary "as a defense against political forays centered on the establishment in Washington."[9]

Some critics of these efforts at congressional reorganization of court governance emphasized the lack of centralized control.[10] But the major problem that gained the direct attention of Congress in the years after passage of the Administrative Office Act was the perceived fail-

[7]For full discussion of these developments, see Peter Graham Fish, *The Politics of Federal Judicial Administration* (Princeton University Press, 1973).

[8]53 Stat. 1224 (1939). For discussion of the current provisions, see Chapter 10.

[9]Fish, supra note 7, at 145.

[10]Franklin D. Roosevelt's attorney general, Homer Cummings, had advocated concentrating overall supervision of the federal judiciary in the office of the chief justice of the United States. See Peter Graham Fish, "The Circuit Councils: Rusty Hinges of Federal Judicial Administration," 37 *U. Chi. L. Rev.* 203, 205 (1970). In the 1970s Judge J. Clifford Wallace commented about the absence of central authority in the Judicial Conference of the United States, likening its participants to a "Board of Directors without authority to enter orders." See J. Clifford Wallace, "Judicial Administration in a System of Independents: A Tribe with Only Chiefs," 1978 *B.Y.U. L. Rev.* 39, 47.

ure of many of the judicial councils to fulfill the objectives of the legislation. In 1959 a field study of the operations of the federal courts conducted by Paul J. Cotter for the Senate Appropriations Committee severely criticized the circuits for their indifference to the 1939 legislative requirements. Cotter found "a grave lack of administrative direction in the business of the United States courts, with resultant serious, and in some cases, shocking conditions of delay and neglect of cases on court dockets."[11]

A year after the Cotter report, Chief Judge J. Edward Lumbard of the Second Circuit provided an important evaluation from within the judiciary. In an address to the National Conference of Judicial Councils, Lumbard bluntly urged the judicial council members to meet the challenge of circuit management, which had for two decades "fallen far short of what was hoped and expected." Failure to do so "might ultimately become a real threat to judicial independence." Lumbard ended his appeal with the admonition that "if we continue to do little or nothing to keep our house in order Congress will intervene in the public interest and establish non-judicial controls which may well go beyond what is necessary or desirable." A year after its presentation, Lumbard's speech was reproduced in the *American Bar Association Journal*, there receiving wide dissemination among legal professionals.[12]

Failure to properly implement the act of 1939 was a national problem, but other issues of judicial administration also received some attention both within the judiciary and from Congress during the postwar years. Because district judges were excluded from direct supervision of judicial administration of the circuit, their role in circuit governance aroused concern. Significant recommendations also concerned the sensitive issue of disciplining judges for behavior not serious enough to warrant impeachment but serious enough to impede the performance of the judicial function.[13]

---

[11]Paul J. Cotter, "Report on the Field Study of the Operations of the Federal Courts to the Senate Appropriations Committee," Staff of the Senate Committee on Appropriations, 86th Cong., 2d Sess. (Committee Print, 1959), at 1.

[12]J. Edward Lumbard, "The Place of the Federal Judicial Councils in the Administration of the Courts," 47 *A.B.A.J.* 169, 169–70 (1961).

[13]One of the most important of these efforts was initiated by Chief Justice Earl Warren after the resignation of Associate Justice Abe Fortas. On May 22, 1969, Warren called a meeting of the Committee on Court Administration of the Judicial Conference to draft a code of ethics and financial reporting for federal judges. Six district judges and five court of appeals judges, including Browning, were named to the committee. *New York Times*, May 23, 1969, at 1 and 41.

Among these other issues, the concept of dividing circuits to reduce both the number of judges and geographic size was destined to become one of the most important and persistent with respect to the Ninth Circuit. As early as 1941, Circuit Judge Bert E. Haney circulated a pamphlet proposing a division of the Ninth Circuit in which the northwestern region of the circuit (Alaska, Washington, Oregon, Idaho, and Montana) would comprise a new Eleventh Circuit. A pamphlet opposing division was prepared and circulated by Judge William Denman.[14] Denman conceded that he had advocated a division of the circuit in 1935, a realignment that would have split California. But after saying that he was "now wiser," Denman provided a detailed explanation of why the division was no longer necessary. The main thrust of his rebuttal was that, as a result of 1937 legislation increasing the number of judges to seven, the Ninth Circuit had effectively managed a larger caseload and reduced the complaints of northwestern judges, lawyers, and litigants about lengthy travel to San Francisco, where the court of appeals regularly sat. This exchange did not attract the nationwide attention aroused by later efforts to split the Ninth Circuit, but it does indicate the persistence of the idea.[15]

The combination of issues involving circuit division, occasional intransigence by district judges over administrative matters, and the ever-growing caseloads helped to set the stage for greater congressional scrutiny of the Ninth Circuit after the late 1950s. One able observer described the judicial councils of the circuits as "rusty hinges of federal judicial administration."[16] From the 1950s through the early 1970s, some may have thought that the Ninth's was the rustiest. As legislative concerns over judicial administration mounted, the Ninth Circuit responded in much the same manner as the other circuits, but the general judicial indifference to calls for reform was accentuated by a regional tradition of independence and by occasional strained relations between chief judges and the other judges within the circuit.

It was in this setting that James R. Browning was chosen by Presi-

---

[14]William Denman, "How the Accomplishment (of the Ninth Circuit's Judges) Will Be Destroyed by an Unwarranted Division of the Circuit into a Shrunken Ninth and a Grossly Overstaffed Eleventh Circuit" (San Francisco: privately published, August 20, 1941).

[15]In 1954 Denman changed his mind again and supported a proposal for dividing the Ninth Circuit, this time without splitting California. He explained that the volume of business in the four northwestern states and Alaska (then still a territory) now warranted creation of a new circuit.

[16]Fish, supra note 10.

dent John F. Kennedy for the Ninth Circuit Court of Appeals in 1961.[17] Fifteen eventful years intervened before Browning had the opportunity to take on the mantle of chief judge. During that period the leadership of the circuit was in the hands of Chief Judge Richard H. Chambers.

The Office of Chief Judge and the Administration of the Ninth Circuit, 1948–76

The internal leadership of the circuit embodies several concepts, the most important of which is the position of chief judge. Until 1948 there was no such office as "chief judge" of a circuit. Such leadership functions as existed were exercised by the "senior circuit judge." Among many other changes, the Judicial Code of 1948 created the position of "chief judge of the circuit," to be filled by "[t]he circuit judge who is senior in commission." Until the enactment of the Federal Courts Improvements Act of 1982, a chief judge could serve until the age of seventy. Today the term of a chief judge is limited to seven years.[18]

Some of the chief judge's powers and duties are defined by statute; some are not. By statute, the chief judge presides over the judicial council of the circuit and serves as a member of the Judicial Conference of the United States. The chief judge also presides over court of appeals meetings and, with the aid of the executive committee, sets their agendas. He is responsible for carrying out the policies adopted by the court, principally through coordinating the work of the various court offices, whose senior staff report to him.

From 1948 to 1988, six men served as chief judge of the Ninth Circuit, but only three had tenures long enough for them to exercise substantial influence: William Denman (1948–57), Richard H. Chambers (1959–76), and James R. Browning (1976–88).[19] Unless Congress

[17]Browning received his commission on September 18, 1961, but did not take the judicial oath until October 23. In the meantime, Judge Ben Cushing Duniway had taken the oath of office. However, because Browning was senior in commission to Duniway, Browning had precedence.

[18]After stepping down as chief judge, a judge may continue in active service, as Browning did.

[19]The first chief judge was Francis A. Garrecht, who died in 1948 after serving less than two months. Between 1957, when Denman reached the statutory age limit of seventy, and 1959, when Chambers took over, Albert Lee Stephens and Walter L. Pope each served brief terms as chief judge. Alfred T. Goodwin succeeded Browning on June 15, 1988.

changes the law once again, no future chief judge will enjoy the opportunity to exercise leadership for the extended periods of time that were available to these three men—nine years for Denman, seventeen years for Chambers, twelve years for Browning.

Each of these three chief judges exercised his authority in quite different ways. Denman undoubtedly represented the older, highly individualistic tradition of the circuit. As chief judge he did not share decision making with the other judges on the court and did not seriously seek to use the institution of the judicial council. Chambers, whose service in the Ninth Circuit included several years under Chief Judge Denman, reported that when he joined the court of appeals the judicial council met "maybe" once a year. Chambers recalled that he and Judge James Alger Fee gained passage of a resolution for more meetings of the council. Regarding leadership style, Chambers wrote that "[a] predecessor of some years back would tell the district judges what they had to do. (That system took little time.) As a consequence, most of the district judges' meetings were spent in pouring vitriol on him." Since one of the major purposes of the 1939 statute creating the judicial councils was active participation of the court of appeals judges in the governance of each circuit, Denman's tendency to concentrate administrative decision making in himself not only engendered division among the judges, but also thwarted congressional intent.

Chambers's seventeen-year role as administrative leader of the circuit coincided with the beginning of a long era of increased congressional interest in judicial administrative reform. His first year, 1959, was the year of the Cotter report; in his second year, Judge Lumbard delivered his influential criticism from within the judiciary.

Chambers's third year as chief judge brought an internal innovation that was to grow in importance over time. Several judges on the court of appeals successfully pressed for the establishment, on a regular basis, of an informal institution for open discussion of institutional change that would help to develop and maintain a tradition of collegiality and innovation. The idea appears to have originated with Judge Charles M. Merrill, who suggested an occasional retreat because he was "convinced that this court operates too much as a mixture of uncondensed individuals."[20] Thus "it might be a good idea for us occasionally to withdraw to some secluded resort for a seminar or retreat and there to discuss the work of the court and how it might be

[20]This particular phrase came to mind as the result of a chemical patent case Merrill had been working on.

improved, methods of operation, etc." Merrill noted that Judge Frederick G. Hamley had originated the New York University Seminar for Appellate Judges, which could serve as a model for internal emulation. The idea was enthusiastically endorsed by other members of the court, including Browning, who had taken his seat on the Ninth Circuit only a few weeks earlier. Chambers responded by appointing a committee composed of Merrill as chair and Hamley and Browning as members to organize an informal session or retreat. Thus Browning was, from the inception, directly involved in the development of the retreat or Symposium as a vehicle for the informal exchange of ideas and the enhancement of collegiality.

The annual Symposium has retained its original character as a manifestation of the good fellowship of the judges on what was, from today's perspective, a comparatively small court of appeals. But from its first two days of sessions and recreation at the Wawona Lodge in Yosemite National Park in May 1962, the Symposium also served as a fairly accurate barometer of the internal cohesiveness and intellectual flexibility of a court under increasingly severe external and occasional internal pressures. By the early 1960s, the workload of the judges was rapidly growing. As one of two major external influences on the court, the increasing caseload has been the constant. As Browning put it in his initial State of the Circuit Report in 1976: "Since 1960, we've had a 500 per cent caseload increase and a judgeship increase of 44 per cent." But it was the second of the external influences, the Congress, which stimulated a good deal of discussion and debate among the judges. As a result, issues involving the internal administration of the circuit increasingly shared place on the agendas of the annual Symposia with matters related to potential congressional action.

By the early 1960s, it had become evident that, in contrast to Denman's era, long-range decision-making authority would no longer be concentrated in the chief judge, although the day-to-day administration of the circuit would continue to be handled that way. Chambers generally cooperated with his fellow court of appeals judges, though he sometimes disagreed strongly with their ideas about administrative reform and occasionally did not immediately implement policies that had been adopted by a majority of the judges. His style of administration has been described by some judges who served with him as a "carrot and stick" approach. Those judges who accepted tough assignments were subsequently rewarded by more desirable ones.

As the possibilities for potentially disruptive congressional intervention increased in the 1960s and early 1970s, more action in restructuring the administrative organization of the circuit was requested by some of the appeals judges. Conversely, Chambers became increasingly reluctant to respond, partly because he did not view the possibility of congressional intervention seriously, but also because he sometimes disagreed with the remedies proposed. For example, in 1964 Chambers resisted a suggestion by one of his colleagues for the appointment of an administrative assistant who would take over the handling of routine administrative matters. Five years later, Judge Hamley warned that federal legislation requiring greater supervision by the judicial councils was imminent. He suggested that the chief judge be required to call a council meeting at the request of five circuit judges. Chambers objected to this proposal as well, adhering to his view that "one judge should handle the agenda." More fundamentally, he "refuse[d] to accept the proposition" that more federal legislation was "in the offing which directly [will] require the exercise of the Council's supervisory functions."

Chambers's denial of the seriousness of the threat of congressional action in this as well as in other matters involving the Ninth Circuit was viewed with increasing concern by some court members because proposed legislation regarding division of the circuit and discipline of judges appeared to be nearing enactment. The Ninth Circuit became a natural target for division because of its geographical size, the rapid increase in the number of judges, and the circuit's historical reluctance to develop more effective and expeditious procedures.

The circuit's responses to these criticisms were generally deemed unsatisfactory by members of Congress and their staff. As early as the beginning of the 1960s, serious attempts to divide the Ninth Circuit were made. One such effort arose out of unusual circumstances. In 1961, H.R. 6690 provided for district judge representation on the judicial councils of the circuits. The bill was opposed by the Ninth Circuit. This opposition brought a sharp rebuke from a key Senate staff member, Hubert H. Finzel, chief counsel to the Senate Judiciary Subcommittee on Improvements in Judiciary Machinery. Writing to Chambers, Finzel bluntly stated that the opposition of the judges of the Ninth Circuit to H.R. 6690 in the 87th Congress "resulted in focussing attention on the advisability of creating smaller circuits." According to Finzel, the judges of the Ninth Circuit opposed the resolution because of the "impossibility or difficulty . . . of the vast geographical distances in the Ninth Circuit." Finzel then wrote: "In other words, when legislative measures designed to improve the efficiency of the administration and operation of our judiciary are opposed because of the size of a Judicial Circuit the apparent result could only be to decrease the size." The result was the introduction of S. 1876, which provided for the creation of a new Eleventh Circuit comprising Alaska, Idaho, Montana, Oregon, and Washington. The bill was sponsored by Senators Olin D. Johnston of South Carolina and Warren G. Magnuson of Washington and cosponsored by four senators from Ninth Circuit states.[21]

By the 1970s, the prospects for division had become greater. The traditional responses to caseload growth, such as adding more judges to reduce the workload or reassigning judges from regions with lighter caseloads to those with heavier ones, were no longer accepted so readily by Congress. Influential critics such as Chief Justice Warren E. Burger and Solicitor General Erwin N. Griswold pinpointed the Ninth Circuit as too large, both numerically and geographically, and too unwieldy administratively. The conventional wisdom in that period was that nine judges were optimum for the size of an appellate court.

These developments came to a head in the work of the Commission on Revision of the Federal Court Appellate System (Hruska Commission). Chambers's statement to the commission in Seattle, filed on August 27, 1973, was a classic statement of the old regional tradition. He bluntly asked for more judges and rested his case for retention of the entire circuit on the argument that a large, geographically diverse circuit provided needed "back country" regions from which judges with light caseloads could be temporarily reassigned to districts with heavy caseloads when needed.[22] Chambers himself, however, recognized that the "back country" was disappearing. His own state of Arizona had, within the years he served in the Ninth Circuit, been catapulted from a region of modest litigation activity to one of intensive court business.

---

[21]Sponsorship of the bill by Senator Johnston of South Carolina, a state remote from the Pacific Northwest, almost certainly can be traced to the controversy over H.R. 6690. In 1962 Johnston, who was then chairman of the Subcommittee on Improvements in Judicial Machinery, took to the Senate floor to condemn judges, including Chambers, who had waged an active campaign against the earlier legislation. Fish, supra note 7, at 311. The cosponsors of S. 1876 were Senators Ernest Greuning and E. L. Bartlett of Alaska, Daniel K. Inouye of Hawaii, and Henry M. Jackson of Washington. The legislation died a quiet death after the Judicial Conference of the United States, at the urging of Chief Judge Chambers, expressed its opposition. See Deborah J. Barrow and Thomas G. Walker, *A Court Divided: The Fifth Circuit Court of Appeals and the Politics of Judicial Reform* 63 (Yale University Press, 1988).

[22]Commission on Revision of the Federal Court Appellate System, Hearings First Phase 662–67 (1973) (hereafter cited as First Phase Hearings).

The Hruska Commission's draft report, entitled "The Geographical Boundaries of the Several Judicial Circuits: Alternative Proposals," was adopted in substance as its final report on December 18, 1973.[23] Rejecting Chambers's exhortations, it recommended dividing the Ninth Circuit into a smaller Ninth and a new Twelfth Circuit. The reorganization would have allocated the judicial districts of California between the two circuits. Although the recommendation was controversial, to many observers the division of the circuit seemed inevitable.[24]

The three years between the Hruska Commission's investigations and Browning's assumption of the office of chief judge were marked by intense self-examination of the circuit's mode of operation and a good deal of uncertainty about the potential consequences of particular choices. Some of the ideas discussed in this period were sharpened, developed, or later seen in a different light. For example, in 1973 Judges Browning and Duniway submitted detailed statements to the Hruska Commission supporting the division of the circuit. At that time Browning believed "wholeheartedly" that a court of even twelve judges was not only "too large to function efficiently" in its performance of its adjudicative responsibilities, but also "too large to do an effective administrative job."[25] Two years later Browning joined several of his colleagues in supporting S. 729, a bill that would have established two "divisions" within the Ninth Circuit instead of splitting it into two separate circuits. Interestingly, Browning favored the legislation because it would have created two appellate structures that were substantially independent of one another; other Ninth Circuit judges, including Chambers, liked the bill because it avoided actual division of the circuit. However, Judge Shirley Hufstedler and others strongly opposed this approach as well as the possibility of formal division.[26]

[23]This was the first of two reports issued by the commission in accordance with its statutory mandate. A later report presented recommendations on a wide array of topics relating to the structure and internal procedures of the federal court appellate system.

[24]In March 1977 a member of the House Judiciary Committee reported to Browning on a breakfast "hosted by Attorney General [Griffin] Bell for the Judiciary Committee . . . shortly after Bell took office." He said that Bell "seemed to take it for granted that the circuit should be divided though he seemed to have no particular concept in mind."

[25]First Phase Hearings, supra note 22, at 907–8.

[26]See Circuit Realignment: Hearings on S. 729 before the Subcomm. on Improvements in Judicial Machinery of the Senate Judiciary Comm., 94th Cong., 1st Sess., Part 2, at 145 (1975) (letter from Judge Browning); id. at 156 (statement of Judge Duniway); id. at 125–26 (statement of Judge Chambers); id. at 88 (statement of Judge Hufstedler).

It was in 1976, during this period of ferment and uncertainty, that Chambers reached the age of seventy and assumed senior status. For several years before that, Browning had been in the forefront of those judges who were actively seeking meaningful administrative reform in the court. In particular, he played a leading role in a lengthy and difficult struggle to establish and maintain a case-screening program using a small, centralized group of law clerks. This effort proceeded in the face of strong opposition from the chief judge, who acted with characteristic zeal and ingenuity to forestall the proposed experiment. The confrontational style of leadership and the rancorous atmosphere of the debates might well have provided a negative model for Browning as he took over the helm of the circuit. As will be seen, Browning followed a very different approach from that of his predecessor.

Browning's Background and Career

James R. Browning was born on October 1, 1918, in Great Falls, Montana, to Nicholas Henry and Minnie Sally Browning. Nicholas Henry had served as an apprentice blacksmith before establishing his own successful blacksmith business in Belt, Montana, in the Great Falls region of that state. When autos, tractors, and trucks began to replace horses, he became the owner of Belt's Ford agency, which he successfully managed until World War II. Minnie Sally was educated in a state teachers' college and was active in women's organizations and in the community affairs of Belt.

James attended Belt Elementary School from 1924 to 1932, and Belt Valley High School from 1932 to 1936. His undergraduate education comprised two years at Montana State University (now the University of Montana) in Missoula, September 1936 to June 1938. He was then eligible to enter law school at the university, where he became the second editor of the fledgling law review (his brother having been the first). His law-school years, 1938 to 1941, were influenced by one of his mentors, Professor David R. Mason, who encouraged him to join the ranks of other eager New Deal attorneys in the Department of Justice. Browning joined the Justice Department's Antitrust Division in Denver, Colorado, in October 1941 and served for two years. Then he was called to military service and was stationed at U.S. Army Headquarters in Honolulu, Hawaii, from October 1943 to September 1946. Afterward he returned to the Justice Department, where he served in the Antitrust Division in Washington, D.C., until August 1948.

In the Justice Department, attorney Browning's career was influenced positively by the guidance and assistance of Holmes Baldridge, the chief of the General Litigation Section of the Antitrust Division. Although only thirty, Browning was placed in charge of the Seattle, Washington, office of the Antitrust Division, where he served from August 1948 to April 1949. He then returned to Washington, D.C., as assistant chief of the General Litigation Section of the Antitrust Division for two years. From April 1951 to August 1952, he served as first assistant in the Civil Division of the Department of Justice, and from August 1952 to April 1953, he was in the Attorney General's office, where, until the end of the Truman administration, he served as executive assistant to Attorney General McGranery.

With the transition of the Justice Department to the Eisenhower administration, Browning stayed on briefly under Deputy Attorney General William P. Rogers. At Rogers's request he prepared a wide-ranging (and soon implemented) set of recommendations for administrative changes within the department, work that in many ways anticipated some of the reforms he set into motion at the Ninth Circuit. After leaving the department, Browning went into private law practice in Washington, D.C. In 1958 he became Clerk of the Supreme Court of the United States, serving there until his nomination and appointment as judge of the Court of Appeals for the Ninth Circuit by President John F. Kennedy in 1961.

Some of the qualities that have characterized Browning as jurist and administrator can be traced to his early upbringing and career. Although his family maintained comfortable economic circumstances, the region in which he was born, raised, and educated had experienced great economic changes. These were vividly described by another contributor to the New Deal, the appellate judiciary, and legal advocacy, Thurman Arnold. Although Browning has not made a similar autobiographical commentary, his "passion for antitrust," as one observer has described it, may derive from similar personal acquaintance with the impact of monopoly on the small, independent businesses of his region. In his autobiography Arnold wrote a chapter titled "Law and Politics in Wyoming, and Why I Left." In it he observed that,

> As the years went by it became increasingly apparent that the West and the South were becoming afflicted with an economic blight known as absentee ownership. . . . It was plain murder for small business. . . . Local lawyers were as ignorant of the anti-trust laws as they were of the laws of

the Medes and the Persians. . . . Giant corporations continued to absorb local industry, draining off to the big cities the purchasing power of the West and the South. . . . I saw no future under these conditions.[27]

Browning's "passions" have not been limited to issues affecting his region. Philip Elman's recently published oral history, for example, indicates that Browning was an unsung hero in facilitating the filing of the first brief from the Justice Department in *Brown v. Board of Education* in December 1952. Elman, then a staff attorney in the solicitor general's office, had the completed brief ready for filing. It had been signed by Attorney General James P. McGranery and by Elman himself. Because the leadership of the solicitor general's office was in transition from Acting Solicitor General Robert Stern to newly chosen Solicitor General Walter Cummings, Jr., Elman was uncertain whether the brief should be printed and filed as is. Elman recalls that he called McGranery's executive assistant, James Browning, "who was very much with us on this whole enterprise," asking "What do we do?" With decisiveness Browning told Elman to send it to the printer "just as it is." Thus the Justice Department's antisegregation brief became the official position of the Truman administration in December 1952.[28]

Perhaps the most important legacies of Browning's experiences in the Justice Department were his successful administrative roles, roles that often involved the management of attorneys and staff members older than himself. Of particular significance, Browning served as the number-two man in several of the offices, an experience that plunged him into what he later described as "the nitty-gritty of administrative work," with responsibility for "keeping a large office functioning." The years in the Justice Department also provided experience in dealing with Washington bureaucracy and with members of Congress and their staff. These abilities were to prove invaluable in the twelve years of his chief judgeship.

The Challenge of the Omnibus Judgeship Bill

Less than a year after Browning assumed the office of chief judge, the long-pending issue of circuit division took on new urgency. With

[27]Thurman Wesley Arnold, *Fair Fights and Foul: A Dissenting Lawyer's Autobiography* 30–37 (Harcourt, Brace and World, 1965).

[28]Philip Elman, "The Solicitor General's Office, Justice Frankfurter, and Civil Rights Litigation, 1946–1960: An Oral History," 100 *Harv. L. Rev.* 817, 827 (1987).

the presidency and both houses of Congress controlled by the same party for the first time since 1969, prospects for legislative action on an omnibus judgeship bill brightened substantially in the Congress that convened in January 1977.[29] The response from the Ninth Circuit on a matter that could have fragmented the court provides a good demonstration of Browning's manner of leadership.

Browning's principal aim was to secure additional judges for the circuit, including ten for the court of appeals. To succeed in this effort, he found it essential to keep this goal separate from the question of circuit division. He recalled all too clearly that linkage between the two issues had led to an impasse between Senator Quentin Burdick, who had served on the Hruska Commission, and the California delegation.[30] Now the strategy of separation was necessary not only because Congress was considered to be leaning favorably toward circuit division, but also because the judges themselves were then still closely divided. Thus, when Browning polled his colleagues by questionnaire in late 1976, he included a carefully worded memo that not only requested each participant's position on division of the circuit, but also asked those supporting circuit division whether or not California should be divided.

In pursuing the strategy of giving unencumbered priority to securing the new judgeships, Browning subordinated his own views about the future of his court. He had testified in favor of dividing the circuit at the hearings of the Hruska Commission, and when speaking for himself during this period he made clear both to his fellow judges and to members of Congress that he adhered to his earlier position. But in appearances before committees in both houses and in conversations with influential congressmen and senators, he repeatedly emphasized the unanimous position of his court that creation of new judgeships should not await action on division of the circuit. He also assured Senator John L. McClellan, another member of the Hruska Commission, that when the judgeships were provided he would work to implement a plan advocated by Chief Justice Burger for establishment of administrative units within the circuit.

With Browning's example before them, it is not surprising that most of the judges who took competing positions on circuit division united to assist their chief in urging Congress to meet the need for new

[29]Barrow and Walker, supra note 21, at 184–89.

[30]Omnibus Judgeship Bill: Hearings on S. 11 before the Senate Committee on the Judiciary, 95th Cong., 1st Sess. (1977) at 241 (testimony of Judge Browning) (hereafter cited as 1977 Hearings).

judgeships without delay. Several members of the court spoke or wrote to senators and congressmen they knew personally to put forward the united circuit position.[31] From time to time, at formal and informal meetings, the judges discussed the strategy of separating the effort to gain more judges from the issue of dividing the circuit and related issues of internal reform. Ideas were exchanged concerning the best way to approach members of Congress in order to avoid antagonism while pursuing the circuit's goals.

Browning was keenly aware of the fact that some members of Congress from the Ninth Circuit, such as Senator Henry M. Jackson of Washington, had already committed themselves publicly to dividing the circuit and were thus unlikely to change their position on that issue. State bar groups like the California State Bar Association and politically astute attorneys such as John P. Frank of Arizona had been marshaled in behalf of the circuit's goal.[32] Browning coordinated his efforts with a politically unlikely pair of bipartisan supporters of the circuit, his friend and home-state senator, Lee Metcalf, and a knowledgeable Republican congressman from southern California, Charles Wiggins (now a court of appeals judge in the Ninth Circuit). One important unifying factor was the concept of a western regional culture that was closely tied to California. For example, in his testimony before the Hruska Commission, Frank opposed circuit realignment because "the legal life" of Arizona "as well as [its] economic life is wholly tied to California . . . Justice Traynor is just as authoritative in our state as he is . . . in your state [California]."[33]

Browning's decisive achievement in this carefully coordinated effort was gaining the support of the entire senatorial delegation from the

---

[31]In a two-month period in late 1976 and early 1977, Browning himself met with Senator Cranston and Congressmen Charles Wiggins, George Danielson, and Don Edwards; Judge Merrill wrote to Senators Howard Cannon and Paul Laxalt; Judge Otto Skopil met with Congressman Robert Duncan and Senator Mark Hatfield; Judge J. Blaine Anderson met with Senators Frank Church and James McClure; and Judge Goodwin wrote to Senator Robert Packwood and Congressman Duncan.

[32]Frank later recalled that, in the aftermath of a conference on appellate justice held in Coronado, California, in January 1975, "there was a breakfast meeting [with] some people from Arizona [and] some people from California. . . . We entered into the pact of Coronado, which is that we would use our Senatorial influence and the Californians would use their House influence to make sure that the circuit was not divided. We have diligently supported Jim [Browning] in this regard. I have made lots of telephone calls myself to helpful people and have gotten others to do so who have local influence." Conference on Empirical Research in Judicial Administration, 21 *Ariz. St. L.J.* 33, 97 (1989).

[33]First Phase Hearings, supra note 22, at 1009.

Ninth Circuit. On February 24, 1977, all eighteen senators from the nine states in the circuit signed a letter to Senator McClellan, in his capacity as chairman of the Subcommittee on Criminal Laws and Procedures of the Senate Judiciary Committee, urging approval of Amendment 42 to S. 11, "to implement the Judicial Conference recommendation that 25 new judgeships be created for the Circuit Court of Appeals, including ten new judgeships for the Ninth Circuit."[34] The senators urged that the need for new judgeships be separated from "the difficult problem connected with the geographic reorganization of the Circuit."

The fact that eighteen senators of widely different partisan and ideological views were united on this issue had an especially effective influence on the consideration of the judgeship bill. These were the men who signed the letter to Senator McClellan:

California	Alan Cranston (D)	S. I. Hayakawa (R)
Alaska	Mike Gravel (D)	Ted Stevens (R)
Idaho	Frank Church (D)	James A. McClure (R)
Hawaii	Spark M. Matsunaga (D)	Daniel K. Inouye (D)
Oregon	Mark O. Hatfield (R)	Bob Packwood (R)
Washington	Warren G. Magnuson (D)	Henry M. Jackson (D)
Nevada	Howard W. Cannon (D)	Paul Laxalt (R)
Montana	Lee Metcalf (D)	John Melcher (D)
Arizona	Dennis DeConcini (D)	Barry Goldwater (R)

Daniel J. Meador, who was an assistant attorney general at the time the division of the Ninth Circuit was under consideration, has given a vivid account of the impact this communication had at the Justice Department.

> I will never forget the day [the] letter arrived on my desk. It was very short, only a few sentences, and signed by all the United States Senators from the states of the Ninth Circuit. Eighteen United States Senators signed this letter and all it said [was], "Do not split the Ninth Circuit." That was a powerful communication. That letter just sat there on my desk for awhile; it was almost as though it was radioactive. . . . It was a conversation stopper. That was the end of the effort to split the Ninth.[35]

Reflecting later on these events, Browning observed that "Congressional support for division was so strong that because the two

[34]1977 Hearings, supra note 30, at 656.
[35]Conference on Empirical Research, supra note 32, at 96.

circuits [the Fifth and Ninth] opposed it, they were very nearly entirely excluded from the Omnibus Judgeship Act of 1978."[36] Through adroit leadership and united action toward a shared goal, the Ninth gained its full complement of ten judges in the legislation.

One consequence of these and other legislative activities was an increase in recommendations by judges to members of Congress concerning proposed judicial legislation. This development, in turn, aroused some academic criticism of so-called judicial lobbying. For example, Charles Halpern, of Georgetown University's law faculty, argued, "There is something unseemly . . . for judges to ginny up a letter writing campaign or phone call campaign."[37] Many members of Congress and judges, sensitive to the continuous interrelationship of Congress and the federal courts, disagreed with that criticism. By 1980, Browning was being described as "one of the more active appellate judges." In response to a *Congressional Quarterly* interview, Browning noted,

> I have not hesitated to write or call whether [a member of Congress] inquired or not, if legislation affects the operation of the courts in this circuit . . . I cannot believe that the public interest is served by saying "Do not speak until spoken to" about legislation that directly affects the administration of the courts. No one questions Congress' ultimate authority to make decisions, but surely they want to make them with the facts.[38]

The ultimate success of the effort to gain new judges did not settle the issue of circuit division. From 1970 into the 1980s, Chief Justice Warren E. Burger was a consistent advocate of splitting the circuit. For example, in his report to the Judicial Conference in 1980, Burger applauded the decision of the Fifth Circuit to divide and urged Congress to continue on that path by carving three full-fledged circuits out of the Ninth.[39] In that same year, supporters of division gained a

[36]Cited in James R. Browning, "Report to the 1981 Circuit Conference," at 12 (June 29, 1981).

[37]Nadine Cohades, "When Federal Judges Lobby, the Congressmen Usually Listen," 38 Congressional Quarterly Weekly Report 3167 (October 1980).

[38]Id. at 3168.

[39]Cited in Browning, supra note 36, at 12. In 1988, after both men had stepped down from their leadership positions, the former chief justice paid a backhanded tribute to Browning's successful effort to keep the circuit intact: "Like Gorbachev, you didn't want to split up your empire. But you will ultimately have to." *Los Angeles Times,* Oct. 9, 1988, Part II, p. 2 (quoting letter read at special session honoring Browning).

champion in Congress when the voters of the state of Washington elected Slade Gorton to the Senate. Gorton reopened the debate early in 1982 by proposing a bill that would create a new Twelfth Circuit out of the five northern states of the Ninth. By that time, however, Browning had changed his mind about the desirability of a split. From his new perspective as chief judge, he had concluded that the large circuit could work; he had seen that a large number of new judges could be integrated into the operation of the court of appeals; and he had become more aware of the national implications of creating new circuits.

The impending introduction of the Gorton bill prompted an extended discussion at the March 1982 Symposium held in Indian Wells, California. This time the judges appointed to the court under the 1978 act took part. As in previous debates, support or opposition to division did not break on party or ideological lines. No formal vote was ever taken, but a majority of the judges appear to have favored retaining the Ninth as a single circuit.

Starting in 1982, members of the court moved on three fronts to resist pressures for division. Even before the Gorton bill was introduced, judges traveled to Washington to meet with key members of Congress and their staffs. Institutionally, the judicial council and the court of appeals prepared and circulated a "biennial report on the implementation of section 6 of the Omnibus Judgeship Act." This report (like its three successors) enabled the court to tell its story directly to Congress without having to depend on committee hearings; it also served as a device for rallying support within the circuit. Outside Congress, individual judges communicated with lawyers in each of the states of the Ninth Circuit to persuade the organized bar to oppose the legislation. These efforts succeeded in halting whatever momentum the proposal may have had. When Gorton finally introduced his bill in April 1983, it had no cosponsors.

The discussions within and outside the court helped Browning to prepare a strong statement for submission to a Senate Judiciary subcommittee in March 1984. In that statement Browning marshaled the arguments against division of the circuit:

> The size of the Circuit permits flexible and efficient use of a large pool of district as well as circuit judges. At any time, some of the fifteen district courts in the Circuit have more judge-power than work, while others have less. Because the fifteen districts are part of the same circuit, judges

may be readily assigned to follow the work. Similarly, the number of circuit judges from one part of the Circuit rarely matches the number of appeals originating from that area. A single court of appeals permits even distribution of appellate resources. Division of the Circuit would foreclose these efficiencies.

The people in the area encompassed by the Ninth Circuit have important social, political, and commercial interests in common. Existence of a single Circuit and a uniform body of federal law facilitates commerce and strengthens social and political unity in the area. A vital purpose of a federal court is to give expression to such regional viewpoints while fostering the national interest. . . .

A large and vigorous Circuit strengthens the decentralization of the federal court system deliberately ordained by the Congress. Congress may conclude that reduction in the size of the Circuit would accelerate control and administration in Washington, contrary to that principle.

. . . [D]ivision of the Ninth Circuit would destroy the laboratory in which innovations are being developed to test whether a large circuit, and particularly a large court of appeals, can function effectively.

The outcome of this experiment has important implications for the future organization of the federal judicial system. If it fails, there is no alternative to continued multiplication of circuits and courts of appeals, entailing, among other adverse consequences, an inevitable increase in conflicting rulings by different courts of appeals that must be resolved by the Supreme Court itself, or by the creation of either additional specialized national courts of appeals or a new national intermediate appellate court below the Supreme Court. If the experiment succeeds and the effectiveness of a large circuit is thus established, conflicts can be contained and resolved within existing circuits and no further division of the circuits will be necessary.[40]

Gorton's bill was never reported out of subcommittee. The Ninth Circuit remained intact, and a large majority of the judges support its continued unity.[41]

---

[40]Oversight on the Federal Court of Appeals and U.S. Claims Court Workload and a Hearing on S. 386, S. 677, and S. 1156 before the Subcomm. on Courts of the Senate Judiciary Comm., 98th Cong., 2d Sess. 86–87 (1984).

[41]In May 1989 Gorton revived his proposal to divide the circuit. See Chapter 1, note 38. This time the bill had seven cosponsors. Again the judges of the circuit launched a vigorous counterattack, including the preparation of a "section 6 report" that attempted to rebut arguments made by supporters of the legislation. A Senate subcommittee held hearings on the bill in March 1990. Former Chief Justice Burger spoke in favor of the proposal, as did a district judge and an attorney from Oregon. But California's two

Leadership in a Changing Circuit

In the aftermath of the Omnibus Judgeship Act of 1978, the Fifth Circuit chose to divide. The Ninth opted instead for internal reform. Detailed analysis of the most important elements of the Ninth Circuit's program are found in the preceding chapters, but three features warrant special mention here.

First, the court gave broader powers to its executive committee, including authorization to decide many questions that would formerly have been decided by all the judges. The executive committee also assists the chief judge in setting agendas for court meetings and presents recommendations that have already received a good deal of fine-tuning, thus reducing the amount of discussion by the full court.

Second, the "court" has been sharply differentiated from the "council," and the council now includes only five circuit judges among its nine members. This transformation began with a self-conscious separation of court and council agendas; eventually, the two bodies were made entirely separate. The result is that a majority of the circuit judges no longer have any direct responsibility for council matters. In addition, a smaller council can undertake projects that would have been impossibly cumbersome for a body that included all the active circuit judges.

Third, when the court votes to hear a case en banc, the decision on the merits is made by an eleven-judge panel rather than by the full court.

What these innovations have in common is the delegation and concentration of responsibilities other than the decision of individual cases by three-judge panels. Without that reallocation, it is doubtful that the court could have operated effectively with twenty-eight active judges; other duties would probably have overwhelmed the function of deciding cases.

These and other changes were primarily the result of two major developments, both of which have their roots in the explosive growth in the court's caseload. The first and most important was internal to

---

senators—one a Republican, the other a Democrat—testified in opposition, along with Chief Judge Goodwin and representatives of environmental groups, who saw the bill as an attack on Ninth Circuit rulings affecting the timber industry. See *New York Times*, Mar. 9, 1990, at B6 (New York edition). At this writing it appears unlikely that the legislation will pass. For a brief discussion of the merits of the proposal, see Chapter 13.

the Ninth Circuit; the second was external. The internal impetus was the often intensive self-examination by the court of appeals judges, a scrutiny that extended to their court's procedures, their own work patterns, and the structure and effectiveness of the circuit's institutions of self-government. The external influence was the interest and oversight of the Congress. One of Browning's key contributions was the constant attention he paid to maintaining the underlying atmosphere of mutual trust, respect, and professionalism which provides the basis for effective group decision making, whether of cases or of administrative issues. Effective leadership also entailed handling internal and external issues simultaneously and with full appreciation of their interrelationship; and in that effort Browning was notably successful.

The dynamics of change in the Browning court were most prominently manifested in the process through which the court adopted its limited en banc rule. The history of the rule is traced in detail in Chapter 3. Our interest here is in understanding how so substantial a reform could be accomplished with so little friction, yielding an arrangement that has remained in place despite the passage of time and changes in the court's membership. Several clues can be found. First, the process was a long one. To some extent this was adventitious; in particular, the delay in filling the new judgeships meant that the court could not adopt the rule for more than a year after the extended discussion at the 1979 Symposium. But the length of the process gave the judges ample opportunity to consider the merits and drawbacks of possible approaches, and often they ended up rejecting ideas that had initially seemed attractive. By the time the judges actually voted on the rule, the decision seemed almost anticlimactic.

Second, the process was structured in a way that avoided confrontation and enabled judges to modify their views without having to give up positions to which they had formally committed themselves. All of the extended discussion took place at Symposia rather than at court meetings. The informal atmosphere encouraged give-and-take, and because no binding votes were taken, judges could easily announce afterward, as they did, that further reflection had changed their minds on key issues.

Third, the discussion remained free of ideological overtones. Even before the new positions created by the 1978 judgeship bill were filled, it must have been apparent that the Carter appointments would be of a distinctly more liberal bent than most of the judges already on the court. Nevertheless, judges on all points of the political-ideological spectrum ultimately became convinced that the ad hoc method of selection was preferable, largely because it would minimize result-oriented votes on granting en banc rehearing.

In contrast to the extended debates over the size and composition of the limited en banc court, the process that resulted in the restructuring of the circuit council consisted of two distinct phases: a lengthy period of intermittent general discussion, followed by a relatively brief stage devoted to formulation of the rule. Moreover, during the first phase the court as then constituted did not reach a consensus in favor of reform; on the contrary, the sentiment was predominantly one of opposition to change.

As early as February 1978, the court considered a proposal to amend the Judicial Code to provide for district judge representation on the circuit councils.[42] The suggestion was prompted by the then-pending Nunn-DeConcini bill, which would have given the circuit councils new responsibility in matters of judicial discipline. Proponents argued that, if the council was to discipline district judges, district judges should be represented on the disciplinary body. Other judges voiced opposition to change, insisting that discipline of lower-court judges was a supervisory function that was appropriately vested in the members of the circuit court. The subject was discussed again the following year, and nine of the thirteen active judges expressed opposition to any change in the structure of the councils.[43]

The debates within the court became moot on October 15, 1980, when the legislation requiring some district judge representation on the council was signed. Within six weeks, a committee chaired by Browning had drafted a plan for a nine-member council with four seats allocated to district judges. The draft was discussed at one meet-

---

[42]As noted in Chapter 10, the restructuring of the council was preceded by a period in which Browning carefully separated the "court" agenda from the "council" agenda, even though the same individuals composed the two bodies and the meetings generally took place sequentially in a single block of time. The bifurcation may have helped to persuade the circuit judges that the two institutions were separable and that it was not important for the members of the court of appeals to play a dominant role in the business of the council. From this perspective, it could be said that the first phase of the restructuring began in 1977.

[43]By this time, Browning had begun the practice of inviting district judge representatives to the portion of the court's meetings devoted to "council" business. See p. 260. This development helped acclimate the judges to the prospect of change. Although the documentary evidence is conflicting, it appears that at least some of the judges who opposed the membership of district judges on the council did not object to their attendance at council meetings as observers.

ing of the court of appeals and was circulated to all judges in the circuit. One substantive change was made to accommodate concerns expressed by the court of appeals judges. After a few additional modifications, all of them quite minor, the plan was submitted to the court, which approved it on April 17, 1981. Barely six months had elapsed between the enactment of the statute and the court's acceptance of a structure that went much further than most of the other circuits in giving a voice to the district judges and reducing the role of the circuit judges.[44]

Yet another pattern can be seen in the process that led to adoption of the innovations program lauded by the Federal Judicial Center report in 1985.[45] Although the problem of backlog was discussed in general terms for quite some time before the court decided on a course of action, the gestation period was not nearly as long as that of the limited en banc rule. More important, the details of the program were worked out primarily by the court's staff and a Federal Judicial Center consultant, with relatively little direct participation by the judges. The sharpest break with existing modes of operation, a screening procedure modeled on that of the Fifth Circuit, was not presented to the court as a concrete proposal until two weeks before the meeting at which it was adopted. Judge Browning, who remained largely on the sidelines in the interchanges over composition of the en banc court, took an active role in the shaping of the innovations program; he gave direction to the work of the staff and worked closely with the FJC consultant.

Browning's differing approaches to these various issues can be attributed in part to the differences in the situations that confronted him. The court reached an early consensus that it would adopt a limited en banc rule, so there was no need for Browning to exercise his powers of persuasion on that question. The issues on which the judges did differ—the size and composition of the panel—were not ones on which he had strong feelings. Thus he could stand back and encourage open debate, confident that whatever rule the court adopted would accomplish the purpose in a way the judges would feel comfortable with.

At the other extreme, there was no consensus on the need for measures such as screening to increase productivity; on the contrary,

---

[44]From the start, the process was attended with a sense of urgency: the statute required that the number of circuit judges and district judges on the new council be fixed by April 1, 1981. However, the initial restructuring could well have been more modest.

[45]For a more detailed account of the process, see Chapter 5.

even after an initial report on the FJC innovations study, a majority voted against a plan to assign lightweight cases to special panels. Browning thus saw it as his task to educate his colleagues on the magnitude of the backlog and the extent to which the Ninth Circuit lagged behind other circuits in judicial output. From his perspective, the FJC study served as a mechanism for advancing an objective that was arrived at independently. Once the judges were persuaded that less drastic means would not bring the Ninth Circuit even to the national median, resistance to screening crumbled.

The restructuring of the circuit council represents a third kind of situation: an external stimulus—congressional legislation—gave the court no choice but to act, and Browning's role as leader was to guide his colleagues toward a plan that would be good not only for the court of appeals but for the circuit as a whole. He discerned (correctly, as events proved) that the appeals judges would be willing to cede a substantial role to the district judges as long as they were assured that the council would not interfere in the work of their own court. The very first sentence of the plan drafted by the committee he chaired provided that assurance. With that basis for objection removed, the plan had clear sailing and could receive rapid approval notwithstanding the drastic change it introduced.

Conclusion

Judge Browning was aware from the outset that the Ninth Circuit's success in gaining new judgeships would create challenges both for the court as an institution and for his own role as its leader. A large number of new judges joined the court within a short period of time; moreover, the newcomers tended to be quite different ideologically, politically, and doctrinally from the judges already serving. Browning's basic approach was twofold: to emphasize the importance of collegiality and mutual respect, and to keep matters of administration and governance separate from the legal issues on which disagreements were inevitable.

The commitment to collegiality was manifested in several ways. In contrast to the case in some earlier courts, the new judges were not confronted by a policy of "sink or swim,"[46] but instead were provided a carefully designed orientation program with guidance and assis-

[46]Robert Carp and Russell Wheeler, "Sink or Swim: The Socialization of a Federal District Judge," 21 *Journal of Public Law* 359 (1972).

tance free of any attempt at doctrinal influence.[47] Browning openly
and forthrightly addressed issues relating to collegiality in his reports
in the mid-1980s and in major portions of the Symposium sessions,
which were important vehicles for problem solving under his leadership. Over time, the members of the court engaged in structured
discussion of such questions as the appropriate tone for written exchanges, the degree to which an opinion should reflect the author's
personal views as distinguished from those of the panel, and the
necessity for giving proper respect to other panels' dispositions.

Browning's approach to the threat of potentially rancorous doctrinal
division was firm and realistic. In contrast to Justice Felix Frankfurter's
often-cited conception of judges as "disinterested," Browning recognized that judges have deeply held doctrinal positions. Rather than
attempt to discourage diversity, a difficult if not impossible goal, he
sought, with a high degree of success, to encourage the judges to
handle disagreement with sensitivity and mutual respect. When a
subject was especially divisive, like the death penalty, he encouraged
candid discussion of the fundamental bases for such differences so as
to foster greater knowledge and understanding.[48]

Throughout Browning's tenure on the court, the Ninth Circuit never
lacked members who possessed both ability and interest in the realm
of judicial administration. Reform-oriented judges could be found in
every cohort of presidential appointees, and more important for the
unity and collegiality of the circuit, the key administrative reform
decisions never split along partisan lines but reflected the considered
judgment of judges primarily concerned with the effective operation
of their court and their circuit. Judges of quite different political and
ideological backgrounds could work together on matters of administration, in part because they could be confident that Browning would
keep his leadership role separate from his views as a judge deciding
cases.[49]

In conclusion, all of Judge Browning's attributes as a successful
innovator and circuit leader—skilled manager, keen negotiator with
Washington's judicial bureaucracy and with Congress, respected judicial craftsman—were enhanced by his great sensitivity to the funda-

---

[47]For a detailed account of the program, see Stephen L. Wasby, "Into the Soup? The
Acclimation of Ninth Circuit Appellate Judges," 73 *Judicature* 10 (1989).

[48]At one Symposium late in Browning's tenure, a panel composed of three judges led
a discussion on the question, What are our obligations in reviewing death penalty cases?

[49]See Mary M. Schroeder, "Jim Browning as a Leader of Judges: A View from a
Follower," 21 *Ariz. St. L.J.* 3, 7 (1989).

mental necessity for collegiality based on mutual trust and respect. The annual Symposium was Browning's particular vehicle for fostering and maintaining this kind of collegiality. Judge Otto Skopil's excellent summation of the nature of the Symposium under Browning's leadership is a fitting description of the spirit and purpose of the Browning era:

> The Symposium is vital as an open avenue of communication. The larger the number of judges in the Circuit, the greater the need for the annual Symposium. I am pleased and proud to be a member of a court where each member feels free to express, openly and candidly, his or her views with confidence that our relationship with one another will not be destroyed or diminished, but will be strengthened by an exchange of conflicting views.
>
> Despite the exchange of conflicting views, we enjoy a complete unity of attitude and purpose in our dedication to dispensing the highest quality of justice in all matters that come before us, as well as a unity of purpose in administering our judicial process in an efficient manner.
>
> Our individual differences tend to arise from the different way we strike the balance between justice and efficiency in dispensing justice. We should be sensitive to each others' differences in how we strike that balance. Our goal remains the same, however: the highest quality of justice in the shortest period of time.

The Authors

MICHAEL A. BERCH is professor of law at Arizona State University. He is coauthor (with Rebecca White Berch) of *Introduction to Legal Method and Process*, published by West (2d ed. forthcoming 1991), and the author of a study of Arizona's court system. In 1990 he was appointed a pro tem judge of the Maricopa County Superior Court.

PAUL D. CARRINGTON is professor of law at the Duke University School of Law, where he served as dean for ten years. He is coauthor (with Daniel J. Meador and Maurice Rosenberg) of *Justice on Appeal* (West Publishing, 1976) and author of numerous other books and articles, and serves as Reporter for the Advisory Committee on the Federal Rules of Civil Procedure.

THOMAS W. CHURCH, JR., is professor of political science and director of the Court Systems Management Program at the State University of New York at Albany. He is editor of *The Justice System Journal* and author of articles and monographs in the field of judicial administration, including *Justice Delayed* (National Center for State Courts, 1978).

JERRY GOLDMAN is professor of political science at Northwestern University. He has written several monographs on appellate settlement conferences and other aspects of appellate judicial administration, and is the coauthor (with Kenneth Janda and Jeffrey M. Berry) of *The Challenge of Democracy: Government in America* (Houghton Mifflin, 1987).

ARTHUR D. HELLMAN is professor of law at the University of Pittsburgh School of Law. He is the author of numerous articles on the

The Authors

work of the federal courts and has served as director of the central legal staff of the Ninth Circuit and as deputy director of the Commission on Revision of the Federal Court Appellate System (Hruska Commission).

A. LEO LEVIN is the Leon Meltzer Professor of Law at the University of Pennsylvania Law School. He served as executive director of the Commission on Revision of the Federal Court Appellate System and, from 1977 to 1987, as the director of the Federal Judicial Center. In 1987 he was elected president of the American Judicature Society.

DANIEL J. MEADOR is the James Monroe Professor of Law and the director of the Graduate Program for Judges at the University of Virginia School of Law. He is coauthor (with Paul D. Carrington and Maurice Rosenberg) of *Justice on Appeal* (West Publishing, 1976) and the author of numerous other books and articles. He served as assistant attorney general in the U.S. Department of Justice, 1977–79.

JOHN B. OAKLEY is professor of law at the University of California at Davis. He is coauthor (with Robert S. Thompson) of *Law Clerks and the Judicial Process* (University of California Press, 1980) and (with Edgar Bodenheimer and Jean Love) of *An Introduction to the Anglo-American Legal System* (West Publishing, 2d ed. 1988).

DORIS MARIE PROVINE is professor of political science at Syracuse University. She is the author of *Case Selection in the U.S. Supreme Court* (1980) and *Judging Credentials* (1986), both published by the University of Chicago Press, and of *Settlement Strategies for Federal District Judges* (Federal Judicial Center, 1986).

JUDITH RESNIK is the Orrin B. Evans Professor of Law at the University of Southern California Law Center. She is the author of many articles on the federal courts and adjudication and is coauthor (with Robert Cover and Owen Fiss) of *Procedure*, published in 1988 by Foundation Press.

MAURICE ROSENBERG is the Harold R. Medina Professor of Procedural Jurisprudence at Columbia University School of Law. He is coauthor (with Paul D. Carrington and Daniel J. Meador) of *Justice on Appeal* (West Publishing, 1976) and author of numerous other books and articles. He served as assistant attorney general in the U.S. Department of Justice, 1979–81.

JOHN R. SCHMIDHAUSER is professor of political science at the University of Southern California. He is the author of *Judges and Jus-*

376

tices: The Federal Appellate Judiciary (Little, Brown, 1979) and many other books, book chapters, and articles.

ROBERT S. THOMPSON is Legion Lex Professor at the University of Southern California Law Center. He is coauthor (with John B. Oakley) of *Law Clerks and the Judicial Process* (University of California Press, 1980) and served as a justice of the California Court of Appeal from 1968 to 1979.

STEPHEN L. WASBY is professor of political science at the State University of New York at Albany. He is the author of several books on the federal judicial system, including *The Supreme Court in the Federal Judicial System* (Nelson-Hall Publishers, 3d ed. 1988), and of a series of articles on communication among judges in the Ninth Circuit.

Index

Abuse of discretion, 46–51, 131–32, 200
Adjudication
  alternatives to, 328–29
  and governance, 247n
  and judicial administration, 245–46
Administrative agencies, 326–27
Administrative chief judge, 241–42
Administrative Office Act, 14, 250–52, 349
Administrative Office of the U.S. Courts
  and budgeting, 271–72
  legislation creating, 251
  powers of, 222, 349
  statistical reports, 113n
Administrative units
  operation of, 235–40
  origins of, 227–35
Adversary system, 94, 133–34
Advisory Committee on Rules of Practice and Procedure, 313–14
Alternative dispute resolution, 328–29
American Bar Association, 166n
American Mariner Industries, In re, 179–80
Annual action plan, 265, 269
Appeal
  decision to, 46, 54
  frivolous, 126
  right of, 185n, 324–25, 328–29
  values of, 100–101
Appellate magistrates, 136–37
Arizona, District of, 236n
Arizona Court of Appeals, 188, 191n
ARMS (Appellate Records Management System), 114–16, 120
Arnold, Thurman, 359–60

Article III courts, 185n
Article III judges
  alternatives to, 327–30
  and bankruptcy judges, 185n, 214
  management problems of, 270
  and non–Article III judges, 249, 275
Attorneys. *See* Lawyers; Staff attorneys

Baldridge, Holmes, 359
Bankruptcy Amendments and Federal Judgeship Act (BAFJA), 171
Bankruptcy Appellate Panel
  backlog, 174–75
  effect on appeal rates, 175–76
  evaluation of, 95, 184–86, 198–99
  history of, 168–72
  law-deciding function of, 181–84
  opt-out provision, 172–74, 212–14
  precedential effect of decisions, 182–83, 211–15
  and predictability, 211–15
  reversal rate in court of appeals, 176–81, 185–86
  view of bankruptcy bar, 184
Bankruptcy Code, 168
Bankruptcy courts, 168–69
Bankruptcy judges
  appointment of, 173n
  and circuit conference, 292–93
  and circuit governance, 264, 275–76
  reversal rates of, 173–74
Bankruptcy Reform Act, 169–70
Bell, Griffin, 231, 357n
Belloni, Robert, 262n
Bremson, Francis, 266n

Browning, James R.
on administrative chief judges, 242
background and career, 358–60
and bankruptcy courts, 270
and circuit conference, 285, 300, 303, 307
on circuit division, 357, 365
on court of appeals governance, 243
and decentralized budgeting, 272
influence of, 241n
and judicial council reorganization, 259–67
on judicial lobbying, 364
leadership qualities of, 368–73
and non–Article III judges, 275
and omnibus judgeship bill, 360–64
on panel autonomy, 88
philosophy of administration, 331–34
on predictability, 189–90
proposal for specialist panels, 167n
on role of circuit, 11, 223
and screening, 143–45, 358
strategies for reform, 370–71
testimony of, 365–66
see also Chief judge
Budgetary process, 271–72
Burdick, Quentin, 229, 361
Burger, Warren E., 356, 361, 364–65, 366n

Calendaring, 58n, 110–11, 144n, 245–46, 335–36
California
Central District of, 269n
and circuit realignment, 6, 229, 339–40
Carrington, Paul, 19–20
Cartwright, United States v., 28
Case weights, 110–11, 155–57
Caseload, 3–6, 30, 206–7, 211
Cecil, Joe S., 148
Central staff. *See* Staff attorneys
Chambers, Richard H.
as chief judge, 352–58
and circuit conference reform, 284
and circuit division, 354–57
Chief judge
and circuit conference, 288
and circuit governance, 241, 257
powers and duties, 352
see also Browning, James R.; Chambers, Richard H.; Goodwin, Alfred T.
Circuit conference
district meetings at, 303–4
evaluation of, 314–18
goals of, 284–85
and judicial council, 251, 289

lawyer participation, 286, 300–301, 304–7
lawyer representatives, 293–99
meetings during the year, 307–10
membership, 289–99
organization, 287–89
origin of, 251, 284
program of, 299–301
reform of, 224, 284–87
resolutions process, 301–3
selection of lawyer representatives, 293–99
size of, 289–93, 315
Circuit council. *See* Judicial council
Circuit executive, 235n, 254, 264, 269, 271–72
Circuit government
and accountability, 277–78
evaluation of, 276–80
judges' views of, 273–76
in operation, 267–73
structure of, 262–67
Circuit realignment
congressional debates, 228–32
criteria for, 339–40
proposals for, 225, 338–41, 356–57
see also Ninth Circuit
Circuit size
as catalyst for reform, 7–8, 221–22, 331–33
and circuit conference, 315–16
and consistency in the law, 55–56, 90, 195–96, 209–11
and court of appeals governance, 243
and judicial council, 262
problems of, 224, 334–38
Circuits
budgeting in, 271–72
early history of, 11–12, 346–47
role in federal judicial system, 11–16
role in governance of judiciary, 248–51, 278–80
see also Law of the circuit; *entries for individual circuits*
Clerk of court, 235n
Clerk's office
and decentralization, 233, 235–40
and inventory process, 111n
Collegiality, 148, 336, 371–73
Commerce Court, 188
Commission on Revision of the Federal Court Appellate System. *See* Hruska Commission
Committee on Evaluation of Lawyers and Judges, 312–13
Common law system
changes in, 96

and evolution of legal rules, 78–79, 81–82, 88–89
predictability in, 88–89, 96, 203
Computer systems, 239
Conference of Chief Judges of District Courts, 259
Conference on Empirical Research in Judicial Administration, 106n, 167n, 236n, 246n, 362n, 363n
Conflict. *See* Intercircuit conflict; Intracircuit conflict
Congress
  and judicial administration, 348–50, 354
  and structure of federal courts, 11–13, 346–47
  see also entries for specific statutes
Consistency. *See* Intercircuit conflict; Intracircuit conflict
Cotter, Paul J. 350
Counsel. *See* Lawyers
Court law clerks. *See* Staff attorneys
Courts of appeals
  creation of, 12–13, 348
  function of, 97–101, 240
  see also entries for individual circuits
Critical Legal Studies, 204
Cummings, Walter, Jr., 360

Davies, Thomas Y., 130–32
Davis, William E., 264–65
De novo review, 37–40, 198
Death penalty cases, 276, 372
Decentralization
  in court of appeals
    evaluation of, 222–23, 240, 246
    origins of, 227–35
    in practice, 235–40
    purposes of, 232–35, 240
  in judicial governance, 14–16, 251–56, 278–79
DeConcini, Dennis, 261
Denman, William, 351, 352–53
Dictum, 80, 81, 199–200
Discretion, 46–51
Discretionary jurisdiction, 324–25
District judges
  and courts of appeals, 255–56
  meetings with lawyers, 307–10
  participation in judicial council, 259–64
District of Columbia Circuit, screening in, 109
Diversity cases, 51–53
Douglas, William O., 347
Duniway, Ben C., 357

Egan, Michael, 231n

Elbow clerks. *See* Law clerks
Electronic mail, 148, 238–39
Elman, Philip, 360
En banc
  effect of decisions, 76–77
  fate of requests, 73–75
  history of, 13
  and intracircuit consistency, 74–75, 197
  origins of Ninth Circuit rule, 62–70, 368–69
  procedures governing, 70–73
  reasons for granting rehearing, 74–75
Evarts Act, 3, 12, 25, 182n, 348

Federal Bar Association, 294
Federal Circuit, 321n
Federal courts
  early history of, 346–47
  role of, 327–30
Federalism, 346
Federal Judicial Center
  and Bankruptcy Appellate Panel, 172–74, 184
  establishment of, 267n
  and Ninth Circuit screening program, 143–44, 370
  studies, 18, 107n, 334–36, 345
Federal Rules of Appellate Procedure
  and en banc hearing, 62
  Rule 34(a), 106, 112, 133–34, 141
  and screening, 106, 112, 133–34, 141
Federal Rules of Civil Procedure
  and local rules, 253, 271, 323–24
  Rule 11, 42–46, 198
  Rule 56, 36
Fee, James Alger, 353
Ferguson, Warren J., 275
Field, Stephen J., 347
Fifth Circuit
  administrative units in, 245n
  division of, 6, 228–32
  and Rule 11 sanctions, 44–45
  screening in, 108–10, 140–41
Finzel, Hubert H., 355–56
First Circuit, 170n
Fish, Peter, 14, 274
Forum shopping, 28, 182–83
Frank, Jerome, 48
Frank, John P., 106n, 362
Frankfurter, Felix, 19, 372
Friendly, Henry J., 13, 228n

Garrecht, Francis A., 352n
Germany, appellate courts in, 203
Goodwin, Alfred T., 166n, 242n, 352n, 366n
Gorton, Slade, 340–41, 365–67

Governance
  bar's role in, 281–318
  of court of appeals, 241–46
  of Ninth Circuit, 247–80
  regionalism in, 14–16, 251–56, 278–79
Grey, Thomas C., 20n
Griswold, Erwin N., 20n, 28, 356

Halpern, Charles, 364
Hamley, Frederick G., 354, 355
Hand, Learned, 165
Haney, Bert E., 351
Hruska Commission
  and circuit realignment, 5–6, 228–29,
    338–40, 356–57
  and limited en banc, 63n
  and rulemaking process, 313, 341
Hufstedler, Shirley M., 95–96, 163–64,
  357
Hughes, Charles Evans, 14, 21, 258, 348–
  49
Hunter, Elmo, 261

Ideology
  and en banc process, 71n, 77, 368–69
  and judicial reform, 371
  and unpredictability, 87–88, 208
Immigration cases
  and intracircuit conflict, 85–86
  and screening, 121–22
Inconsistency. *See* Intercircuit conflict; Intracircuit conflict
Infield fly rule, 71n
Innovation
  conditions fostering, 333–34, 336–37
  patterns of, 367
Intercircuit conflict, 28, 57
Intercircuit panel, 9, 55
Intracircuit conflict
  defining, 78–83, 199–200
  extent of, 83–86, 199–200
  mechanisms for avoiding, 57–62, 337–
    38
  significance of, 196
  and unpredictability, 86–89
Inventory, staff attorney
  and issue coding, 58–59
  and screening, 110–12
Issue classification, 58–59

Jackson, Henry M., 362
Jackson, Robert H., 178n
Johnston, Olin D., 356
Judges

appointment of, 187–88
case disposition statistics, 270
Judges' Bill, 13
Judicial administration
  Browning's influence, 241n
  Browning's philosophy, 331–34
  innovation in, 221–25, 333–34, 341
Judicial Conference of the United States
  and circuit governance, 222–23, 247–
    48, 251, 349
  district judge membership, 258–59
  meetings, 332
Judicial council
  and circuit conference, 289
  composition, 322
  district judge representation, 259–64
  duties of, 268–69
  lawyers on committees of, 310–12
  and local rules, 323–24
  membership, 265
  origins, 14, 251–52, 349
  reform of, 223–24, 262–64, 369–70
  selection of BAP judges, 171
Judicial Councils Reform and Judicial
  Conduct and Disability Act, 14, 254,
  260–61
Judicial discipline, 261, 268, 324, 350
Judicial independence, 248–49, 279, 322–
  23
Judicial misconduct, 261, 268, 324, 350
Judicial selection, 187–88
Judiciary Act of 1789, 3n, 11, 346
Jury, role of, 38

Kastenmeier, Robert W., 260, 261
Kennedy, Anthony M., 189
Kennedy, John F., 359

Large circuits. *See* Circuit size
Law clerks, 59n, 146–47, 154, 217. *See
  also* Staff attorneys
Law of the circuit
  coherence in, 26–27, 55–90, 195–205,
    211–15
  and opinion writing, 217
  role in federal judicial system, 13–14,
    27–29
Lawyer Representatives Coordinating
  Committee, 289, 311–12
Lawyers
  and Bankruptcy Appellate Panel, 173–
    74, 184
  on circuit committees, 310–14
  and intracircuit conflict, 56, 196, 199–
    200, 208

and screening, 133–34, 162n
and standards of review, 27
see also Circuit conference
Legal realism, 204
Legal rules
changes in nature of, 96, 209–10
fact-specific, 82
Lieber, Francis, 209–10
Limited en banc. *See* En banc
Litigant attitudes, 158–63
Llewellyn, Karl, 189, 208
Local rules, 256, 271, 323–24
"Luck of the draw," 86–89, 189
Lumbard, J. Edward, 350

McClellan, John L., 361–63
McConney, United States v., 34–36, 41, 50,
76
McGranery, James P., 359–60
McNichols, Ray, 262n
Magistrates
in appellate courts, 136–37
lobbying by, 269–70
role of, 173n
Magnuson, Warren G., 356
Mason, David R., 358
Matter of McLinn, 51–53, 76
Meador, Daniel J., 168, 191, 210, 338
and omnibus judgeship bill, 231n, 363
Merrill, Charles M., 353–54
Metcalf, Lee, 362
Miller v. Fenton, 33, 50
Mini en banc, 56n, 87–88
Motions panels, 143
Motions practice, 237
Multiple-precedent issues, 82–83, 85–86,
89, 200

NewAIMS, 239
Ninth Circuit
distinct from court of appeals, 321–23
origins, 347
patterns of government, 272–73
patterns of reform, 367–71
proposals to divide
analysis of, 338–41
and circuit conference, 317
before 1970, 351, 355–56
in 1970s, 6–7, 228–30, 356–57
after 1978, 16, 364–67
and omnibus judgeship bill, 360–64
Ninth Circuit Court of Appeals
delays in disposition, 334–46
executive committee, 241–45
General Orders, 61, 70–72

governance of, 241–45, 264
rules of, 32, 63, 112, 313–14
see also Administrative units; Calendaring; Clerk's office; Decentralization;
En banc; Intracircuit conflict; Staff attorneys; Symposium
Nonaffirmance, 126
*Northern Pipeline Construction Co. v. Mar-
athon Pipeline Co.*, 170–72
Nunn, Sam, 261

Omitted precedents, 84
Omnibus Judgeship Act of 1978
Browning's role in, 360–64
history of, 229–31, 360–64
Section 6 of, 7, 63–64, 231–32, 240
Opinions
circulation of, to nonpanel judges, 59–
60, 197
citation of, 156–57
publication of, 126–28, 151–57, 216–17
writing of, 58–60, 99n, 197
Oral argument
denial of, statistics on, 113
and judicial efficiency, 142
and opinion publication, 154–57
and screening, 104n, 106, 140–42, 149–
50
value of, 139–40, 155, 216
Overruling, 56

Panel autonomy, 87–88
Panner, Owen, 287
Pasadena
clerk's office in, 238
courthouse, 234n, 235, 236, 238
Peckham, Robert, 262n
Pierce v. Underwood, 50–51
Pope, Walter L., 352n
Posner, Richard A., 11, 160n, 167
Precedent
scope of, 79–82
theory of, 78–83
Predictability, 86–89, 202–5, 207–11
Pro se cases, 134, 160–61
Procedural fairness, 158–62
Public opinion, 159–62

Regional sittings, 246
Regionalism
and court of appeals calendaring, 246
and governance, 14–16, 251–56, 278–79
Rehnquist, William H., 10, 11, 347
Resnik, Judith, 138, 164n

Reversal rates
  of Bankruptcy Appellate Panel, 177–79
  in diversity cases, 52–53
  and screening, 126–28, 151–53
Right of appeal, 324–26
Robel, Lauren K., 276n
Rodgers, United States v., 28n
Rodino, Peter, 230
Rogers, William P., 359
Roosevelt, Franklin D., 250

Sanctions, 42
Scalia, Antonin, 139, 167n
Screening
  alternatives to, 215–18
  and bureaucracy, 104–5
  cases rejected from, 124–29
  defined, 98
  in the federal courts of appeals, 106–9,
    113–14
  justification for, 98, 104, 142
  and legitimacy, 134–35, 158–62
  origins of Ninth Circuit program, 142–
    45
  and predictability, 215
  recommendations for improvement,
    129–35
  serial and parallel panels, 110, 128–29,
    147–49, 156–57
  staff attorney role, 145–47
  statistical analysis of Ninth Circuit pro-
    gram, 114–29
  testing effects of, 149–57
Second Circuit
  judicial conference, 287
  "null" model of screening, 106–8
Section 6. *See* Omnibus Judgeship Act of
  1978
Section 6 reports, 232n, 365
Senior advisory board, 296, 312, 325
Senior judges
  and en banc process, 63n
  and judicial council, 264
Separation of powers, 346–47
Settlement, 207–11
Seventh Circuit, judicial conference of,
  293
Sixth Circuit, screening in, 108
Skidmore v. Baltimore and Ohio Railway Co.,
  48
Skopil, Otto R., 262n
  standard of review outline, 32, 37, 49
  on Symposium, 373

Sneed, Joseph T., 262n, 263
Specialist panels, 95, 186–91, 200–205,
  214–15
Specialized courts, 9, 166–67, 186–91
Staff attorneys
  and decentralization, 233–40
  and intracircuit consistency, 58–62,
    190, 196–97, 237
  memoranda by, 217
  and screening, 109–12, 130–34, 145–
    47, 159–60
  and unpublished opinions, 159–60
  see also Law clerks
Standards of review, 26–27, 30–54, 197–
  98, 203–4
Stare decisis, 56–57, 77–78, 87–88
State law, 51–53
Stephens, Albert Lee, 352n
Stern, Robert, 360
Stevens, John Paul, 103n
Stop-clock memos, 71–72
Subject-matter panels, 95, 186–91, 200–
  205, 214–15
Summary judgment, 36–42
Supreme Court
  and courts of appeals, 13, 19–20, 25,
    195
  oral argument in, 139–40
  public perceptions of, 159
Symposium (court of appeals)
  and circuit division proposals, 365
  and collegiality, 372–73
  and intracircuit consistency, 77
  and limited en banc, 63–69
  origins, 354
  and screening, 143

Tax cases, 191, 213
Tax protestors, 124
Third Circuit, screening in, 109
Thomas v. Capital Security Services, Inc., 44
Tyler, Tom R., 158–61

Uniformity. *See* Intercircuit conflict; Intracircuit conflict.
U.S. attorneys
  and circuit conference, 297
  and district meetings, 308
United States v. ———. See name of opposing
  party
Unpredictability. *See* Predictability
Unpublished opinions, 89

Wald, Patricia M., 231n
Wallace, J. Clifford
  and circuit conference, 284–87, 305
  and judicial councils, 252–53, 261,
  262n
Wallace Committee, 284–85, 287–88,
  289–90, 293, 295, 297–98, 305, 314

White, Byron R., 28n
Wiggins, Charles E., 43, 231, 362
Williams, Spencer, 260
Windmill Farms, Inc., In re, 182

Zaldivar v. City of Los Angeles, 43–46
Zuboff, Shoshana, 276

Library of Congress Cataloging-in-Publication Data

Restructuring justice: the innovations of the Ninth Circuit and the future of the
federal courts / Arthur D. Hellman, editor.
    p.   cm.
    Includes bibliographical references and index.
    ISBN 0-8014-2405-4 (cloth : alkaline paper). — ISBN 0-8014-9686-1 (paper : alkaline
paper)
    1. Courts—United States.   2. Judicial process—United States.   3. Court
congestion and delay—United States.   4. United States. Court of Appeals (9th
Circuit)   I. Hellman, Arthur D., 1942–   .
KF8752 9th.R47   1990
347.73′2—dc20
[347.3071]   90-55129